Critical Acclaim for Christopher Darden's

IN CONTEMPT

"[Darden] has given us new insights into a trial
that has become a defining part of American legal
and racial history. *In Contempt* is not a bitter book.
Rather, it is one man's account of the experience of
his lifetime. Other O. J. Simpson books are on the
way; I doubt they'll be more honest or personally
insightful than this one."
—*The Los Angeles Times Book Review*

"Though Mr. Darden gives the reader his own
candid impressions of the Simpson case . . . [this is]
the story of his own coming of age, as a lawyer
and as a black man."
—*The New York Times*

"Brooding, complex, ambitious . . . Details of the
lawyers' behind-the-scenes machinations remain
strangely compelling."
—*Time*

"Whether one believes in O. J. Simpson's guilt or
innocence, prosecutor Christopher Darden's book, *In
Contempt*, should be a must read. It's lucid, concise,
graphic, factual, and not without suspense and
insights. [It] takes the reader into the heart
of the prosecution and its case."
—*Amsterdam News*

D0288645

Critical Acclaim for Christopher Darden's
IN CONTEMPT

Powerful and powerfully written . . . precisely because his personal dilemma was so squarely in the center of the debate about race that the Simpson saga embodies . . . Darden's book is the story of his journey on that electrified path, the path of self-definition."
—*The Philadelphia Inquirer*

"The most fascinating . . . Darden's fans will love his book, which is both an emotional account of the trial and his personal story of growing up black in America during the last four decades. . . . Some of the most moving parts of Darden's book, however, have nothing to do with The Trial. His personal story is the tale of the road not taken, of the decisions along the way not to follow the path of his beloved older brother Michael, whose petty juvenile crimes and recreational drug use escalated into addiction, AIDS, and death."
—*The Washington Post*

"A detailed, passionate, and disarmingly self-deprecating account of a life far more representative of the black experience than the famous defendant's."
—*The Indianapolis Star*

"Darden reveals important facts and events that failed to surface during the trial and brings readers in on closed-door prosecution strategy sessions, out-of-court interviews with witnesses, and the private 'sidebar' conferences at Judge Ito's bench and in his chambers."
—*Black Media News*

IN CONTEMPT

IN CONTEMPT

CHRISTOPHER DARDEN

with Jess Walter

Published by Graymalkin Media

www.graymalkin.com

Copyright © 1996 by Christopher A. Darden

Originally published by HarperCollins

This edition published in 2016 by Graymalkin Media

ISBN: 978-1-63168-074-8

Printed in the United States of America

1 3 5 7 9 10 8 6 4 2

IN MEMORY OF

MICHAEL VIRGIL DARDEN

January 2, 1953 – November 29, 1995

NICOLE BROWN

May 19, 1959 – June 12, 1994

and
RONALD GOLDMAN

July 2, 1968 – June 12, 1994

Behold, I shew you a mystery;
we shall not all sleep,
but we shall all be changed,
In a moment, in the twinkling of an eye,
at the last trump: for the trumpet shall sound,
and the dead shall be raised incorruptible,
and we shall be changed.

1 CORINTHIANS 15:51-52

CONTENTS

PART 1

DARDEN

As I like to say to the people of Montgomery: "The tension in this city is not between the white people and the Negro people. The tension is, at bottom, between justice and injustice, between the forces of light and the forces of darkness."

—*STRIDE TOWARD FREEDOM*,
MARTIN LUTHER KING JR., 1958

ONE

The clerk, Deirdre Robertson, stumbled over his name, and for just a moment, a last bit of hope hung there on her voice. But I knew. I'd known from the beginning, from the moment I walked into that courtroom a year earlier and saw that jury. I could see in their eyes the need to settle some score. And I was the only prosecutor who knew what the score was. Still, to hear it announced like that was like a swift baseball bat to the stomach.

"We the jury in the above entitled action, find the defendant, Orenthal James Simpson, not guilty of the crime of murder . . . upon Nicole Brown Simpson, a human being . . ."

A human being.

"My God," I muttered. "My God, my God, my God." Next to me, the other lead members of the prosecution team, Marcia Clark and Bill Hodgman, whispered after me, "My God." I watched Simpson and his lawyer Johnnie Cochran pump their fists and smile fiercely and I wanted to scream.

I turned to face the jury, to show them my disgust. My eyes caught those of Juror 247, reportedly a former Black Panther. Earlier in the trial, Judge Lance Ito had asked Cochran to get tickets to the UCLA-Miami football game for Juror 247, and Simpson's lawyer had gladly obliged. That's what this trial was about. Juror 247 and I stared at each other while the courtroom erupted, all at once, in a collective gasp, a rejoicing shout, and the tortured hiss of Fred Goldman: "Murderer!" Finally, Juror 247 looked away from me, at the floor. As he left the courtroom, he raised his fist in a black power salute, and I was saddened that one of the symbols of my idealistic youth was being used to celebrate a killer's release. As the jury filed out of the box, my head swung around the courtroom until I settled on O. J. Simpson.

He turned to Kim Goldman, made eye contact with her, and smiled slyly. He'd done it. He'd killed her brother and, in spite of all the evidence against him, had gotten away with it. His eyes swept past the Brown family too. He'd won. He had told Nicole that he could kill her anytime, anyplace, and that he could get away with it. Well, he'd done it. And now it was over.

I stood, trying to get my bearings. One of the defense attorneys, Robert Shapiro, walked toward me, but I brushed him aside. Judge Ito immediately left the bench, locking himself in his chambers, which was where he belonged. I wanted nothing to do with him or the "Dream Team." I reached the door and looked back with disdain at the courtroom where I'd spent the last nine months. Alone, I turned away, walked through the double doors of Criminal Department 103, and never looked back.

I never got a chance, of course, to cross-examine him. And as I stood in the hallway, waiting for an elevator, I didn't want to anymore. I just wanted to talk to him, make sure he knew that he hadn't fooled all of us and that his "Dream Team" hadn't fooled most Americans. A criminal defendant, much like a lawyer, can forget sometimes that what is admissible in court isn't necessarily true and what is inadmissible isn't necessarily false, that a not guilty verdict doesn't mean you are innocent.

I wanted to tell him that there was another court that would hear his case one day, with a judge who would try racist cops and murderers separately. A court where everyone will have to account for his actions alone, without lawyers or jurors or overworked prosecutors. A court where there will be no need for DNA, gloves, or Akitas, and the only witnesses will be the eyewitnesses, Ron Goldman and Nicole Brown.

As I stepped on the elevator, I thought about Ron and Nicole and was filled with images that continue to haunt me. I could see exactly how it happened, in fact I see it still, much more vividly than I'd like, much more often than I want to. And every time I see it, I want to confront him, to tell him that I can see inside his heart and that I know what happened:

Through the window, you watched Nicole put away the dishes, didn't you? She finished and then she lit some candles and you watched her, the way you had watched her so many times before, on so many dry runs. She stopped suddenly and looked out the window, but she couldn't see you, because it was dark outside and well-lit inside. All she could see was her own reflection and, for just a moment, you both stood staring at the same thing: her frightened face. She reached into a drawer and grabbed a long kitchen knife, her knuckles white around the handle. You were impressed. You knew how afraid she must be to grab a knife. Nicole had told you and everyone else how frightened she was of knives, that it was her worst phobia, this irrational fear that one day she would be killed with a knife. She looked around the condominium and then set the knife back on the counter. And she went back to lighting candles.

Candles! That really got you, didn't it? You couldn't believe that she would light candles. That was your ritual, something that let you know she was ready to be taken. It infuriated you that she might be lighting candles for someone else. You moved along the bushes outside the window, watching her, the way you had watched her before. Was there a voice pulling you? Pushing you? Goading you? Or was it just matter-of-fact, slow and measured?

Was it because you owned her? I know you believed that she was yours from the time you first saw her in 1977, in that Beverly Hills restaurant where she was a waitress. You believed she was yours on that first date, when you tore at her pants to get at her more easily, when she seemed to like that. You could see beauty in a blond, small-chested, suburb-pretty girl, and so you set out to make her what you wanted her to be. You gave her an apartment and filled it with furniture. When you told her what to wear, she wore it; when you told her what to do, she did it; when you wanted her, you had her; when her hair wasn't blond enough, you told her to dye it.

From the beginning, she had a way of getting under your skin, didn't she? After she flirted with another man, in 1978, you smacked her in an elevator and told her that it was part of a normal relationship. That was just the beginning, of course. Everything she did on her own upset you. When you drank, she was afraid of you. You threatened to kill her when she talked about leaving you, and when she divorced you, she was so afraid, she hid all your guns.

Sure you loved her. You love a lot of your possessions. You even married her after it was clear the people at Hertz would rather have a married spokesman, especially if that spokesman was black and had a reputation for sleeping with every woman he met. And at first, the marriage was great and she knew who was in charge. After she had children, and didn't lose the weight fast enough, you told her she was too fat and you complained to her parents. What kind of impression did that give corporate America, a successful man like you with a fat woman? She had to understand that she was nobody without you. When you tried to make her understand, when you pushed her or knocked her down, she would just cry, so you would slap her again; you would stand above her, with your hand raised, and you would threaten to slap the living shit out of her if she didn't shut up. And she did.

One time, in 1985, you took a bat to your own Mercedes, the one you'd given Nicole, after she came home late. She called the police and you couldn't believe it. This was no matter for the police. This was how normal families behaved! You handled the officer who showed up with your charm and humor: "Can't a man beat his own car?" Of course. A man has a right to beat anything he owns. And that's why you had a right to beat her, isn't it? Because you owned her.

"Stop by anytime," you said to the cop that day, and then you shut the door slowly and went looking for Nicole again.

Maybe even you would agree that you went a little too far in 1989, when she accused you of sleeping around. You didn't deny it. Why should you? "Look at me," you told her. "You can't handle all of this."

Then you hit her. But that time, she didn't cry. That time, she ran out of the room and called the police, while you chased her around the house, beating her. When the police came, she was dirty and bruised, wearing only sweats and a bra. Nicole hid pictures from that night in her safe-deposit box, a trail of evidence pointing to you, a warning to whoever would listen.

Even the jury wouldn't listen. Just as they wouldn't listen to the desperate 911 call she made three years later: "You know who he is. He's O. J. Simpson. . . . He's going to kill me!"

Did you think at all about those other times as you stood outside her window? Or did you simply wonder how she could break up with you? How she could take your wealth and your children? You had taught her which fork to use at dinner. You had created her and bought everything she had, her clothes, her car, even her breasts.

At times, you were OK after the divorce, right? It had to be nice to not have to hide your many women in the maid's quarters anymore. But then she began dating—mostly young, white men—and that was too much for you. You couldn't imagine your property in the hands of another man. Remember *the night you followed her home from a club and watched through the picture window as she was with another man? You were enraged and devastated.*

You tried a few times to get back with her, but she wouldn't have you. She was afraid of you. She told all her friends that you were so possessive, you were going to kill her one day. And you would get away with it. Don't be crazy, they told her.

So what went through your mind that day? Were you planning it at the recital, where you stared at her coldly and then put on your public face as soon as you got outside? Or was it after the phone call from your new girlfriend, Paula Barbieri, who left a voice mail message that day, announcing that she was breaking up with you? Is that why you tried to call Paula so many times before the murder?

It was everything, wasn't it? It just built up inside you until you were afraid you were going to burst. It was a dizzying mix of anger and sorrow, a surreal feeling of being alone, the world moving in slow motion and the bottom coming up to meet you.

How long were you planning to do it? When did it stop being a day-dream and become a challenge—"Can I get away with this?" Maybe you didn't even know when you got there that night. Maybe it was like other missions, and just watching her like this made you feel better. Maybe when you told Ron Shipp about your dreams you were telling the truth. Maybe it felt like a dream to you, standing out there, all in black, in quiet, rubber-soled shoes, with dark gloves over your hands and a cap on your head.

You'd carried the knife plenty of times, hadn't you? Did you search your dreams just before you acted, wondering what would happen next?

You watched her walk out of the kitchen and you shadowed her outside, onto the walkway, past the windows, to the front steps that led to the gate. There, you rang the bell and you knew she had to come outside because the intercom was broken. But she didn't come out, did she? Instead, she took the knife again and peered out the window.

The Akita came over and sniffed you. He cocked his head in silent recognition. You watched her set the knife back on the counter, blade facing out (strange with the children home). And then she came running out to the gate and you were filled with rage. Whomever she was expecting, she knew him well enough to answer the door barefooted, in the skimpy black dress she'd worn at the recital. You were furious. Your wife, the mother of your children, was wearing that dress and expecting a man to come over while the kids were asleep. Was it more than you could take?

It was so dark behind the trees, under the steps, that she didn't see you. Instead, she walked right past and you could have emerged from the shadows and grabbed her then if you wanted to. But you waited a second. Did you feel some remorse? Was there a chance she could've been spared just then? She opened the gate, but there was no one there, and when she turned back, you saw her standing in front of you, the way you had dreamed it.

You came out of the shadows so quickly, so smoothly, you must've surprised yourself a little. You hit her with your fist and with the knife handle, right on the crown of her head. Then you grabbed her by the arm and drove the knife deep into her neck, four times. We've all seen those scenes a hundred times on television. But you knew what to do. You were an actor. You had played this part before. You had learned the correct way to kill someone with a knife: not just to stab, but to draw the knife all the way through.

Were you shocked when the gate opened and that white boy walked in on you? That was just the kind of guy Nicole had been seeing. You must've been furious. In fact, you'd seen this one before, driving Nicole's car. Ron Something. He didn't know what was going on at first, did he?

"Hey," he said, "Hey."

You yelled back, but it wasn't really words, just pure, vocalized anger. And then you pulled him inside the gate and lifted him to the left, where he was cornered by the fence and by the shrubs. Ron put his hands up to protect himself, but he had no chance against you. What did he have? A pair of glasses he was trying to return to Nicole's mother? A key chain? Not much help against the blade you swung like a scythe. You were in a pure fighting rage by that time, an athlete bred on controlled anger and violence, operating without control.

Still, the boy fought. You stabbed him over and over, until his bloodied arms finally fell. And then you grabbed him by the shirt and stabbed him more deeply. You moved in behind him and brought the knife across his throat, deep and straight, your own eyes closing with the release of rage. You dropped him like trash.

". . . A human being," the court clerk said. But not to you. Not tonight.

Then you turned back to Nicole, that little black dress pulled up around her thighs. This was all her fault. You grabbed her by the hair and pulled her head back, put the knife to her throat, and drew it back toward yourself with even more force, cutting all the way to her spine. You damned near cut her head off. It was freeing and painful at the same time, wasn't it?

You had finally taught her to listen. What better listener could there be than someone you silenced forever?

Was the boy still whimpering? That must've pissed you off. Is that why you returned to his body, gave him a halfhearted stab in the thigh and another, deeper cut to his chest? Were you slowing down, coming out of the dream? You walked up the stairs as the Akita barked at your feet. Blood dripped from your cut finger. Your arms were at your sides and you stared straight ahead as you walked slowly down the dark walkway, toward the alley, where your Bronco was parked. And then you paused, as if you'd forgotten to tell Nicole something. You walked a few more steps toward the back gate and paused again. One glove was missing. And your hat too. You must've lost them when you fought with the boy. And so you walked back to the bodies, unaware of the bloody footprints you were leaving. You couldn't find the hat and glove, but I'll bet you stared at her for a moment, slumped at the bottom of the stairs as if she'd just fallen asleep. It was her fault, wasn't it? You owned her now. Completely. Forever.

But it wasn't quite like your dreams. It was messier and harder, and at night—when your lawyers aren't around to convince the world that you didn't do it—I'll bet you ache a little bit. But not that night. That night, you turned and walked back toward the Bronco, a bit faster; after all, you had a plane to catch.

The conference room next to Gil Garcetti's office—like everything in this case—was smaller than it looked on television. I stood behind Gil as he praised our efforts to the dozens of cameras fanned out before us and the reporters wedged in next to one another—waiting to see how we would respond to the verdict, gawkers at the scene of an accident.

I hadn't wanted to be there, so soon after the verdict, but Suzanne Childs, the director of communications for the D.A.'s office, had insisted.

"Not me," I said. "I don't feel up to it."

"If you're not there," Suzanne said, "the public might get the impression that you are angered by the verdict."

So there I stood, staring past the reporters to my clerks, who lined the walls and wiped at their wet eyes. This was their case too. I had coerced, cajoled, and browbeaten every one of them to tap their last ounces of energy, their good ideas, their sweat, and their inspiration. Now they looked at me for an explanation and I didn't have one, except that, sometimes, the world is unjust.

Marcia spoke and I watched her warmly; for months, she had given more than she had. Raked by the media because of her painful divorce, she had battled harder than anyone I'd ever seen, and I could see the fatigue on her face as she thanked the victims' families.

"Their strength and dignity have been a source of inspiration," she said.

And then it was my turn. I had no idea what I was going to say. Should I admit that I was angry, furious with the jury, the judge, the media, the defense, the whole damned country?

Should I confess that I was haunted by my mistakes, errors that might have contributed to losing this case, that might have allowed a double murderer to go free?

Should I say that, above all, I was ashamed of a jury that needed just four hours to dismiss the lives of two people and a year's work, a jury that picked a dreadful time to seek an empty retribution for Rodney King and a meaningless payback for a system of bigotry, segregation, and slavery?

I stepped up to the microphone. This was the part of the trial I had never been comfortable with—the public spectacle, the entertainment for millions of people. The case shouldn't have been about ratings and book deals; it should have been about Nicole's children, Sydney and Justin, who were about to be returned to their murderer/father; it should have been about Kim Goldman, who stood with her own father trying to be strong.

Early in the case, I had avoided meeting Kim because she reminded me so much of the photographs I had seen of her brother, whom I never met in life and could only see lying broken and drained of his blood. I saw Ron in Kim Goldman's face, and when she looked to me for explanations, I felt as if Ron were asking too. On the podium that day, I was speaking to my clerks and fellow prosecutors, to the Browns and the Goldmans, and to my clients, Nicole and Ron.

"We came here in search of justice," I said into the sharp strobe of flashing cameras. My throat constricted and I struggled to finish. "I'm not sure whether we got any."

What could I say to Nicole and Ron? That I was sorry their murderer went free because of the deep chasm that racism and slavery have carved in this country? That I was sorry Johnnie Cochran had dragged them into that dark pit? That I was sorry about the gloves and the other mistakes I had made?

"I'm not bitter," I said, hoping to convince myself. "I'm not angry." I scanned the people lining the walls, the earnest faces of law clerks who spoke of justice without a hint of cynicism, the professional faces of lawyers who had worked until they could barely stand, and the anguished faces of the Browns and Goldmans, who had deserved so much more. "I am honored to have—"

And then I broke down. I gave in to the hollowness inside me. Like a man standing for hours in a strong current, I gave up and allowed myself to be swept away by my own sorrow and sacrifice. I had taken this case because I believed that my duty was to seek justice, no matter how famous, rich, and black the defendant. I had naively believed my presence would, in some way, embolden my black brothers and sisters, show them that this was their system as well, that we were making *progress*. I had believed that African Americans were the most just people on the planet and that they would convict a black icon when they saw the butchery, the pattern of abuse, and the overwhelming evidence.

Instead, I was branded an Uncle Tom, a traitor used by The Man. I received death threats and racist letters from blacks and whites alike. As the case became more and more about race, I watched helplessly as it ripped the scabs off America's wounds, which will now take even longer to heal, assuming they ever do.

I slumped into the arms of my colleagues and they helped me out of the conference room. I had no idea where I was going; I couldn't see through my bleary eyes. I stumbled through Garcetti's outer offices into a twenty-five-foot hallway that led to my cramped office, the only place I could think to go. Before I could get there I felt two small hands on my shoulders.

"You have to let go, baby," she said. "It's over."

I couldn't see her face, but I knew the voice. I knew the voice very well. "I can't, Marcia." And I just kept walking until I was alone in my office, where I collapsed in my chair.

I suppose people who watched the trial on television and who watched me break down that day thought they knew me and knew what I had been through. But I don't think they did.

My law career was over. I couldn't go back into another courtroom expecting justice when there had been none in the strongest murder case I ever prosecuted. I was alone, isolated from a community I had served so honestly for the last fourteen years. Reporters were going through my trash, looking for scandals in my family, and chasing the women I had dated. While Judge Ito moved the trial at glacial speed, my brother was dying of AIDS four hundred miles away, near the city where my daughter was growing up without me.

Most of all, I had become the lightning rod for the bigotry, insecurity, and misunderstanding of an entire nation. The civil rights movement and the sense of black solidarity and pride that had saved me from a meaningless life of poverty and crime had been reduced by Johnnie Cochran to nothing more than the taking of two sides, nothing more than a lawyer's trick, a smooth bit of strategy.

For everyone in that case and everyone who watched it on television, the Simpson trial was a long, arduous journey. For me, it was even longer, its roots and shadows extending back to my childhood and earlier, to the moment my grandfather's grandfather's grandfather was sold as a slave. I wept that day for Ron Goldman and Nicole Brown and I wept for myself, for the place I had come from and for a journey that I had honestly believed had meant something.

TWO

There was this white kid with a crooked leg who lived near where my father grew up in Gilmer, a dusty farming town on the eastern side of Texas, near the city of Tyler. This kid had a little tree house, and most days, when my father would walk past, the kid would pull himself up into his tree house, wait for that little nigger kid to walk past, and then spit on him.

As soon as that kid came down from his tree house, my father would beat his ass, but two weeks later, that white boy would drag his weak legs into his tree house and would proceed to spit on him again. My dad would wait for him to come down from his tree house and then beat his ass again. Didn't matter. The next day, that kid would be up in his tree house again.

It says something that, in America, a lame white boy would suffer a beating just for the chance to spit on a black kid. That's how important it has been, after slavery in this country, for whites to put blacks in their place, how important it has been to replace a codified social hierarchy with a lawless one, how important it has been for many white people to have someone beneath them.

Stokely Carmichael wrote in his book *Black Power* that it was important that we change from "Negroes" to "blacks" because of the deep need to define oneself. I've always believed that. To allow others to define us is to be shackled always to the past, to be chained to old stereotypes. To allow white people to define us is to be slaves forever, to be beneath whites on some artificial social order. I guess for a little white kid with birth defects, with warped and tired legs, well, for a kid like that, I guess that social order was invaluable. I guess having someone beneath him was worth a routine beating.

When he wasn't beating their asses, my dad played with white kids while growing up, and he especially liked a couple of children who lived between his house and the one-room general store. But one day one of the children, a little girl about twelve, wouldn't come down from her porch to play with my father.

"I cain't play with you no more, Eddie."

"Why not?"

"I just cain't."

It wasn't until later that my father figured that the girl's parents didn't want their twelve-year-old girl having anything more to do with him. She was a young woman now. And in the South, white women didn't roll around in the dirt with niggers.

When you're a kid, you don't know anything about race. You don't think, I'm black and he's white and she's yellow. Not until someone decides that they must tell you. And when you're young and black, they might tell you from a tree house or from their front porch. They might even tell you with the word "nigger." It's an experience you can never forget. The details become a part of you, indelibly etched in your memory. And then you know your race and you know your place. When a white person decides it is time for you to know those things, when a white person looks you in the eye and calls you nigger, you're never able to forget.

I never met my father's father, Miles, never even saw a picture of him. He was a farmer initially, in that East Texas town of Gilmer. He was married at age thirteen, had ten children by the time he was twenty-five. One day, Miles said he had received his calling from God and he began farming less and preaching more until soon he stopped farming altogether and left his family to preach on the road. From that point on, he was something of a jacklegged preacher—a nomadic rookie preacher who moved from church to church, preaching one-Sunday stands and then moving on to the next community. Every month, he sent a little money to his family, but he never came home. My own father has always seen a certain hypocrisy in churches, and I believe that losing his own father hardened him to religion.

My dad said that it wasn't until he was a father himself that he understood his own father. He realized that Miles, married at thirteen, didn't figure his children needed him around once they reached age thirteen themselves. Grandpa Miles died in Monroe, Louisiana, in 1963, when I was just seven. But I got the feeling my father had given up on his dad long before that.

My father has worked as long as he can remember, since the time he was five years old, picking cotton in hot, East Texas fields. My father was a hard worker, but his sister was the best cotton picker in Texas, he would brag, a girl who could pick more than any man. Four hundred pounds a day, my father used to contend, which gives you an idea of the lack of shame with which my father will stretch a good story.

He also could tell you about the first nickel he ever earned, when he was five. He picked cucumbers all day and sold them at a nickel a peck. He got that nickel, went home, and showed it to his mother, Viola, whom we called Big Mama. He asked her to keep his nickel for him and so she tied it into the corner of her apron. But that made my daddy nervous and so he went back and asked for it. He didn't want to lose that nickel and so he put it where it would always be safe, where he could always find it. He put the nickel in his mouth and was going to hold it there as long as he needed to.

Instead, he swallowed it.

"Don't worry," Big Mama said. "You can get your nickel back when you go to the outhouse."

But Eddie was smart. He wasn't going to take any chances and he wasn't about to go digging around in someone else's shit. And so when the time came, he went to the bushes and squatted down there, dug around, and got his nickel back. My daddy can still pinch a nickel better than anyone I know.

When my father was twelve, Big Mama walked down a country road with him and talked about his future.

"Boy, when you get old enough, you leave the South," his mother said. "It ain't for you."

Daddy didn't say anything. He just kept walking, his head down, looking at the East Texas dirt. There was nothing to say. Big Mama was right. He was nobody's boy except hers. And on that day he began thinking of a way out of Texas, a way out of the poverty that he associated with the South.

My mother's family, the Robertsons, had already left Gilmer by then. Like thousands of other families—black and white—they moved west with the war effort.

My mother, Jean Robertson, was seven when her family left Texas. They ended up in Richmond, California, on the northeastern shore of the San Francisco Bay. Before the war, Richmond had been called Petroleum Town, and most of the Italian and Greek immigrants who lived there worked either for the railroad or for Standard Oil. In 1940, there were 23,000 people in Richmond.

A year later, the shipyards were churning out ships up and down the East Bay, from Alameda to Richmond to Vallejo. By 1944, there were 100,000 people in Richmond, many of them poor, many of them black, many of them from the South.

From the beginning, Richmond was poorer than the rest of the Bay Area. It was a city with services and infrastructure for 23,000 people with a population that—even after the war ended and the shipping jobs left—never dipped below 70,000.

My mother's father was Marvin Porter Robertson, and he showed up at the Alameda shipyards in 1942 to work on the Victory ships, moving his family to the most affordable town in the Bay Area: Richmond. We used to call him Grandpop. Grandpop had one leg shorter than the other; he had busted it in a car accident and had gotten the kind of medical treatment black people often got in that day, the kind that left you with one short leg. But Marvin Robertson was as successful as any black man I'd ever known. He wore a suit every day, ran a floating craps game in the projects, and went down to the golf course to sell barbecue to the white folks. He was an entrepreneur and a hustler. But his real job was operating a bail bonds business and a real estate company out of his house. "If you land in jail," his business cards read, "let Robbie go your bail."

My dad didn't show up in Richmond until 1951.

Eddie had joined the army a couple of years earlier and was sent to Korea. He always called it the best time of his life, and when I was growing up, every story, every lesson seemed to be based on the military. It was my father's mantra: "In the army . . ." My father hardly ever had any visitors at the house. One day when I asked why his friends rarely stopped by, he said he lost most of his friends in Korea. He too was hit with shrapnel and sent stateside to the navy hospital in Vallejo. When he went home to Texas on a forty-day leave, Eddie ran into my mother's grandmother, who was called Miss Pearl, a fitting name for a woman so light-skinned. She was a friend of my father's mother and she got to the point quickly.

"Where are you stationed?" Miss Pearl asked.

"Vallejo," my daddy said.

"Ain't Vallejo near Richmond?"

"I don't know," he said.

"Well, Jean is in Richmond. Here's her telephone number. You should call her." As my father walked toward the door, Miss Pearl cried after him, "Call me and let me know when y'all get married."

"Miss Pearl," my father said, laughing, "the last thing I plan to do is get married to anybody." He was going to be a career soldier. He loved the army life, and even after being wounded, he said he needed to go back to Korea. "I heard my comrades calling me back."

My mother was divorced and already had a baby—my oldest sister, Angie—when Eddie came to visit her, sometime in 1951. They drank coffee and talked about the closest thing they had to old country—East Texas. And because they had that history, my mother's parents allowed my father to stay overnight on the couch—in plain view of her parents' bedroom—when he came to visit. It wasn't until some lipstick showed up on Eddie's cheek that he was no longer welcome in the Robertson house. But by then, he was in love with my mother.

While Eddie waited for a transfer back to Korea, he and Jean were married. My brother Michael was born in January 1953 and my sister Edna was born in December of that same year. And then my father returned to Korea for the tail end of the war. He came home two years later and then, on April 7, 1956, I was born.

When you talk about Eddie Darden, you're talking about an Old-School Pops. Old-School Pops works hard all week and will take off his belt and bust your ass if you do something wrong. Then, on Saturday evening, Old-School Pops slips on a pair of Stacey Adams, the kind with the long, pointed toe, and a suit, and he grabs his hat, a black fedora with a red feather, and he heads for the door. We usually cut him off to ask where he was going, but his raspy answer was always the same. "I'm goin' to see a cat about a pair of kitten mittens." Or he might say, "I'm goin' to see a man about a dog." And he'd look real serious saying it. We'd stand there totally confused and baffled by his answer and he would slip out the door. Old-School Pops always has a fifth of Ancient Age or Wild Turkey or a bottle of gin in a brown paper bag in the trunk of his big, old-steel car, and he drives down to the parking lot of some store, where he hangs with his friends, talks about his army days, and drinks out of the bottle cap. Old-School Pops is fair. He can be the sweetest man and can tell a story that would have you screaming with laughter. Or he can lift you by the arm and bring down his belt so hard, you run out of breath to cry.

People raise their children differently now. Back then, when we misbehaved, we were spanked, slapped, hit, belted, whatever it took to make sure we got the message. It has a definite stigma now, but everyone smacked their kids when I was growing up. You didn't storm out of a room. You asked permission, unless you wanted a steel-toed boot up your tail. Kids didn't misbehave in the malls and on television like they do now. And while I can't defend smacking your children, it's hard to argue that in the neighborhood where I grew up, heavy discipline was important for the people who were eventually successful. There were strict, definite rules when I was growing up. We knew what was expected, which behavior would be tolerated and which wouldn't. Our family life was based very much on Eddie Darden's success in the army. At home, we were his little army, his baby soldiers. Mom was in charge of the day-to-day operations of the barracks; Dad was there for the major decisions. He was the C.O., the commanding officer.

As such, my father was the main source of discipline, although my mother was very capable of beating our asses alone, and she did when it was necessary. But the worst punishment was when she would say, "Wait until your father gets home." I'd be downstairs in the bedroom I shared with my brothers, shaking and scared, trying to sleep. Pops would come home from work at two o'clock in the morning from swing shift and I'd hear him coming up the outside steps, his work boots foretelling my punishment on the fourteen steps that led up to our front porch. It was like the executioner was coming.

I'd hear the tumblers in the lock open and there'd be a three-minute delay as he got the reports from my mother, the longest three minutes there ever were. And then the interior door at the top of the stairs would open and I just knew I was dead. Those boots would pound down the stairs to the family room and this arm would slide into our room, flick on the light, and then he'd follow the arm inside.

"OK, Daddy I won't do it again. I won't do it again." I was always moving backward, unlike Michael, who knew it was no use. It wasn't like today. They used belts then.

My father and mother bought their first house in Richmond in 1958, for $10,550. My dad put $50 down. It was in the shadow of downtown Richmond, a neighborhood of World War II-era laborers' houses, a tiny, three-bedroom, one-bathroom house that looked like a mobile home covered in stucco. The children were born in two groups; I was the youngest of the big kids: Angie, Michael, Edna, and me. Next came the little kids: Debbie, Larry, Rosalind, and Anita.

And so my mother had eight children before she was thirty years old. She had so many kids and we were so young, she couldn't work until we were older, when she got a job in a school cafeteria. My father worked three jobs sometimes, but they always kept us fed and in clean clothes.

After being discharged from the army, my father was a welder at the Mare Island Naval Shipyard, a laborer, and a part-time bail bondsman in Grandpa Marvin's business. My father knew a little about a lot of things and he even had a reputation as an old, blue-collar lawyer. He'd help workers or sailors file lawsuits if they were being discriminated against or in some other way treated unfairly. Once, he won twenty-one days of overtime compensation for himself. He's assured me often that he is a better lawyer than I am.

He even took a business law class once and suggested that, had he not had so much responsibility at such a young age, maybe he would have tried to be a lawyer. But he said someone stole his law book. He always figured it was me, because for as long as anyone could remember, I was walking around saying I was going to be a lawyer someday.

I didn't know any lawyers, but I read about them and I knew they made a lot of money, dressed nicely, and had power, commodities that I had in short supply. When you grow up in Richmond, it can be intoxicating to imagine a way out. Being a lawyer was like that for me. I had no sense of what a lawyer did; it was like imagining some far-off place you'd never been, some fantastic land where you could drive whatever you wanted and eat as much as you could.

When you're a kid, you think about food all day long. I wonder now if we were as poor as I thought, or if a child's hunger will distort his memory. It seemed to me that my parents provided enough to stay full and healthy, but there was no more than that. Bowls of food weren't set on the table at dinnertime; my sisters would take our plates into the kitchen and come back with our ration of food. That was it; there were no seconds at the Darden house, no heaping plates of food left over as on *Father Knows Best*. I was a kid; I was always hungry. And so I'd steal food—crackers and apples and whatever else I could liberate from the pantry.

That was when you learned who your true friends were, when you looked over your shoulder Sunday morning at 5 A.M., perched on the top shelf, your hand around a beautiful Saltine cracker, all six squares just for yourself, and saw your sister, staring up at you with a crazy, toothy grin.

"I'm telling Mama."

And so you crept back down to the chair and onto the kitchen floor and you broke the cracker in half, offered her some of it. But there weren't enough Saltines in the world to keep a Darden sister from telling on one of her brothers.

The first time I really saw anyone steal anything, it was food. And— as was true for most of the lessons I learned—it was my older brother, Michael, who taught me how *not* to steal. He and I walked from our house on Sixteenth Street in Richmond up to the Golden Rule Market, on Sixteenth and Cutting. He went straight to the cookie section, grabbed this package of Mother Oats Oatmeal Cookies, and just broke for the door. "Come on!" he yelled.

I was only about seven and I had no idea why I was running. The white store owner jumped into his car and chased us as we ran down the street. Finally, he cut us off with his car, leaped out, and caught Michael. I just stood there crying.

The white man put us in his car, drove us back to the store, and locked us in a room while we waited for the police. The officers arrived, spoke to the store owner, and placed us back in their patrol car. We thought we were going to jail, but it was far worse than that. They took us home. The officers knocked and my mother answered the door. Her face went from shock to anger in a blink. She looked us over and yelled,

"Eddie!" My father came to the door then. I couldn't see his face. I was crying too hard. Miraculously, one of the officers came to my defense. "This little one here, he didn't steal anything," he said. "He was just with this other one over here."

I just rolled right over on my brother. "I didn't know he was gonna do that. He did it. He stole the cookies." Of course, they beat the crap out of Michael and I had my lesson: You have to be a smarter thief.

My brother taught me a lot that way—through his failures. I watched him constantly screw up and constantly get caught, get a whipping, get grounded, and then screw up again.

I have always felt guilty about Michael because he always got the worst of everything. Michael was the gentle one and was never violent, but he got in more trouble than anyone I ever saw. It was like he was walking through this minefield, just ahead of me, blowing up all the mines and showing me where not to step. Some part of me wonders if I was able to escape that life only because he lived it.

But Mike and I were partners in crime. There were Mike and me, our brother Larry, who was too little to get into trouble with us, and our sisters, the snitches, the rats, the informants. As soon as we did something, they'd be there to sing it to the world, like a Greek chorus: *"Mama! Chris stole a cracker!"*

I spent much of my childhood criming and conniving. It was how I existed. Cynics might say my lawyer character developed early. All I knew was that I wanted to be just like Grandpa Marvin, to have clothes and money and to eat what I wanted. I never got exactly what I wanted as a child for Christmas; I always figured I'd have to get it myself.

I stole in elementary, junior high, and high school, and I didn't stop stealing until I was in college. I was always scheming to get an extra cinnamon roll or some clothes I just had to have, a few cents here, a buck or two there.

Michael was my role model in thieving and I even replicated his oatmeal cookie heist. Once, when I was ten, my mother sent me to the store to get some baking powder for dinner. I walked to Frank's Market on Thirty-fifth Street, and as soon as I saw it, I was in trouble. I loved Hostess fruit pies. Those, to me, were French pastries. I grabbed that pie, stuck it in the tight blue sweater I was wearing, picked up the baking powder, and walked calmly to the counter.

The store clerk gave me a chance. "Just this baking powder?"

With a pie outlined in my sweater like a baby kangaroo, I nodded dumbly. "Yeah."

"That's all."

"Uh-huh."

Then he reached over and pulled out my sweater and a flattened lemon pie fell to the floor. He kicked me out and told me never to come to his store again. Of course, I didn't want my mother to find out, so I ran all the way down to the store on Twenty-eighth Street to find baking powder. They were out. Mama's homemade cornbread wouldn't rise without baking powder, so I had to keep looking. I ran to every store in a twelve-block radius just to find the right kind of baking powder. Nobody had it. I was gone an hour and a half. Finally, I went home empty-handed.

"Where have you been?" my mother asked.

I lied. I said I'd gone to Frank's and he'd accused me of being there earlier in the week and stealing a pie and then he ordered me out of his store forever.

My mother was furious. "How dare he!" Tottering on high heels, she grabbed me by the wrist and dragged me down to that store. I was beginning to get nauseated.

"How dare you falsely accuse my son!" my mother yelled, not letting the clerk get a word in. "He is not a thief. He is not the boy who was in here earlier this week, you racist son of a bitch!"

Finally, my mom talked herself out and while she was coming up for breath, the clerk said, "Ma'am, I didn't accuse him of stealing something earlier this week. I accused him of stealing this Hostess pie on the counter about an hour ago."

She turned to me, as slow and deliberate as a sprinkler head. "Is that true?"

I started crying. "Yeah, that's true."

Then she dragged me home by the wrist, all the way asking how I could embarrass her like that. I'm not sure the beating that night hurt as much as my guilt. Mama grounded me for the rest of the summer, six weeks. And when Mama handed down a sentence, there was no probation.

I have also felt guilty because so much of what Michael was blamed for, I actually did. I had any number of scams going and sometimes Michael was blamed for them.

My father used to collect fifty-cent pieces—the old Kennedy half-dollars. Dad would bury those Kennedy halves in a sorry collection of piggy banks, jars, and bottles in the corner behind the shoes and boxes piled up in his closet. There must've been five, six hundred dollars in shiny half-dollars in that closet.

Pops would work graveyard or swing, and by the time I got ready to go to school, he'd be asleep already, snoring like a horse. I'd sneak into his room, sneak into his closet, and grab those Kennedy halves. By the time I hit junior high school I must've had seven, eight dollars. I was stealing them weekly. There was a major manhunt for those Kennedy halves. My parents looked everywhere but they never found my hiding place.

We had bunk beds—the three of us boys packed into a small bedroom with two beds stacked and the third against the wall. There were wood slats between the bunk beds and I would raise the mattress a little bit and put a couple of those halves underneath the slat. Eight kids in two bedrooms, there weren't a lot of places to hide things, and my parents turned our room upside down looking for those coins. They'd rip the bedding off, tear everything out of our drawers, look under the bed, even under the mattress. But they never looked under those slats. They're tearing up the house and I'd laugh, knowing I had seven, eight bucks stashed right in front of them.

Of course, I blamed Michael. Anything bad happened, Michael was blamed for it. Not long ago, as Michael was lying sick in a convalescent home, blind and unable to swallow food, I talked with my sisters and my brother Larry and I admitted that I was the one who was actually stealing those Kennedy halves.

"I was stealing those!" My sister Anita laughed.

"Me too!" my other siblings said.

Looking back, Michael was probably the only one who *wasn't* stealing those coins. That would figure. Anyone with siblings knows how everything you do is somehow connected to your brothers and sisters. At times, it seems, your success is built on your siblings' sacrifice.

Michael always and gracefully took the blame in my family. Sometimes he deserved it, other times not. In a sense, he suffered for our sins.

People ask me often why I never smile.

I had bad teeth as a kid. By the time I was twelve, my front teeth were beginning to rot. And then I got hit in the face with a baseball bat and my teeth just cracked. They were cracked and rotten and they were decaying from the center of the tooth out. One of my sisters called me Crunchy because she said I had teeth like Cap'n Crunch. At school, they called me Corn Nuts, Toofy Thompson, and Snagglepuss. By the sixth grade, my parents took me to the county dentist, where they didn't spend much time talking about my options. Instead, they pulled my front teeth. There I was, twelve years old, with partial false teeth.

I was so embarrassed by the spaces that once held my front teeth that I never saw anyone unless my partial was in my mouth. When I was younger, I was afraid to even take it out to clean it. Once, I leaned back and yawned and the girl I was with said, "You have your name written on the top of your mouth." She'd read my name on the partial. Another time, I was on the bus for a football game and I stood up to yell and my partial went flying out, right in front of the football team. I had to bend over and pick it up off the floor, with all the other players just tearing into my ass over it.

I guess, after a while, I stopped smiling. I didn't want to draw attention to the fact that my teeth were missing. And after the humiliation, I didn't have much to smile about. When you smiled, they called you Snagglepuss; when you opened your mouth, a girl saw that your teeth were missing. And even though, later in life, I spent thousands of dollars for crowns on my teeth and bonding, I have never been able to get over that. Twenty-seven years later, I still find it difficult to smile.

My world then was pretty well-defined: To the north was Macdonald Street, which cut through the middle of downtown and was strung with all manner of businesses: beer-and-shot bars, grocery stores, and the places that today would be called ethnic delis: warm, familiar shops with pig's knuckles behind the counter.

To the east were the hills overlooking Richmond—Richmond Heights and El Cerrito, winding streets and driveways leading to split levels and ranchers, houses that looked like mansions to me, with their groomed lawns and manicured shrubs. In every city, there is a heights, and in every city, the heights is where the rich people move, like feudal castles above the serfs.

To the northwest was North Richmond, the unincorporated part of town that was, literally, on the other side of the railroad tracks, out by the dump. There were rutted streets with tired bungalows, no sidewalks, burned-out streetlights, and aimless people on corners. At night, it always smelled like someone in North Richmond had left the lid off a cold pot of collard greens.

My father would tell you that I was on the lazy side, but what he means is that I had little patience for manual labor. It's hard to argue with that. It seemed to me that my five sisters were coddled, while my brothers and I were loaded down with work. I had to dump the trash, clean the upstairs bathroom and the downstairs bathroom, sweep and mop the kitchen. And we all had to make our beds, because if we didn't, Mom would grab our sheets and blankets, take them outside, and dump them in the garbage can.

My other job was walking the dog, a stocky black mutt with a white throat. In my neighborhood, all the male dogs were named King and the female dogs Queenie. And so we named our dog Maharaja and called him Raja for short. But no one in my neighborhood knew what that meant and everyone called him Roger. I always suffered my neighborhood's lack of imagination.

I also suffered that dog and his walks every evening. We'd go about seven o'clock, before the good shows came on television, his long chain wrapped around my wrist. My parents would tell you that I noticed girls more often and at a younger age than other boys; again, hard to argue. I remember once spotting a girl while walking Raja. I took that slow, casual look over my shoulder and Raja took his long chain right off the sidewalk and into traffic. There was a thunk and a yelp and I realized the dog had been hit by a car. But he stood up on wobbly legs and seemed to be OK. The car kept driving and I just picked him up, carried him home, and gently put him in the backyard. As far as I knew he was fine.

We had a small backyard, nestled in behind a six-foot fence, and Raja's personal mission was to fill that space with his droppings. And one of my other jobs was to bury Raja's contributions in the backyard, so I'd trudge out there with a shovel, look for a fresh piece of ground, and bury the dog shit. Pops had impossible demands: He wanted a dog and he wanted grass too. So, once every few weeks, he'd send me or my brothers out to "dig up the backyard." It was that awful hybrid of punishment and chore, a mindless, pointless, all-day affair. I'd push my shovel into the ground and turn over a bit of sod, usually unearthing the dog shit I'd just buried two days before. But my old man didn't care. "Come on, boy, get out there and dig up the backyard."

I hated that kind of work, couldn't understand it, and wasn't very good at it. My family said I took after my Grandpa Marvin, my mother's father. Maybe that's when I began looking for a way to make money without manual labor. It's hard to spot the seeds on a grown plant, but maybe it was the dog shit that made me become a lawyer.

Or it might have been Nanny.

My grandmother made the best coffee you ever tasted. Every day, Grandpa Marvin would eat beans. He'd have black-eyed peas, vegetables, and those damned beans. And every day, he'd drink Nanny's coffee.

I'd look over at the can and it would read Maxwell House or something, so Nanny must've done something to it, because I've never found a can of coffee that tasted like the liquid, black candy that Nanny served. Nanny was a hairdo over five feet tall, with the clearest complexion I ever saw on a woman. She always wore a wiglet—a hairpiece—and it wasn't until years later that I realized she was probably losing her hair. But the thing I will always remember about Nanny is her laugh. She didn't drink, but she had the laugh of a hardy drinker, deep, from the chest, full of warm bourbon and meandering stories. I used to wonder how such a big laugh came out of such a little woman. I only heard that laugh one time after Nanny died, and when I saw the woman who unleashed it, I very nearly married her.

Even though my grandfather was something of a leader in the community, he knew better than to go against Nanny. She was the matriarch of the family, and even if other people feigned to make decisions, everyone knew who had the final say. It wasn't because of force; it was because Nanny was just the wisest person anyone knew. Even my father knew better than to go against Nanny on anything important. He could bitch and complain, but, in the end, Nanny got her way.

She was everything to my mother: her best friend, her confidante. With eight children on a welder's wages, you aren't sneaking the family off to Disneyland very often, and so, on weekends, we'd go over to Nanny's. On vacation, we'd go over to Nanny's. We'd pack in the 1960 Oldsmobile, four in the front seat, six in the back, stacked like wood. The worst spot was backseat, bottom middle, where you're seemingly touched by all your brothers and sisters. We'd get cleaned up, dressed up, and then we'd fire over to Nanny's house.

Nanny's decor was French provincial, all the chairs, furniture, and pillows fitted with plastic covers. There were crocheted doilies everywhere. The dining room was grand and could seat ten people. The table was always draped with a white tablecloth, with tight lace and little doilies along the edges. There was a china hutch and a tea service—silver, always polished—although no one ever had tea. Everything at Nanny's was accompanied by a stern "Don't touch that!"

Nanny served the most incredible sweet potato pie—harder on the top than the sweet potato pie they make now, firmer. And I'd sneak a half-cup of that incredible coffee when no one was watching.

I was a cranky kid for a while—messed-up teeth, guilty conscience, and a lack of space. I was going completely nuts in that crowded house with all those people. Sunday nights, we spread out like a deck of cards in front of the TV, watching *Lassie* and then *Bonanza,* eating popcorn from pink porcelain bowls that Mama called her china. Other days, I was stuffed into a small bedroom with three beds and barely enough floor space to lie down, my head pressed against the stereo speaker, listening to the Delphonics as quietly as I could, so that my father couldn't hear. But in that house, with informants everywhere, Pops seemed to hear everything.

"Turn that down!" he'd yell, until only dogs could hear my little turntable and shoebox speakers. There wasn't even a place to do homework, except the kitchen table after supper and dishes, and even there, you could hear the television and your brothers and sisters fighting. We fought over everything. Someone spit in your food? You fought. Someone played with your toys? You fought. And you held a grudge and did everything you could to get back at the sibling you just fought with. I remember once, I saw that Michael hadn't made his bed and I was so angry with him over something, I decided to pee in his bed. I knew that peeing in your bed was one of the most serious crimes in the Darden house and so I quickly ran and told my mother that Mike had wet the bed. She stormed to the room, with me gleefully behind her, and it took her only a few seconds to realize that the top cover had been peed through as well. It was clear that someone had done it from outside the bed, and she turned, red-faced, to glare at me. Needless to say, I got no revenge that day.

It was like that, like *Lord of the Flies.* It was noisy and crowded and we fought over crackers and over space and we peed in each other's beds. What Nanny's house meant to me was space, quiet, a place to think and talk. And so she would invite me over sometimes by myself and I would stretch out there and talk to her about things no one else seemed to understand. Like becoming a lawyer.

I couldn't talk to my parents then; they were overwhelmed with the business of raising a family, and so I talked to Nanny, especially when I started my teenage years. I felt as if my parents and siblings didn't understand me at all, as if I spoke a different language than they did, a language only Nanny understood.

Sometimes Nanny would let one of us kids spend the night on a Saturday, then get us up for church the next morning. Grandpop was a steward at Davis Chapel, a CME church, where women would start shouting and trembling, shaking and chanting: "O Jesus! O Lord! Hallelujah!" One time I burst into laughter and Nanny reached over and slapped me right across the face. Of all the beatings I'd gotten or seen, that was the worst. I was so embarrassed. That was the only time Nanny ever hit me.

I think Nanny knew that I needed to get out of my house. Sometimes she would call over to my house and say she needed some weeds pulled, and I'd race over there and she'd pay me a dollar and a half. Later she gave me money to buy myself cologne and we'd talk a lot about girls, Nanny and I. When I was in high school and college, I'd bring the girls by to meet Nanny and she would tell me if this girl was going to hurt me or if that girl was playing games. I still miss her judgment and I miss the pride she showed in me.

"This is my grandson Chris," she'd say to her friends. "He's gonna be a lawyer someday."

* * *

I paid for integration. Fifteen cents every day. That's how much it cost to catch the Alameda County Transit bus at the corner of my neighborhood and ride it up into Richmond Heights to go to Adams Junior High School. We moved in 1966, when I was ten years old, a few miles down the street, to a bigger, $18,000 house, the house my parents still live in today

In 1969, my neighborhood was 75 percent black. The heights, which loomed over our neighborhood and where my daddy always dreamed of owning a house, was 90 percent white. According to the census figures, the median income in the heights was almost twice what it was in my neighborhood. Only 7 percent of my neighborhood went to college. I don't know how many graduated or how many went on to graduate school or law school, and it's probably a good thing I didn't know the odds then.

The social engineers of the day were probably looking at the same numbers when they decided that the black kids from the flatland ought to be exposed to better education through integration and that we ought to ride the bus up the hill, three miles away, and go to a school where they didn't seem to want us.

In 1969, fifteen cents was a candy bar and change, and it was hard to spend that money on a ride to school. Even then, it didn't make sense to me that the poor kids—the ones who were discriminated against and who could least afford it—would have to pay to integrate the schools. It hurt to pay that fifteen cents. And so we didn't. We'd show up at the corner early, pitch coins against the wall; if you match, you win. Or we might sell our bus tickets for a dime. You'd go there, flip for your bus fare or sell your ticket, and then you'd be without a bus ticket thirty minutes before school started.

So, whatever shoes we had on, we'd run from the bus stop, all the way up the hill, on the winding roads of Richmond Heights, past houses that seemed like mansions. It was three miles. We'd try to beat the bus, passing it at each stop, watching it pass us in between.

Adams Junior High School was my first real exposure to white people because it was the first time I felt like a minority. At Nyestrom Elementary School, only the teachers were white. At Adams, however, in 1968 and 1969, the teachers and three-quarters of the students were white. Unfortunately, it was almost as segregated as if we'd been in different buildings.

You'd take the bus with your friends, hang out with your friends, and go home with your friends. They weren't like us, we weren't like them, and we left it at that.

Even the teachers didn't seem thrilled to have us there. Many of them didn't quite know what to do with us. I remember one counselor, a short, white woman with light red hair and an Oklahoma drawl. We called her Bulldog. She was chubby and wide with a face that did justice to her nickname. I was always scared of Bulldog because she was so mean-looking and she seemed to know things about you that you didn't know yourself.

She took one look at my grades from elementary school—mostly A's—my interest in reading and writing, and quickly put me into the classes she figured were appropriate for a bright young brother: wood shop and metal shop.

I had no talent for mechanics, no interest, no proclivity, no future. I couldn't draw a straight line. But I went down there to metal shop, made a bolt and a nut. My bolt never fit my nut. And so I got my first D in metal shop. But Bulldog said that's where my aptitude was. I was a smart young black kid, and the educators at my school knew what that meant: laborer, or if I got lucky, mechanic.

I wonder how many future black doctors and lawyers, politicians, and writers have been sent to auto shop or food service classes. I didn't like it then and I don't like it now, someone looking at the color of my skin and deciding what my life will be, what my opinions should be, on which side I should be.

I had a close bunch of friends growing up: Kenneth, Keith, Harold, Rusty, and Baby Brother. Harold was the oldest and, along with me, the leader. He was light-skinned with bright green eyes and a bad right leg that he carried over sideways, instep first. It's wonderful to be a kid; I never needed to ask what happened to Harold's leg.

Most days, we'd walk to the park near my house, where we played a thousand innings of baseball—Harold and I the captains—with the kind of rules born of too few players—right field's dead, got to beat it to first before the ball gets back to the pitcher. We'd play touch football in the street with the least traffic. Sometimes, we'd climb the railroad trestle near my house or look for tadpoles in the ponds that formed alongside the tracks.

Whatever you say about those days, you had to be thankful that everyone watched out for everyone else. It wasn't just my parents making sure I did right, it was every parent in the neighborhood, the parents of all my friends. I guess there is something to the old saying that it takes an entire village to raise a child, because back then I was raised by the six or eight blocks that constituted my village, the flatland of Richmond.

In those summer days, you left the house at eight in the morning with your baseball glove and bat and, if everything went well and your sisters didn't come outside screaming—"Chri-i-i-is! Ma-a-a-ma wants you!"—you could stay out playing until dinner.

On one of those summer days in 1968, when I was twelve years old, Harold decided we ought to catch the bus to San Francisco. Although it was just across the bay, San Francisco might as well have been on another planet. None of us had ever been there. It took some courage, knowing that at any time, one of my sisters could come outside and call me in for the day.

Baby Brother, Keith, Kenneth, Harold, and I caught the 72 M bus on Macdonald Street and rode it through Berkeley to San Francisco, as calm as if we had some business there. We got off near Market Street in San Francisco and walked up Market, staring at the windows and the skyscrapers.

We were a million miles from home; it was TV. We walked through downtown San Francisco and along the water, staring at the people, the cars, the buildings, a world we couldn't even have imagined in Richmond. I don't think we talked much, just walked and looked and played it cool. But I doubt any of us ever forgot that day

I never would've gotten permission to do that, never would've gotten the money. I'm sure the money I spent that day was from my father's collection of Kennedy halves. Amazingly, we made it home with no trouble and my parents never knew we'd gone anywhere.

But that trip was rare, because, usually, my friends and I stayed in our universe, between Macdonald and Cutting and always on this side of San Pablo Avenue. That was because on the other side of San Pablo, the white neighborhoods began and it was just always understood that San Pablo was a border of some kind.

Occasionally, we'd get daring enough to cross that border, like one time when I was about twelve. Rusty, Kenneth, and Keith were about my age; Harold was the oldest, thirteen, and Baby Brother was the youngest, seven.

For some reason that day, a few of us walked right across San Pablo and went to Alvarado Park. We played that day, and on the way home, we stopped at a vacant lot, where there was an apple tree, tempting us. There was only one apple left on that tree and we did what we always did—we began racing for that apple.

Next door, there was a house with a white picket fence, and as soon as we hit that tree and began climbing, a man came out of it.

"Hey, you niggers! Get out of that tree!"

We all jumped down and began running and I looked back over my shoulder to see one of the neighborhood kids lagging behind like a short-legged dog and to see that white man huffing up behind him with an automatic pistol. He caught one of us and wouldn't let him go. "You niggers better come back," he yelled, "or you ain't never gonna see this one again!" And so we had to go back. That man called the police, and I took my second ride in a cop car, back to my house, where they told my parents I'd been caught stealing. Didn't matter that we were only stealing an apple from a vacant lot. Back in that day, a thief was a thief.

Your first friends have a way of drifting on you. Keith played AAA baseball in the Mets organization. Baby Brother, I believe, lives near his mother. I lost track of Kenneth. There was another kid named Fella; who knows what happened to him? I know Harold died of kidney failure a few years back. And Rusty, I heard, killed a guy, stabbed him to death. I still remember those summer nights, sitting on the porch and watching nothing happen in my neighborhood, watching the same nothing night after night, people walking from house to house with nowhere really to go, people living and dying in a two-mile radius of the house they were born in, people dying over an ounce of dope or a flirtatious glance. I watched my parents struggle to get a decent meal on the table and watched the ten people in my family packed into a house like ants.

I think for anyone who grows up believing he's poor, the drive to succeed is always touched by economics. But that doesn't necessarily make it shallow. For me, it has always been about space, about having enough space to figure out who I wanted to be. People who have never been without don't understand the claustrophobia of poverty.

I'm not sure I understood it until the end of ninth grade, when I sat on my parents' front porch, waiting for another summer of nothing in that crowded house. That semester, I'd gotten three A's and three F's, the first time I'd ever failed anything. The schedule at Kennedy High School allowed you just three failures over four years, and I'd gotten them all my freshman year. I didn't even bring my report card home and, somehow, in the summer-vacation crush of eight children, my usually diligent parents didn't ask for it.

But I sat outside at the beginning of that summer knowing that I was letting my chance slip away. I had no more leeway at school. One more F and I'd be just another high school dropout, hanging around the neighborhood, hoping to get on with the county or to get into the service.

I can't say it was an epiphany. Who has epiphanies on lazy summer days in Richmond, California? And it certainly wasn't prescience. Sitting on that square-posted porch, I didn't know Rusty would end up in prison or that Harold would die without having seen much of the world. I certainly didn't know what would happen to Michael. I only knew that I had to get out of there. I wanted to see places like San Francisco every day, to pick out my own clothes, drive my own car, and be whatever a man could hope to be, not *just* a black man, not *just* a man from the flats of Richmond. I wanted no limitations. I wanted to be whatever a *man* could hope to be.

THREE

"Nobody ever beats the Temptations." Michael leaned back into his pillow. His head was right next to mine as I lay in my bed, while our baby brother, Larry, snored away in the third bed in our little room. One of Michael's old radios—which he'd rescued from some garbage can or junk pile—buzzed on KDIA, Lucky 13 AM.

"Yeah, the Temptations are cool," I said to my big brother.

At night, KDIA played the battle of the bands, one R&B song after another, and then the station would wait for telephone calls to determine which was the best group. So the Miracles might battle the Four Tops or the Supremes might fight the Marvelettes. And, it seemed to me then, Michael was usually right about such things. Nobody ever beat the Temptations.

The radio was barely at a whisper, so my father wouldn't hear, but Michael and I would stay up late listening to music, just hanging together. There was only one official, government-sanctioned radio in the house—Mama's plastic, fuchsia-colored radio, with the big round dial with numbers written on it. Perched on a kitchen cabinet next to the bread box, it played R&B on weekday mornings and gospel on Sundays.

But in the basement, we had Radio Free Darden. Michael would dig these broken radios and turntables out of the garbage, take them to our room, and set to fixing them, combining pieces from one into another until he'd pronounce some pile of tubes and wires a completed radio. Typically, it would have no cabinet and would be tied to one ugly speaker with a twisted wire, but when Michael plugged it in—assuming it didn't pop and smoke and burst into flame—we'd hear music.

Michael introduced me to R&B, soul, and funk that way, our heads back on our pillows, tapping the songs on our legs and staring at the ceiling of our bedroom. Sometimes he tried to show me how to put the radios together, but I was afraid of getting electrocuted and so I didn't really want to know. Every once in a while, Michael would buy a 45 RPM and, since we usually didn't have one of those little yellow disks to make the single play like an album, he'd press the 45 hard into the turntable, so that it stuck, and then he'd lift the scratchy needle and set it down on some incredible jam. He taught me to appreciate everything about music just by playing it.

Back then almost everything Michael did automatically became cool with me. One summer, when he was in high school, Michael got his first job ever, and he began buying the clothes of that day and style; tight and shiny hustler's threads.

He came home with these silk slacks—pink, yellow, and pea green; pointed lizard-skin shoes; and pimp socks, sheer, with vertical stitching running up the sides. He'd put on his black leather jacket and head out with his friends, and I'd watch him from the porch at dusk, strutting down our street toward downtown. I'd look down at my faded corduroys and button shirt and feel like the biggest bumpkin in the Bay. Sometimes, when Michael wasn't around, I'd reach up into his closet and just feel his silk pants.

Back then, the brothers in Richmond also wore Levi's, starched and creased until they had the general consistency of pressed wood. They'd cut the bottom, split them up the vertical seam a couple of inches, and roll them up as tight as a drum. Michael would spend half an hour on his jeans, spreading them out on the ironing board and ironing them into starched submission. He'd press them with liquid starch and then cover them until the bottom of the iron turned black and my mother yelled at him. Some of his friends would buy powdered starch and put it in a bucket with their pants before ironing them.

I'd see those young men walking down the street, their pants shiny and crisp because of all that starch. They were clean. Like my father, Michael never told me where he was going when he left the house with those guys. His curfew was ten o'clock, two or three hours earlier than any of his high school friends'. It was practically impossible. So Michael would stagger home drunk at one or two, and by the time he got to the door, my father would be so furious, he'd have dead-bolted the door and Michael would have to curl up and sleep on the porch.

My father says I was a backpedaler, trying to explain myself with each disciplinarian step he took toward me. Michael stood his ground, took his beating, and, the next time, came home fifteen minutes later.

"Man, why don't you just come home on time," I'd whisper afterward, when we were lying in our abutting beds.

He'd just laugh and turn on one of his Frankenstein radios and I'd hold my breath until I was sure it wasn't going to explode.

We always had the same taste in music then, but he was older and I guess it couldn't last. I kept up with Michael when Jimi Hendrix started making his sky turn hellfire red and when he bobbed his head to Funkadelic's "Maggot Brain." But I missed the old R&B battles of the bands. And I started to miss Michael.

His musical tastes were becoming harder and more acid and I couldn't hear the rhythm or the melody anymore. I found out later that his drug usage was changing then, too.

At first, he only smoked pot, which I thought was pretty cool because all the big guys in our neighborhood did it. And it wasn't like it ever made anyone violent and it certainly didn't seem addictive. Michael said that smoking a little reefer was "a victimless crime." For a while, Michael even dealt marijuana out of the house and he cut me in on some of the action—letting me watch a few of his deals—although I don't recall him ever cutting me in on any of the profit.

Michael had taken some of his summer money and bought a pound of dope. Back then, you could get a pound of reefer for a hundred bucks. He divided the pound into ounces—each in its own sandwich bag—and sold it out of our downstairs room. Each bag was a lid. The math was simple: sixteen lids, that's sixteen ounces at ten bucks a lid, plus whatever he cut it with, minus the little bit he smoked; Michael could make sixty or seventy bucks on that pound.

I have to say, in those days, if you sold dope out of your house, it really increased your popularity. People who had never been over to our house were suddenly stopping by, and I was happy for Michael. Back then, Michael was cool, but he was never the coolest. He never had a lot of girls around. He was so skinny, some of the kids called him Spider;

and his ears were so big, some of the other kids called him Monkey. Michael was the guy who ran out to watch two other guys fight, laughed at one of them, and then got beaten up because of it. Even though he was my big brother, I never felt as if he was really bigger than I was. Just more unlucky. Early on, I knew I had to watch out for my older brother, that he was one of those people you know is too stubborn and free to stay out of trouble. Yet when he began selling weed, Spider all of a sudden seemed like a cool nickname.

It was pretty bold, selling dope out of our bedroom. It was also incredibly stupid. For one thing, it was a felony, and who knows what would have happened if the police had found out and tried to raid our house, back in the days of Black Panther-style shoot-outs. But even more fearsome was what would happen if our father found out. Daddy was an anti-drug fanatic, and a shoot-out with the cops would've been a birth-day party compared to what Eddie Darden would've done to us.

Even though I had serious misgivings about the whole thing, I kept my mouth shut and watched out for Michael. Even so, Daddy almost caught Michael a couple of times. Once, I was in the room with Michael when our dad came thundering down the stairs. Michael had just lit up a joint.

"Tell him I'm asleep!" I cried, burying my face in my pillow.

By the time Pops came in, that reefer had gone the way of the nickel he'd swallowed when he was five years old, and Michael was sitting there, digesting a lit joint and trying to look smooth about it. Daddy sniffed and looked everywhere for evidence but found none.

I sat up and wiped my eyes as if I'd just gotten up. "Hey, what's going on?"

That was enough of the retail marijuana business for me. Long before it became fashionable, I was scared straight, by my foot-pound-ing, belt-swinging father.

Michael, of course, responded the other way, getting deeper and deeper into drugs. Soon, he was into other stuff: pills, bennies, acid. Even heroin.

And that's when Michael first left me. I see now that it was the only thing he thought he could do, distance himself from me. I would learn later that my big brother had been a junkie since the eleventh grade. Yet he never offered me a pill or a hit of acid or anything like that. At our school, every day, someone on red devils would just fall the hell out of his chair and slap against the floor like a raw burger on a grill. Drugs were everywhere then. It would've been understandable if Michael had wanted to get his little brother baked with him. But he never did.

"Don't you mess with that shit," Michael told me in 1970, when he was a senior and I was a freshman. "It ain't cool."

"You're messing with that shit," I fired back.

"Don't worry about what I'm messing with," he said. But I worried anyway.

Michael was high all the time then. We both ran track and I'd show up for practice and see him with his buddies sprawled out in the grass, stoned out of their minds. Michael was a track man; he was Spider. That was what Michael Darden was known for. He was a force in East Bay track, a great 100-yard sprinter who, if you put a gun to his head, might even run a 440 or a relay.

"That's just Spider," people would say as he lay down in the track infield and slept off whatever he was on.

I remember one day in 1970, when I was working out with the freshman track team and the coach was running us around like ponies, intervals of 440, 330, 220, and 110 yards, with an easy jog between each race.

Michael came strolling up, wearing his leather letterman's jacket—red, with white sleeves and a big red "K" with white trim. He plopped down in the grass and watched me run. At the ends of races, when I ran out of juice, my form would always go to hell. My knees would be pumping high and my thighs were very strong, but when I got tired, my head would go back and my chest would go forward, so that I was running straight up instead of leaning forward. It is not a very efficient way to run.

From the infield, Michael leaned up on one elbow, almost as if he were leaning on his bed at home, telling me no one ever beat the Temptations.

"Man, what the hell was that?" he asked. "You're never gonna beat anybody unless you work on your form. Keep your head straight, arms even, chin down." The next 220 was better.

"Do that Friday and you might beat somebody," Michael said. Of course, I listened, and not just because he was my brother. Michael was one of the best sprinters in the city; I was nothing, a lowly freshman, Spider's brother.

But even on the track, you were always afraid Michael was going to unravel in front of you. And even when things went well for him, they had a way of falling apart.

The track at Kennedy High School was called the beach because it was a dirt track covered with sand. As you might guess, it wasn't very fast. Michael was one of the best sprinters in the conference his senior year, second only to a guy named Sammy Barnes. That year, Michael was running the 100 and he just tore away from the field. When they checked his time, Spider had run the 100 in 9.8 seconds. He was smoking. The people watching stared at one another. If he could run a 9.8 on the beach, he could easily run a 9.5 on tar. Those were almost world-class times. It was in the newspaper—"Michael Darden runs 9.8"—and everyone was congratulating him.

It wasn't until a few days later that one of the coaches went back and noticed that the finish line was chalked in a little short. It seemed Michael hadn't run a 100 in 9.8, he'd run a 90 in 9.8. The newspaper ran a correction, and Michael shrugged it off. By that time, he already understood that sometimes, through no fault of your own, you just come up a little short.

I was twelve when they shot Martin Luther King Jr. and I think of him now the way people think of a grandfather who dies before you can really learn from him. Martin's death wasn't like the death of John F. Kennedy five years earlier, which I remember vividly, when the teachers in my school hugged one another and I found my mother slumped on our sofa, crying as she watched the news. When Dr. King was killed, April 4, 1968, people stood in small groups in the street talking seriously, but, for the most part, life went on. We'd become used to losing heroes.

Sadly, by the time Dr. King was killed, I—like many other young blacks—had already given up on nonviolence as a solution to the problems of race and poverty. If we needed another indication that nonviolence wasn't working, Martin's murder was it. I'd watched the news coverage of protests that quickly dissolved into fire hoses, dogs, and cracker police officers with nightsticks. Nonviolence was an admirable, right-minded idea, but it didn't work fast enough for young people like me, people excited by the word "revolution."

By then, the Black Panthers were thriving in the Bay Area. I don't remember the first time I saw the black leather jackets and black berets, the loose Afros and combat boots. But suddenly here was something that made sense: brothers who weren't going to take shit, who were going to take what was owed us. I began cutting the covers off Panther magazines and taping them to my walls: "Today's Pig Is Tomorrow's Bacon." I found out what was happening through the Panther publications: People's Park, Kent State, the 1968 Chicago convention. I started dressing like a Panther, except for the leather jacket, which I couldn't afford. I was a "baby Panther," an evolving militant. It was the first time I developed a sense of politics and a stand on the issues of the day. My stands then were simple: The white man was a racist oppressor. The government conspired to jail and kill the brothers who stood up to it. And it was my duty to stand up, like the Panthers.

Before that, I guess my heroes were athletes. Everyone on the football team wanted number 32 and I was no different. That was the running back number, like 12 was the quarterback number. I wanted to be a running back. Thirty-two was O. J. Simpson's number, and if you were from the Bay and fancied yourself a running back, of course you wanted the Juice's jersey. I first heard of Simpson when he was at USC, and then I followed him at Buffalo too, where he ran the way we all wanted to run, fluid and powerful. He was a hell of a football player.

But he was never my hero, despite the media's simplistic analysis of it during the trial. I'm sure I respected him for making it out of his rough Frisco neighborhood, but had he really wanted to impress me, he would have opened a free clinic in the neighborhood or bought guns for the militants.

Other kids hung posters of athletes on their walls—Willie McCovey, Willie Mays, Walt Frazier, and O. J.—but I had political posters, Stokely Carmichael and Huey Newton. I respected those athletes, but even then, I realized that athletes weren't people to model your life after. My real heroes were the Panthers, because they weren't sitting around whining about civil rights. They were standing up like men and doing something.

About that time, I began dating a girl named Kelli. I'd had other girlfriends before that. In fact, if you believe my sisters, I spent most weekend nights apologizing to some young girl for something I'd done,

holding the telephone up to one of Michael's bad turntables, playing the
Delphonics' "I'm Sorry."

But Kelli was different. Kelli was white. And in Richmond, California, in 1971, there weren't a lot of interracial couples. Kelli lived on
a hill with her grandparents above Arlington School. Her parents were
separated. They were from Oklahoma and her father hated black people.

She was a year older than I was, in tenth grade while I was in ninth.
I don't remember how Kelli and I met, but we just started hanging
around, seeing each other at school and on weekends, doing our best to
avoid her father. I don't remember any other interracial couples in our
school, and people hassled me at first about dating a white girl.

I was used to taking shit. You don't go to school wearing partial
dentures at twelve and not learn how to take shit. I had a tough exterior,
and since I was considered a bright kid, the tough guys didn't mess me
up too badly, because they might need help one day on a term paper
or some homework. After a while, it seemed, people got used to seeing
Kelli and me together.

By then, I had heard from the Panthers and Muslims that white men
were devils, but no one ever told me how white women fit into the puzzle of racial politics. I knew that, in the South, dating a white woman
would draw the Klan to your door before the date was over, but I didn't
think about what it *meant*—except in the crude language of Kelli's dis-
approving father.

It wasn't until later that I realized that, as a potentially successful
black man, I had more than myself to think about. I was a black man
who would graduate from college, who wanted to be a lawyer. For too
many years, black women had watched such men rise out of poverty
and reward themselves with a white woman. For too many years, black
women have since told me, they'd seen white women who were interested only in successful brothers. I soon realized that I had a responsibility to try to breed success in my community, to strive to become one
of those whole black families I'd seen in church, families that moved me
greatly. I still take that responsibility seriously.

If two people fall in love, of course, they owe it to themselves to be
together, no matter their color. But sometimes white women were seen as
trophies of success and achievement by black men, and I vowed never to

fall into that game. I had dated black women before, and almost all the women I dated afterward were black women, but if I liked someone and her skin was green, I wasn't going to stay away from her because of that.

I would never date a woman because she was white. And I would never *not* date a woman simply because she was white. I dated Kelli because she seemed kind and pretty. But I had ulterior motives too. Kelli taught me how to drive.

My father had tried to teach me. He threw me in his huge 1960 Oldsmobile, took me out to North Richmond, to the dump, and switched places with me. I fired up that twenty-five-foot beast and drove slowly, keeping it at fifteen miles per hour, my hands gripping the wheel as tightly as I could.

But fifteen mph was not in the Old-School Pops Driving Manual. "Come on! Get us goin'!" He slammed his foot onto the gas pedal, onto my foot, until we were careening down the street at sixty. That was our last driving lesson together.

Kelli had a Ford Tempest, and since she was a year older than I was—sixteen when we started going out—she let me drive around the parking lot at Kennedy High School and around my neighborhood. And pretty soon, we began driving out to Berkeley, home of the University of California's best and most liberal campus, where an interracial couple went unnoticed or sometimes was encouraged with kind looks and nods.

I'd gotten a job at the Bubble Machine car wash and so we'd save our money for a couple weeks and drive over, taking the 17 Freeway to the 80 to Berkeley. We'd park near Durant Street and Telegraph, which was the counterculture headquarters then, and we'd just walk around, looking at the hippies and the militants, the street musicians and head shops, people smoking weed right out in the street.

I had a little facial hair that I'd managed to sneak past Pops, and Berkeley was so free then, they'd serve a young brother alcohol without batting an eye. If we'd saved enough money, Kelli and I would go to Larry Blake's Rathskeller, where we'd order spaghetti and meatballs and a bottle of wine.

Durant and Telegraph was the spot, though. Leopold's record store was just down the street, along with Gray Wolf's and Blue Beard's, where I began buying my clothes from these cool women in velvet hip huggers.

I'd get crushed corduroy bell-bottoms with two-inch cuffs, or a velvet suit, green, with a white silk shirt festooned with green and yellow roses, a yellow bow tie, and yellow platform shoes. I also had an orange leisure suit—real imitation leather—under which I wore a brown shirt and two-tone brown Flagg Brothers platforms with dark brown stars sewn on them. Back home, I dressed in my new threads, put on a wide brown hat with a chain-link band, and ventured out in the street, walking around the 'hood, taking the most circuitous route I could imagine to Nanny's house. It was as if Bootsie Collins himself was walking down my street.

People would come out and stare at me, and I was so proud. I was going somewhere. One woman came out of her house and just watched me. "Goddamn," she said as I passed. "You sure are cool."

Kelli and I sort of drifted apart when she became a senior. Well, actually she drifted. Right into the arms of an older man, another brother who was twenty and drove a new Mercury Cougar. I found out after getting a busy signal on her telephone for a couple of weeks. When I finally talked to her, she was ice-cold. I played it cool too, and said maybe she should find someone else.

"I already have," she said.

It was my first heartbreak and it lasted the entire summer of 1972. But I continued going to Berkeley and imagining the world that the hippies and militants were promising. Berkeley reinforced my belief that there was a world outside Richmond, and past my parents' porch. It's sad that people look at those times as naive and corny. Because there was a message, an idealism, that would be valuable today. We protested Vietnam and fought racism; we bucked the establishment. Nobody cared about race or age. Not on Telegraph. I don't know. Maybe we need a little naïveté today, a little idealism.

I began going to summer school after ninth grade, trying to make up those three F's I'd gotten. I was a hard worker in school, but I wasn't a genius. My siblings were all bright and hardworking, driven by our parents' desire for us to succeed. Anita has an MBA and a bachelor's degree from Cal Berkeley, Debbie also has a bachelor's from Berkeley, and all the rest have good jobs. But only my older sister Edna was a truly brilliant student; she graduated from high school two years before me—a year after Michael—and was immediately accepted at Dartmouth, where she received her degree.

I knew that if I wanted to succeed, I'd always have to work harder, like Michael, and so I went to summer school every year. The faster I got my diploma, the faster I could get out of my house and out of Richmond and out there in the boundless world.

Back then, my success was one part hard work, the other part hustle, and I was not shy about my scams. Once, I had to take a Renaissance art class over the summer. I had about as much business being in art as I'd had in metal shop, but I needed the credits and I needed the grade. So I scammed the teacher. When she called on me to explain the brushstrokes in a particular painting, I just looked down at my tennis shoes and shrugged.

"I'm sorry," I said quietly. "I'm color-blind." She felt so bad, she gave me a B.

My senior class yearbook shows a serious young brother with a decent Afro (despite scurrilous media reports otherwise). Beneath my name are the words: "track, football, cross country captain, National Honor Society, the letterman's club, home room representative and CRC"—whatever the hell that is.

But, in some ways, that senior picture is a lie. By the time the 1974 Kennedy High yearbook came out, I was long gone.

It had taken me no time at all to make up those fifteen credits I'd lost. And I just kept going to summer school, until I got ahead, so that by the time I became a senior, I needed only one semester to graduate. I'd had a disagreement with a coach, and so, when spring came around, I decided I wouldn't run track. I was a very good quarter-miler and relay leg, but I needed to get ahead and so I enrolled in junior college, ran track there, and had twelve college credits by the time my high school class graduated.

During those summer school days, I would stop by and visit another girlfriend, a beautiful young girl named Pamela, who was home alone in a big house during the days. She would make me breakfast and set me a place for dinner. Her daddy was a deacon at the St. John's Missionary Baptist Church, where the pastor was a man named R. L. Johnson, one of those men who preached loud, sweaty poetry, like the old preachers used to do. I went to church with them sometimes and finally decided

I wanted to be saved before I made any important decisions about my life. First, I accepted Jesus as my personal savior in front of the whole congregation, then I agreed to be baptized. "Come as you are," the pastor told me.

I wore red shorts and a red T-shirt. Everyone else who was going to be baptized that day wore white, and as we all began to walk toward the pool beneath the floor of the church, I felt badly. But the pastor said God wanted me however I was. So, in front of the girl I loved then, in front of her parents, in front of the world and God, I was baptized.

Sometimes, you can see your young self as someone else entirely. I think about the thieving and hustling and I wonder where I hid my shame. I also wonder how I can explain this stuff to my daughter. All I can say is what I believed: that the world was an inherently dangerous place, and in a city like Richmond, it felt as if you were at evolution's ground zero, where the fittest survived and you had to do whatever you could to improve your life and get out. I know that doesn't justify some of the things I did, but I know, too, that it is good to look back and remember that there were days when I felt that, ultimately, I had a good heart. I had promise. And, Pastor Johnson told me as he leaned me gently back in that pool, I also had a calling.

The Ivy League schools weren't calling this Darden. My father was urging me to stay at the junior college I'd attended during my senior year in high school. But that wasn't far enough away. I really wanted to go to Cal Berkeley, where I'd been awakened just a couple of years earlier. But I couldn't afford to go to school there and my father made just enough money that I didn't qualify for financial aid. My father's extra jobs and overtime had kept us clothed and fed, but they also kept us from getting very much help for college. And I knew he and Mom couldn't help me very much.

So I applied at San Jose State, where tuition was something like $68 a semester. But I didn't think I could afford even that. I had pretty much resigned myself to joining the army.

There was no reason to *want* to attend San Jose State University. It was an unimpressive and depressing urban campus in the middle of a place I'd never even visited. I knew only one thing about San Jose State. Tommy Smith and John Carlos had trained there. The heroes of the

1968 Olympics in Mexico City, Smith and Carlos had raised their fists as a symbol of black power—black solidarity!—that gave us all hope and inspiration back in the 'hood. I knew those guys had gone to San Jose State, or Speed City, as they called it. I hoped the school would make me faster.

When San Jose State University accepted me, I just packed my things into my 1963 Dodge Custom 880—white with red interior and push-button transmission—and headed out. First, I had to figure out where the campus was. I drove around San Jose and found it, finally, this nondescript urban campus where only 1,600 of the 30,000 students were black. I had $300 when I arrived at San Jose State.

While I was there, I heard about a meeting of the track team and so I crashed it. One assistant coach, Don Riggs, was a cruel little man, and he looked me up and down and realized I wasn't one of his scholarships. "Who the fuck is this guy?" he asked.

"I'll be the best quarter-miler you've ever seen," I said. He didn't seem convinced.

But there was an assistant coach, a man named Larry Livers, who had been a top hurdler at Villanova and who had two brothers nationally ranked in the triple jump and high jump at San Jose State. We called the Livers boys the Philly brothers, because they were from Philadelphia. Larry Livers worked in the financial aid office, so I went to see him.

"I need to go to school and I ain't got no money." I told him where I was from, and told him my best quarter-mile times. If he could just help me out, I said, I would do everything I could to help the track team.

He listened, talked to me, and finally gave me some applications for financial aid. I think now about the breaks that young black men need sometimes and how little it can take to help someone. Coach Livers showed me that I was eligible for some financial aid that I hadn't considered and, just like that, I was in school. While I waited for my aid check to come in, I slept in my car the first couple of nights in college, until my money showed up.

The coaches had some scholarship athletes coming in: a guy from Sacramento named Calvin Cazenave and a guy from Pasadena named James Austin, whom we called Pete. There was another walk-on, a brother from Richmond named Daryl Austin; and the four of us moved into a two-bedroom apartment in San Jose together. We were all dead broke. Daryl and I would go out and get emergency food stamps, sixty bucks each, and then we'd buy groceries. Even at 1974 prices, that would feed a houseful of runners for only a week. And then we'd be a week without food, until food stamp time came around again.

When there was food in the house, we'd kill for it. Once, Calvin and I were running home from track practice and one of us remarked that there was a half-can of Hi-C punch in the refrigerator. We looked at each other for a second and we both just took off running. Calvin Cazenave was a physical specimen, a cut, lean, muscular man who seemed to be built for running. He'd finished second in the 440 in the state championship meet. We flew over curbs and around fences, past garbage cans and parked cars and, somehow, I beat him up the stairs and to the refrigerator. That Hi-C was gone in one swallow. Calvin picked up a cake cutter and fired it at me and it stuck in the wall.

We all learned expansion cooking. My specialty was meat loaf. I'd take a pound of the fattiest beef in San Jose, a third of a box of oatmeal, an egg, a bell pepper, and an onion. By the time I finished stirring, my pound of hamburger was three. We would also make Hamburger Helper and a pan of cornbread. You chase that with a glass of milk and you're full for a day. Sometimes a day and a half. Every once in a while, we'd splurge on a couple of steaks, round steaks usually. Never mind that it was the toughest piece of meat on the herd, it was also the cheapest and biggest. And if it tasted like a shoe, who minded? At least it was a steak.

There I was, far from home, but in the same place: broke and always searching for food. We started stealing almost right away, almost always food. We'd go down to the market wearing an army fatigue jacket and just grab a pot roast, or we'd take a shoulder bag and fill it with bread and cereal.

Even when we stole other things, it was usually to buy food. Once we heard there was this white boy living in the dorms with a pound of weed under his bed. If we could steal that dope, we knew, we could sell it and make a lot of money. So we ran over to the dorm at 9 P.M. and we made a plan. Calvin, who was taking Tae Kwon Do, would kick the door in and we'd rush in, trying to look like scary black men. In the confusion, I was to look under the bed and grab the weed and then we'd all run away. Calvin was always wearing his karate clothes: black Chinese jacket, with the shoes and everything.

We got to the dorm room and Daryl leaned his head against the door, listening to see if anyone was inside. That's when Calvin decided to kick the door in. Boom, the door crashed open and Daryl fell backward. And, of course, everyone in the dorm burst out of the rooms and there we were, wearing our San Jose State track sweats, no masks, in the middle of the hallway. We ran inside the room and, luckily, it was empty. I looked under the bed. Nothing. All we could find was a stereo amplifier and a hair dryer, which we were using then to blow out our Afros as big as they'd go. So we grabbed the hair dryer and ran out of the room, through all those screaming students.

We piled into a little Volkswagen like a bunch of felonious clowns, and drove off. There I was, a criminal justice major, committing residential burglary over a stupid hair dryer.

After a while, we became even more brazen in our thievery. For me, I guess the seeds that had been planted in my Hostess-pie-thieving days were sprouting.

That winter, in my freshman year, Calvin, Pete, and I were sitting around the apartment, trying to figure out what to do. The scholarship guys had just gotten their money a couple of days earlier and so they wanted to go buy some clothes.

We drove down to the mall, where Calvin already had bought a pair of those orange, clunky-looking earth shoes. He was the first black man I ever saw in a pair of earth shoes. Pete had just gone through surgery on a torn ligament in his knee, and so he was on crutches, lagging behind us at the mall, while Calvin and I were popping from store to store, daring each other to steal something.

It became a contest, who could steal the most clothes. We went into Chess King, grabbed shirts and pants and socks and shorts and went into the changing room. We were wearing our San Jose State sweats and it was easy to pull them over a couple pairs of pants and two shirts. There we were again, stealing clothes in sweat suits marked with huge gold letters: SAN JOSE STATE TRACK. We were not smart thieves.

We waddled through Sears on our way out of the mall, our stealing contest a virtual draw. But tying was never good enough for me. Ahead of us, I could see that it was raining outside, and I realized we didn't have an umbrella. A rack of umbrellas was coming up on my right.

"We ought to have one of those umbrellas," I said.

"Come on, Chris," Calvin said. "We got this far, let's not push it." That sealed it for me. Calvin's fear meant I was a lock to win the thieving contest if I just grabbed one of those umbrellas. "Don't do it, man."

I didn't even break stride, just brought my arm forward and lifted one of those umbrellas, a walnut-handled honey, a real elegant piece. Calvin was looking toward the glass doors ahead, when suddenly he got huge eyes.

"Don't panic. And don't look over your shoulder."

I looked over my shoulder. There was this huge guy in a suit that didn't fit at all, walking toward us with his arms swinging.

I just took off. There were double doors ahead of us and as I reached them, I saw a handful of San Jose police outside, waiting for us. I still didn't hesitate, piling into the crush of shoppers trying to leave the store. The doors flew open and the shoppers were pushed into the cops, who were also surprised by a direct frontal assault. The next thing I knew, Calvin and I were in the parking lot, with a Three Stooges pileup of people behind us.

It was winter, the beginning of the track season, and we were in pretty good shape, lean and fast, even with three sets of clothing. We hit that parking lot like idling sports cars. Boom, we were gone. Our knees were flying high, our arms were pumping, and we were running through that parking lot. The cops got to their cars, but it was like chasing a couple of motorcycles through rush hour traffic. We squeezed between some parked cars and ran over others, until we broke out of the mall and onto the street. We were just gone. We couldn't have caught ourselves. We were blazing.

A half-mile away, we slowed down and were slapping hands and talking smack, so impressed with ourselves. I looked down and realized that umbrella was still in my hand and we howled with invincibility. But there must've been one ex-athlete in the bunch, because one red-faced cop suddenly came up behind us, on foot, and lunged at me. I threw down the umbrella and bolted again, toward the expressway.

"What are you doing?" Calvin asked. I was about to step in traffic when Calvin reached out and got one hand on my shoulder. He spun me sideways and the car that I was about to step in front of—the car moving sixty miles per hour—just grazed me.

I ran across the expressway anyway, much to Calvin's amusement. He bent over to pick up the umbrella and then a hand landed on his shoulder, and he turned to see the cop, whose face was even redder. Just like that, we were off and running again.

We ran across six lanes of traffic, causing cars to brake, skid, and swerve, and then we climbed a fence and dropped into a muddy field, an orchard. We ran deep into the trees and stopped, catching our breath. We could hear the cop cars screaming around and when we peeked out of the orchard, we could see police officers everywhere. They had us sur-rounded. We stripped down to our stolen clothes, took those off and put our sweats back on. Then we dug holes in the mud and buried the clothes we'd worked so hard to steal.

I lay there in that muddy field, cold and miserable, marveling at how stupid I was. I was so close to getting out of that nowhere life and what did I do? I acted like a common thief. It was ridiculous. I was con-stantly endangering everything I'd accomplished, everything I wanted, over a hair dryer or a pair of new pants. I don't know that I ever disliked myself again as much as I did that rainy day. Finally, after three hours, darkness set in and the cops gave up their search, probably convinced that we were gone. We sneaked out of the wet, dirty orchard and walked two miles back to our apartment. Calvin's new earth shoes really were earth shoes. They were so covered in mud, it looked like he was walking on two chocolate cakes.

That's when I had realized we'd left two things at the mall: my car and Pete.

Pete was also wearing his blue track suit with the gold SAN JOSE STATE lettering, the same lettering a half-dozen angry cops had seen running away from them. It was like leaving one guy behind at the bank wearing a stocking on his head. When we got home, Pete still wasn't there.

"Come on, Calvin," I said, "let's go down and get my car."

Calvin took off his dirt shoes and climbed into his bed. "No way, man. I'm never going to that mall again. It's your car."

So I changed clothes and Daryl and I drove down to the mall in his car. There was only one shopper's car in the mall by this time: my 1963 Dodge. On either side of it was a San Jose police car. Pete sat on the hood of my car with his head in his hands.

As we pulled up, I turned to Daryl. "You weren't there. You drive my car home."

He just laughed. "I don't think so. I don't need that trouble."

So I got out myself and walked over to the car. "Come on, Pete," I said. I climbed into my car, started it up, and we drove away. For some reason, the cops never stopped us. Lying in bed that night, I felt as if I was back on my porch at home again, staring out at that empty neighborhood, at all that failure. I was nothing more than a criminal. I was out of Richmond but I'd brought the worst parts of it with me.

I've wondered since then if I was subconsciously self-destructive. Years later, a dear friend would tell me that I was a victim of my own guilt and that I was most afraid of success. She said I didn't think I deserved it. I think that has probably been true at different times in my life. I've received more blessings and breaks than anyone I know, and when the day was darkest, I've always been delivered. There were other guys in the neighborhood smarter than I was, guys like Harold Cordier and Clarence Bolton. What happened to them? And then there was Michael. I spent so many days setting him up for my crimes. Michael deserved so much better and yet it was always me with the opportunities, always me trying to blow it by becoming a petty thief.

I wish I could say that I suddenly understood what crime victims felt, how it must be to have something stolen from you, but that depth wouldn't come until later, when I became a prosecutor. Before I could understand my responsibility to others, I had to grasp my responsibility to myself.

And so I remembered the indignity of lying in that muddy field, like an animal, waiting to be arrested for a crime embarrassing in its stupidity. I remembered that car brushing me and Calvin grabbing my shoulder, probably saving my life, keeping me from dying over a pair of stolen jeans. I remembered going back to get my car in front of those cop cars, realizing that a criminal justice major would be expelled for shoplifting and eluding officers. I remember those things today.

I decided that, from that day on, I would do my best to carry myself with the self-discipline and pride my parents instilled in me, the promise Nanny saw in me, and whatever calling God had for me. I remembered to study the lessons that Michael inadvertently taught me. And that was the last time I ever stole anything.

FOUR

Gloria Alibaruho was all of five feet tall. She was an intense woman, dark-skinned, with a round, smooth face and electric eyes. She dressed like a hippie and often wore African head-dresses to class, wearing them with a complete lack of self-consciousness that intrigued me from the beginning. She was married to a Nigerian intellectual and was smart, strong, and always one step ahead of the schemers and hustlers in her classes, no matter what kind of scam we tried to pull on her.

She was a professor in the Afro-American Studies Department at San Jose State University, the first person to teach me what it really meant to be a descendant of Africans. I first met Gloria when I took her Intro to Afro-American history class as a way to get past a history requirement. It became much more than just a requirement to me.

The Afro-American Studies Department was in a small, converted Victorian house on the south end of campus. Between classes, Calvin and I would go there just to hang out sometimes and listen to her philosophy. She spoke in words we could understand about things we'd never imagined. We called her Ali.

"You are the direct descendants of kings and queens," Ali would say. When she had something important to say, whether it was in class or just walking down the street with us, she'd lean toward whoever was listening, and enunciate every word.

"They didn't load just anyone on those slave ships," she'd say. "They stole only the best and they stole only the brightest. They took the strongest physically and mentally. They took royalty and that's why you are the sons and daughters of kings and queens. You are the princes and princesses of Africa."

I had never been exposed to African history before, to anything but a surface examination of slavery, emancipation, and racism. And I'd never made a conscious decision to study those things, to figure out where I fit in American history and society. It was overwhelming to find the history beyond George Washington and Thomas Jefferson, to realize that the fathers of my country *bought and sold* my fathers' fathers.

My eyes opened like slipped blinds and all of a sudden my own life was explained to me. Martin Luther King had taught me what was fair; the Black Panther newspapers screamed at me what was unjust; but it was Gloria Alibaruho who taught me who I was. It was like discovering gravity. It explained the universe to me. So, this is why people treat me the way they do. This is why women grab their handbags when I get on an elevator. This is why I paid fifteen cents to catch a county bus to an integrated junior high school and why Bulldog told me I ought to be in metal shop.

I took almost every class the Afro-American Studies Department offered and every class Gloria Alibaruho taught. I could've majored in it or gotten a degree if I'd wanted to take a couple more courses. In a college that was 5 percent black, the Afro-American Studies Department gave us somewhere to feel proud and to discuss issues and ideas that white students weren't comfortable with or able to talk about. We read black writers like W. E. B. Du Bois, Ralph Ellison, and Richard Wright. I wasn't just instructed in these classes, I was defined by them.

Gloria herself was like no one I had ever met. She had a double Ph.D. from Cal Berkeley; I didn't know anyone with so much as a master's and here was a woman with a double doctorate from one of the most prestigious universities in the country. She was the first person since Nanny who didn't bat an eye when I said I wanted to be a lawyer. In those classes, filled with other awakening black students, what had always seemed like a dream—law school and some vague notion of success beyond—suddenly became expected. "You can do it, Chris. Apply yourself." She pushed me and prodded me and listened to me and did everything a teacher and friend could do.

My God, she'd been to Africa! When I was a little kid, I thought, "Why would anyone want to go to Africa and get eaten by the savages there?" To a kid in California, Africa was just the jungle where Tarzan lived.

In Afro-American studies, I learned that my people didn't live in grass huts. I learned that we had science and astronomy, art and music. Man originated in Africa and there were times in history when the most advanced civilizations in the world were from that continent. It was something like rummaging in your parents' attic and finding evidence of a life you never imagined for them—that your father was an astronaut and your mother a movie star. In my attic, I found nobility, humanity, and achievement where I imagined only slavery, injustice, and sorrow.

Suddenly, my eyes were opened and I was seeing everything differently. Even track and field. Where once I ran just because it was fun, now I watched the business of college athletics, coaches whose jobs were won or lost based on the score of some game or meet. Too often, the currency in that economy was young black men. Instead of being served by the higher education system, the athletes were swallowed by it—devoured, chewed up, and spit out.

It hit me one day in the beginning of the 1976 track season—my second at San Jose State—when the coaches handed out report cards to all the guys on the team. Looking around, I was shocked to see that I had the highest grade point average. There were some incredibly bright guys on the team, like my roommate Calvin, who was an aeronautics major, and yet for Calvin and many of the others, it was a struggle just to pass. I remember once, he had an exam in aeronautics and he didn't buy the textbook until the day before the test. He still got a C. That was all the coaches wanted from him—enough work to stay eligible to run. That was their expectation, and so Calvin never worked as hard as he could in class.

By all rights, Calvin should have been much faster than I was too. He had a perfect runner's body; it was as if he'd been designed specifically for the 440-yard dash. But by our sophomore year in college, his confidence, like his grades, began to lag. You can't serve two masters, and the coaches seemed to me to have no interest in Calvin's other responsibility—his grades.

The coaches fostered in Calvin, and in all of us, the firm belief that running was all that mattered. The scholarship athletes, especially, were told in no uncertain terms that they were brought to San Jose State to run, and if they weren't running well, the coaches chipped away at their self-esteem and wondered out loud if they weren't spending too much time and energy off the track. In other words, in school.

By the 1976 season, I was beating Calvin in the 440. He had so much raw talent and speed, but they stripped him of his desire and his self-esteem under the guise of motivating him. And they didn't give him an alternative, an education. They should have been trying to lift him up with positive reinforcement. Instead, they tried to motivate Calvin and others through intimidation, by taking away their choices.

"If you don't run faster this week, you're gonna lose that scholarship," they would say. "You're gonna lose that money. Why do you think we brought you here?"

In some ways, college athletics seemed to me no more than an updated system of sharecropping. *This isn't your education, boy. You are just borrowing it for as long as you can produce. And if you don't produce enough, then you're gone.*

For a handful of athletes each year, there are financial rewards at the end of a college career. But for more than 99 percent of college athletes, there is no professional contract, no Olympic medal, no competitive future beyond college. Instead, they can expect lower graduation rates and less earning potential than the students who don't play sports. Yet, somehow, Deion Sanders is the expectation for young people instead of the aberration.

I'd suspected earlier that, at some level, athletics was just another system that siphoned the energy and talents of young blacks without giving a reward. That was another of Michael's lessons.

By the time Michael was a senior in high school, he was having serious trouble in his classes. He was smart, but he had no attention span and was brash and stubborn enough to believe that he didn't need to show up for class or do his homework. But he was on course to graduate, as long as he passed a government class. When he flunked the final exam, the track coach—the same one who had coached me in cross-country—went to the government teacher and asked if Michael could retake the test. He explained how busy Michael was in track, how hard he'd been working, and how close he was to graduating.

"I'll give him the makeup test on Friday," the teacher said.

The coach winced. "The state meet is on Friday." Michael's mile relay team had made it to the state meet, and Michael was, arguably, the strongest leg of the team.

The government teacher was adamant. "The makeup test is on Friday."

The coach left the meeting with the teacher, went to track practice, and never told Michael when his makeup test was to be held.

The Kennedy High School mile relay team didn't even win a medal at the 1971 California high school track and field championships. Who would have remembered even if they'd won? Probably no one. Yet Michael would always remember that he wasn't able to graduate with his senior class. It wasn't fair. I was proud of the way Michael worked through summer school, but I was furious with the track coach.

The next year, I got the nerve to ask him about what he'd done to Michael.

"It was for the good of the team," he said. Then he added, "I'm sorry about that. It was wrong."

"Don't tell me," I said. "Tell Michael."

San Jose State had the same attitude. An athlete's worth in college sports can't be separated from his performance on the field or court or diamond or on the track. We were commodities, and as a young black man coming to terms with the legacy of slavery, I did not want to be a commodity.

I ran the rest of the 1976 track season, but my attitude was different. I no longer cared about winning. When the gun sounded, I ran and ran and ran but I stopped competing; I stopped playing the game; I stopped being a commodity. I was still part of the team, but I was distancing myself from it, preparing to emancipate myself.

When the spring of 1977 came around, Calvin and Pete and some other guys asked if I was getting in shape.

"No," I said. "I'm done."

So I ran the last competitive race of my life in the spring of 1976, at the peak of my abilities and training. I finished the 440, slowed down, took a leisurely lap, and then stopped. I walked off the track and never went back.

With my criminal career thankfully over and my athletic career unfortunately behind me, I attacked school at San Jose State. I didn't go home in the summer, but stayed in school, just as I'd done in Richmond. I had come into San Jose State with twelve junior college credits and I worked so hard, so fast, I was soon on track to graduate in three years.

I was a professional, serious student. Early in the fall of my third year, I began seeing notices posted all around the college by the Black Law Students Association, saying that if we wanted to go to law school, we should apply right away, because by the next year, there might be a decision in the case of *Bakke* v. *University of California at Davis Law School*—a reverse discrimination case that would begin closing the door to affirmative action and minority admission programs in California.

"If you're really going to do this, you'd better get serious," Gloria Alibaruho said, in that direct, patient voice. I signed up for the Law School Admissions Test, a requirement to get into law schools, and took it without any preparation. In fact, I stayed up until 3 A.M. the night before, and my score reflected it. But I did well enough to get into most schools, and so, with Gloria's help, I began applying to law schools at the age of twenty.

Here I was, just two semesters from graduating, and I still didn't feel as if I'd gotten the full college experience. Two years of college life hadn't done anything to improve my sullen (often nonexistent) social skills. I was a chronic introvert so driven by some intense desire to succeed that I wasn't enjoying the things I was working so hard to achieve. I knew that I could spend the rest of my college years living on meat loaf in a dark apartment or I could get to know people, gain confidence speaking, and network with people from all over campus.

I could join a fraternity.

One of the guys I'd met in my Afro-American studies classes was a bright, friendly guy named Phil Brown. Phil had the sweetest disposition of any man I'd ever met. He was from Vallejo, just up the bay from Richmond. And he was a member of Alpha Phi Alpha.

Like the Afro-American Studies Department, the black fraternities and sororities were great places for young black students to congregate and get to know one another. When you took classes from Gloria Alibaruho and then went to a function held by one of the black fraternities, it was almost as if you were going to one of the all-black schools in the South. It was comforting and wildly entertaining at the same time.

I went to a smoker for Alpha Phi Alpha during the first week of classes in January 1977. Immediately, I saw the other students waiting to pledge the Alphas. Most were young, freshmen and sophomores, but I remember spotting a student even older than I was and I quickly got to know Luis Silvestri, a black Puerto Rican from New York. Luis was twenty-eight years old, with a junior college degree in refrigeration and a tour in the army. Luis was one of the guys who would become a life-long friend. I thought about it for a few days, and when Phil Brown was selected as dean of pledges for the Alphas, I pledged.

In some ways, the entire purpose of pledging a fraternity is the initiation. There are lessons—pride in your history, brotherhood, and discipline—but for the most part, it's just a chance to engage in that most natural of activities: tormenting someone you like.

We were called pledges or line brothers, and as a "line" we had to wear similar haircuts and absolutely no jewelry, to dress all in black and gold. We could never wear colors associated with another frat. The Kappas were red and white, the Qs were purple and gold, and we were black and gold from top to bottom, from our gold hats to our black shoes.

Alpha pledges like myself were Sphinxmen, so named because we had to wear a four-inch sphinx head—a wood carving hung with leather—around our necks at all times. It identified us as Alpha wannabes and helped define the sport of pledging. We were also called little brothers, and the Alphas were our big brothers.

If one of our line lost his sphinx head, he wouldn't be allowed to pledge. And, since we were brothers, we couldn't pledge either. And so, just to make our lives a little worse, the big brothers would try to steal our sphinx heads. Most of our entertainment for the next few weeks involved trying to keep from being isolated by a pack of Alphas eyeing the wood carvings around our necks. That and the constant beatings and harassment were how we were narrowed from seventeen pledges to eight.

It might seem strange that a journey of self-discovery would lead to the rigidity and raucousness of fraternity life, but it was just what I needed at the time. I needed to subjugate myself, to learn discipline, and to be thrown together with other young men, to open myself up to other people. In many ways, I was still that stubborn eleven-year-old, keeping my scraggle-toothed mouth tightly shut and grimly going about the business of scheming my way through life. Only now, my schemes were legitimate: graduate from college, get into law school, succeed. In the fraternity, I had to do things I didn't want to do. I was forced to do irrelevant, crazy things and to make the kind of friends I'd never had before, friends who see you at your weakest and most vulnerable.

The requirements were exhausting mentally and especially physically. We had to learn a piece of frat history every week and we had to keep a personal history (brothers, sisters, parents, major, hometown) of all seventeen of our line brothers. When I was elected line president, I felt even more pressure to make it through the constant initiation. There was Tar-and-Feather Week, Hell Week, weeks when I was bruised and other weeks when I was just embarrassed.

The older frat brothers would lead us wherever the hell they wanted to, threatening, pushing, yelling at any moment: "Give me your history!" Often, they would try to separate us. If we were separated from our brothers, we were helpless, easy to beat, berate, and break.

Finally, after thirteen weeks of intense pledging, Hell Week, the final week, had come. Those who survived became brothers. Those who couldn't handle it were "turned back" and returned to civilian life.

For the big brothers, every weekend had been a chance to humiliate and harass the Sphinxmen.

At one point, they shaved the beard off half my face and left it on the other half, then forced me to dress in Alpha colors: one black sock, one gold sock, and a beanie, carrying a black brick. Throughout Hell Week, we had to carry this black brick—always at shoulder level—a symbol of the fraternity that would also be with us at all times.

One night, they blindfolded us, tied our hands behind our backs, and put us in the rear of several cars. They drove us around and messed with us all night and then we ended up somewhere rather cold. We were still blindfolded and they pushed us forward a few steps. I stepped forward and fell into a swimming pool, into ten feet of water. I'd never learned to swim. The other blindfolded pledges scrambled toward the sides and felt their way out of the pool. I thrashed around a little, swallowed as much water as I could hold, and then sank like a stone. The frat brothers stood on the side laughing until they realized one pledge was unaccounted for. Finally they dove in and pulled me out of the water. I lay on the side of the pool, coughing and spitting until it was clear to my brothers that I wasn't going to die. Then they laid me on the ground next to the other shivering wretches. That's what brotherhood is, having people to be utterly miserable with.

Another time, they drove us out of town, stripped us to our underwear, and poured molasses, syrup, oatmeal, flour, rice, and spaghetti
sauce all over our bodies. Then they covered us with manure and made
us eat whole, raw onions. And then they drove away.

We were sitting out in the middle of nowhere, twenty-five miles
from San Jose, in our underwear, covered in cow shit and syrup, with
no money and no way back to town. This was the social life I'd come
looking for?

Luis immediately found an irrigation sprinkler, kicked the head off,
and washed a little bit of the gunk off his body. But most of the rest of
us were too cold to stand in that freezing water and I was afraid of getting pneumonia. I rummaged through a trash can until I found a plastic garbage bag, and I covered myself with that. Someone in one of the
farmhouses set back from the road must've been scared out of his wits
when he saw ten naked, shit-covered black men walking through rural
northern California, because the police showed up soon after that.

We were walking slowly toward town, like a disgusting parade,
when four or five police cars came screaming up. As long as they didn't
shoot us, it seemed, we would be saved. If nothing else, they'd have to
give us rides back to town.

"What the hell is going on here?" asked the first officer to roll down
his window.

"What's that smell?" his wrinkle-faced partner asked.

"Oh," the other one said, "it's just a goddamned fraternity. Shit, you
guys stink." And then they drove away.

The women who associated with our fraternity were called Alpha
Angels, and, finally, a couple of cars full of Angels found us and picked
us up. I had them drop me off at the apartment of a woman I was seeing,
a student named Beverly.

She wouldn't let me in.

"Hey, I need some help here."

"Oh, man," she said. "You smell like shit!"

"Please, Beverly, this isn't funny."

She turned away from the door, breathing through her mouth.
"No," she said, "it is not funny."

Finally, I talked my way in. I got in the shower, but the caked manure
and syrup wouldn't come off. So, still covered in this shit, I went to the

store and bought some vinegar. I filled the tub with vinegar and, finally, got the slop off. But the smell didn't go away. I stank for days. And after you eat a whole raw onion, you can brush your teeth five times a day and you won't get rid of that smell. I talked into my hand for the next month.

But I felt a real sense of accomplishment; I'd done something that I never would've even tried before, did something completely out of character. I even thought it would make me a better lawyer, being forced to socialize and compromise. But the best thing I got out of the fraternity was a group of lifetime friends—guys like Luis and Maurice "Mo" Sullivan, a smooth, muscular, Barry White-voiced brother.

One night, the Alphas were having a party south of San Jose and I went with some of my line brothers. The party ended about two-thirty in the morning and we were caravaning back to town. I was in Mo's old Pontiac GTO, screaming along the freeway. In the car in front of us were a couple of brothers we called MicroMac and MiniMac and behind us was a brother named Reggie, who was blind as a mole even with his Coke-bottle glasses.

Just before we got to San Jose, the car in front of us slammed on its brakes and swerved out of the way of something. Mo did the same and as I looked out the window, I saw a confusing blur of colors and what looked like people. As happens with such visions, it took a few seconds for my brain to assemble the unrelated images. I had seen people running on the freeway, what looked like an overturned motorcycle and a woman lying in the middle of the freeway, right in the lane we had been driving in. It looked as if her head was split wide open. Behind us, blind Reggie didn't veer out of his lane an inch.

We got off the freeway and Reggie followed us.

"Man!" I yelled as I got out of Maurice's car. "Did you see that?"

"See what?" Reggie asked. I was afraid to think of what might have happened.

"You hit that woman."

"No I didn't," Reggie said. He insisted that he hadn't hit anything. But Mo and I looked at the side of Reggie's car and found blood all over it. I realized that if that woman was somehow alive when I passed her (which was terribly unlikely after falling off a motorcycle onto her head with no helmet), she would probably have died if indeed Reggie had run her over.

We went back to the scene of the accident and there was a sheet lying on top of the woman. Since then, I have seen hundreds of murder victims, corpses bloodied in every imaginable way. But that woman, lying on the freeway with her head opened like a discarded purse, has haunted me, and that blurry car-window picture has stayed with me always. I guess she was a precursor to the bodies I would see later in my life, a hint that I would soon be trafficking in blood and tragedy. I still see her when I'm tired and I'm driving late at night and I feel all over again the helplessness.

But the worst thing that happened while I was at San Jose State had nothing to do with college. I answered the telephone early one morning, when I was still living with Calvin, and it was my sister, using one of those voices that you recognize right away, even if you've never heard it before.

"Chris, Nanny is dead."

She had been very sick with diabetes for some time and we'd gone to visit her in the hospital the last time I was home. I remember that everyone else was crying, "Oh, Nanny; oh, Nanny," all clustered around her hospital bed. But I just stood back against the wall. Other people thought I was being cold or detached—the way some people describe me now—but Nanny always knew who I really was.

"What's wrong?" she asked from her hospital bed. "Why are you afraid to come over here?"

I *was* afraid. I was deathly afraid and I have hated hospitals ever since then. I could see her dying. Maybe not that day, but some time soon. For the first time, I understood the temporary nature of our lives, and it killed me to see it first in the face of this woman I loved, this woman who had, in a sense, raised me. I knew then, months before she actually died, that Nanny wouldn't see me graduate from college or law school. The only person who believed I could be a lawyer wasn't even going to see it.

I went over and kissed her on the cheek that day and I couldn't believe how soft her face was. I couldn't tell her what I thought as I stood back, watching the rest of the family hug her and talk to her and comfort her. It was as if I could see her funeral.

Now, a few months later, my sister was telling me that Nanny was dead.

"How did it happen?" I asked, shuffling in my college apartment.

Nanny had awakened with a stomachache and said she didn't feel well, my sister said. "I'll go make you some tea," Grandpop had said. When he came back, she was gone.

I had taken my track teammates to meet Nanny and they had liked her as much as I did. And I used to take all my girlfriends over to meet Nanny because she was such an incredible judge of character. I had a tendency to be attracted to destructive women, but Nanny could spot them before they got halfway inside the front door. I had no filter beyond Nanny.

I stood in the filthy apartment I shared with my track teammates and held the phone to my head, wondering how I would live without her. She was my best friend, the person in whose eyes I wanted to be successful.

That weekend, I went home for the funeral, which was held in the church where Nanny had slapped me once for laughing at people overcome with the Holy Spirit. When someone like that dies, you go through the lessons she tried to teach you for the strength to go on, and it seemed to me that Nanny was always trying to teach me that I had to expect as much *from* myself as I did *for* myself, that all the success in the world was empty without an unfailing moral core, an absolute sense of right and wrong. That's what Nanny had always tried to instill in me.

That is the problem I have struggled with and the one I will probably struggle with my entire life. For just when I think I've come close to finding some answers, someone seems to have changed the questions. Sometimes, they even change the rules and your moral core feels slightly off-kilter from the rest of society, when being honorable and good just doesn't quite fit with being black or being a man. During those times, you do your duty, the best you can. But in those cases, you can never make the right decision. You can never win and even if you do your best and come out on top, someone will always be there to point out that you just ran a 9.8-second 90-yard dash.

And other times, my failures have been mine alone, failures of intelligence, energy, and spirit. But by far, the worst have been my failures of character, like the one Nanny once tried unsuccessfully to slap out of me.

* * *

I graduated from San Jose State in the spring of 1977, after just three years, with a bachelor's degree in criminal justice and a minor in criminology. I called my parents and told them when I was graduating and they said they would try to drive the fifty miles for the ceremony. But on graduation day my father had to work overtime and my mother didn't come because she didn't drive. So I just sat in the stands with Luis, surrounded by other people's parents and well-wishers, and watched the ceremony the way I had done most things in college, detached from it.

I applied to the University of California's Hastings College of the Law, a well-respected school in San Francisco, and was accepted. The first year of law school was intense and difficult and I found Hastings to be about as unfriendly a place as there was in the world. There was only a small percentage of black students at Hastings, and the other students didn't go out of their way to make us feel at home. With the *Bakke* decision, affirmative action was in the news almost every day, and I felt as though black students were looked down upon by the white students, as if we hadn't deserved admittance to the school. I knew that I was there because I was bright and had worked hard, that my grades and scores had gotten me into school and that I was ready to prove it.

Those first few weeks, I noticed which students wore sweatshirts with their undergraduate alma mater on them: Princeton, Yale, Berkeley, Stanford. I didn't see any San Jose State sweatshirts. And I certainly didn't wear one. These guys with their huge egos and $80,000 educations were always posturing and posing and doing their best not to talk to me.

In high school, I had gotten partial scholarship offers from Claremont and Occidental, two good Los Angeles colleges, but I had never heard of those schools and so I had gone public, to San Jose State. Now, my choice of a college embarrassed me. I was intimidated by those sweatshirts and the square-headed geeks who wore them. But San Jose State was all I had and I was going to succeed no matter what was written on my sweatshirt.

My law school education is one of the most valuable things I ever earned, and I was educated by some of the best professors in law. But the environment was difficult—not exactly hostile but not friendly or nurturing either.

To be in law school is to be completely isolated. It was like being back in my supposedly integrated junior high school.

Everyone at Hastings seemed to slog to class every day, hang out only with the people like themselves, and then slog home alone. Bill Hodgman, who would later work on the Simpson case with me, was at Hastings at the same time I was, but I never met him. That's how closed and isolated we all were. Law schools have an inherent, destructive competitiveness, and the students eyed one another suspiciously. If you helped someone else, you might be hurting yourself. I sat at a lunch table with other black students that first year; 1952 Mississippi, I imagined, couldn't have been more segregated. And so I just studied and worked and tried to adapt to the increased pressure and academic demands of law school.

For about eight weeks, I lived back with my parents in Richmond, but I could tell right away it wasn't working. I couldn't live with my father's rules anymore, and without Nanny around, everything seemed empty. So I moved into a small apartment in Richmond and commuted to San Francisco.

I saw Michael a little bit during that time and it was clear that he wasn't doing well. Michael had gone to junior college for a short time and had quit, had joined the air force for a short tour and had been discharged. He came back to Richmond and fell right back in with his drug-using and dealing friends. It was amazing how quickly the streets absorb someone like Michael.

Once, during law school, my mother called me and said that no one had heard from Michael for several days. I knew he was living in North Richmond at the time, near the dump, and so I drove there looking for him. I found his apartment, but it looked vacant, dark and boarded-up. It was about 6 P.M.; the drug users, hookers, and pimps were coming out of the shadows and North Richmond was starting to smell like it did every night, like a pot of collard greens. I stood outside Michael's ground-floor apartment, the paint chipped and peeling. I didn't want to go inside.

"Michael?"

When he didn't answer, I grabbed a flashlight, pushed the door open, and stepped inside. "Michael?" Still no answer. I shone my flashlight down and realized the floor was covered with an inch of water.

There were two-by-sixes placed like a bridge over the water and I walked carefully on them. "Mike?" The bridge led from the front door to a bedroom with nothing in it except a mattress lying on top of soap boxes, just above the water level.

I walked into the bathroom and just stared. The toilet had been ripped out of the floor—perhaps to sell for scrap to get drug money—and water was running from the exposed pipes onto the floor. I stood there, amazed that Michael would live like this. I waited, but he didn't come home.

It was a few days still before he showed up at my parents' house. "What the hell are you doing?" I asked. I told him I had visited his apartment.

"Oh," he said, adopting his con voice, his Spider smoothness and nonchalance, "it ain't that bad. I hardly ever stay there."

Looking back, I can see the steps Michael was descending and it frustrates me that I didn't do more. Later, I gave him money whenever I saw him and whenever I had it; I gave him clothes, and when he acted like he was getting his act together, I helped him rent an apartment. But in 1977, when he began slipping deeper and deeper, I was in no position to help him. I was barely living above the water myself. And it was about to get worse.

At San Jose State, I had dated a lot of women, but had become most serious with a petite, fiery girl named Pathenia. We'd broken up about a month into my second year of law school and I was sitting in my cold apartment in Richmond, studying at the kitchen table for the next week's final exams when the phone rang.

"Chris?"

"Yeah?" I concentrated on the book in front of me. Pathenia was always trying to draw me into a deep discussion of why we'd broken up, but I was in no mood for that.

"I have something I need to tell you. Could you come down?" Pathenia asked.

"Are you OK? You're not sick, are you?"

"No."

"Then why don't you just tell me over the phone." I was very busy and I didn't have time for her games.

"No. I have to tell you in person."

San Jose was over fifty miles away and there was no way I was driving down there. So, I got abrupt with her. I can't do it, I said. Just tell me.

The sarcasm dripped from her voice. "Well, come down whenever you get the time then."

I kept studying, took my finals, and did well. But the phone conversation was always in the back of my mind. So, as soon as I was done with finals, I drove down to San Jose and knocked on her door. The thing that bothered me most about Pathenia just before we broke up was that she seemed to be retreating from the world. The curtains in her apartment were always drawn, and it seemed as if she spent most of her time in her nightgown, either getting out of or going to bed.

I knocked on the door, girding myself for another let's-get-back-together argument.

She unlocked the door and let me in. It was early evening and her apartment was completely dark except for a light in her bedroom. She was in her robe and nightgown.

"How are you?" I asked.

"Fine." She was very tense. She didn't offer me anything.

"So, what did you want?"

She stood there, looking at me blankly, and then she just blurted, "I'm pregnant." She said it matter-of-factly in a low voice, but she might as well have said it with a megaphone from the Goodyear Blimp.

"What?"

"I'm pregnant."

"How . . ."

She just kind of gave me this smirk.

I've thought a lot about the next question I asked, and if I could rephrase one sentence in my life, it might be the one I said to Pathenia that day.

"What are you going to do?" I asked. It was a huge question, a hundred questions wrapped into one: Am I the father? Are you sure? Do I have to be responsible? Are you going to put the baby up for adoption? Should we get married?

What are *you* going to do? No words could've isolated her more, made her feel more like she was alone in this. I was twenty-two. She was twenty-one. I had thought of having children and knew that I wanted to one day, but not then. And I had never really thought about what it would be like to be a *father*. Making a baby and being a father are nothing alike.

I remembered a high school teacher, John Goaia, who told me I had great promise but that I might be sunk by my already voracious dating habits. "You are smart enough and talented enough to do whatever you want," he said, "as long as you don't impregnate one of these girls you're seeing." Now, it seemed, he was right. Everything I'd worked so hard for was disappearing, and in a flash I saw myself dropping out of law school and getting a job at a Burger King to pay for my child and wife. I guess that's where the question came from, the part of me that would scheme and steal just to rise above the place I had come from. Suddenly I felt as if I was about to be dragged back down again. "What are you going to do?"

Her entire expression changed. "What do you mean by that?" I backpedaled but she got angrier and angrier.

I guess I wallowed in self-pity for a day or two. The day after she told me, I went to my parents' house for dinner and I tried to tell them, but I couldn't. I knew how disappointed they would be. I was totally overwhelmed and confused, staring off as I poured ketchup onto my French fries.

"What's the matter with you?" my father asked.

"Nothing," I said.

"Then why don't you stop putting French dressing on your fries?"

A father! The more I thought about it, the more I realized that I had as big a role in this as Pathenia. So I tried to call her. But she wouldn't take my calls for about a week. I went to her apartment, but no one answered the door. I found out she'd left college and moved home to East Oakland with her parents.

She wouldn't take my phone calls there either. Finally, I got hold of her and repaired some of the damage; we were ready to communicate at least. I asked her to marry me, but she said that I really didn't want to get married. "I'm not going to marry someone just to be married when the baby is born," she said. But I'd thought about it and I was sincere. It was true that much of the reason I wanted to marry her was a sense of responsibility, but I was willing to give it an honest try. She still said no.

A few months later, I decided I had to let my parents know. I took Pathenia to Richmond with me, and it was clear that she was pregnant.

My parents didn't say anything until the next day, when I was sitting outside with my father, drinking a beer.

"What are you gonna do?" Eddie asked. "Don't you think you ought to marry this girl?"

"Well, no, Daddy. I asked her to marry me but she said no."

"Well, then you ought to start giving her two hundred and fifty a month," he said. My whole income then was $350 a month. I was basically living on an Arco card in a one-bedroom apartment with no carpet and rented furniture.

I had somehow survived the first year of law school, when most blacks get weeded out. I had stayed off academic probation and my grades were beginning to follow the same pattern I'd taken in high school and college. I had just finished my fall semester of my second year, and my grades were excellent. I was breaking away from the pack, a little more than a year from the goal I'd chased since childhood.

I was a second-year law student! People saw me differently; spoke to me differently. "What do you do?" they would ask.

"I'm a law student," I said proudly. I was somebody. But now, here I was, shooting myself in the foot again, mortgaging my future. I had almost made it and now I was going to lose it because I couldn't afford law school and a baby.

After Jenee was born, I went to Pathenia's to see the baby and to talk to Pathenia's parents. I drove over there that afternoon and her father was waiting outside for me. I got out of the car, and he marched down the walkway toward me. He was a longshoreman and he seemed huge to me, six feet, four inches tall, 260 pounds. "Hey," he said, freezing me at my car door.

"You don't have to go into that house," he said. "You don't ever have to see that child, OK? You don't have to buy diapers or milk or do anything. You can turn around, get in your car, and never look back and we won't ever bother you or ask you for anything."

We stood there staring at each other for a moment and then I just walked past him into the house and he followed me in. Nobody was going to keep me from seeing my baby. The only other conversation he and I had that day was about how beautiful my daughter was and how special she was. Even though I couldn't yet afford to pay $250 a month then, I knew I was a daddy.

You notice babies when you have one of your own, and I began to notice a hell of a lot of *ugly* babies. They say every parent believes his or her child is the best-looking one in the world, but I swear I was looking objectively, like a scientist almost. Other babies were just ugly. Jenee was a gorgeous baby. And smart? I would talk to her and swear she understood. And that wasn't all. She would exude a kind of charm that always calmed me. I'd look in her eyes and it was as if she were saying, cool as lemonade, "Hey Dad. It's OK." Every time I saw her, there was a new beginning and all the bullshit was behind me. It was an overwhelming sense of love, not like any kind of love I'd ever felt before or since. I can't imagine a greater passion than loving and protecting my daughter.

That's why it's so hard to explain what I did a year and a half after she was born.

In May 1980, I graduated from law school. It was a momentous occasion for me, the completion of a ten-year dream. Some of the brothers from the frat came to my graduation, and one of them sidled up to me and slapped me on the back.

"I want to tell you how much I respect you," he said. "You walked over a lot of motherfuckers to get what you wanted." It stunned me. I didn't know what he was talking about. I gave it some thought and realized what he meant. I had always put relationships on the back burner. First with Calvin, Pete, and Daryl, and later with my fraternity brothers, I put my schoolwork (and therefore myself) first at all times. If the Alphas called for a party, I didn't go much of the time. I went about my business, studying. I had every reason in the world not to succeed. There were girls and track and my petty crime ring. Later, I had a fraternity, and, finally, I had a baby, but I was single-minded and tireless in my efforts to become a lawyer.

That summer, I took the California bar exam, a three-day marathon, probably the toughest in the country. Fewer than half the students pass. I passed the first time. I was a lawyer.

The same single-mindedness caused me to take a job in Los Angeles, four hundred miles from Jenee. I had tried unsuccessfully for four months to find a job, and now I was broke. I took a job with the National Labor Relations Board in L.A., but I didn't enjoy the work and still wasn't making enough money to help Pathenia very much with our daughter. So I applied for a job with the Los Angeles County District Attorney's Office and got it.

I visited Jenee as often as I could, driving the freeway between L.A. and Richmond in six hours. I would look forward to the trip all week, but when the weekend came, I would spend a few hours with Jenee in her grandparents' living room and then the weekend would be over. It was like visiting someone in jail, behind glass. We smiled and cooed and then went back to our separate lives. Immediately, I realized I didn't like being an absentee parent. When Pathenia pierced Jenee's ears, I couldn't believe it. "No one asked me about piercing my baby's ears." But when you're an absentee father, you have no standing. You are the father, but you are not the daddy.

After a while, I began to feel some degree of uselessness, as if my only purpose was the money I gave. Leaving Jenee was the hardest and stupidest thing I have ever done. What does it say about a man's character? It says I was a coward, it's proof of my immaturity and selfishness. If you're not man enough to be a presence in your kid's life, how can you call yourself a man? Real men, I knew, support their children and stay home with them when they can. But I left. I ran away. And while I know that I had my reasons, it is still the worst mistake I've ever made and my deepest failing. I have looked at my father recently and remembered the way we used to argue sometimes, but I have also realized that he stayed and raised eight kids when it would have been easier to just run away. I would never do that again and I have done my best to see my daughter as often as I can and to be a presence in her life, to let her know how much I love her and that there's nothing in the world I wouldn't do for her. But I'm not there. In that sense, Eddie Darden will always be a better man than I.

FIVE

I got my first assignment in the Los Angeles County District Attorney's Office in the fall of 1981 and couldn't believe my luck. I was going to someplace called Huntington Park. Could there be a more placid, evocative name? It must be a resort town, I thought, green and friendly, nestled in some quiet ocean cove, a city of harmonious young people and happy retirees whose biggest worry was getting a good seat on Main Street for the weekly parade.

But Huntington Park was a hole, just another of those deceptively named Southern California towns, any quaintness and charm long since devoured by the sprawl and spread of Los Angeles, just another place with too many gang-bangers, too much smog, and not a great deal of hope. I arrived there in October, moved into a roach-infested apartment in Koreatown, and set to work.

I really hadn't given much thought to the kind of work I would be doing in the D.A.'s office. I was a lawyer but I didn't understand how the law worked and didn't really consider the people affected by its practice. Like most recent law school graduates, I thought about the law as little more than a series of answers to a series of questions on a series of tests, topics to be mastered so I could finally become a lawyer. I had considered the journey for so long, I hadn't given any thought to the destination. Well, now I was there. I was a lawyer and I was about to find out that the law is a living, breathing system of criminals and victims, actions and reactions. I was about to find out that it often cannibalized its practitioners and traumatized crime victims, and that the threat of punishment wasn't much of a deterrent at all. I was about to find out that three years of college, three years of law school, and two months of intense studying for California's grueling bar exam was the easy part. Almost anyone could become a lawyer. Justice was the real accomplishment.

It started that first day in Huntington Park, with my first preliminary hearing. We handled the misdemeanors in our branch office, but the felonies were sent to another office. So our only job on those serious, violent crimes was to hold the preliminary hearings, present a bare-bones case to establish suspicion of guilt, get the suspects held over for trial, and move on to the next case. My first prelim was for a carful of gang members, one of whom had randomly fired a shotgun at a car. Inside the car was a couple, kissing good-night after a date. I still see the pictures of the victims and the troubling, dead-calm faces of the suspects. I have seen those pictures and those faces reproduced so many times, I should be immune to their power, like many of the other people in my office. But it's an immunity I never acquired.

It wasn't just the felonies passing through our courtroom, either. Many of the misdemeanors have stayed with me as well, like snapshots in a wallet. In 1982, I prosecuted a case involving three women and a man who lived in a house with five children, the oldest four, the three youngest just babies. By the time the health department and children's services got involved, they found the kids living in filth, in a house with no running water, heat, or electricity. The toilets overflowed with feces and so the adults had been using the bathtub, which was full of waste too. The children ate whatever they could find among the garbage. There were no bed frames and so the mattresses were just set on top of piles of trash. I saw the pictures: babies in diapers that clearly hadn't been changed in days, older children with rashes, with feces and dried urine caked to their bodies. There was no refrigeration or milk and the babies were suffering from malnutrition.

The man in the house wasn't the father of any of the children; he had moved in only a couple of months before and the women were trying to nurse him back to health from a gunshot wound to his leg. The man had not had antibiotics in weeks and the wound hadn't been properly cleaned and nursed, and so it oozed with infection. The women couldn't understand why the man seemed so dazed and why his injuries weren't healing.

They offered no excuse for the house except a shrug and an admission that they were drug addicts.

They were charged with child endangerment, a misdemeanor, which had a maximum penalty of a year in jail. Their lawyers knew they couldn't go to trial. One look at those photographs of the children and a jury would convict them in a hot second. And they would be looking at "a bullet"—a year in county jail. So when the attorneys for the three women said they wanted to talk in the judge's chambers, I smelled plea bargain. I figured they'd want me to go soft on jail terms for the mothers. No way. Fortunately, the Department of Children's Services had already taken custody of the children and put them in foster homes.

"We'll plead to child endangerment," one of the lawyers said. "A year each."

I was confused. They were asking for the maximum sentence. "Because they feel guilty?" I asked.

The public defender shook his head. "Because they can get three squares and a warm place to sleep for a year. Beats the outside."

"But what about their kids?"

He didn't say anything. The kids were better off without these mothers. He knew it. The judge knew it. Even the mothers—when they weren't stoned—knew it. After they entered the guilty plea, one of the mothers looked at me and said, "Thank you."

I started in Huntington Park with a group of young deputies and we quickly gained a reputation throughout the D.A.'s twenty-six branch offices for our irreverence and cockiness. We were hired at a time when the D.A.'s office was experiencing huge growth and was hiring a herd of young lawyers. There was Nick Koumjian, an intellectual, unpredictable Armenian wildman who was all head and torso, with stubby legs like Barney Rubble. There was another guy in the office named Wayne Sato, a short Japanese guy with a wide body, who was from El Cerrito, the upper-middle-class suburb just above Richmond.

We had a brash camaraderie in the Huntington Park office—like soldiers at war—because we were stuck there in East Hell together. Nobody but us cared what happened out there. We served the cities of Huntington Park, which was heavily Hispanic, and Firestone, which was mostly black. Our jurisdiction also extended into parts of the Watts area of Los Angeles to the west and the rough towns of Vernon, Bell, and Bell Gardens to the east. There were always murders and gang violence, but no one paid attention to our office. As long as we moved the misdemeanors along and got the felonies to superior court, we were blissfully ignored.

Our deputy-in-charge was John McDonald, a classically trained D.A., who insisted that he looked like the actor Chuck Norris. He taught us the subtleties of the criminal justice system and, more important, which liquor stores would extend us credit. We'd just go into the store around the corner—where we had a standing account—and the clerk would see us in line and just hand us a bottle of Johnnie Walker Red. Every day after court, we'd sit around and drink Scotch, McDonald's drink, and talk about our cases. It was the kind of training that lawyers rarely get now.

The Huntington Park Police Department was in the same building as our office, and one day a detective showed us a substance they used to train officers about the smell of marijuana. He lit it, and some disgruntled secretary called downtown and said the arrogant new deputy D.A.'s were smoking marijuana in the office. Of course, it wasn't true, and we denied it, but we were suspicious when, a few days later, toward the end of 1981, a new deputy showed up, a serious, sloppy-looking Jewish guy named Alan Yochelson.

We were so sure Yogi—as we called him—was a snitch sent from downtown to spy on us that we teased him about it all the time. "How do we know you're not a rat?" We offered him a stiff shot of Scotch one day, just to see if he'd drink it.

"No thanks, guys," Yogi said. He sighed and shrugged his shoulders. After that we designed a test for him. The ultimate test. If he failed to go along, we'd have conclusive proof that Yochelson was sent from downtown. McDonald was having a birthday, so we asked Yogi to come with us to get his present.

Koumjian, Sato, and I piled into my 1976 Toyota Corolla, along with Yochelson, and we headed toward the city of Bell. I had recently filed a case there involving a place called Suzette's Modeling Studio, on Florence Avenue. The "modeling studio" was on the top floor of a split-level building, and on the bottom floor was an X-rated film parlor and a little shop with an impressive inventory of sex toys. We parked the car across the street, and I told Yochelson, "You're the new guy; you have to go in and get McDonald a gift."

"Get the biggest dildo you can for twenty bucks," Koumjian said from the backseat. "Otherwise, how will we ever know if you're a snitch or not?"

Yogi took the money and shuffled across Florence, all six lanes of traffic. He walked into the porn store right in front of a guy in a sailor suit, and we were dying in the Toyota, rocking it with laughter. It was ten minutes before we saw his pudgy hands push open the curtain that served as a door to the dildo shop. He came out with this eighteen-inch phallus, long and pink, too big to put in a bag, I guess. He weaved his way across the traffic, and we were laughing so hard, I could barely get the car into gear.

As soon as he got to the car, I took off, leaving Yogi standing in the middle of the street, holding that big, pink dildo for six lanes of traffic to admire. He was laughing and good-natured when we picked him up a few minutes later.

"OK," I said. "You're clean."

When we came into the D.A.'s office, we were given a three-week crash course on trial advocacy—practice doing preliminary hearings, making objections, the mechanics of doing a jury trial. It helped, but it couldn't prepare us for the reality of what was coming next. It couldn't prepare us for making objections in front of a judge or persuading a jury to convict someone. In the field it was trial by fire, and in the harsh courtrooms of Huntington Park, I developed a fiery, aggressive style.

After a year in Huntington Park, management began transferring my young group of prosecutors, moving us up the always-present political ladder of the D.A.'s office. I had spent a year and three months in Huntington Park when I was transferred to the other end of the world, Beverly Hills.

I arrived at the Beverly Hills office in 1982, in the municipal court there. There was a judge in Beverly Hills named Andy Weiss, whom we used to call Crazy Andy. He would have these fits in which he'd just light into some poor lawyer; for ninety seconds, he'd just attack you and berate you, snarling, making all these faces, and then, all of a sudden, he would turn back into a sweet man. He was always fair and honest, but no one wanted to go into Crazy Andy's court. You would make some standard objection, a no-brainer, and Judge Weiss would argue both sides of the argument for you—on the record. He'd be talking about the defense counsel's side of the argument and you would be thinking, "My

God, he's going to rule for them." Then he'd take you all the way back, arguing your side better than you could, and you'd think, "OK, that's more like it," and then, boom, he'd reverse his field and come back the other way.

"But then again," he'd say, and you'd slump back in your chair, certain that an entire trial with this judge would leave you dead. But when Weiss made a decision, it was usually the right one.

I'd been successful in Huntington Park, but I was getting killed in my first few months in Beverly Hills. I had hung juries on the first four cases I'd tried and was doubting my abilities. I even worried that it was the way I spoke.

It had always been tough for me to get in front of a group of people and speak. I often took longer than other lawyers to warm up, to get comfortable. I had never been trained in public speaking and I worried about my speech, that I didn't enunciate as well as I should or speak as clearly as I ought to. I heard in my voice a lisp and the traces of a black, Southern drawl that I feared might hurt my effectiveness in court.

During the Simpson trial, Johnnie Cochran would argue that you can't hear a difference between the voices of a black person and a white person. I think that insults our intelligence. That isn't to say all black people sound alike; of course not. But who can deny that we have our own dialect and our own accent? It is a large part Southern—where most of our grandparents lived; a little bit urban—where most of us live now, and a little bit African—where we all come from ultimately.

It seemed to me that by the time I got to college, we were given a choice. We could learn to speak more mainstream, to sound more white, or we could be proud of our heritage and acknowledge that culture extends to language as well as paintings and books. I was proficient in English. I could read it and write it expertly, and I knew the rules for speaking it. And so I felt no need to change the way I spoke, to ignore the heritage and the background that formed my diction, my speech patterns, and the phrases I used.

If the jury didn't like the way I spoke, they probably didn't like other things about me: that I was urban, that I was black. I was not going to change those things about myself. I couldn't. That was who I was. I could speak like Sean Connery and I would still be a black man. If the juries didn't like me because I was black, perhaps I was in the wrong line of work.

"That's not it," Judge Weiss said in his chambers one day. He had called me into his office to talk about my awful record. "You're just not doing very well," he told me.

"I should be winning these cases," I admitted. "I don't know what it is."

"Let me tell you," the judge said. "This is Beverly Hills. That aggressive, obnoxious style of trying cases that you may have learned in Huntington Park doesn't work here. The people you are prosecuting here are, for the most part, the jurors' neighbors, people like them. Jurors don't like you to be confrontational and sarcastic with their neighbors."

At first, I blanched from Judge Weiss's advice. I was outraged by crime; I wasn't going to pretend I wasn't.

"Sometimes, you look like you have a chip on your shoulder or some personal animosity toward the defendant," Judge Weiss said. He told me to modify my trial style to fit the environment, in that case Beverly Hills. "People here are laid-back, tolerant. They will convict a defendant if there is sufficient evidence, but they don't ever want to get caught up in some vendetta.

"Calm down," he said, "and make sure never to appear angry or confrontational. Don't take these cases personally. Treat the witnesses in a dignified manner and treat opposing counsel the same way, no matter how much you may dislike them."

I took his advice and quickly got guilty verdicts on some of the cases I'd hung before. Soon I was running off a long string of convictions in Beverly Hills.

Judge Weiss's advice stayed with me. I agreed with him, but I have reserved the right to lose my cool sometimes. On occasion, I do take these crimes personally, because sometimes, they are an affront to my humanity and are so brutal and unforgiving that they sicken me.

And, sometimes, the defense attorneys come after me personally, challenging my ethics, my abilities, even my heritage. Maybe it's not the best strategy, but at those times, I still take it personally.

The goal of most young deputy D.A.'s was to get downtown, to the Criminal Courts Building—the CCB. By definition, that was where the biggest and most interesting cases were tried. In addition, most of us figured that the best way to move up in the system was to practice down-town, where the top brass worked.

Yochelson had already been moved downtown, along with some other deputies I had worked with, and—worried that I was somehow falling behind—I began pushing to get from Beverly Hills to the CCB.

By the end of 1983, I got my wish. It took a couple of months, but I was finally transferred downtown to Central Trials. As a Grade 2, I was assigned to a Grade 5, the top level of civil service management below the D.A. himself. My Grade 5 was a smooth, silver-haired lawyer named Gil Garcetti—a finely dressed, well-spoken man, a sort of Joe College all grown up. Gil offered me a choice of two Grade 4 deputies to work under: Phil Halpin, the prosecutor of the famous Onion Field case, a very experienced, fiery lawyer with a temper and a low threshold for patience; or Joe Martinez, another experienced and talented lawyer who didn't quite have Halpin's reputation.

"You've got to go with Halpin," Yochelson said to me. "Man's a leg-end."

So I chose to work for Phil Halpin. He was a very fine lawyer, with some of the best cross-examination skills I had ever seen. He was incred-ibly quick-witted and he'd use his loud, raspy voice to set a guy up and then would drop him with a question as nasty as an uppercut.

We were assigned to superior court commissioner Sam Bubrick's courtroom. Sam was my kind of judge. He was a throwback to the days when judges swung their power like clubs. Sam could be heavy-handed with lawyers, and he refused to take any crap from them. He also was the kind of guy who couldn't stand wasted time. If you were arguing before him and you weren't ready or you weren't framing the argument correctly, Sam would stop you, pick up where you left off, and frame the argument for you. If you were arguing something stupid, he would stop you right there and that would be it. Sam worshipped efficiency. Under him, the Simpson case might've lasted all of two months.

The only problem with Halpin and me was that we were both noto-riously late for work. One of us was supposed to be in superior court every morning at eight-thirty or nine, when the judge came out to hear the morning calendar. But Phil and I routinely strolled in at nine-fifteen or nine-thirty. I figured it was his responsibility. He was the Grade 4, the calendar deputy One day I wandered in at nine-fifteen and found Gil doing the calendar for us. He dragged me upstairs and gave me a serious lecture about my responsibilities in the office, then gave Phil a similar lecture when he came in. Two days later, I showed up late and Gil was doing our calendar again.

"I'll do better," I promised. But I still believe the best lawyers get to work late.

Between 1983 and 1985, I prosecuted the first of my career's twenty murder cases, all but the last of which would result in strong convictions. There was the guy who shot a man, his wife, and his five-year-old son and then hid in New York for eight years before he was arrested; the crack dealer who shot a businessman and father of two, yelling "I got him" after the shooting; the man who shot an ex-girlfriend while her eight-year-old daughter looked on; and, in 1985, a Belize native who strangled his live-in girlfriend while she lay in bed, then covered the body with a blanket. Then he invited a sixteen-year-old girl into his apartment and strangled her too, covering her with the clothes of his girlfriend. A few days later, he invited some friends over to play dominoes while the bodies decomposed in a room nearby.

These cases warranted nothing but the briefest mention in the Los Angeles media, and similar murders took place there, literally, every day. But these cases outraged me, from the gruesome crime scene pictures to the cold stares of the murderers. When you learn that a man is capable of calmly playing dominoes while the bodies of two women rot in his bedroom, you understand the darkest part of our human nature and you can easily imagine a celebrity, a football player perhaps, walking slowly away, driving off, and casually catching a plane after murdering his wife and her friend.

I was becoming pretty successful in the office, one of the rising stars, I suppose. But Halpin and I had our share of run-ins. Once, I was assigned a rape case that seemed suspicious to me.

I thought about the case for a while and finally I went to Garcetti. We had a standing rule in the D.A.'s office: If we didn't believe in a defendant's guilt, we didn't try the case. Garcetti disagreed with me about the case. He thought it was a good case. And when Halpin heard I'd gone to Garcetti, he exploded.

"Who the hell is this Grade 2 telling me he's not going to try a case!" He ordered me to take it.

"I can't," I said. "I don't believe it."

Later, when some people would allege that I was only on the Simpson case for my career, that I didn't really believe that O. J. Simpson was guilty, I would think about cases I have turned down or decided to drop. There have been several. I have never taken the power of the prosecutor's office lightly. Prosecutors have the discretion to charge a case or reject it, to plea-bargain or go to trial. With a signature, a prosecutor can end a case before it ever begins, free someone if he believes the person is innocent. There are few things I feel more strongly about than a prosecutor's duty to work only those cases he believes in. I would like to think that I only plea-bargained cases when it was the ethical and moral thing to do, because I believed that no one should be allowed to plead to a charge that was less or greater than the crime they'd committed. At the same time, I didn't overprosecute, like some deputy D.A.'s, figuring the system would automatically compromise the defendant to the charge that fit. I looked at every case carefully, and if I believed in it, I went after it with my full energy. After all, as prosecutors, we make far less money than many defense lawyers. One of the few perks of the job is the chance to stand on principle.

Defense attorneys don't have that luxury. They *have* to defend guilty people. If they only defended innocent people, there would be only a handful of criminal defense lawyers (which might not be a bad world). But prosecutors—if they are honorable and if they haven't become too cynical—can go to work every day and honestly say their job is to seek justice.

I guess we carry our childhood with us wherever we go.

If you had stopped by my house in the mid-1980s, you might think five men lived there. There were usually six boxes of cereal above the refrigerator. In my closet were forty starched and pressed white dress shirts (not counting colored shirts or shirts with stripes) and twenty suits. The cupboards bulged with food, cookies, crackers—always something to snack on. I loaded up on everything I thought I was deprived of as a child, every kind of food that I muttered about as I skulked back to my bedroom as a kid ("When I get big, I'm gonna have a million graham crackers!").

I'd always loved music, ever since the days Michael and I stayed up late listening to his reconstructed radios. But I never had the money to buy all the records I wanted. When I began making money, I assembled quite a music collection. Friends say my back room looks like a Detroit radio station, with stacks and stacks of every jazz, gospel, R&B, soul, funk, disco, rap, and hip-hop record, tape, and CD I could imagine. I lived in apartments in L.A.'s Crenshaw area and, later, in Carson, just south of Compton, on the edge of the 'hood, I guess, in a blue-collar neighborhood. In 1989, I bought a house in Carson, just before the housing market plummeted.

I dated quite a bit in the eighties, and got serious a couple of times. I fell deeply in love with a slightly older woman I met my first day in the D.A.'s office, and I almost married another woman, Judi, in 1987. Judi was a superior court clerk from Compton, a feisty, beautiful woman who went out of her way to remind me that she could kick my ass if she wanted to. She had a wonderful toothy smile and deep brown eyes.

That year, I asked Judi to marry me. She said no. I was too intense, too serious, and I never took vacations or seemed to relax. Twice I had asked women to marry me and twice they had said no. But I understood.

There was always a part of myself that I kept out of these relationships, and probably do still. When Jenee was born, I struggled with two feelings. The first was that no woman could make Jenee and me the family that I wanted us to be. I had already blown that opportunity. The other, stronger feeling was that I couldn't bear to let anyone down the way I had let Jenee down. A deep relationship meant deep commitment, which meant deep hurt. Jenee has grown into a beautiful and smart young woman: student body vice president at her high school, yearbook editor, student minister, and a member of the National Honor Society. But I hurt Jenee by leaving, and while I saw her as often as I could—taking wild, late-night drives to the Bay Area after work on Fridays—I could see how an absentee father had affected her.

I have always ended every telephone call to Jenee with "I love you." And I have always provided for her financially and with advice and guidance. But Pathenia has been the strongest influence, and I am grateful for the wonderful job she has done with our daughter.

No matter how much I've done, I am not there. When I hear of young men who father children and complain about the financial responsibility I want to shake them and tell them that is only a small part of it. I have realized that children really do need both parents. And more than that, they have a right to both parents. It took two people to make Jenee. It takes two people to watch over her, support her, teach her, counsel her, and help her develop. I just couldn't do that as well from Los Angeles.

I visited home often in the 1980s, watching my sisters and my brother Larry graduate from high school and college and sometimes grad school, watching the usual parade of weddings, births, and holidays like a photo album, the pages turning in my memory, immediately blending together and passing the time faster than anyone likes.

I saw Michael occasionally during those years too. He was so proud that I was actually a lawyer. While the rest of the children filled out (some more than others), Michael just seemed to get skinnier and skinnier, his eyes pulling back in his head and the shadows lengthening beneath his cheekbones. It wasn't until later that my mother would tell me how bad it was getting.

She and Pops would help him get an apartment but Michael wouldn't allow them to visit. They would set up his monthly check from the government in a direct deposit account, and he would go to the cash machine several times a day until the money was all gone just a few days into the month. Once, my mom bought him a toaster because he complained that he had no way to cook food. A few days later, he was complaining again, and Mama asked about the toaster.

"Oh, it broke," he said.

She bought him a microwave a little later. Still he complained that he had no way to cook food.

"Michael, what happened to your microwave?"

"Oh, it broke," he said.

The pawnshops wait for someone like Michael, an addict so desperately in need of a fix that he'll sell anything to get enough money to buy one hit.

"Did you sell the microwave, Michael?" Mama asked.

"Yeah," he said in one of his rare, straight moments. Mama looked at him but didn't complain. She had already resigned herself to the fact that drugs owned him. Mama only wanted to make sure that he ate well. Michael stared at her. "Don't give me nothing else, OK?"

But they did. And I did too. I gave him money every time I saw him, hoping that it might go for food or clothing. I realize now that we could never give Michael enough to fill the hole he was making inside himself.

I despise gangs.

I grew up in a time when one black man walked down the street, saw another black man, and said, "What's up? How you doin', brother?" Or, "What's happenin', blood?" back when "blood" didn't mean that you got capped if the guy you said it to happened to be a Crip. Blood meant kin. You never knew when you might be talking to someone from the same village or the same tribe and so you treated everyone like a brother. We were so full of optimism! The future to us was *Star Trek*—a multiracial, educated bunch of people who just went around the universe doing good deeds.

But the young brothers who were terrorizing Los Angeles in the 1980s and their younger brothers who are terrorizing the country today felt no kinship, no solidarity with anyone. They saw a young black man, they pulled a Glock 9 mm pistol from their sagging waistband and they shot him for the unforgivable offense of wearing the wrong cap or standing on the wrong corner. If they had ever heard of a time when black people stood together and tried to raise not just *themselves,* but everyone around them, these gangsters had long since forgotten it. More likely, no one had ever taught them.

In 1985, I was transferred to the hard-core gang unit of the D.A.'s office, a special branch of the prosecutor's office set up to hit gangs hard, to coordinate prosecution and specifically target the young men involved in the drug trade, in the random robberies and constant murders of gang life. The year I joined the unit, 1985, there were 271 gang murders in Los Angeles County. The next year, there were 328. By 1991, there were more than 700. Police estimate there are 143,000 gang members in Los Angeles.

I drove home at night through neighborhoods in various states of warfare with gangs, some in which the families were held captive behind barred windows because of packs of fifteen-year-olds with semi-automatics; other neighborhoods in which the families just gave up and moved farther away and the houses, duplexes, and apartments dissolved into bullet-pocked crack houses and shooting galleries. At the time, L.A. was beginning the decline that everyone talks about now; I honestly thought that if we could just get rid of half the gangsters, it would make a huge difference, the kind of difference people would notice.

One of my first cases in hard-core involved James Hegler, a Rollin' 60s Crip gangster. In 1985, Hegler shot and killed a local businessman after a bad crack deal. Hegler sold a rock that wasn't cocaine, just a plain, white rock. When the victim demanded a refund, Hegler shot him in the chest.

I filed murder charges on Hegler, and the case took a year to wind its way through the preliminary hearing, arraignment, pretrial hearing, and, eventually, a jury trial. During that time, I got to know the victim's widow, a medical student and victim's advocate named Norma Johnson. Norma and other women were the founders of a fledgling nonprofit group called Loved Ones of Homicide Victims (LOHV). Norma harassed me every time I saw her at the courthouse. "Come down to the LOHV offices and check it out. Maybe you can join the board of directors."

One day, while I was making the rounds in South Central, I walked into a church on Eighty-seventh and Budlong, deep in the worst part of L.A. Inside the church there were sofas on the left and, on the right, a large poster board covered with photographs, mostly of young people between the ages of twelve and twenty-five. There must've been hundreds, senior class pictures, snapshots, pictures of smiling boys with football helmets tucked under their skinny arms, girls in marching band outfits or bobby socks, little boys on bikes, prom pictures, and pictures of kids at their first jobs. Also pinned to the board was an obituary for each of these young people.

They were primarily black, with a few Hispanics; I couldn't believe the number. These were just neighborhood kids, the ones they'd lost. And they were all homicide victims. I covered my mouth. Above the bulletin board was a sign that read: LOHV.

I noticed other pictures, older women and smaller children, some two or three years old. People outside South Central dismiss the victims of gang murders, assuming the gangsters only kill other gangsters. God, I wish that were true. But most of the victims, like the ones in these pictures, had done nothing except go outside at the wrong time. Sometimes, they didn't even go out; the bullets came crashing through their walls, like uninvited guests.

Farther back in the church were a couple of women who did all the work for LOHV, contacting the families of the latest murder victim and helping to arrange counseling, funerals, whatever they need. I talked with them about some of the pictures, and they told me about cases I had never heard of before. Four young teens on their way to school are shot in a drive-by. A couple on a date is shot twenty-four times. The stories went on and on, and then I began noticing them, in tiny articles in the *L.A. Times,* buried on back pages while they devoted the front page to a car bomb in Beirut that injured four and a woman from Beverly Hills who was carjacked at gunpoint. There were just so many gang deaths in these neighborhoods, they went mostly unreported. It was like discovering a civil war in your own backyard.

Even then, people sometimes asked me how I could work so hard to put other brothers in jail. I was always amazed and sometimes angered by that question. This wasn't an issue of solidarity or brotherhood! This was the murder of the weakest in our society by bullies, the terrorizing of entire neighborhoods and communities. The victims in these cases were usually black, and they were often old people or children. How could I put other brothers in jail? How could I not? As long as they were victimizing old people and making orphans of black children, how could I not?

That day, when I walked into LOHV, a kind of transformation was completed in me. I stopped being a lawyer for myself and started being a lawyer for the people I represented, the victims and their families.

All the lessons of my life ran through neighborhoods like that one, through faces like the ones I was staring at, faces like mine. All the lessons from my parents, Michael, Nanny, and Gloria Alibaruho came together in front of that bulletin board, in all those faces of innocent people. I ached for those people and was ashamed of the system I worked in, which rarely offered solace to them or—more rarely still—justice. I recalled the days that I believed I had a calling and knew that, here, there was work I could do that would actually help people. These people in this rodent-infested church were standing up in defiance and saying they would do something; even if it was small, they would do something.

I have been a board member of LOHV ever since that day.

* * *

I was a whirlwind in hard-core gangs. When I was working a gang case, no one could talk to me. I visited my family less and had little time for my friends.

"Hey, G! 'Sup?" I'd say, greeting one of the police officers from the CRASH unit, the special gang intelligence and enforcement division of the LAPD, with whom I worked closely.

I was determined to stop as much of the violence as I could, one asshole at a time if necessary. I worked fourteen-hour days, prosecuted cases, wrote search warrants, and began spending a lot of time in the field, researching gangs and hanging out with the cops. I learned the language and the graffiti and the players. I began carrying a gun.

"You're starting to sound like a gang member yourself," said the woman I was dating at the time.

In late 1985 or early 1986, I inherited a case involving a hard-core gangster and ex-con known on the streets as No Brain.

No Brain had pulled up at a corner and threatened an eighteen-year-old girl named Erica Johnson. Erica was standing with a group of people when No Brain drove up, got out of his car, took her aside, pointed a pistol at her head, and accused her of snitching on him.

"The only reason I'm not gonna blow your head off right now," he said, according to the police report, "is that all these people are around. But I will at some point. You can count on it. And you better not tell anyone what I said, or I'll have you killed from county jail."

None of the other people present would talk to the police. Erica was our only witness. I talked with my supervisor who said that No Brain was a major player, a Playboy Gangster Crip who served as a special bodyguard for a notorious prison gang, the Black Guerrilla Family, and a guy whose moniker was Doc Holiday. Holiday was eventually convicted on a murder charge by a prosecutor named Marcia Clark.

The No Brain case was trouble from the beginning. All we had was Erica Johnson's frightened testimony. "Nobody's corroborating what she says," I said.

"But No Brain has a horrible record," a supervisor said. "Let's start a file on him and keep him in custody for ten days, just to throw a scare into him, teach him a lesson."

So I charged him with assault with a deadly weapon and asked for a monster bail. Now we had ten court days to haul him out of his cell and hold a preliminary hearing.

The hardest thing about gang cases can be convincing the witnesses to testify. There was no shortage of shootings on crowded streets where— miraculously!—no one saw a thing. Yet I had become something of an expert at getting people to testify. I pleaded: "How are we ever going to rid the streets of these gangsters if good people like yourself won't stand up in court and do the right thing?" I made deals: "I can make your own court case easier if you'll just stand up and do the right thing on this one." I threatened: "I'm going to lock you up as a material witness until you're ready to stand up and do the right thing." And it usually worked.

But with Erica Johnson, we didn't need to do anything. She was brave and she wanted to testify against the jerk who'd threatened her. She thought her life depended on it. No Brain had been charged with murder or attempted murder twice before, and each time the case was dismissed. Each time a witness came close to testifying, he or she was stabbed or shot and either didn't show up for court or changed the testimony.

On the eighth day of No Brain's confinement, the LAPD served Erica with a subpoena to testify. The cops drove out at ten o'clock that morning and gave her the paper. At eight o'clock that night, a car drove up to where Erica was walking. A man got out and shot her four times in the face from just a few feet away.

No Brain was in jail, of course, but it seemed he'd done just what he'd promised he would do: have her killed from inside jail. I was sick with rage that day. I got a search warrant and went with the cops over to the house where No Brain lived with his mom. There was a chance that the person he had called to put out the contract was living in his house. And even if he wasn't, there was a chance we'd find some names or indication of who ran in No Brain's crew. I couldn't see straight as we drove over, and the sound of my own breathing filled my ears.

We parked outside his mother's house in West L.A. and the cops prepared to go in. The adrenaline was coursing through my blood as we ran for the door. One cop burst in and I went in second, the only person not wearing body armor or carrying a gun.

There was no one home. I stormed through the house until I got to a small area next to the kitchen. There was a chalkboard there, with a picture of No Brain in a stocking cap and the names of two guys—Bond and Martel—along with their telephone and pager numbers.

We found Bond and Martel and arrested them even though we had little probable cause. One of them had a blue car, and a blue car was observed at the scene. They both had gang histories. But that was about it. Out of desperation, I came up with a plan. We'd leave them together in the basement of the Criminal Courts Building, in a sheriff's car that was wired for sound.

"Crippin's a hard job," one said to the other when they were alone.

"Yeah. Who you think snitch on us?"

"I don't know. No Brain would never snitch us out."

And he didn't. I presented the case to my boss, and he tried it himself. We never got enough to charge No Brain, but Martel and Bond were convicted of first-degree murder.

I think often of Erica Johnson and of hundreds of people like her, people so vulnerable and afraid. People like Erica got beaten up by some guy, and when the police came, the police were suspicious because the victim was black and lived in this awful neighborhood. Someone like me would try to convince the Ericas to testify by getting tough with them, threatening to lock them up or prosecute them for some probation violation. She would agree, and the guy who beat Erica up would come back and kill her. A defense attorney always talks about his client, but I had clients too. Erica Johnson was my client. I was paid to represent all of the Erica Johnsons. Was I doing the best for my client?

That was the system I worked in. I sat across from those people and lied to them, told them that the best thing they could do would be to testify against the No Brains of the world. It was the best thing for me, but was it the best for them? Not usually. Gangs were a process, a machine. We fed victims and suspects into the machine, and it only created more victims, more suspects, more death. And every time I got an asshole off the street, three more replaced him.

Midway through 1986, I had been a prosecutor for five years, eighteen hard months in the gang unit.

I was exhausted. I had achieved much of the material success I wanted. I was a lawyer and a successful one. I had discovered inside myself the capacity to care for others and the calling that I always knew God had for me. I had worked as hard as I possibly could and now I was tired and confused.

Soon after, one of the deputies assigned to the unit came into my office after interviewing a gang member. The gangster had apparently snitched on his homies—but anonymously—and the case was falling apart. She needed him to testify if she was going to win at trial.

"What did he say?" I asked.

"He won't do it," she said. "I did everything I could, but he just won't do it."

"Well, he still has to walk the streets out there."

She shook her head. "I was so pissed, I told one of his homeboys that he was the one who snitched them off."

My mouth fell open. I couldn't believe it. She had signed some guy's death warrant after we had promised him anonymity. I shook my head, gathered my belongings, walked into the secretary's office, and signed out for the rest of the day. I had to get out. Either these people had no clue what they were doing or—worse—they didn't care. I was tired of "justice" that made life worse for these people. For the first time, I seriously considered leaving the D.A.'s office.

SIX

D arden. Come in. I want to introduce you to someone."
      I stepped inside my supervisor's office and he introduced
      me to two detectives from the Robbery/Homicide Division of
the LAPD.

Jerry Stephens was about five feet, eight inches, with sandy gray-blond hair and a mustache. A motorcycle cop back in his patrol days, he was raucous and friendly, working on a new marriage, one of those guys who could stand at a bar for twelve hours and never pull his wallet, one of those guys you never minded buying a drink.

Addison "Bud" Arce was a Spaniard who couldn't speak a *por qué* of Spanish. The steady and reliable one, Bud planned retirement parties in the office, dated the same girl for ten years, and was known as the kind of guy who wouldn't cheat at anything. With their soft-edged suits, cop hair, and rubber-soled shoes, neither guy could've passed for anything but a detective.

"Congratulations," Arce said that day in 1988. "You've been given a really important case."

"Really?" I asked. "What?"

Jerry nodded in my direction. "You ever hear of the Koreatown Slasher?"

I'd read about him in the *L.A. Times.* He was a nut who had been stabbing transients to death in the Koreatown area, following them, coming up from behind and driving a kitchen knife into them with such force that twice he'd gone all the way through his victims. By the time the police caught him, he'd killed six and wounded seven, all with the same knife. Arce and Stephens had investigated the guy, and we began working together on the case. I had come back to central trials from the hard-core gang unit, and it was a great case to pick up. Even from the beginning, Arce and Stephens were great cops to work with.

In court, during the arraignment, I saw the Koreatown Slasher for the first time: Joseph Danks, twenty-six, of Saginaw, Michigan. He wore high-top tennis shoes with yellow flames wrapped around the backs. Otherwise, he was the classic Hollywood image of a psychokiller, eyes set back deep in his head, blond hair on a hairline set mid-dome, as far back as his eyes, which were red and beady like the heads of two matches.

At the same time, Richard "the Nightstalker" Ramirez was on trial for crawling into open windows during a hot Los Angeles summer and killing thirteen people. Danks was jealous of the media attention Ramirez received. He called him "Hollywood" and bragged that he could easily kill the guy if we'd just leave them alone together for a few minutes.

Danks was a diagnosed paranoid-schizophrenic. After he was arrested, a deputy joked with Danks that he had masturbated in Danks's food, and Danks became so paranoid, he demanded that he be allowed to pick his sandwich from a hundred in the jailhouse cafeteria every day. He didn't figure any man could produce enough semen to taint one hundred sandwiches. If he didn't get to pick his own sandwich, he became uncontrollable. "I'm gonna kill all six of you," he told a half-dozen jurors one day.

"Goddamn," he said to one juror, "you are one ugly-assed bitch." She immediately declared herself unable to be fair and impartial in the case. Danks would amuse himself every day by belching and farting and became so disruptive, the judge had him taken out of the courtroom. When he came back, his arms and legs were bound and his face was covered with a muzzle, like you might put on a Doberman pinscher. Somehow he got out of the muzzle, though, and just kept saying "Fucking cunt" over and over to the female judge.

When Joe Danks looked at you, you felt kind of cold and sometimes you couldn't help shivering. There were nights when I would see his face in my nightmares, following me, so that I had to walk backward, because he liked to stab people from behind. Some nights, after court, I would believe he was the devil. Joe Danks was also crazy, of course. Three times, a judge ruled that Danks was mentally incompetent to stand trial. There was nowhere to go on the case. We'd spend five weeks selecting a jury and then, suddenly, dismiss them because Danks was so disruptive and insane.

No judge could handle him. Few were willing to try, to spend six months listening to this nut, only to have him end the trial with his antics.

Danks was one of those criminals who was too crazy for prison and too dangerous for a mental hospital. They sent him to the state mental hospital at San Luis Obispo anyway, and he was tied down most of the time, but he still managed to stab a guy in the eye with a pencil.

In 1989, we got another chance to try him, and this time, he was found competent. But Danks didn't like his public defender, Larry Rivetz, and on more than one occasion, he told the judge that if he didn't remove Rivetz, Danks would remove Rivetz himself. Once, he buried a razor blade in a toothbrush, demanded a new lawyer, and, when the judge said no, pulled out the toothbrush and slashed Rivetz across the nose.

Rivetz was a fighter and he refused to be taken off the case. So the judge ordered Danks shackled every time he was in court. But one day, Danks wiggled out of his chains and ran toward Rivetz, who backpedaled like an NFL safety. They moved toward me and I moved away. Who wouldn't? It was the devil. Danks took a swing and knocked his lawyer to the floor, then jumped on top of him and started punching him. It took two of us to pull him off.

Rivetz sprang to his feet and said, "May the record reflect that I was never knocked to the ground or struck by my client!" In hindsight, I think that is the ultimate expression of what it means to be a defense lawyer.

The judge was smarter than some judges I would see later, though. She quickly set the record straight. "Counsel, that is not true. In fact, you were knocked down by your client."

Finally, in August 1989, I convinced Joe Danks to plead guilty to six murders, and he was sentenced to six sentences of 25 years to life plus two full life sentences, a total of 150 years to life. If anyone deserved to die, it was probably Danks, but there was no way I'd ever get his case to the death penalty phase. This guy would never be well enough for a trial, and we'd screw around with him for years while witnesses died or forgot. Our most important witness then was a seventy-year-old man living on the street, and he wasn't going to be a good witness for long. I was happy just getting Danks put away forever.

He was sent to the inmate reception center at Chino and then to the state prison at Tehachipi. But apparently Danks's file didn't make it, because they placed him in a cell with a guy in his sixties who was in on a domestic violence charge, and who looked a little bit like a transient himself.

In his statement to police, Danks said that they ought to just let him out and let him start a business: bum busters. That way, he said, he could kill seven bums a day. Joe Danks hated dirty people.

At Tehachipi, the other inmates made fun of him. They laughed at him. "You don't look like no slasher," they howled. "You ain't shit."

One night, that old man was in the top bunk and Danks wrapped a sheet around the guy's neck and swung off the top bunk from the other end of the sheet, strangling the guy to death. When the guards came running, Danks proudly showed them what he'd done. He said he could hear the guy's heart beating as he killed him.

When you work on a case like that, you tend to get close to the detectives who worked it, in this case Stephens and Arce. You get drunk and joke about a guy like Danks, but I think, deep down, you all know you've seen real evil. Fortunately, it doesn't happen often.

I first met Johnnie Cochran in 1983, in the Beverly Hills office. He was representing Don Cornelius, host of the television show *Soul Train*. Cornelius had piled up a stack of parking tickets on his Excalibur. Normally, I wouldn't work a traffic case, but Cochran wanted to meet in the judge's chambers and I guess they wanted a prosecutor there when they cut a deal on the fines.

All I really knew about Cochran was that he was a prominent black attorney, but that was enough for me to respect him. He had his own firm, the most visible black law firm in L.A., and he gave opportunities to good, young lawyers. I knew that it was hard enough being a black lawyer, but for a black man to rise to the heights Cochran had, to build his own firm and become as influential as he had, was worth admiration. I'd heard that Cochran took cases that others wouldn't; along with celebrities like actor Todd Bridges, who was acquitted of an assault charge, and Michael Jackson, who was investigated for child molestation, he

IN CONTEMPT   93

represented black people with nowhere else to turn, people victimized by the system.

Of course, like other prominent civil attorneys, he extracted a healthy 30 or 40 percent from those victims—at least the ones who got big settlements.

Cochran was friendly enough, if a bit smooth, and he seemed to take a professional interest in someone he saw as an aggressive, young black prosecutor. He had been a prosecutor himself and had left the Los Angeles County District Attorney's Office just a year before I started.

I noticed how the judge, Charlie Boags—who was later convicted of fixing parking tickets—sat up when Cochran came into his chambers. Judges were that way in Los Angeles toward the big-name lawyers. And it wasn't just Cochran. I'd seen another lawyer bring a pair of wing-tip shoes once to a judge in chambers during a case the judge was hearing.

"Judge, I got those shoes you like," the lawyer said. He gave the judge the expensive Johnston and Murphy dress shoes.

"What's that all about?" I asked the lawyer later.

"Hey," he said, "that judge takes care of me."

Boags gave Johnnie the kind of break that judges give to big-name lawyers, knocking the parking fines down about 80 percent.

After that, I'd see Cochran around the courthouse occasionally and we became more friendly.

But I didn't really get to know him until I moved from the central trials group to the Special Investigation Division in February 1988. SID was one of the most demanding divisions in the D.A.'s office, where public officials, primarily police officers, were investigated for crimes they might have committed. I took the transfer happily. Prosecutors in SID worked closely with the top brass of the prosecutor's office, including the district attorney, Ira Reiner, and it was a good place for an ambitious prosecutor looking for paths to promotion.

I had worked with a lot of good cops and, when I went to SID, I had no comprehension of the crimes being committed by police officers. Like any black person in L.A., I could feel the antagonism growing between African Americans and the police, but I didn't think a lot about it until it was my job to investigate and prosecute the police.

In 1988, the Los Angeles Police Department began a program it called Operation Hammer, an attempt to slow the incredible spread of crime and—especially—gang violence. For several years, the fear of crime had grown louder, like an approaching storm, until, by the mid-eighties, it was deafening. Exacerbated by newspaper headlines and television reports of wild shoot-outs, brash carjackings, and unprecedented butchery, crime was winning in L.A., driving out more people than the sun and beach were attracting.

It was out of Angelinos' collective fear that programs like Operation Hammer were born. It was simple, really: Isolate an area with gangs and heavy crime, sweep through with as many officers as possible, harass the locals, and arrest everyone who seemed out of place. If police were enough of a nuisance, the theory went, they could pester and intimidate the gangs into submission.

The police chief in L.A. was a throwback named Daryl Gates, who had started in 1978 and who had the tough, no-nonsense support of his police officers. Operation Hammer was Gates's kind of policing, aggressive, take-back-the-streets, take-no-prisoners, open warfare.

But there was one big problem with Operation Hammer. It assumed that everyone in a bad neighborhood was bad, that everyone who dressed like a gangbanger was a gangbanger, that only criminals lived in the parts of town where there was crime. The neighborhoods strafed by gangs were almost exclusively black and Hispanic, and the people in those neighborhoods didn't have to worry just about the gangs; they had to worry about the police too. Officers would swarm into the worst divisions in the city—77th, Newton, Rampart—and arrest anyone who looked suspicious, anyone who talked back, anyone in the wrong place with the wrong people.

Operation Hammer would lead to the arrests of 300 people in one night in a few-block radius. In neighborhoods like Westwood, where the cheapest gated houses went for $400,000, the frightened villagers would cheer the courageous police, and very few would notice that 297 of those arrested were allowed to go free the next day because there wasn't enough evidence to hold them. But in the D.A.'s office we noticed. As a black man, I noticed.

The relationship between police officers and blacks—especially young black men—was tentative enough as it was. Most black men knew what it was like to be driving lawfully down some street when you caught the eye of a police officer, who spun around and pulled you over.

In a few minutes at least one other cop car would show up. You didn't see white people stopped on the street with two or three cars lined up behind them.

"Keep your hands on the wheel!" the cop would say over the P.A. system from his car. His spotlight would hit your mirror right at eye level, to keep you disoriented, and then he'd shine his flashlight around your car, looking for the pile of rock cocaine and the semiautomatic rifle that every black man obviously carries wherever he goes.

"You got a bad taillight," the cop would say. Or, "You were weaving a little." But you knew what the real crime was: suspicion of being black. And there were other stories too: stories of people beaten, kicked, and knocked around by LAPD officers; stories of a police officer who planted so much evidence his colleagues called him Farmer; stories of other cops who flat-out lied on the stand to get a conviction. There were even stories of racist cops, guys who collected Nazi paraphernalia and tossed around vicious racial epithets like gossip at a barbershop.

Most of the cops I knew and worked with were good, conscientious officers, committed to serving the community. But even among some of those guys there was something of a bunker mentality, the sense that it was them against the world and they needed to do whatever they could to protect their own and to get convictions, to put away the assholes.

You can't just toss out the kind of anti-crime rhetoric that was fashionable in the 1980s ("This is a war on crime!") without expecting some casualties. In this case, the casualty was African Americans' trust in the police and the judicial system, which was frail enough anyway. By 1995, I wasn't surprised at all that a mostly black, L.A. jury could be convinced that the police would go to supernatural extremes to frame a prominent black man. In some small way, the police were to blame for that irrationality. There were simply too few black people in L.A. who didn't have a story about being hassled, or a story about their son or husband or nephew being hassled. There were few African Americans who didn't know someone arrested in Operation Hammer or pulled over for a phantom blinker. In some parts of L.A., people smiled and were relieved to see a police car. In others, they tensed up and were afraid.

In SID, I quickly found out there was plenty of reason to be afraid. There was a small percentage of cops so dirty, you couldn't imagine a crime they hadn't committed. The files fell onto our desks like dirty snow—rape, embezzlement, fraud, theft, bribery, intimidation, black-mail, assault, even homicide. And that same bunker mentality, that code of silence, allowed them to get away with it more often than other crim-inals.

The neighbors hated the two duplexes at the corner of Thirty-ninth and Dalton in Southwest L.A. The gang members stood there all day and night, selling drugs openly in front of the porches. There was so much traffic—people on foot, on bikes, in cars—you might think there was a McDonald's behind the two-story cinder-block apartments.

The duplexes were just a few blocks from the police precinct on King Boulevard—the Southwest Division—which some officers called the "Wild, Wild West," after a song by rapper Kool Moe Dee. One of the worst corners in the Wild Wild West was Thirty-ninth and Dalton. The openness with which drugs were dealt so close to the station and the frequency of drive-by shootings was an embarrassment to the precinct's new captain, Thomas Elfmont.

A Hispanic family living between the two duplexes installed exte-rior lighting on their garage to discourage drug dealing, but the local gang, the Rollin' 30s Crips, immediately shot out the lights. The family replaced the bulbs and the gang members threatened to firebomb their house. One of the cops at Southwest Division dated a woman in the house between the duplexes, and she lodged a complaint with Captain Elfmont. Finally, on August 1, 1988, the officers at the Southwest Pre-cinct got a warrant to raid the duplexes at Thirty-ninth and Dalton.

At roll call, Elfmont told the officers they had "carte blanche" to do what they needed to do and that they had "bureau backing."

"If a Crip gets dumped," Elfmont said, "the bureau will look the other way." But, he cautioned, "what's said in this room stays in this room." By the time roll call ended that night, eighty-five police officers left the precinct house and headed for the two duplexes. They were car-rying battering rams.

I first heard about the raid at Thirty-ninth and Dalton about a week after it was over, when the head deputy of SID, Steven Sowders, poked his head into my office. I knew he had something interesting for me. As the head deputy, Sowders supervised fifteen attorneys and fifteen inves-tigators and was responsible for assigning all the cases.

"I got a call from the LAPD," Steven said. "Something about some damage to some apartments during the execution of a search warrant. Can you go down there and take a look at the place?"

"Yeah," I said. "Why not."

"Let me know what you see," he said.

The duplexes at Thirty-ninth and Dalton didn't look much different from any other abandoned apartments in the city of Los Angeles, just two more buildings with busted doors and boarded-up windows. The difference was that these apartments weren't abandoned. They had been occupied until just a few days before.

I met the police Internal Affairs investigators out front and we made the usual introductions and passed around business cards.

"Well, let's go inside," one of the officers said.

It was heart-wrenching, like a bomb had been dropped in the middle of these people's lives.

Doors and windows were broken. The doors had been chopped off the kitchen cabinets. A refrigerator door was hacked off. Furniture was cut up and smashed, clothes and other belongings were strewn about the apartment.

There seemed to be a hundred holes poked in what was left of the walls, some of them big gashes in the plaster, each of them framed with bits of red paint from whatever had been used to punch the holes. There were also big square holes framed in black paint, and it wasn't difficult to discern what had caused those: handheld police battering rams.

I went into the bathroom. Someone had taken an axe to the side of a bathtub and had completely destroyed the toilets. An outside staircase was ripped away from the wall of the building and nearly knocked to the ground.

"The officers at the scene say some Crips apparently came by after the raid and busted the places up," one of the detectives said.

"Yeah, right," I muttered under my breath. I could tell the detective didn't buy it either. It didn't seem likely that Crips would use police battering rams and then scrawl "LAPD Rules!" on the walls. A few days later, a police spokesman would acknowledge that "most" of the damage was done by police.

I shook my head as I looked around at the devastation. These apartments were uninhabitable. They must've run into an army of gangsters here. They had waited to execute the raid on the first of the month, when the residents would have received their county checks and would have more than the usual amount of crack cocaine. They must've found several pounds, I guessed. But when I checked the file, I couldn't believe it.

That night, the Kevlar-vested police officers of the Southwest Division had set up a perimeter in a two-block radius of the duplexes and detained anyone who seemed to be going in that direction. Soon they had forty people sprawled out on the ground—most of whom didn't live there and were just passing through.

In the end, they arrested only eight people and seized some nickel bags of marijuana and a Baggie of white powder that they thought was cocaine but turned out to be the flour someone had used to make fried chicken.

They arrested only one person who actually lived at the duplexes they'd raided. That night, the cops had destroyed the homes of families with small children and of women in their sixties, people who went to work every day and to church every Sunday and were no more drug dealers than I was. One woman said she was grabbed naked out of her bathtub and separated from her four-year-old daughter and two-year-old son while police went through her duplex, destroying everything. The gangsters were selling drugs in front of these destroyed apartments, but the cops didn't stop to think: *They don't necessarily live there.*

First the gangs victimized this neighborhood by setting up shop near these duplexes and now the police had victimized it again by destroying their homes.

To me, this was just the type of case SID needed to prosecute. I worked the case as aggressively as anything I'd ever prosecuted. This was a chance to send a message to the community about police accountability. But before I could proceed, I had to wait for Internal Affairs to finish its investigation and I had to wait several weeks for my boss, D.A. Ira Reiner, to decide what to do with the case.

It was July 29, 1990, two days from the two-year anniversary of the raid, and people in the community were becoming anxious to see if anything was going to come of this case. That afternoon, I met with D.A. Reiner and two other top prosecutors, who had been looking at the results of my investigation for weeks. I could see they were expecting me to file misdemeanor vandalism charges against the officers.

But my report on the case recommended felony vandalism charges.

Reiner studied each word carefully and looked over the tops of the pages at me. "Why felonies?"

I told him that office policy dictated that when the damage exceeded $100,000, we had to file a felony. This was clearly more than a hundred grand. But there was a deeper moral issue. "To do anything less would be to ignore established policy," I said. "We would be treating these officers differently than other defendants."

There were also extenuating circumstances. The damage was incredible and the cops had been malicious. One had even filed for overtime to make the battering rams from scrap iron and metal. They tore up family photos and poured bleach on the victims' clothing. They tried to cover up what they'd done, first by blaming the damage on gangs, and then, I found out, by dumping one of the battering rams down a manhole.

Reiner thought for a minute and we talked some more about the case. The meeting lasted about an hour. "File a felony tomorrow morning," Reiner said.

Fortunately, I had already thought to ask one of the SID secretaries to remain in the office until the meeting was completed. We began right away filing the charges in a felony complaint: conspiracy to commit vandalism, a felony violation of Penal Code section 182(1). The complaint named three officers as defendants, along with their captain, Thomas Elfmont.

I knew right away that it was going to be a difficult case. There were some eighty-five officers at the scene. Thirty-eight had already been disciplined by police brass, the largest number of officers ever punished because of an Internal Affairs investigation. The challenge for me was proving which officers were responsible for approving and supervising the vandalism.

It was unprecedented that a captain was charged, and it sent shock waves through the LAPD. But I was convinced that Elfmont was ultimately responsible. I'd heard that he told his cops to level the duplexes and make them uninhabitable.

After a couple of hours of fitful sleep, I arrived at work the following morning at six. The complaints were ready to be filed and the defense discovery material was being copied. All I had to do was wait until the documents were ready and file them with the clerk of the court at eight.

I was bushed and I leaned back at my desk and finished the last sips of a twenty-two-ounce coffee. The phone rang.

"Yeah?" I recognized the twang immediately. It was Curt Livesay, Reiner's assistant. Curt prided himself on being an Oklahoman, and he spoke with a smooth drawl.

"The man wants you to file misdemeanors."

Reiner? I was stunned. "Misdemeanors? We never even talked about misdemeanors."

"The boss doesn't want to leave you with your ass out flapping in the wind on this one," Curt said.

My ass? Now I was angry. This had nothing to do with my ass; this was Reiner caving in to police pressure. "Tell him not to worry about my ass, I can take care of myself." But I knew I was trapped. There was nothing I could do. "OK, Curt. Misdemeanors it is, but this is wrong."

We had to work quickly to file misdemeanors. As I filled out the paperwork, I couldn't concentrate. If these officers were convicted of felonies, they would have to surrender their badges. That was very important to me. These guys didn't deserve badges. They weren't serving the public. They had destroyed the property and trampled the rights of these people. They had intimidated innocent citizens, painted graffiti on the walls, lied about what they'd done, and tried to destroy evidence. They were acting just like the people they were supposed to be catching: the gangs.

Filing misdemeanors meant the officers had little to lose. I didn't have much chance of winning this one anyway, and even if I did, no judge was going to jail cops found guilty of misdemeanors. Judges need the support of the police, and the police union was firmly behind the officers. Yet there was nothing I could do. It was Reiner's decision.

Pretrial hearings began in the fall of 1990 and were incredibly contentious. We squabbled over every conceivable legal issue. The officers and their defense team were funded by the Los Angeles Police Protective League and were told not to spare any expense. And so we went at it, day after day, over discovery of LAPD documents, immunity for some of the eighty-five officers present at the scene, and whether to admit the battering rams into testimony. Internal Affairs had convinced the officer who dumped the battering rams that he should come clean, and so he led them to the manhole where he'd concealed them.

But the cop's attorneys claimed his rights were violated and that recovery and concealment of the rams should not be admitted at trial. It was so hypocritical. An LAPD officer who admitted lying and concealing evidence was now claiming that his rights had been violated? The rams were admitted.

But the primary difficulty we encountered was the lack of cooperation from the LAPD. At one point, we learned from an anonymous police officer that a management study of the vandalism was kept from us. Even after we requested it, they still dragged their feet. When I heard that a police sergeant was allegedly aiding the defense, while on city time, I threw a fit. Most defendants didn't have the expertise and protection of the entire police department.

Apparently, Police Chief Daryl Gates got wind of my somewhat aggressive style of seeking discovery and wrote a letter to the D.A., complaining that I was overly aggressive. At the end of the typed letter, Gates added in his own hand, "This guy has gotten personally involved in this case and I'm sick and tired of this guy and the nasty things he says about this department."

A copy of the letter was passed on to me and I was instructed not to deal with the LAPD in such a heavy-handed manner. The letter was also published in the *Los Angeles Times*.

By the time the Thirty-ninth and Dalton case got to trial, it was humongous, more than 150 potential witnesses, each with multiple statements. Typically, in a complex case, the investigating police officer sits at the counsel table with the D.A., assisting him in the presentation. But not in this case. The LAPD issued an order directing Internal Affairs officers not to sit at counsel table or to help in any way in the courtroom. Outside the courtroom, the City of Los Angeles settled a lawsuit brought by the occupants of Thirty-ninth and Dalton by paying out $3.4 million.

On April 1, 1991, the jury began hearing evidence in the criminal case, and although it was just a misdemeanor, everyone paid attention. Just a few weeks before the start of the trial, LAPD officers had pulled over a driver named Rodney King and had beaten him while someone videotaped it nearby. The public was enthralled by anything that had to do with police abuse.

The Thirty-ninth and Dalton trial lasted three frustrating months. Nobody wanted to testify in the case. Many cops refused outright to do so. When they did testify, they changed their stories and contradicted their Internal Affairs statements. One officer told IAD that he smelled bleach on a pile of clothing, an odor so strong he had to leave the room. Then, on the stand, he denied ever smelling bleach, even after I played an audiotape of him describing the smell.

Yet a few officers took the stand and told the truth. One testified that, during a roll call three days before the raid, Elfmont said that "shooting a Crip gang member would be a cherry on the cake." Another admitted that three days prior to the warrant service Elfmont said they should "leave the place uninhabitable. He might have been trying to get our adrenaline up for it," the officer said.

But most of the cops were determined to stick together, to not implicate one another. It was a stark example of the code of silence. At one point, one detective, Robert Clark, insisted that gang members had threatened officers a few days before the raid. In the middle of his testimony, Clark dramatically pulled out a Polaroid photo showing gang graffiti that read: "Southwest KillA [*sic*] Police." He tried to insinuate the graffiti was a threat to police, but I contended that it was a statement of the police department's reputation. Still, I was worried about the photo. As the jury filed out for the day, IAD investigators and defense attorneys descended on the clerk, all wanting to see the photo.

I looked too, then turned to Monroe Mabon and Suni Cookson, the Internal Affairs investigators. "Date this thing."

My intuition was right. The film was manufactured a year after the raid at Thirty-ninth and Dalton. Clark may have perjured himself. The following day Detective Clark did something I had never seen an LAPD officer do before and wouldn't see again until Mark Fuhrman testified in the Simpson case. Detective Clark exercised his Fifth Amendment privilege not to incriminate himself.

The jury was out fifteen days. I knew we'd proved the cops destroyed the duplexes, but had we determined which officers were ultimately responsible? Finally, the jury came back with acquittals. At the time, it was one of the few losses I'd ever experienced in court and probably the most disappointing.

The West Covina police were looking for a shotgun and they thought Darryl Stephens might have it.

Stephens was an ex-con who had been fingered by a police informant as the owner of a shotgun used in a brutal mass murder at a shopping mall. So the police stopped by Stephens's home and asked if they could search for the gun. Stephens told them he didn't have any shotgun and that if they wanted to search his apartment, they should come back with a search warrant.

So three days later, at two o'clock in the morning, the West Covina SWAT team lined up outside Stephens's door, knocked, then used a battering ram to bust open the door. They threw an explosive inside, then ran into the dark, smoky apartment, yelling "Police officers! Down! Down!" Beams of light from the SWAT team rifles cut the darkness in the room as they made their way back to Stephens's bedroom. The bedroom door was locked and so they kicked it open.

Two officers burst inside. "Get your ass down, now!" one officer yelled.

Stephens was lying in bed on his stomach, with his hand under the covers. "All right!" he yelled back. "Goddamn it, motherfuckers."

And then they opened up on him with fully automatic rifles. One officer shot him four times. The other officer emptied his clip, hitting Stephens with twenty-four bullets. Stephens died instantly. The officers said they worried that Stephens was reaching beneath the covers for a handgun. So they shot him twenty-eight times.

Police found no gun under the covers and they never found the shotgun or any other evidence that Stephens was connected to the murders they were investigating. One of the SWAT team members had left his radio microphone on and as I listened to a tape of the search, I thought I heard one of the police officers yell "Nigger!" just before they fired.

Like the other D.A.'s in SID, I investigated the hell out of cases like Darryl Stephens's. I took taped statements, commissioned charts and diagrams, subpoenaed records, served search warrants, and interrogated witnesses before the grand jury; basically, I mowed over anything or anyone that got in my way.

Civil attorneys like Johnnie Cochran came along after we'd done all the work in such cases. They represented people like the family of Stephens and often instructed their clients and some of the witnesses not to cooperate with us. Then, they took our research and filed lawsuits against the police. The cases would end with some backdoor, million-dollar settlement brokered by Cochran or another lawyer, and the officers would still be working.

I was frustrated by the work in SID. These cases were difficult to win, because they often became a choice between the officers and the people whose rights had been violated. The victims in these cases almost always had criminal records, and jurors had little sympathy for someone like that. There are few things more difficult than convicting a police officer of a crime. But to me, it wasn't about sympathy for the criminals, it was about accountability of the police. If they could violate a criminal's rights, they could violate anyone's rights.

At times, I felt blocked on one side by the law enforcement code of silence and on the other by overprotective defense attorneys like Cochran.

But a few times, I was glad Cochran at least got some compensation for the people whose brothers, fathers, sons, sisters, and daughters were killed by police when the amount of force didn't fit the alleged crime.

That was the case with the Stephens investigation. His family seemed so nice and they believed Darryl was turning his life around, yet I knew I would have had trouble prosecuting the officers who killed him. Stephens was a former gang member who had done time. He was no Boy Scout.

To prove the officers guilty of murder or manslaughter, I would have to prove criminal intent and show that a reasonable person would've acted differently. The officers thought Stephens had threatened a police officer in an earlier telephone conversation, when, in fact, the threat had come from someone else. Before the search, the officers had been told in a briefing that the residents of the apartment would get in a gunfight rather than surrender. The officers clearly believed their lives were in danger. If the word "nigger" really was on the tape, then that might show a motive for shooting Stephens, but tests of the tape were inconclusive.

My supervisors agreed with my pained assessment: We couldn't prove criminal intent. That was the way SID was. We were able to charge people much less often than other units.

It seemed so unfair. I knew Cochran was representing Stephens's family and that he wanted a copy of the tape of the SWAT team entrance. I agreed to meet with Cochran and the attorney for the West Covina Police Department, George Franscell, who also had the tape. I couldn't ethically turn my tape over to Cochran, but I could use it to encourage a settlement for Stephens's family.

We sat down and talked about the tape and whether I would prosecute the officers.

"I don't hear racial slurs," Franscell said.

"I'll show you on my copy," I said.

"That's OK," Franscell said. He wanted to know if I would make my decision about the case before the next election.

"I have no idea," I said.

"I hope you do prosecute this case," he said. "You'll lose."

I didn't say anything.

Franscell got down to business. "I just want to settle this case now," he admitted. Johnnie and I exchanged a quick glance, and my silence was tacit approval, an indication that I wouldn't stand in the way. In the end, Cochran was able to get a decent settlement for Stephens's family—minus his high fees, of course.

That was the basis of our relationship; Cochran and I were often working on the same case, approaching it from different angles. The phone would ring and I would know that Cochran had signed as a client someone involved in one of my cases.

"Chris. It's Johnnie Cochran. How've you been, my brother?"

It strikes me now that Cochran was only as effusive with me as he was with everyone else. It's what he does.

I could see problems in the Rodney King beating case even before it was moved to Simi Valley—the community where 25 percent of police officers and retired officers lived. Still, I wanted it.

By all rights, the King case should have been mine. I had been in SID for three years and was up in the rotation. But I was in the middle of the Thirty-ninth and Dalton case and so they assigned it to another prosecutor, Terry White. I was only upset until I saw what Terry would have to deal with.

First, there was Simi Valley. There wasn't a community more friendly to police in the entire country. But the case itself had problems too. Clearly, the jury would want to hear Rodney King, but he wasn't going to testify. He couldn't. King had made so many inconsistent statements, he was essentially worthless as a witness. And I had seen him. Rodney

King was a huge man. The jurors might measure him against the normal-sized cops, consider his criminal record, and side with the cops, no matter what they'd done.

The defense in the Thirty-ninth and Dalton case had been poor training, the claim that they were never trained *not* to break doors, rip toilets out of the floor, and punch a hundred holes in apartment walls. The Rodney King beating defense was the same. And if they could get around criminal intent by blaming their training—we were never trained *not* to beat a man senseless—they had a chance of winning. I especially felt bad for Terry when I saw the entire home video. Television news programs had aired only the portion in which King was beaten, but before that, the tape clearly showed him fighting back, kicking at the officers and moving toward them. It still didn't justify the beating he'd received, but when a jury saw the entire video, it could reverse the way they saw the case.

On April 29, 1992, I was in front of the Los Angeles County Grand Jury, working on the Stephens case, when I heard a woman bailiff yelp outside the chamber: "Not guilty!" I knew what that meant. The Rodney King case. Acquittals in Simi meant riots in L.A. Anyone with half an ear to the streets knew there would be riots. All you had to do was listen to rappers like Ice Cube to know how blacks under age thirty-five were going to take the verdict.

"It appears the officers in Simi Valley have been acquitted," I said carefully to the jury foreman. I told him there could be riots. "May I suggest we adjourn these proceedings forthwith."

The foreman just sat there staring at me.

"I would suggest that, for your protection, you take the freeways," I said, nodding toward the rest of the grand jury. "Stay off the surface streets, OK?"

Back in the office, there were sullen looks throughout SID. I took the freeway home, turned on the TV, and watched the riots grow. The images are familiar: screaming teenagers, people ducking through broken windows into stores, a man being pulled out of a truck and beaten with bricks.

A liquor store was being looted at Florence and Normandie. Mexicans were being dragged from their cars or were being pelted with rocks. Korean businesses were looted and black-owned businesses were torched. For days after the riots, black people couldn't buy a bag of groceries because they'd burned down the ten supermarkets that would do business in the 'hood. The mail stopped and people had to stand in long lines to get their checks. Meanwhile, business in Simi Valley went on uninterrupted. This was getting back at the Man?

I agreed that the verdict was wrong, but this was insane. How did any of this get back at corrupt or violent police officers? How did the lives of dozens of innocent people and property loss of nearly $1 billion make anything better?

The city has been a powder keg ever since the beating. Since then, I have told people, "We're just one officer-involved shooting away from another riot."

The first night of the riots, my law clerk, Michael Curls, came over to watch the incredible scenes on television. Curls was a big, engaging young black man from Kansas City who had come to Los Angeles to go to law school. When he'd started in the D.A.'s office, Curls told me later, he thought I was the biggest asshole he'd ever met. He would work himself to death on some motion or a bit of research and I would take it from him and say, "Hmm," and turn around and go back to work. For the first few months, I didn't say a word to him, and every day, he wondered if that was going to be the day he finally told me off. Finally, after working particularly hard on a motion for me, Curls decided he was going to let me have it. The hell with his job.

I realize I can be icy at times, especially when I first meet someone. But I had no idea how upset Curls was getting. I took the document from him and looked it over, just as he opened his mouth to tell me what a cold, heartless bastard I was and that I was too hard on other black men.

"Want to go to lunch?" I asked, before he could say anything.

"OK," he said. After that, we became good friends and we joked about my early coldness. The night of the riots, he and I sat there watching the television and shaking our heads. As usual, I had nothing in the house to eat and Curls—at six feet, four inches, 250 pounds—wasn't the kind of guy who settled for finger food.

"Hey," I said, "I'm sure there's no rioting in Torrance. We can go out there and grab a bite at a diner."

About nine o'clock, Curls and I climbed in his orange Datsun 260Z and drove west toward Torrance, a sprawling suburb near Carson, with low crime rates and few people like Curls and me. When we reached Hawthorne Boulevard, the main drag in Torrance, I noticed that there wasn't much traffic. We pulled up to a red light just as a patrol car appeared in the intersection, stopped suddenly, and shone its spotlight in our direction. By the time our light changed to green and we turned onto Hawthorne, Torrance police cars swooped down on us and pulled Curls's car over. Within minutes, there were four cop cars behind us.

They ordered Michael out of his car and ordered me to keep my hands on the dash. They took Michael to the rear of the car and began questioning him, while I sat there, the lights from the patrol car illuminating me. You could tell that these cops were incredibly edgy. I had learned the rules of the game years before, and I put them to work instinctively: Don't move. Don't turn around. Don't give some rookie an excuse to shoot you. Don't ask questions, no matter how badly you might want to know the answer to "Why are you stopping us, but no other cars on this street? Why aren't you stopping any of those white people?"

I am always amazed when I get stopped by the police. It happens about five times a year and yet I rarely get tickets. I don't speed and I certainly don't drive recklessly. I am a firm believer that no one should drink and drive. And yet I always seem to get pulled over by some cop who is suspicious of a black man driving a Mercedes.

In Torrance, the cops didn't even pretend we had a bad blinker or a missing taillight.

Behind the car, Curls nervously told the officers that we were employees of the L.A. County D.A.'s Office.

"The city of Torrance has imposed a curfew," the cop said, as other cars rolled past us unhindered, their white drivers staring at us, relieved that the police were protecting them. Apparently, this was a curfew based on color. But we weren't about to say anything that night. They let us go and we turned around and headed back to my house. We didn't say anything. And we didn't get anything to eat. Our hunger was gone.

Sonji Taylor was the twenty-seven-year-old single mother of a three-year-old boy named Jeremy. A week before Christmas, 1993, Sonji brought her son into a department store in West Covina. She bought three kitchen knives, a knife sharpener, and a troll doll for her son, for a total of $120. Sonji took a twelve-and-a-half-inch knife from the package and cut the price tag off the doll. Then she went to a restaurant and bought a pizza.

A few hours later, Sonji and her son were spotted in the hallway of Saint Vincent's Medical Center. About eight o'clock that night, a medical technician heard a child crying and followed the sound to the hospital roof.

Sonji was standing on the helipad, in the center of the circle where the choppers usually landed, holding her whimpering son in a headlock and waving the foot-long knife around. "Blood of Jesus," Sonji moaned over and over. "Blood of Jesus." She threatened to stab the hospital security officers if they came any closer and said, at one point, "Call your mama." When Jeremy cried, she became more agitated and brought the knife closer to him.

In the dull light of the helipad, police officers tried to talk to Taylor, but she waved the knife in their direction and threatened them. When they shone flashlights on her, she didn't seem to notice, and they figured she was high on something. Finally, officers sprayed her with pepper spray and pulled Jeremy away from her.

And then they shot her nine times, seven in the back.

When one of the deputy D.A.'s from our office—a husky, ruddy-faced ex-cop named Scott Gordon—arrived at the hospital, police wouldn't let him go up to the helipad. Finally they took him up and showed him around the scene. Police said they'd shot Sonji Taylor only because she'd rushed officers after being sprayed with pepper spray and having her son wrestled away. Gordon was the most conservative lawyer in SID, and he was eager to believe police officers' stories. We were poles apart, but I'd grown to like and trust Scott and we became friends. Even he admitted there was something strange about the case. But when Gordon was promoted, the case made its way to my desk, like many of the most difficult cases in SID, the ones in which it was difficult to prove the officer's criminal intent.

I took over the Sonji Taylor case in February. It was a mystery in our office. Several witnesses, besides the police officers, said that Taylor was moving toward the cops when she was shot and no one saw her fall or turn away until after she was dead. Yet seven of the nine shots hit her in the back. Again, most of the officers refused to testify unless they were all guaranteed immunity from prosecution.

Before I could deduce what had happened, I tried to figure out why Sonji Taylor went to that hospital, what caused her to snap that night. She wasn't the kind of person I expected to find with a knife near her own son's throat.

Her friends and family said she was a part-time child-care worker and full-time churchgoer who was waiting to hear about a job as a corrections officer. Her family offered no help. When I asked for any medical records or personal effects, they said that they'd destroyed all of them. The hospital's records showed that Taylor and her son had never been treated at Saint Vincent's. She had absolutely no connection to the hospital, except that the father of her baby had been born there. We didn't know if she even knew that, though. We reviewed her driving record to see if perhaps she'd gotten a parking ticket near the hospital. No luck. We watched hours of hospital security tape, but saw no trace of her. There was no reason for her to go to that hospital. Unless she was looking for help.

The police had guessed she was on drugs, but the tests came back negative. There was simply no explanation for what Sonji Taylor did that night.

Hospital employees, security guards, and police said she attacked the officers and never turned her back to them. Yet there were seven slugs in her back. None of it made sense.

We talked about it in the office. We couldn't go to a jury and say, "This is damned confusing." If she was indeed attacking police officers with a butcher knife in such tight quarters, they were well within the police department's deadly force policy. All the defense had to prove was that the officers reasonably believed their lives were in danger, whether they actually were or not.

During the summer of 1994, I realized we couldn't prosecute the officers who killed Sonji Taylor. I decided that would be the last SID case I would ever work on. As I prepared a memo on the case, my career was in flux. I had been trying for the top position in SID, a managerial job that would take me out of the courtroom forever.

But my zeal in pursuing the police and my aggressive style seemed to be hurting my chances. I had even turned to Cochran for help and he'd promised to put in a word for me. As far as I know, he never did.

When I found out Allen Field had been named the head deputy in SID, I was happy for him. Allen was a great man and attorney and

I knew he would make a good manager. I accepted a transfer to the Inglewood office, where I would supervise other prosecutors. But inside, I was beaten. I was thirty-eight years old, at the top of the pay scale for my position, but hitting my head against a glass ceiling. There were only a handful of head deputy positions, and once you were passed up, it was too easy to sink into your chair and wake up thirty years later at sixty-five, retired in the same position where your progress stopped. I was afraid I was losing momentum.

I was also losing enthusiasm for the job. The compromises and realities of the law were draining. You could look at only so many pictures of the Erica Johnsons, or look into the eyes of only so many relatives of Darryl Stephens, before you wondered whom you were helping. In SID, there were just too many Sonji Taylors.

Prosecutors, like all lawyers, can be a hypercompetitive, small-minded group of people, easily caught up in the game of it all. When some prosecutors won a death penalty case, and the judge signed an order of death, the prosecutors framed the order and hung it on their walls like a trophy, like a deer head or a stuffed fish. That made me sick.

And defense attorneys were worse. They talked of their love for justice and their clients, yet many of them operated with the integrity and tactics of used-car salesmen. After thirteen years in the D.A.'s office, I was tired of playing a cynical game in which the lawyers are contestants and the defendant is just a ball.

So I considered quitting the D.A.'s office and moving up to the Bay Area. I had already missed too much of Jenee's childhood and, if I hurried, I might be able to catch her last couple of teenage years. And then there was Michael.

That Christmas, Michael had gathered the family together and told us what we'd feared for a while. He had AIDS. He'd gotten it from a dirty needle, probably eight years earlier, he said. I couldn't believe how brave he was, the same brash little boy who stood right in Daddy's face and admitted he'd done wrong. Maybe, I thought, I could move home, be with Jenee, spend Michael's last months with him. Maybe I'd given enough to my calling and had grown into the man Nanny envisioned.

No matter what happened, I was done in the courtroom. Or so I thought.

PART 2

SIMPSON

"When you have eliminated the impossible, whatever remains, however inprobable, must be the truth."

—SHERLOCK HOLMES, *THE SIGN OF FOUR*,
SIR ARTHUR CONAN DOYLE, 1890

SEVEN

When police reached O. J. Simpson in Chicago on June 13, 1994, and told him that his ex-wife had been killed, he was hysterical. But afterward, the detective who had spoken to him realized something. Simpson hadn't asked which ex-wife was murdered. He hadn't asked how his ex-wife had been killed or by whom.

Before he left the hotel room, Simpson made thirteen telephone calls, to airlines and his personal assistant, to the police, to Hertz, and to Nicole's parents' house.

There, Nicole's sister Denise grabbed the phone. "You killed her, you brutal motherfucker!" When Nicole's mother came on the phone, Simpson asked, "What are your girls trying to do to me?"

He packed, went downstairs, and demanded a Band-Aid. As he waited for his ride to the airport, Simpson paused to sign an autograph.

He made fourteen more telephone calls on his cell phone on the way, to Hertz, to his business partner, and to his houseguest and soon-to-be alibi, Kato Kaelin. At seven-fifteen that morning, he caught a flight for Los Angeles.

Several miles away, in Beverly Hills, police were wading through ponds of blood at 875 South Bundy Drive, collecting evidence of the murders. One victim, the twenty-five-year-old waiter and aspiring model Ronald Goldman, was lying on the ground next to the walkway, slumped against the bars of the fence, a brown glove and knit cap at his feet. Among his sixty-four knife wounds were deep slashes to his lungs and clean slices across his neck and throat. Nicole Brown Simpson, thirty-five, was curled up at the base of the stairs near him, her throat slit nearly ear to ear. Leading away from the body and then back and then away again was a trail of bloody footprints—remarkable in that they were size 12, but the stride was short, as if the killer had walked away calmly, amazing after such butchery.

When O. J. Simpson arrived from Chicago at his Beverly Hills mansion later that day, police put handcuffs on him and then drove him downtown. He agreed to talk to Los Angeles police detectives Phil Vannatter and Tom Lange.

"All right," Vannatter said. "We're investigating, obviously, the death of your ex-wife and another man."

"Someone told us that," Simpson said.

The detectives asked about their divorce, and Simpson said Nicole had recently tried to reconcile with him but they had both realized that it wasn't working out. They asked Simpson about their first separation.

"Uh, for me it was big problems," he said. "I loved her. I didn't want us to separate."

He said he last drove the Bronco "maybe seven, eight, nine o'clock. I don't know, right in that, right in that area."

The police said it was parked at a strange angle.

Simpson stammered, "It's parked because when I was hustling at the end of the day to get all my stuff, and I was getting on the phone and everything, I forgot to pull . . . when I pulled it . . . bringing it out of the . . . out of the gate there . . . it's like . . . it's like, it's a . . . it's a tight turn."

"So you had it inside the compound?" one of the detectives asked.

"Yeah, yeah."

"OK," the detective said.

"Yeah."

"O. J., what's your . . ."

Simpson interrupted. He was still sorting out his last answer, the Bronco. "I brought it inside the compound."

"OK."

"To get my stuff out of it," Simpson continued, as if he was telling himself.

"OK."

"You know, and then it . . ." Simpson paused.

"And then you brought it out?"

"And I put it out and I run back in the gate before the gate closes."

They asked Simpson how he'd cut his hand.

"I don't know," he said. "Not the first ti— . . . I know I've had. . . .
When I was in Chicago I know how, but at the house I was just running
around and . . ."

"How did you do it in Chicago?" one of the detectives asked.

"I broke a glass. I just was . . . you had . . . one of you guys had just
called me and I was in the bathroom and I just kind of went bonkers for
a little bit."

"Is that how you cut it?"

He thought. "It was cut before," Simpson said. "But I think I just
opened it again. I don't . . . I'm not sure. I'm not sure. I didn't feel it."

"Do you recall bleeding at all in your truck?" one of the detectives
asked. "In your Bronco?"

"I recall bleeding at my house," Simpson said, "and then I went to
the . . . went to the Bronco. The last thing I did before I left, when I was
rushing, was went out and got my phone out of the Bronco."

The detectives nodded.

"I knew I was bleeding," Simpson said later. "But it was no big deal.
I bleed all the time. I mean, I play golf and stuff, so there's always something. Nicks and stuff."

It was quiet for a second while the idea of chronic, bleeding golf
injuries settled on the interview room. Later, the detectives asked about
domestic violence. "Did you ever hit her, O. J.?"

"That night we had a fight," he answered, bringing up an incident
from 1989. "Hey, she hit me . . . You know and, as I say, they never took
my statement. They never wanted to hear my side . . . Nicole was drunk,
she did her thing, she started tearing up my house, you know. And I . . .
I didn't punch her or anything but I . . . I . . . I . . . you know."

"Slapped her a couple times?"

"No," Simpson said. "No, I wrestled her is all I did . . . Nicole is a
strong girl . . . one of the most conditioned women. Since that period of
time, she's hit me a few times, but I've never touched her after that. And
I'm telling you, this is five, six years."

They asked him about taking a lie detector test.

"Should I talk about my thoughts on that?"

"Well," the detective said, "I mean, it's up to you."

"No," Simpson said, "I mean, I'm sure eventually I'll do it. But it's
like, hey, I've got some weird thoughts now. And I've had some weird

thoughts—you know, you've been with a person for seventeen years, you think everything. And I don't . . ."

Some weird thoughts.

With that, he went silent, and a few minutes later, the interview was over. O. J. Simpson walked out of the police department's Parker Center headquarters. Waiting for him were thirty years' worth of friends, employees, and confidantes, and several million dollars' worth of lawyers and experts.

Everyone sees a different L.A.

The tourist saves money all year long to go on vacation here, to search out Mann's Chinese Theatre, to see Hollywood Boulevard the way it looked on *I Love Lucy.* What a shock it must be when they finally see that part of the city, run-down and dirty and no place to be after dark.

It is pretty fashionable now to dump on the city, but some people still see the L.A. of the fifties, the natural, inherent beauty, the palm trees and beaches. I do, sometimes. More often I see other things, the filth and poverty, the young men in sweatshirts on warm summer days, the gun-shaped bulges beneath their shirts a warning. I see the bangers and the players and their gangster version of E-mail. I see graffiti.

I learned to read graffiti from the cops when I worked in the hard-core gang unit and now I read graffiti on the way to work, like other commuters read newspapers.

In the summer of 1994, the freeways were so bloated with morning traffic, I often took Main Street north to downtown, catching it right outside my little stucco house in Carson. I followed the street twenty miles as it carved a path from the South Bay sprawl where I live, through some of the toughest neighborhoods in L.A., through the Garment District, past Skid Row, and finally to the Los Angeles County Criminal Courts Building.

Along the way, I read the graffiti instinctively. It was painted on the sides of warehouses and apartment buildings, on freeway underpasses, medians, curbs, houses, fences, walls, cars, Dumpsters, trucks, trains, and buses, on freeway signs so high you couldn't imagine how they got up there. Some of it was obvious: the colors, red for Bloods; the gang names marking territory or declaring war, "Rollin' 60s" and "8 Trey Gangsta Crips." Sometimes, it would be one gangbanger's moniker or the moniker of a subset within a gang, like "Seven Deadly Dwarves."

Often there were threats or common braggadocio. Sometimes, the graffiti would just be a list of names preceded by the initials "RIP."

There are many subtexts in a city, and this one depressed and infuriated me. Graffiti is such a waste. It cheapens and diminishes everything it touches, makes every building it covers seem abandoned and condemned, and reminds people living in a neighborhood that they don't own shit. It's as if they have only a tenancy in life, they can be totally evicted; their lives, like their neighborhoods, don't really belong to them.

You notice a change as soon as you leave the industrial area of North Carson and hit the unincorporated county area, which looks just like every other block—industrial parks and small storefronts, strip malls bleeding away into residential neighborhoods, rows of cinder block and stucco—until you pass beneath the 91 Freeway and the first seedy motel, planted like a mushroom in the shadow of the underpass. Now you're at the edge of L.A. and you pass some of the most famous streets in the 'hood—Imperial, Century, Manchester, Florence, and Slauson—streets that wrap through the city from the projects in Watts and South Central and end up in suburbs like Ladera Heights, Culver City, and Westchester.

You drive along a stretch of Main Street called Dodge City because of all the shootings and shoot-outs between rival gangs. You pass a Catholic church where the teenage funerals are too often interrupted by drive-bys, and you pass the liquor store at Imperial and Main, which sat for months like a monument, a burned-out shell from the 1992 riots. Just east of the intersection is the Imperial Garden Housing Project, the "jects." Even the cops won't go in without backup.

Most people think of Main Street as the character and center of some small town, the hardware store and city hall and all of that. This is Main Street L.A., and so it's twenty miles of the entire world, every language and color and nationality, natives of everywhere except Los Angeles, the very poor slamming every day against the very rich.

The cars rolling past all this on their way to work are nice, splayed along four lanes of steady traffic, but the ones parked on the curb are buckets, cardboard-for-windows, dented-door buckets. There are only two kinds of cars in L.A., and you see them both on this Main Street— nice, expensive new ones and the ones that just ought to be junked. At eight in the morning, you don't see any tricked-out Jettas, with their tinted windows and low profiles, no bass-pounding Jeeps, no restored

Impalas. It's too early for the gangsters to be out, but the addicts and prostitutes are out on foot, coursing up and down Main, looking every day like this will be their last.

Past King Boulevard, the terrain is more relaxed. Just to the west looms the Sports Arena—where the NBA's Clippers play basketball—and the Coliseum, where the Raiders once played football games. Next is the University of Southern California, where O. J. Simpson carved up opposing football teams.

You hit the garment district next. At one end, illegals walk head-down between dirty sweatshops, while at the other end, closer to down-town, women walk with a flourish, ridiculous hats in their gloved hands. The drivers are insane in the Garment District, insistent upon turning their 500 SL's left across double yellow lines and across three lanes of traffic. They don't care. As long as they can stop traffic, they don't care.

And then it begins to get seedy and you hit the homeless area—Skid Row. The bus station is two blocks south and there are a number of flop-houses and waves of people who have given up and have been given up on. You see the remnants of the mental health system here, people wandering in clothes held together only by the dirt on them, people lost in their own minds.

At first, the Civic Center area doesn't look much better than Skid Row. But things brighten up when you pass the bus station. And then you hit the Criminal Courts Building, a dark, twenty-story egg carton that contains the District Attorney's Office, my office.

That's all I did in the summer of 1994. I went to work.

The traffic in L.A. is nothing compared to the wait for an elevator at the Criminal Courts Building. A hundred people stood clustered in front of a bank of ten elevators, like slots players in Vegas, hoping they picked a lucky machine, hoping they're standing in front of the next elevator to open. Otherwise, the wait might be fifteen minutes to get upstairs, stand-ing there watching everyone else pack in shoulder to shoulder, as another group takes their place waiting for that same elevator. I could've taken the stairs, seventeen floors through landings filled with every smoker in the building, the air in that stairwell worse than any L.A. smog.

By the summer of 1994, I would rather wait. I finally caught an elevator and made my way upstairs, a little after nine. I walked past the barrel, a glass-encased information and security desk, down a hall, and into the reception area for my office. I moved the little oblong magnet by my name from "Out" to "In" and said hello to the office assistants, Amelia Garay-Ellis and Martha Mosqueda. Martha was a true homegirl, as skilled an office worker as I've ever seen. She looked like a gangster herself, but wasn't. She had a round face and the letter "M" tattooed between her thumb and finger. Nobody messed with Martha. Well, except me. She and I had a pact: You watch my back, I'll watch my back too.

"Hey Darden, what's up? 'Bout time you got your ass in here."

She and Amelia had the bad habit of running the television all day—watching soap operas, game shows, and news programs on this small, black-and-white, nine-inch TV wedged between their desks. Usually, that bugged me, but that week, just a few days after the murders of Nicole Brown and Ronald Goldman, everyone wanted to know what was going on with O. J. Simpson. I craned my neck as I passed to see what was happening, but it was just some lame-ass soap opera.

I stuck my head in my old friend Alan Yochelson's office, right next to mine. His office looked, as usual, like shit, paper and boxes strewn all over, binders in every open space so that there was nowhere to sit. Alan had recently begun decking his short, slightly overweight, Jewish body in $1,000 Hickey-Freeman suits with custom, Egyptian-cotton shirts, his initials sewn onto the French collar.

"Why would someone spend a grand on a suit when he won't even do his sit-ups? That's a waste of a good suit."

"I don't know," Alan said, "you could stand to spend a little on clothes yourself. And do a few thousand sit-ups."

I was wearing chinos and a white oxford shirt with a button-down collar then—soft, comfortable cotton stuff, much more casual than the rest of the office. Earlier in my career, I could have shamed a guy like Yochelson with my suits. I guess I was beyond that stage in my career, when I needed to wear a suit. Now, I was dressing like my attitude— down. I didn't think I needed a suit. I was certain that I was never going to do another trial.

My office was next door, small and cramped, but it had a window that looked out on the hills behind L.A. and, right across the street, the majestic Hall of Justice, which had been damaged in the earthquake and closed down.

I sat down at my cluttered desk and buzzed Martha. "Any messages?"

"Why didn't you just grab your messages when you were in here?" Martha shot back.

In the office, like anywhere else in the country, we talked about the O. J. Simpson case. Earlier that week, I had been talking to a guy at the LAPD and I asked about O. J.

"Well, do you have him?"

"Yeah," the guy said, "we have him."

There was a ton of evidence, an unreal amount of evidence.

"He did it then?" I asked.

"Yeah, he did it."

O. J. Simpson was a murderer. Perhaps I'd been a deputy D.A. too long, but even that didn't surprise me. I'd seen him around Beverly Hills a few times, always a new blond on his arm, and, if you live in L.A., you learn quickly that some celebrities aren't who they seem. "How'd the interview go?"

"He's lying like a rug."

But I had less interest in the Simpson case than other prosecutors. I was thinking about the Black Panthers again.

One of the leaders of the Panthers was a man named Geronimo Pratt. In 1972—back when Panther newspapers lined my bedroom wall—Pratt was convicted of murder, the shooting death four years earlier of a twenty-three-year-old college student during an $18 robbery on a tennis court in Santa Monica. The key witnesses in the case were a Panther who later turned out to be an FBI informant and the woman's husband, who first identified another man as the killer. For years, there have been indications that Pratt's conviction was tainted by the FBI's notorious COINTELPRO investigations. And yet Pratt remained in prison. When I was a young man, the Geronimo Pratt case was one of those that had inspired me.

Pratt's attorney had been an up-and-coming young black lawyer— Johnnie Cochran. Cochran's key piece of evidence in the case was a Polaroid photograph that purported to show Geronimo Pratt with a beard and mustache just a week before the murder—during which he was described as clean-shaven. The only problem was, after the photograph was introduced as evidence, the film was dated as having been manufactured months after the killing.

I didn't know whether Geronimo Pratt had killed that woman, but it seemed to me that his conviction might have been affected by unethical law enforcement and the false evidence presented by his own lawyer.

That was the case I was considering in June 1994, while the rest of the world was wondering who killed O. J. Simpson's wife. I was preparing to ask the District Attorney of Los Angeles, Gil Garcetti, if I could review the Pratt case and offer a recommendation about whether he should be pardoned, be paroled, or remain incarcerated. He'd already spent twenty-three years in prison—the first eight in solitary confinement—and yet people still talked about Geronimo Pratt. It seemed to me that his case should be resolved once and for all.

I had no authority to review the Pratt matter. There was a retired appellate prosecutor, Harry Sondheim, who had begun tackling the humongous case file. I was just one Grade 4 deputy district attorney in an office of nine hundred lawyers. It wasn't my job to worry about the civil rights of those defendants already convicted. It was my job to add to the list of prison inmates. Still, I wanted to try.

That morning of June 17 ground away just like the others. The D.A.'s sparse, industrial offices take up three floors in the Criminal Courts Building, a maze of cramped offices filled with two hundred cynical, unappreciated lawyers. The lawyers upstairs, in Major Crimes, were busy working on the Simpson case, but in the other departments, like mine, our involvement was the same as that of everyone else in America. We watched it on TV.

Of course, that was the day Simpson was supposed to turn himself in, and his lawyer, Robert Shapiro, had made a special deal with the cops to give Simpson some more time and privacy. Shapiro called the cops every fifteen minutes, saying Simpson was almost ready, that he would bring him to police headquarters soon.

I was walking through the reception area when I saw Gil Garcetti on television, followed by an LAPD commander named David Gascon, and the two of them seemed furious. Simpson had promised to turn himself in, but, apparently, he and his friend Al Cowlings had gone on the run.

"The Los Angeles Police Department right now is actively searching for Mr. Simpson," said Gascon, tight-lipped and angry. "We hope to have him in custody soon."

I was impressed. Gascon, especially, was about to burst a blood ves-
sel. I'd never seen any official, let alone a cop, that angry in public. Yet
it was no wonder; they'd been tricked. Cops and prosecutors are not the
type to appreciate being tricked.

"O. J. is dead meat," I told Martha. "They're going to get him one
way or another for making them look like fools." The police had broken
a basic rule of criminal apprehension: Never make special rules or excep-
tions for a potential suspect. But Simpson was a celebrity, and celebrities get a break on everything in L.A. Still, it seemed like a bad idea to
me. With his money and connections, Simpson had a better chance of
running than most people in trouble, and only a fool would waste the
opportunity to get away.

We were enrapt in the office as Simpson's attorney, Robert Shapiro, and his friend, Robert Kardashian, came on television together to
explain what had happened and to read O. J.'s "suicide" note, in which
he proclaimed his innocence, and which he signed with a happy face
drawn inside his "O." A suicide note with a happy face. *Right.* Simpson
wrote:

> Unlike whats [*sic*] been in the press. Nicole + I had a great rela-
> tion for most of our lives together. Like all long term relation-
> ships we had a few downs + ups. I took the heat New Years
> 1989 because that's what I was supposed to do.
>
> I think of my life and feel I'v [sic] done most of the right
> things so why do I end up like this? I can't go on, no matter
> what the outcome. People will look and point. I can't take that
> I can't submit my children to that.
>
> I'm sorry for the Goldman Family. I know how much it
> hurts.
>
> Don't feel sorry for me. I've had a great life made great
> friends. Please think of the real O. J. and not this lost person.

Even then, I wondered, why apologize to the Goldman family if he
was innocent? And why write a suicide note at all?

Afterward, Shapiro answered questions from the reporters. A reporter
asked if Simpson had done anything to indicate he might be suicidal.

"From Tuesday on, he has been exceedingly depressed," Shapiro said.

"He has been under a doctor's care, medicated and sedated, and we have had a very real concern that this might be an avenue he would choose."

Another reporter asked if Shapiro or Kardashian had received any communication whatsoever from Simpson.

"None since this morning," Shapiro said.

It was incredible. I kept one eye on the television all afternoon. As a supervisor in SID, I was responsible for investigating officer-involved shootings. Now that Simpson was a fugitive in a double murder case, the police had legal standing to shoot him if they caught him, and judging by the anger in Commander Gascon's voice, a shoot-out seemed to be a distinct possibility.

If they shot him, we'd be called to investigate the shooting. We wanted to be ready. I would have to go to the scene along with the head deputy in my division and a senior investigator assigned to SID. We waited until about six o'clock that night and then I left for home. There were wild rumors but still no sign of him and Cowlings.

I thought about Simpson as I drove home, thought about him as a successful black man from San Francisco and about my own journey out of the Bay Area. The Juice. It was sad. I figured he'd either kill himself or get out of the country. Hell, Roman Polanski skipped out and he's still free in Europe. Besides, this was O. J. Simpson. He was too far removed from the 'hood to be able to make it in prison; a life without parole wouldn't be much of a life and might not even last very long for someone like him.

It took forty-five minutes to get home in the traffic of the Harbor Freeway, and as I opened the door to my one-story, gray house in Carson, the telephone was ringing.

"Turn on the TV," said whoever was on the line.

It was on every channel and it was hypnotic—that white Bronco meandering up the freeway with something that people in L.A. have never seen before: no traffic. He passed near my house and onto Highway 91, crossed over Main Street and onto the 405. I was spellbound and I turned to every channel to find that they'd all switched to the chase. Even the finals of the National Basketball Association had been interrupted. We'd all been swallowed whole by this thing.

As soon as I set the phone down, it rang again. And again. Friends called from all over the country, fellow lawyers talking about the murder case, college pals trashing L.A., everyone shouting either for or against Simpson.

He was headed for his house on Rockingham and I assumed there would be some sort of standoff. That would make it my responsibility again; to make sure that if the cops blew up O. J., everything was done by the numbers.

Helicopters were following him and police cars cleared traffic in every direction. It seemed that would only make him believe there was no way out. Nowhere to go. I remember thinking: I hope he just kills himself. It seemed like his only choice, which is strange because I believe suicide is wrong. But I could well imagine the horror his two children would feel if they discovered that their father had killed their mother.

The Bronco—its long shadow tailed by rows of police cars—tooled past freeway exits that were familiar to me, places I'd lived, where friends lived. A. C. drove past Manchester, and I couldn't believe what I saw, people holding up signs—GO JUICE—standing on the side of the freeway, cheering him on. It was the most outrageous thing I'd ever seen. I figured those people must not realize how much evidence there was against him. Those people must have no idea how Nicole and Ron were butchered, I thought. As I watched the bizarre procession down the 405, I began to think about the Rodney King beating and the riots and now this—people cheering a double murderer. I wondered what the rest of the world must think of Los Angeles.

The Bronco parked at Rockingham and Simpson's adult son, Jason, ran out. I couldn't understand it. Why would O. J. wait and kill himself at home, blow his brains out in front of his family? It seemed cowardly and stupid.

They negotiated with Simpson, talked him into giving up his gun, and then he was arrested. I was relieved in a way. It was over. But I was also exhausted and confused, a feeling I will always associate with this case. It was dark in the bay south of Los Angeles, and I had been on the telephone with my colleagues all evening. On the television, reporters and talking heads were swarming in front of Simpson's mansion like buzzards on road kill, already sensing that this story was huge. I sighed, leaned back into my couch, and rubbed my bald head.

"Now someone's got to try that poor bastard," I said. "Thank God it's not me."

EIGHT

H ow come you never get any big cases?" my sister Debbie asked
when I went home to Richmond that weekend, after the
Bronco chase.

My family had always been supportive of my career, but I don't
think they truly understood what kinds of cases I handled in the D.A.'s
office. I'd tried nineteen murder cases without an acquittal. I'd tried gang
cases and gone after racist and excessively violent cops. But if you slog in
L.A. and haven't worked a single celebrity case, people start to wonder
if you've ever really done anything. In the L.A. legal community, unless
you can get rappers off murder charges or convict Zsa Zsa Gabor of slapping a cop, you aren't much of a lawyer.

I guess the closest I ever got to a celebrity case was when I prosecuted the guy who stole Tom Petty's guitar. Petty never came to court,
but his roadie did. That's what I got. Roadies.

"So," Debbie asked, "how come you never get any big cases?"

I didn't say anything to my family at first, but I'd begun to suspect
that I was going to have a hand in the Simpson case. I'm not sure what it
was, just a feeling, like the static electricity before you're hit by lightning.
I watched this thing take over our office and I knew I was imminently
available and that I was one of the most experienced litigators in our
office. I figured I'd be dragged in eventually, in a small role. I didn't look
forward to it. I was tired. In thirteen years, I'd never taken a vacation to
anywhere except the Bay Area. I needed a break.

My father is the kind of guy who can fill up any room, head resting
on his barrel chest, arms swinging as he gets excited. He has a great laugh
and is a wonderful, whiskey-voiced storyteller, a man who isn't afraid to

lie for the sake of a story, but a man whose advice always makes more sense at the bottom of your second beer.

"I think I might get the Simpson case," I said, pulling on a bottle of beer on the porch of my parents' house.

"Black folks ain't gonna convict O. J. Simpson," my father said, his voice cracking with emphasis. He and I sat out there that summer, watching the flotsam and jetsam of a decaying neighborhood: do-ragged women standing for hours on the nearest corner, waiting for who knows what; kids cruising in too-big Starter jackets and too-new high-tops; fifteen-year-old putty-colored cars that sounded like a kid's rattle rolling around in a drum, trolling for one of any number of houses that sell rock.

"Black folks want two kinds of justice, like everyone else," my father said on his porch. "One for them and one for the other guy."

I disagreed, silently. This was a strong case and black people are fair. We are repulsed at injustice. Historically, what segment of the American population is more fair than blacks? Fairness is a fundamental part of our nature. A black jury would convict if the evidence was there. I was on the outside, and just the evidence I'd heard about appeared to be more than in any of the murder cases I'd ever prosecuted. It was more than in any case I'd ever seen.

"You'll catch hell if you work on that one," my daddy said. "There'll be hell to pay, you work on that one."

My father and I haven't always gotten along, but I've always valued his opinion. He only had two kinds: completely on and completely off. There were no soft opinions from Eddie Darden. I opened another beer. "So, you think I shouldn't get involved?"

"No," he said. "I didn't say that. You have to do what you have to do. You have to do what you think is right." And then Daddy turned and went back into the house, the screen door banging loudly against the doorjamb.

You could hear Marcia Clark's high heels from twenty feet away, clicking on the tile floor in her purposeful, arrogant walk. She turned sharp corners and disappeared behind her office door, on which were posted signs that made you think there was nuclear experimentation going on behind the door:

DO NOT KNOCK, KEEP OUT. CALL PATTI JO. There was another sign that read, IT IS EASIER FOR MEN TO PRAISE A WOMAN WHO FAILS.

Behind that door, the only experiment Marcia was conducting was one about the disgusting effects of smoking; a long, filtered Dunhill Red cigarette was hanging from her mouth at all times, barely out before she reached for another one from the fancy red carton. On her desk was the Smoke Grabber, a square, smokeless ashtray that didn't work for shit; her office always reeked of cigarette smoke.

Marcia and I were contemporaries. We'd started in the D.A.'s office about the same time and had once been assigned to the same trial court, eight years earlier. We were about the same age (OK, she was a few years older) and were midlevel prosecutors—a couple of ambitious Grade 4s.

Approaching fourteen years in the office, Marcia had learned (as I had) from the older 4s to keep a bottle of booze in her bottom desk drawer. She kept Scotch. I kept tequila. We'd also learned that the meek didn't inherit anything in an office filled with lawyers. So we were also ballers, aggressive prosecutors who didn't put up with shit from anyone. And we were friends.

Part of my job in SID was to review requests from the media for information about police officers in our files. And so, when a public records request came in from Andrea Ford of the *Los Angeles Times* for information about a detective named Mark Fuhrman and an allegation that he'd planted evidence in an earlier case, I pulled the file and decided I'd better tell Marcia.

It was a pretty standard officer-involved shooting investigation. We'd looked into it, rejected it for prosecution, and filed it away. But the shooting victim—who wasn't killed—was suing the city, alleging that Fuhrman had planted evidence on him, and so his letter was in the file as well. I'd heard Fuhrman's name before, from Hank Goldberg and Kathy Mader, two other deputy D.A.'s in our office. Hank had prosecuted a murder case in Santa Monica, a case in which Fuhrman had been involved as one of the lead investigators. At the time, Hank had heard rumors about Fuhrman, that he was called Fuhrer-man and Fuhrman the German, and that he was a racist who collected Nazi paraphernalia.

But Goldberg, who was Jewish, had worked with Fuhrman many times before. He said Fuhrman was a serious, meticulous detective, and he found black officers and crime victims who said they had absolutely no problem with Fuhrman. Still, Fuhrman's name was beginning to surface as a key to the Simpson defense strategy, so I figured I should let Marcia know about the public records request.

I hadn't seen Marcia in some time, not since she'd been made a special assistant to Bill Hodgman, who was the director of special operations. After that, Marcia had left management—"I was tired of dealing with everyone else's bullshit," she told me—and had gone back into Major Crimes, desperate to get back into the courtroom. Now, in early July, she was up to her short skirt in the Simpson case.

Marcia never wanted to meet in anyone else's office. You always had to meet in her office. That was Marcia. A lot of people didn't like her drive and single-mindedness. The world was always on her terms, on her turf.

I grabbed the Fuhrman file and rode the elevator to her office on the floor above mine, and when I walked up to her door, there were people milling around outside. I was slightly envious of the adrenaline of a big case. I ignored the insistent warning signs and knocked on her door.

Her voice came smoky and direct. "Who is it?"

"Darden."

She was sitting at her desk, smoking of course, that worthless ashtray doing nothing to clean the thick air in her office. Marcia's office was two and a half times bigger than mine, fourteen feet by fourteen feet, with a big window at her back and a desk fit for a CEO. Behind her was a life-sized photograph of the Door's lead singer, Jim Morrison.

"How's it goin', big time?"

She just sighed and waved her hands. She leaned back in her huge, brown leather executive chair with the diamond tuck in the back, a chair twice her size, clearly not standard county-issue. Marcia was so small, the chair framed her. She would pull her feet up onto the worn seat like a child at the dinner table. She looked up at me with her big, round eyes.

"Well," I said, "I know you're busy, but I thought you should know there's been a public records request on Fuhrman."

"What do you have?"

"Fortunately for you, all we have is a shooting that we rejected." I handed her a copy of the closing letter, the shooting review report, and a copy of the public records request. "They have a right to get the file in ten days. I'll probably give it to them on day nine-and-a-half."

We both laughed.

Marcia lit another cigarette and blew smoke toward the ceiling. "So what do you think of the case?" I knew what she was really asking. *What were her chances of convincing a downtown L.A. jury?*

I don't always answer right away when someone asks me a question. I am by nature a shy person and I will pause before answering a difficult question.

"Well, to be honest, black people don't think he's guilty," I said. "But black people will do the right thing if the evidence is there."

She just nodded, and after a few minutes, we both went back to work.

It was a couple of weeks later that Marcia called me upstairs again. "So," she asked me in her clipped voice, "if you had the A. C. Cowlings investigation, how would you handle it?"

Simpson's longtime buddy, Al Cowlings, was being investigated for his role in the Bronco chase, for harboring a fugitive. With the Simpson case taking all their time, Marcia and Bill Hodgman had to decide what to do with Cowlings: either drop the investigation completely or find someone else to look into it. The media were reporting a rumor that the D.A.'s office planned to drop the Cowlings case only after using it to gather more information against Simpson. I knew Marcia was leaning toward dropping it. I also knew the difficulties of a case like that: First, you had to prove that he was helping Simpson escape; but you also had to prove that Cowlings knew O. J. was actually wanted by the police. And chances were that Cowlings wasn't just going to admit those things.

A prosecution of Cowlings wouldn't be popular with a black jury either. As I sat in Marcia's office, I thought about my regular Saturday morning aerobics class. It had been empty the day after the chase and people later said they were just too drained to come to class. The consensus among these people and some of my other friends was that Cowlings had done just the right thing; he'd protected his buddy at all costs. That was what we'd be fighting.

"I'd probably take it to the grand jury," I said. My reasoning was that the witnesses in this thing were close friends of Simpson and Cowlings and weren't going to just show up and give us interviews. We would need subpoena power.

We talked about it for a little while and then I started back to my office. I thought about what my father had said—"There'll be hell to pay"—and wondered if it was going to be worth the trouble. I was hoping to slow down, maybe get married, be a dad again, have a relationship beyond the telephonic ones I'd been having recently. I was trying to get off the office treadmill, and there were Marcia Clark and Bill Hodgman, trying to pull me back in.

A few days later, on July 20, Marcia and Bill asked me to handle the Cowlings investigation. After my initial trepidation about anything having to do with the Simpson case, I was ecstatic to have some role, to have something to do other than harass bad cops—as long as I could maintain a limited role and not be dragged in deeper. I thanked Bill and Marcia for their confidence in my skills and accepted.

Marcia said I could have complete access to her files and complete freedom in my investigation. They would do their best to stay out of my way. Hodgman reminded me that we had to keep the investigations separate to ensure the purity of both.

Marcia stood, grabbed a book from a stack of eight photo albums, and handed it across her desk to me. Each page was filled with two-inch by three-inch 35-mm photographs, and I flipped through them slowly. There must've been 150 photographs in that one book alone—more than I'd ever seen in a single case. I'd seen a lot of crime scene photos, containing hundreds of murder victims. In the hard-core gang unit, the prosecutors kept a collage of autopsy photos and murder victims, a mess of photographs so gruesome and offensive, I'd complained to the head deputy that they should take them down in case the victims' family members saw them.

But in thirteen years, I'd never seen such a brutal murder. And I'd never seen a knife wound like the one across Nicole Brown Simpson's neck. It seemed perfectly straight and deep, somehow enraged and matter-of-fact at the same time. I stared at the pictures too long, at Goldman slumped against the wall, his jeans tie-dyed with blood, and Nicole lying at the bottom of the stairs, her hair matted in a deep, red slick. I had never seen so much blood.

I took a thin manila folder, containing a few reports, back up to my office, mostly interviews from the people who'd been at Robert Kardashian's house on June 17, the morning Simpson and Cowlings had run. The official story given out by Robert Shapiro and Robert Kardashian made no sense to me. People come and go all morning long and Simpson is flitting about, being examined by defense experts, saying good-bye to his family, and then, all of a sudden, he and Cowlings disappear so Simpson can kill himself? It made no sense. If their friend was truly suicidal and truly missing, why would Shapiro and Kardashian read his "suicide note" while O. J. was presumably still alive? Wouldn't that push a suicidal man over the edge, to hear his own suicide note on the radio? Unless the note was just a diversion by Simpson to help him and Cowlings get away.

I had a thousand other questions. If everyone knew O. J. was suicidal and he was surrounded by all these friends, how did he get a gun? Why would he have to drive somewhere to kill himself? Why not just do it at the house? Why did he need Cowlings to help him commit suicide? And, most important, if Simpson wasn't the murderer, why commit suicide at all? The night before, Cowlings had taken Simpson's place at the house on Rockingham to fool the media; were they planning their escape as early as the night before?

Of particular interest were the interviews with the forensics specialists, Dr. Henry Lee and Dr. Michael Baden, who had been called in by Shapiro to examine Simpson. According to Lee, Simpson was in the room when someone mentioned that the cops were coming. Clearly, Simpson knew he was a fugitive.

The police interview with the psychiatrist, Saul Faerstein, was intriguing also. He said that Simpson was "nervous, but resigned to what was happening . . . nothing was said about suicide." Yet, on June 15, the same doctor said O. J. was suicidal. Now, on June 17, the day Simpson is supposed to be arrested for murder, Faerstein doesn't bother to have a one-on-one interview with Simpson to assess his mental condition? Hadn't Shapiro and Kardashian described O. J. as just that—suicidal? My suspicions were heightened when Faerstein testified that he last saw Simpson at about 11 A.M. on June 17, a full hour and a half before Simpson and A. C. hit the road.

It made no sense, a shrink with a celebrity client who is suicidal letting the client out of his sight, letting him take off, not checking his bag. Wouldn't you want to make sure a guy like that wasn't armed? Add that to the more obvious evidence found in Cowlings's car: You need a fake mustache and beard to commit suicide? A passport? Nine grand in cash? It was clear there was something wrong with the story.

From the beginning, the people in the house didn't seem to be watching him the way they would if they were truly concerned that he might kill himself. Would they let a suicidal guy run off like that? Probably not. Would they let someone escape who was just trying to get out of the country? Maybe.

It made no sense that he was allowed to be alone if he was in a mood to kill himself. It was almost as if they were turning their backs, hoping he'd run away.

As I was finishing with the photos, I stopped and stared at one of them. There was something about it that seemed out of place, and I moved my finger around the edge of it. It was an LAPD photograph of Simpson's bathroom; next to the hamper were dark clothes, possibly a sweat suit.

Marcia had described the killer's clothes as a dark-colored sweat suit.

I was dumbfounded. Had the LAPD criminalists neglected to seize the clothes used during the murder when they searched O. J. Simpson's house?

I have always worked well with law clerks, always had a relationship that alternated between mentor and tormentor. I'd been blessed with several outstanding law clerks over the years, and I was proud that they'd all passed the state bar exam and become lawyers. I was also proud that many of my clerks were black. Not that it mattered in our working relationship, but I felt it was important to have black prosecutors—to have blacks represented in every part of the criminal justice system. After all the opportunities I had received, I felt a responsibility to help and train young African-American lawyers.

My law clerk at the time was not black, but he was one of the best I ever had, so good, in fact, I had to steal him from another prosecutor, Scott Gordon, after Gordon was promoted. Michael Runyon was a little over six feet tall, Canadian-born, redheaded, and nuts about basketball.

He was also my personal clerk, my indentured servant. No one assigned Runyon work except me. And I gave him plenty.

The day I began the Cowlings investigation, Runyon was on leave, preparing to take the California bar exam. I waited until he was finished before I called him and left a message on his machine.

"Congratulations," I said calmly. "I'm sure you're a lawyer by now. Call me when you get in. We've got a good one."

Since the Cowlings investigation wasn't an SID case, I couldn't use the unit's investigators and would have to find my own. Since the LAPD was already involved, it made sense to get a couple of police detectives, but I needed good cops, smart cops, guys who realized they weren't the only ones who knew something about criminal investigations.

The next week, I called the captain in the Robbery/Homicide Division, William Gartland, and asked for Stephens and Arce, the cops I'd worked with prosecuting Joe Danks, the Koreatown Slasher.

They showed up August 1 at 9 A.M. and sat down in my office across from Runyon, who slurped a cup of Starbucks coffee, and me.

"Here they are," I said, "my two hand-picked detectives."

We bullshitted awhile and then got down to business. We talked about the legal issues and about all the witnesses we needed to interview, mainly the people who were at Kardashian's house that day.

"O. J. is off-limits," I said. I explained the separation between the two cases and said we wouldn't be investigating Simpson. "Life is short enough as it is. We can leave that one to the movie star upstairs."

Even though I hadn't seen Bud and Jerry in a while, the rapport was what I'd remembered.

"Don't tolerate any interference," I told Arce and Stephens. "If they won't talk to you, we'll drag their asses in front of the grand jury." I told them that if they got any hassles from the LAPD brass, I would try to help.

That afternoon, Runyon and I met the detectives at the front door of the Criminal Courts Building. We climbed in the backseat of their four-door, unmarked detective's sedan, pinched by the backs of their seats. (Even short cops move their seats as far back as they'll go, I guess to keep the doorjamb between themselves and the people on the street.)

It was a hot, muggy day, not a day to be riding around in heavy traffic in the back of a cop car. We muddled around downtown and finally got on the 110, heading south. We got off the freeway after five miles, parked at the curb near a large metal gate topped with barbed wire, at Rheuban Motor Tow.

We walked through the gate. To the left was a set of three wooden steps leading onto a porch and into an office. Arce walked into the office and came out a few minutes later. He nodded to the left and we walked over to an unlocked garage door and peeled it open.

Inside was Al Cowlings's Bronco, the second-most famous sport utility vehicle in the world.

It was two-door and white. I was surprised at how big it was; floating alone down the 405, it had looked so small. I looked through the tinted rear window first, at the cargo area, without touching the Bronco.

Jerry was snapping on a pair of rubber gloves when I walked around to the passenger side. He opened the door, reached into the glove compartment, and removed some papers. There was also a brown paper bag in the Bronco, stuff that had been recovered from the passenger-side floorboard. Inside the bag, neatly folded, were four extra-large white T-shirts; an extra-large white polo shirt; a gray undershirt; a Motorola telephone charger; and two gas receipts from June 15, 1994.

My mouth fell open. Why hadn't this stuff been seized by the police detectives?

Another bag contained stuff grabbed from the cargo area: a jacket, two polo shirts, four pairs of socks, and two pairs of underwear. The clothing was fresh, neatly folded. I remembered that Al Cowlings claimed O. J. had pulled the gun out of a towel, and so I unfolded it. It looked like one of the towels that was in Simpson's bathroom in the LAPD photographs I'd seen.

In the center of the towel was a dark stain. It was blood.

"Jerry, Bud, look at this." We stared at the towel in disbelief.

There were other things in the Bronco, things that made no sense for someone about to kill himself: photos of Sydney and Justin (O. J. and Nicole's kids) and two address books—one belonging to O. J., the other to A. C. I couldn't imagine why this stuff wasn't taken as evidence. The towel that hung in Simpson's bathroom, which had an apparent bloodstain? What if it was Nicole's blood? Maybe he had used the towel to dry his hands or wipe down the Bronco after the murder. The Simpson case wasn't my responsibility and there was a good chance that six

weeks in a garage had ruined any forensic value that a bloodstain might
have had. I couldn't help wondering, had the police overlooked key
pieces of evidence in Cowlings's Bronco? What could this mean for the
Simpson investigation?

It made no sense. Why wouldn't they seize the address books of two
guys who were clearly on the run somewhere? If we were going to find
out where they were going, who they were going to see, these address
books could be indispensable. There were also pages of a calendar from
June 1994 to December 1994. In a case that would include premeditation and attempted flight, wouldn't the suspect's whereabouts and plans
before and after the murders be relevant?

We got back to the office about 4 P.M., a time when many of the
judges had already completed their calendars and had gone to their
homes in the hills to sun themselves by the pool, a time when prosecutors and public defenders were eyeing the clock, hoping to skip soon
enough to shave a few minutes of traffic from their commutes. There
were a few reporters sniffing for O. J. leads, but they ignored Runyon
and me.

Runyon had been with me a few months by then and he knew to
hold his opinion until the two of us were alone. Even though he was my
clerk, we were, in a sense, partners, and I respected his intelligence and
loyalty.

My door closed and we started in. "I can't believe that they would
leave all that evidence in the Bronco," I said. "This isn't good." When
they'd arrested Cowlings, he'd been carrying more than $8,700 in cash
and three unopened envelopes, which were rumored to contain checks
to help in their escape. But instead of booking the envelopes into evidence or trying to get a warrant to open them, the police just gave them
back to Cowlings.

Mike nodded. We were both thinking about the larger Simpson
investigation, difficult enough without the cops forgetting to book evidence.

I laughed a little. "I only hope they did a better job handling the rest
of the evidence."

While we were searching the Bronco, I had snapped briefly at Arce and
Stephens about all the evidence left inside it.

They'd both turned and glared at me. "Hey, we're not Tom and Phil." The lead detectives in the Simpson case were Tom Lange and Phil Vannatter.

"I know. But why the hell was this stuff left in here?" I asked through clenched teeth.

Arce stared at the Bronco. "That's a good question, Roy."

They'd been calling me that all day and I wasn't sure why. I didn't think I'd heard him right and so I didn't say anything. In the 'hood, when someone calls you boy, you always give him the chance to back away by asking, "Did you call me Roy?"

It wasn't until later, sitting in the Saratoga—the smoky, red-boothed diner and cop bar where Arce and Stephens basically lived—that I found out why they called me Roy.

There was this officer that Jerry and Bud had known, a big, classic cop named Russell Lee Kuster. Kuster had trained Arce back in 1969 and they'd worked together off and on for the next two decades. Kuster's idol was the country-and-western singer Roy Acuff and so Kuster always called his best friends Roy. In the late 1970s and early 1980s, Arce and Stephens were both working homicide in the Hollywood Division, under Kuster, who began calling all the detectives Roy, which also cut down on the chances that he'd forget someone's name. They would know which one he was talking to by the tone of his voice and his inflection: "Roy!" or "Roy," or "Roy?"

They all moved to downtown Robbery/Homicide over the next few years, and Kuster, Arce, and Stephens remained very close. Kuster was even the best man at one of Jerry's weddings.

One night, in October 1990, just months before his retirement, Kuster was drinking at a bar near his house, a place called the Hilltop Cafe. The thing about L.A. is that there are bars and restaurants for every nationality and ethnicity. The Hilltop was primarily a Hungarian hangout. That night, a drunk Hungarian guy named Bela Marko walked in and demanded to use the telephone to call his mother in Hungary. Marko was a probation violator, an illegal alien with a long record of drugs and violence. He got loud and the waitress told him to quiet down or she'd tell the cop at the end of the bar.

Marko walked out of the bar and came back with a sophisticated 9-mm handgun with a laser sight. He began training the laser on people in the bar, threatening them, yelling at them. He even rested the laser on Kuster, who stood and tried to talk Marko into putting the gun down. Instead, Marko opened fire, shooting Kuster through the knees.

They drew down on each other, firing back and forth from six feet away. Kuster hit Marko twice but the Hungarian kept firing, one bullet hitting Kuster's torso, another tearing through his chest and heart. Kuster fell forward and landed near Marko's feet. He looked up and fired once with his 9-mm handgun. The bullet went through Bela's chin, into his skull, and dropped him like a stone. Legend has it that right before Kuster slipped out of consciousness, he asked if he'd killed the bastard.

Arce and Stephens were the first RHD detectives to arrive at the scene, but their lieutenant told them they were too close to the case. It turned out Arce had busted Bela Marko once before, while they were all assigned to Hollywood. Coincidentally, Kuster had been the officer to sign off on that investigation. But the case had been dropped because of insufficient evidence. All that week, reporters wondered in their news stories if Kuster had recognized the big, surly Hungarian before he killed him.

After Kuster was killed, Arce always wore a black bracelet, like the ones families of missing soldiers wear. He had Kuster's name printed on it with the inscription "EOW"—End of Watch—"10-9-90." And after that, the biggest compliment Stephens and Arce could pay someone was to call him Roy.

"Well, Roy," Stephens said to me late in the summer of 1994, "we got a lot of work ahead of us."

NINE

As soon as the media had reported that O. J. Simpson and Al Cowlings were on the run, the police and the D.A.'s office were buried by every manner of phone call and tip. On August 2, the day after our search of the Bronco, I perused the list of clues, the best information culled from hundreds of telephone calls from people with tips or clues, which had been recorded on a telephone log in military time:

1400—Caller from Laguna Beach says O. J. can leave by boat. 1428—Florida psychic says he's hiding at a place called Markey Dry Cleaners. 1520—Caller says O. J. is in San Diego, headed for Brazil.

On June 17, callers saw O. J. and A. C. in a Mercedes, a blue sedan, a Fiero, a white Isuzu Trooper, a red Toyota, a black Blazer, and a Ford Ranger pickup with lumber racks. Someone saw Simpson hugging a blond woman in Orange County. He was with Magic Johnson; he was with Dionne Warwick; he was with Michael Jackson's older brother Jermaine. Someone had him eating dinner with a former teammate in a French restaurant in Santa Monica; someone else saw him eating alone in a white suit in Winner's Restaurant in Atlanta, Georgia.

Detectives assigned numbers to the better clues (they investigated about five hundred) and passed them on. Clue 56: Former Simpson secretary says Cowlings jealous of Simpson's first wife. Clue 117: Anonymous female says the knife was thrown out the passenger window into some shrubs. Clue 272: Anonymous friend of a friend says A. C. got a call early Sunday morning and rushed out, leaving blood on his sheets.

Most of the clues were investigated and, when they went nowhere— including the tip about A. C. and the bloody sheets—they were checked

with a "closed" mark. But among the early tips from the loony and mis-
guided was one that could potentially answer a vital question: Where
were Simpson and Cowlings going? The deeper I looked, the more I
began to believe that whatever the truth, it wasn't the story they'd been
giving: that they had decided to drive to Nicole's grave, when Simpson
pulled out a gun to kill himself.

To charge Cowlings, we had to prove two important points:

1. That Cowlings knew Simpson was a fugitive. With O. J.
   that appeared easy. Witnesses at Robert Kardashian's house
   on June 17 clearly remembered Shapiro telling Simpson,
   "They're coming to bring you down," just before Simpson
   and Cowlings left. Still, proving that O. J. knew didn't mean
   A. C. knew.
2. That they were actually trying to escape arrest. This one
   would be more difficult to prove. They didn't actually try
   to run from law enforcement after they were spotted. The
   key to proving the second point would be figuring out where
   they might've been headed before they turned around.

That's when I came across Clue 298. I leaned forward on my desk,
pushed my glasses up on the bridge of my nose, and concentrated on the
clue. It was different from any of the others—specific, capable of being
verified, and, on its face, believable.

It was based on a telephone call from a woman in Florida named
Beth Reed. She had called June 18 and left a message saying she had
some information, that she and her husband were in the Bahamas on
June 17 and 18, anchored off Man-O-War Cay. At the same time, a
large yacht, called the *Miss Turnberry,* was anchored nearby, Reed said.
On June 17, the day of the Bronco chase, while in a grocery store on the
island, she overheard a clerk say that the captain and maid on the *Turnberry* were expecting O. J. Simpson to show up on the boat *that day,* and
that they should have their cameras ready.

The following day, June 18, two crew members from the *Miss Turnberry* took a dinghy over to the Reeds' boat and delivered a crate of vegetables and fruit. The crew members were coy, but said their expected
guest hadn't arrived.

I called Robbery/Homicide and asked that any telephone books or
day planners from Simpson and Cowlings be sent over immediately, as
well as any business cards they were carrying when they were arrested.

Simpson's day planner was black, with gold trim and "OJ" printed
in gold in the right-hand corner. I flipped through the letters until I hit
"T" and the book opened to a business card:

Turnberry Associates
19495 Biscayne Blvd., Suite 900
Aventura, Florida 33180

There was a name on the card—Don Soffer—and a couple of
phone numbers. If Turnberry Associates was somehow connected to a
Miss Turnberry yacht, this might be an important clue. But first, I had
to check out Beth Reed's tip, to see if the yacht was where she said it was
on that day.

I called around our office and asked if anyone knew how to check
ports of call, to see if the *Miss Turnberry* had been registered somewhere
on June 17. One of my colleagues suggested checking the Florida Coast
Guard, and so I asked Jerry Stephens to do that.

In the two weeks I'd been on the case, I'd continued to assemble a
picture in my mind of what had happened with Cowlings and Simpson
in the days after the murders. Ostensibly, I was looking into prosecuting
Cowlings. But the closer I looked, the more I could see that there was a
tight web of friends and employees who had been protecting Simpson
ever since he came back from Chicago as the main suspect in a double
homicide. There were threads of questionable conduct from the moment
Simpson got off the plane and handed his Louis Vuitton garment bag
(containing the clothes from the murders?) to his assistant, Cathy Randa,
who handed it to Robert Kardashian. Those threads led through that
entire week until June 17, when Simpson and Cowlings went for a drive.
As I prepared a statement for the grand jury, I left open the possibility
that other people might have aided in Simpson's escape and might also
have earned an indictment on charges of harboring a fugitive.

The strength of Simpson's inner circle and its commitment became
evident on August 12, when Jerry Stephens and some detectives served
a search warrant at O. J. Enterprises, on San Vicente Boulevard. I had

written much of the search warrant, which was designed to gather any notes, memos, diaries, or calendars, anything that showed his activities, appointments, or movements during that time.

Cathy Randa was at O. J. Enterprises when detectives showed up and she quickly called one of the Simpson defense attorneys, Sara Caplan, and the two of them watched closely as detectives fanned out to search file cabinets, desks, and tables. One detective was looking through Simpson's personal desk—covered with pictures of his children—when he found a three-page document, typewritten, having to do with domestic violence. On the first page were two columns, one with the profile of the abuser, the other with the traits of the victim. Handwritten notes— possibly in O. J.'s hand—covered the page.

Caplan reviewed all the items seized by the police but she stopped at this one. This had nothing to do with O. J.'s activities, appointments, or movements, she said. There was a Special Master—an attorney appointed by the magistrate to oversee the search—on the scene, and he agreed with Caplan. It wasn't a calendar or diary. The detectives tried to contact me, but I was out in the field. Yochelson told the detectives to seize the document and turn it over to the magistrate until he could rule on it. But the Special Master declined to do that and instead gave it to Cathy Randa.

Later, during pretrial hearings, Randa's attorneys told the judge she had shredded the document because she didn't think it was important.

I hadn't been in a courtroom for anything important in three years. I straightened my Armani tie and looked over my notes. At one time, trials had been the most exciting part of my job, the place where my competitive spirit would take over and I would feel the adrenaline of working hard on something I believed in. I was a litigator again; this was where I belonged.

"Good morning. I am Deputy District Attorney Christopher A. Darden." I stood at the witness stand and faced the grand jury—twenty-one people seated at desks in four rows cascading from the back of the hall down to the front, like a small college lecture hall. The grand jury met daily listening to evidence in a number of cases, usually to decide whether there was enough evidence to charge someone; occasionally, as in the Al Cowlings matter, to aid in the investigation of a case.

"On June 12, as you know, Ronald Goldman and Nicole Simpson were murdered outside of Ms. Simpson's Brentwood condominium. . . . As time went on, [O. J.] Simpson became the primary suspect in those homicides."

I talked about what happened that week, such as on June 15, when Simpson brought a black duffel bag over to Robert Kardashian's house, and the next day, when Cowlings posed as O. J. to allow Simpson to escape the media and drive to Kardashian's house.

"The evidence will likely show that much of this [Cowlings's posing as Simpson] was orchestrated by Robert Kardashian inside the house," I explained. "After Cowlings and Simpson exchanged clothes, Cowlings practiced walking like Simpson."

I explained the involvement of O. J.'s inner circle the next day, June 17, from Cowlings to Shapiro and Kardashian, who had supposedly made sure the house was clear of any weapons. "During the week, and during the press conference [on June 17], Shapiro—as Kardashian stood nearby—told everyone that Simpson couldn't flee, he only had fifty or sixty bucks on his person. Pocket change.

"He said that Simpson couldn't flee the country because he, Shapiro, had Simpson's passport.

"But when the police searched the white Ford Bronco, they found some interesting things," I said. "First, they found $8,700 on Cowlings. Cowlings later told police detectives that O. J. Simpson gave him that money that day while they were in the white Ford Bronco."

I explained that Simpson also had his passport and a gun, which meant that Shapiro was either lying or mistaken. With a team of five to ten people watching the "suicidal" O. J., I couldn't imagine money and a gun getting past them.

"You don't need cash to commit suicide," I said, "and you certainly don't need a passport."

I knew that as soon as they got a whiff of the Cowlings grand jury, O. J. Simpson's lawyers would come after us. There are two ways to charge someone: first, by filing a complaint and holding a preliminary hearing, usually if there is an abundance of evidence and time; second, by convening a grand jury, which has subpoena power and is supposed to be secret and closed. That meant no defense attorneys, no judges;

grand juries could often be investigative nirvana for the prosecution and a nightmare for the defense.

Simpson had already been through a preliminary hearing (during which he said, "Absolutely, one hundred percent not guilty"), and so it wasn't a surprise when Robert Shapiro and Johnnie Cochran attacked our use of the Cowlings grand jury as nothing more than a fishing expedition in the Simpson case. Of course, the lawyers were also afraid of what we might find; their overreaction deepened my suspicion that Cowlings knew more about the murders.

Our first battle over the grand jury issue came over Robert Kardashian, O. J.'s friend, who also happened to be a lawyer. We wanted to question him freely, but he was claiming to have a lawyer/client relationship with Simpson. Runyon began working on that issue, which was important for a number of reasons, starting with the Louis Vuitton garment bag and ending with the phone call O. J. made to Kardashian on June 17, while he and A. C. were driving away from Kardashian's house. If there was a person besides Cowlings who knew more about the murders than he was letting on—if there was another person who harbored a fugitive—it might well have been Kardashian.

As we squared off with Kardashian's lawyer over the issue, a one-page note worked its way out of our fax machine. The note itself was just four lines:

> *IMPORTANT!* . . . Rb Kardashian cannot assert atty-client privilege as to the Simpson "flight from prosecution" incident or matters leading up to it in that Kardashian's bar membership was inactivated on January 1, 1991 and was not re-activated until June 20, 1994.

The fax had come from the state bar association, but we were never able to determine who sent it.

Unfortunately—while the note was correct and Kardashian wasn't a practicing lawyer until three days after the chase—that alone wasn't enough to prove that he wasn't acting as Simpson's lawyer. Prior cases had established that Simpson had only to reasonably believe Kardashian was representing him when they talked about the murders. Kardashian didn't need to be licensed. So I only asked for limited questioning of Kardashian and I agreed not to ask what he and Simpson talked about.

But his lawyer, Janet Levine, challenged our subpoena of Kardashian and, in a roundabout way, challenged our entire grand jury proceeding. We met in front of another judge and I was surprised to see Simpson at the table next to us, with Kardashian, Levine, and the rest of the Dream Team.

O. J. Simpson was wearing what had to be a thousand-dollar suit. I had seen Simpson on a handful of occasions, each time in Beverly Hills, each time in the company of one or more blonds. Yet this was the first time I had seen him since the murders, and I was surprised at how sinister he looked. He was pale and drawn, with deep-set eyes, and he surveyed the court room in a cold, detached way.

I sat at the prosecution table with Terry White—the Simi Valley prosecutor—who had taken a job as legal adviser to the grand jury.

Simpson looked surprised to see two black men on the other side of the aisle, and he stared at the two of us.

Terry mouthed to Simpson, "It's not me." He nodded at me and mouthed again, "It's him, not me."

"Hey, thanks, Terry."

From his table, O. J. looked away from us and shook his head.

Levine began arguing that Kardashian's testimony was privileged. And then she began challenging the grand jury proceeding as a ruse to gather more information on Simpson.

"The District Attorney's office goes to the press almost weekly and says, 'We are underfunded. Close libraries, close parks, close pools, give us more D.A.'s so we can prosecute more violent crimes, so we can prosecute murders. Give us D.A.'s. And they take Mr. Darden, who has been here for a number of years and they give him a [grand jury on the Cowlings case]." Levine said the D.A.'s office was "abusing the grand jury process and Mr. Darden is a pawn in that. He doesn't have the ability . . . to stop it."

And, finally, she argued that we shouldn't be allowed to conduct a grand jury hearing because we didn't know what we were doing. "This is not an office that knows how to deal with grand juries," she said. "They don't seem to have any idea where they're going, except to get information on Mr. Simpson." As she continued, I could hear Johnnie Cochran's and Robert Shapiro's arguments coming from her mouth. There seemed to be little logic or law in her argument; it was more name-calling and venting. She said we wanted to ask Kardashian about everything, even though I'd made it clear that we would avoid privileged information, anything Kardashian and Simpson said about the murders themselves.

Levine just kept at it, though, with broad, personal shots. "Is there nothing else going on in this country that Mr. Darden can be spending his time on?"

It doesn't take much to make my voice shake. My friend Alan Yochelson was sitting at the table with us as well, and he began to rustle in his expensive suit to argue the point, but before I knew what had happened, I was up and arguing. I responded with as much venting as Levine had used, and it quickly became heated and personal. I paced and scowled and raised my voice above its normal, mellow pitch.

"You are misrepresenting what I have told you," I said to Levine. And then I explained the narrow focus of the grand jury hearing. When I was done, I sat back down and Yochelson said, "Why, thank you. That was my whole argument."

When the hearing was over, I gathered my things and walked toward the clerk, still in a bit of a funk.

I heard a voice, but I couldn't tell at first who was talking to me. I looked down at the table and realized O. J. Simpson was talking under his breath to me. "Man," he said flatly, "you need to learn to control your temper."

Paula Barbieri sat down in front of the grand jury in formal, dark slacks, a high-collared shirt buttoned up to her chin, and a jeweled cross around her neck. In a few weeks, she would pose seductively for a photographer from *The New Yorker* wearing nothing but an open dress shirt, just a minx sprawled on a hotel couch. But on August 22, 1994, she was a schoolmarm.

"You talked to *Playboy*, why won't you talk to us?" yelled a UPI reporter as the quiet Barbieri walked through the courthouse after her testimony.

We'd already called several witnesses before Paula testified, and so I realized how tightly O. J.'s circle had been drawn, how many people were protecting him.

It was like prosecuting a Mafia case. Someone was pulling strings on the witnesses before I ever got to them. The people around O. J. had closed ranks, and I could clearly see Johnnie Cochran's fingerprints all over the strategy. Just as he'd done in the Michael Jackson child molestation case—in which the victim was paid to settle the suit and did not testify in the criminal trial—Cochran tied up every loose end and carefully controlled the testimony. Each witness had an attorney waiting outside in the hallway, and a few of the witnesses had been instructed to ask for a moment to see their lawyers almost on cue, whenever a question got too close to anything important.

There was no better example of the reluctance to testify than Paula Barbieri. Right away, it was clear she wasn't going to answer anything. She wouldn't even answer the simple questions.

"Are you his girlfriend?" I asked.

"I'm his friend," she said crisply.

"The question is: Were you his girlfriend on June 16 or June 17?"

"I'm his friend. OK?"

We went around for several minutes. "You understand the term 'girlfriend,' correct? See, if you don't answer my questions directly, then I have to ask you fifty questions to establish exactly what your relationship is, when there is a term called girlfriend that can explain it easily."

"I need to ask the lawyer," Paula said. "I mean, if you want to make this a girlfriend issue—I'm his friend. I'm there for him."

"If you are not his girlfriend, just say you are not his girlfriend. Just answer the question specifically."

"I'm his friend, specifically."

"Are you his girlfriend?"

"OK. I'll be right back. OK?"

She'd already been outside to talk to her lawyer once. Now, she was allowed to talk to him again. She came back in a few minutes.

I started in again. "Miss Barbieri, are you, or rather were you, on June 16 and June 17, Mr. Simpson's girlfriend?"

"On the advice of my attorney," she said confidently, "I respectfully refuse to answer that question."

Terry White was as dumbfounded as I was by her refusal to answer a seemingly unimportant, obvious question. She had given interviews in which she admitted being O. J.'s girlfriend; now she was being coy. "Miss Barbieri, do you realize that by refusing to answer that question, you can be held in contempt and jailed?" he asked.

"That's what my lawyer told me to do."

"Do you realize that's what can happen?" I asked.

"I'm just going on the advice of my attorney. I need to talk to him some more, then."

White was incredulous. "Miss Barbieri, you have been out to talk to him three times in five minutes."

She never answered the question.

After the trial, in mid-December, I was watching television news and I saw that Paula had been called to give a deposition in the civil case against Simpson. They had been together for a while after Simpson was released from custody, but then Paula broke up with him. During her deposition, she said that she had broken up with Simpson on June 12, the same day Nicole Brown Simpson and Ron Goldman were killed. We'd heard that rumor, but couldn't prove it.

I felt the emptiness I've experienced so many times, the feeling that we were fighting alone for Nicole and Ron and that everyone else was protecting this murderer. Would the jury have understood Simpson's state of mind if it knew that Paula had broken up with O. J. that day?

Robert Kardashian—slick and arrogant, gray-streaked hair forced back on his head—testified before the grand jury on August 31. He wore black socks with a streak of gray—like his hair—and the reporters nicknamed him Skunk Man. We had agreed not to question him about privileged issues and so I worked around the edges. I asked about June 17, about whether he'd talked to Paula Barbieri before she left his house that day, and he said that he had.

"What did you say to her?"

"Just: 'O. J. doesn't want you to be here when the police come. I think you better leave.'" If we needed any more evidence that O. J. knew he was a fugitive, here it was: Simpson telling Kardashian he doesn't want Paula there *when the police come.*

A few minutes later, I asked him about the moments before Simpson and Cowlings ran away. "The last time I saw Mr. Simpson, he was in his bedroom and he was going to get ready to surrender."

And then, Kardashian said, Cowlings gave Paula Barbieri some money and told her, "Here's some money for your plane home. O. J. doesn't want you to be here when the police come."

There it was. Not only did Simpson know the police were coming, but here was the proof that Cowlings knew as well. In my mind, I had proven the first of the two legs, that O. J. and A. C. knew the police were coming to arrest Simpson; that, in effect, he was a fugitive.

But I was no closer to proving where O. J. and A. C. were going.

I asked Kardashian when the police arrived, and he guessed it was between 2 P.M. and 3 P.M.

"What time was it when you realized Mr. Simpson was gone?" I asked.

"It was whenever the police came to the house and then we went to look for him."

"We have reviewed Mr. Simpson's telephone logs . . . and they indicate that he telephoned your home at 1:26 P.M."

I had him. The call contradicted Kardashian's statement to the press on June 17, saying he hadn't heard from Simpson after he left. Plus if the cops arrived at 2 P.M. and Kardashian didn't realize that O. J. was gone until then, how did he explain the 1:26 P.M. phone call?

I was getting used to the calm smile that he flashed me, the smile that hid a well-oiled machine, a moneyed, lawyer-rich, door-slamming machine designed to throttle any honest investigation. "That's privileged," Kardashian said.

Frustrated, I walked into the war room, the cluster of cubicles, file cabinets, and desks that served as the headquarters for the Simpson investigation. In all, fifteen lawyers and ten clerks worked on the case, but there was only one person who was invaluable—Patti Jo Fairbanks.

Patti Jo was everyone's mother, boss, and conscience. Sometimes it seemed as if the Criminal Courts Building had been built around her. A senior legal office assistant with twenty years of experience, she could do in fifteen minutes what it would take a bureaucrat fifteen years to do.

She told me she'd gotten an anonymous telephone call from a local news reporter about a woman who had taped conversations with Cowlings. According to the reporter, Cowlings told the woman that he and Simpson had planned to slip into Mexico until they saw the Christmas lights (police lights) behind them. That's when Simpson and Cowlings concocted the story about the cemetery, the tipster said. He also said that Cowlings told the woman that Kato Kaelin had actually seen O. J. behind the house after the murder. The tipster identified the woman as Jennifer Peace, said she was a porn actress, and provided a phone number for her.

We called the number and Arce agreed to meet Jennifer Peace at seven-thirty that night at the West Hollywood sheriff's station. At eight-thirty, Peace still hadn't arrived. Arce called her house, and a woman said Jennifer wasn't there. He waited another hour and then left. The next day, we got a search warrant.

Jennifer Peace lived in a single-story, coral-colored, stucco duplex in West Hollywood. Arce, Stephens, Runyon, and I pulled up with the Robbery/Homicide commander. A television reporter was standing outside.

Jennifer Peace let us into a small living room with a sofa, a coffee table, and a floor-model TV that was tuned to a game show. She didn't look like I thought a porn actress should look. Jennifer was very pretty, perhaps five feet, five inches tall, with dark hair and large brown eyes. It was clear, even with her loose-fitting dress, that Jennifer Peace was pregnant.

Right away, I smelled something foul. She shrugged and said that her four-month-old German shepherd had the run of the house. In a back bedroom were piles of dog shit. Peace said she hadn't wanted to open any windows because reporters kept pushing microphones up to the windows.

"I don't care," I said. It was a hot Southern California day and we were cramped inside a house with that disgusting smell. "Someone open a window." A sheriff's deputy slid the window open.

I looked around the rest of the barely decorated house and that's when I noticed, on the coffee table, a booklet about AIDS, which made me shiver.

"I know you're looking for tapes," she said. "I don't have any tapes."

We found about nineteen cassette tapes but—as she said—none with Cowlings on them. We did find Cowlings's name and phone number in her address book. And we found an advertisement for a porn movie starring a woman named Devon Shire. The woman in the picture was clearly Jennifer Peace. After some reluctance, she agreed to come back to the office for an interview.

The next day, she was in front of the grand jury.

Jennifer Peace was twenty-three. She said that she was from Kentucky, but had moved to Los Angeles when she was nine. She'd been set up with Cowlings on a blind date by a porn actor and director named Ron Jeremy. They met at a restaurant in West Hollywood in late February or early March 1994. From the first telephone call, Cowlings talked about O. J. and said that he resembled Simpson and that they were best friends.

He asked her out again two weeks later, and they went to the Hard Rock Cafe in his Bronco. After dinner, they went to a hotel, the Radisson in Bel Air. In April, Peace saw Cowlings again, and he talked about an argument O. J. had gotten into with Nicole. Another night, Cowlings called and asked for the phone number of another porn actress, a woman whose stage name was Lyndon Johnson.

"It didn't hurt me," Jennifer said. "We weren't in a monogamous relationship."

Peace said that Cowlings described loud fights between O. J. and Nicole and that sometimes, Nicole would berate her husband with racial slurs.

"What did Mr. Cowlings say Nicole Simpson would say to Mr. Simpson?" I asked.

"Say the words?"

"Yes, please."

She took a sharp breath. "'I can't believe I married a nigger. I knew this would happen to me.'"

"Did Mr. Cowlings say what reaction there was, if any, from Mr. Simpson?"

"Just hurt," Jennifer said. "I don't know if it enraged him because he was already angry because they were fighting." Cowlings then told her he was worried about his friend in the months before the murder. Peace said he told her, "I don't know what he's up to."

After the murders, Peace said, Cowlings met her at a hotel and started crying. He said Nicole didn't deserve what she got and that, just two nights before, Simpson was stalking Ron Goldman.

That day in the Bronco, Simpson and Cowlings were trying to get out, "before it gets too thick and heavy," Peace said.

She said that Simpson talked about going several places, notably, Mexico and the Bahamas, according to Cowlings.

I walked across the empty runway a couple of steps behind the Roys, staring in disbelief at the small, twin-engine prop plane, the kind that is always crashing in cornfields, slamming into the sides of mountains, or dropping like a stone in the ocean. This can't be right, I thought. There were nine seats, with an uneasy tourist wedged into each one. The bucket taxied uncertainly and finally lifted off the ground like a fat man off a diving board. As we rose above Miami, the engine sputtered and coughed and the plane indulged every gust and air pocket, as if we were taxiing forever down an ungraded road.

I could literally feel the wind resistance. It was one of those airplanes in which you begin to question the entire physics of air travel. Surely we weren't traveling fast enough to actually sustain flight. Out the window there was just blue and more blue, more ocean than I'd ever seen. There was no land anywhere. And I don't swim.

And so I closed my eyes and thought about the trip ahead. Jennifer Peace's interview and testimony had iced it for me. Admittedly, she was an awful witness, a porn actress who was fielding tabloid offers for her story and was changing her version of events daily. She would be worthless at trial. But she clearly knew Cowlings, and there were things she knew about the case that hadn't been released to the public. And there were things she said that were just too coincidental to have been fabricated. Like the Bahamas.

I never took real vacations. When I had some time off work, I went home, to see my family, to see my daughter. I just shook my head as I heard people in my office talk about these exotic, far-off places: Cabo, Maui, Fiji, the Bahamas. Except for a couple of afternoon shopping trips over the depressing border at Tijuana, I'd never left the country. I'd never been east of Nashville. I held in my hand the first passport I'd ever gotten.

As I'd packed my files and notebooks, I could already taste my first tropical drink—reclining on the white sands with a beautiful, dark-skinned woman watching me from a sun-drenched veranda: "Oh, Chris darling." I joked with Arce and Stephens and we agreed that this was going to be the best junket in the history of American law enforcement.

Let Marcia Clark deal with aggressive reporters and unethical defense lawyers. I was going to the Bahamas.

The pilot didn't land the plane so much as he parked it, got out, and handed us our luggage, as if we'd landed at a bus terminal. It was muggy and overcast and a handful of people watched us from a random scattering of folding chairs. We had to pay a tax to enter the country, and the Roys and I laughed as we each ponied up $30.

"You need a cab?" a black woman asked through random teeth.

"Yeah," I said.

There were rusted old Lincolns and scratched-up station wagons outside the airport, and we piled into a red station wagon.

"Where you staying?" the driver asked.

Jerry told him, the Great Abaco Hotel.

"Yeah, mon. Sure."

We drove slowly, less than twenty miles per hour, down a road that alternated between rutted dirt and broken pavement. There were no other cars on the road, just a few houses and only a handful of people. The cab lurched to a stop about a mile from the airport, and the driver turned around and smiled. "Seventeen dolla', mon."

We all looked at one another and I paid the fare. I couldn't see the ocean from my $100 hotel room. It faced a hillside, and as I stared, I could see a small shack embedded in the coconut trees. It seemed so out of place. My hotel room had no clock, no radio, and no television. The door didn't fit very well and there were three inches of play, so that the lock didn't really hold the door shut.

Great. I was going to be robbed and killed in my sleep, miles from my home on a tropical island that was basically a third-world country— except twice as expensive. Even if I wasn't killed, I was going to go broke trying to balance these prices against my $50 county per diem.

Arce and Stephens and I went to the pool that night to drink $5 bottles of Miller beer and to talk about where we were in our investigation. In Tampa, we'd already interviewed the Reeds—the people who called in the tip—and they seemed solid. After models and porn actresses, lawyers and nuts, it was nice to talk to people who had no angle, who were just trying to help us find justice. The amazing thing was: When the Reeds heard the discussion in the grocery store, they didn't even know about the Bronco chase. There was a lag in reporting between the mainland

and the Bahamas, so they were shocked the next day to hear that Simpson had been on the run.

We'd seen the seventy-foot *Miss Turnberry* in Miami; clearly it existed. We knew Simpson knew Don Soffer, the owner of the yacht, and that they'd been friends. And our investigation showed that O. J. and Nicole had been on the boat earlier in the spring. One reason the tip was so good was that *the Reeds didn't know any of that*. And they didn't know Simpson was a fugitive. All they knew was what they'd heard that day, two crew members saying that O. J. was coming and, the next day, the crew members unloading food and saying their "guest" wasn't coming.

There was another explanation, of course. Perhaps the crew was joking about O. J. coming, since he'd been on the ship before. But there were problems with that theory. For instance, the *Turnberry* crew wouldn't know any sooner than the Reeds that Simpson was a fugitive. Still, we were willing to consider that it was just a joke, an unfounded rumor.

"It's just too much of a coincidence," I said by the pool at the Great Abaco Hotel. "I mean, the yacht exists. Simpson knows the owner. The yacht was here in the Bahamas on that weekend. A couple with no reason to lie hears the crew say Simpson is coming. Jennifer Peace said their final destination was the Bahamas. . ." I trailed off, knowing we were still far from proving anything.

"Is there a liquor store around here?" I asked the bartender.

"Just down the road."

I must've walked a half-mile, but I was glad to finally find someplace with air conditioning. I put a six-pack of Miller Lite beer on the counter.

"Ten bucks, mon." I ended up taking five of the beers home to L.A. Maybe it was the Richmond, California, in me, but I wasn't going to leave a $10 six-pack behind.

I couldn't sleep that night because of the buzzing of mosquitoes. They were huge, slow-flying monsters, so big you could hear a "swoosh" when one of them flew by. Besides worrying about being robbed and killed, I imagined being sucked dry before morning by these mutant bugs. So I turned on the light in the bathroom and smashed them one by one, for more than an hour. But even then, I couldn't sleep. The Cowlings case— and the larger Simpson case—had a way of getting under your skin. I thought about the reluctance of witnesses and Jennifer Peace's admission that she "didn't want to be the one to convict Simpson." How many others felt that way? Kato Kaelin? Bob Kardashian? Al Cowlings? How much key information was being held beneath the surface? The roadblocks were worse than those in any gang case, any police investigation, any organized crime probe I'd ever seen.

The next morning, we caught a ferry for Man-O-War Cay, a smaller, neighboring island. We were looking for the store the Reeds had been in when they heard the crew from the *Miss Turnberry* say Simpson was coming. They thought it was called Albury's Harbour Store and that it was on Man-O-War Cay.

The ride was beautiful. The water was deep and clear and it was a sunny day. The ride took about fifteen minutes and we docked in the bright, late-morning sun. The ferry captain emerged with a case of beer.

"Boat leaves at four." We all stared at the beer, wondering if we'd want to get on a boat with him in four hours. He just wandered off the ferry, onto the island, and so we followed him.

There weren't really roads on the island, just tracks the width of a one-and-a-half-car garage. But then, no one had cars. There were only white people driving golf carts.

Albury's Harbour Store was a twenty-five-foot by twenty-five-foot room with basic supplies. A clerk called the owner and we sat down to interview him. You could practically see Jeffrey Albury's blue blood. He spoke with a trace of an English accent and was very friendly. He remembered hearing O. J. was coming, yes. Albury had met the captain of the *Miss Turnberry* the week of June 17 and the captain had said that the yacht was anchored just off shore. Then, a couple of days later, Albury met a seasonal visitor who said Simpson was coming to the island if he got off on bail. Unfortunately, he couldn't remember what the man looked like. Albury thought he might have been a white man in his fifties, with dark hair. After that, he remembered other people being in the store and talking vaguely about Simpson coming, including two models that he later found out were on the *Turnberry.* That was all he could remember.

Albury was really a decent guy, a very religious man. He told us about his ancestors, who could be traced to the captain of a ship that had been shipwrecked on this island during the American Revolution.

"How big is the Albury family?" I asked.

"Seventy-five percent of the people on this island are Alburys," he said.

We walked around Man-O-War Cay while we waited for a ferry back, and I noticed that there were almost no black people on this island, while the other island was almost exclusively black.

Back on the other island, our black cabdriver wanted tips on the National Football League. He had a schedule and everything. "Who should I bet on, mon?"

I told the driver about our trip to Man-O-War Cay and that everyone over there was white and was named Albury. "Aren't there any Alburys here?" I asked.

He laughed. "Are there any Alburys over here? I'm an Albury, mon. We're all Alburys."

It was an incredible reminder that we are just a few generations removed from slavery and that its effects continue on today, in places where the rich white people live on one island and the poor blacks live on the other, sharing the same last name because one used to own the other.

Over a bad $125 dinner that night, we talked about the sketchy case. The rumor had been all over the island that Simpson was coming but the evidence was flimsy.

"This is more than a coincidence," I said. "We come all the way across the hemisphere and damned near everything checks out. This is no coincidence."

The next morning, we paid our $30 departure tax and were glad to get off that gouging island. We flew to Miami and interviewed the cook and the captain of the ship. They remembered O. J. and Nicole from the first time they'd been on the *Turnberry,* but denied he was coming there in June. They were strangely adamant. The captain was genuinely concerned that he not do anything to upset Soffer, who called once during our interview.

Then we interviewed Soffer, whose other yacht, the *Monkey Business,* had shown up in photographs showing Gary Hart and Donna Rice, scuttling Hart's 1984 presidential candidacy. Soffer wasn't much help in his interview either. He denied that Simpson was coming. I didn't believe him. But as I flew back to California, I'd already begun to worry that we wouldn't be able to charge Cowlings. I had the sense that, like everything connected to the Simpson case, doors were slamming just as I reached them.

TEN

Marcia took a long drag of a Dunhill Red and blew smoke out the left side of her mouth, in the general direction of the useless Smoke Grabber. I waited, fairly certain why she'd called me up to her office, but wanting to hear her say it herself.

"How would you feel," she asked slowly, "about working on Simpson—as case manager?"

After a time, my friends have learned to anticipate the pauses in my conversation, those points in which I become lost in thought, my mind editing and improving what I am about to say. Sometimes, it is a good check on my quick temper; other times, I pause simply to hear myself out, to weigh what I am thinking, what I should be thinking, and what I am about to say, the length of my silence proportionate to the gravity of my thoughts. But this time, as I sat across from Marcia, trying to decide what to say, my silence was filled with my father's warning: "You'll catch hell if you work on that one." I stared into Marcia's eyes for a long time. And then I smiled.

Marcia said that she and Hodgman wanted someone to coordinate and oversee the young lawyers and clerks, as well as the office investigators, someone to make sure the small stuff was accomplished and that there was a plan for dealing with the big stuff.

"Bill and I are in court all day and trying to get ready for trial," she said. "We could really use the help."

I was about to become free again, the perfect candidate to join the Simpson team. The Al Cowlings investigation was sunk somewhere in the Bahamas, with no way to conclusively prove criminal intent.

Cowlings's version of the Bronco chase was clearly bullshit, of course, but we couldn't charge someone with first-degree bullshit.

I wanted to drag out the case as long as possible though, just in case we received some new information from Man-O-War Cay—some proof that Simpson and Cowlings had been trying to escape there. But my decision on Cowlings was essentially made and was irrevocable.

Marcia and I had begun talking more and more about the Simpson case that October, as I wound up my investigation of Cowlings. I was amazed at her energy, and I could see the clear need for someone to take some responsibility from her and from the other lead prosecutor, a kind, intelligent man named William Hodgman, who was something of a legend in the office.

Simpson had at least nine lawyers working on the front end of the case and who knew how many lawyers, clerks, and investigators working behind the scenes, throwing everything they could at the prosecution. Many of their discovery requests and motions seemed like legal fishing trips and busywork just to keep our side off balance. Yet each document needed to be evaluated and addressed. I had never seen anything like it. It was becoming apparent that this case would have to be prosecuted differently from any previous case in L.A.—maybe differently from any other case in the United States. I still had some trepidation about getting more deeply involved, but it was hard to watch this from the sidelines and know that I could help.

So on October 18, I sat across from Marcia, her offer to join the case still hanging in the air. I glanced around her big office, at the standard metal dividers that served as walls—cold and lifeless in other offices, but painted light blue and covered with photographs in Marcia's. This was clearly someone comfortable at work, unlike other people, whose offices were merely the particular space they took up. This was a woman who took her job and herself very seriously, who invested everything she had. She sat curled up on her knees again, like a tough little package someone had left on the chair. She raised her eyebrows, waiting for me to answer.

"It's a great honor," I said. There were more than nine hundred deputy D.A.'s in L.A. County and Marcia had chosen me for the biggest murder trial in decades, perhaps ever. She told another lawyer that she really didn't know how good I was until she'd read the transcript of the grand jury hearings in the Cowlings case. And that, she said, was when she knew I belonged on the Simpson team.

She smiled at me and raised her eyebrows again. "Well?"

"OK," I said. "Let's do it."

Marcia had intimated that I would present some evidence and handle a few witnesses, but when we told Hodgman that I had accepted, he seemed to go the other way. I would be in the background, cataloguing exhibits, making sure witnesses were in court on time, coordinating investigators, and managing the junior members of the team. I was relieved. That meant no TV, which meant I didn't have to worry that every homie in Southern California would be wondering if I was betraying my race. That made my decision easier.

As I drove home that night along the Harbor Freeway—a million headlights flowing like blood cells through crowded arteries—I knew I could change my mind. My father's words were still with me: "hell to pay." I might be hated and vilified in the black community if I got into that mess. Only a fool would get involved, I thought. Maybe I should say no. But why?

Because I was black? I had prosecuted thousands of black men, yet no one had paid any attention to those cases. Where were the protests for those black men; or did a black man from Inglewood deserve less support than one from Brentwood? No matter how idealistically I looked at this case, though, I knew it was different. It had the potential to become symbolic of things the country wasn't ready to talk about, of deep, illogical prejudices that had nothing to do with the two people murdered in Brentwood. Johnnie Cochran was rarely subtle about his trial strategy, and it could be summed up in one word: race. Cochran was going to use it. He always did. If I allowed the awesome power of the *specter* of racism to drive me off the case, I would be validating their strategy, allowing it to work.

Should I reject the case because of the evidence? Or the cops? I have turned down cases because I believed the evidence wasn't strong enough, and sometimes I have decided not to prosecute cases because I didn't believe the police officers who investigated it. But there was an abundance of evidence here and the case seemed fairly well investigated. The LAPD hadn't done a perfect job, certainly, but its officers had gathered enough evidence to prove that O. J. Simpson was guilty of a gruesome double murder.

Should I say no because Simpson was a celebrity and an icon in the black community? There would be incredible media scrutiny and pressure from black activists, but if there was one thing I believed, it was that nobody is above the law. Not the rich, not the police, not O. J. Simpson. No one. The laws enforced against the minimum wage earner in Compton should be the same laws enforced against the millionaire from Beverly Hills. If it is to work, the law can't succumb to the pressures of media or community. Nor could I.

Still, I was torn. My responsibilities as a prosecutor clearly told me to take this case. But I had other responsibilities as a black man, and they were difficult to sort out.

If I thought I was being named to the case primarily because I was black, I would've rejected it. It was as simple as that. But I knew that wasn't why I had been chosen. I was a strong litigator and an experienced deputy D.A. who had a background in the case because of the Cowlings investigation, and I was floating between positions in SID.

I thought about something else: Was I going to be seen as a brother putting another brother in jail? What did this say to the young black man watching from the outside? Finally, I hoped that young black man would be glad that there was a black man on the other side of the aisle. Perhaps it was naive, but I convinced myself that African Americans had to be represented in all segments of the law if we were to ever believe that the system was ours too.

We have become used to seeing black police officers patrolling 77th and Southeast divisions; we have become used to black public defenders and judges. But if we were to ever have real ownership in the system, we had to have prominent black prosecutors too. They would never really be our laws until we enforced them.

Admittedly, the system was often unfair because of racial bias. That was unfortunate and, at times, criminal. But that had nothing to do with this case. Should blacks take themselves out of the justice system because it is sometimes unfair? Or should we work within the system to change it?

This was a case about rage and obsession, evil and murder, not racial prejudice. This case was about someone who had money and celebrity and thought he didn't live by the rules that the rest of us do.

And when I was done wrestling with myself, there was only one thing left to think about, one set of painful and conclusive images: Nicole Brown Simpson, lying in a pool of seven-eighths of her blood, her throat slit all the way to her spine; and Ronald Goldman, his hands diced by the knife that killed him, finished off with one last plunge of the blade into his chest. How could such intense rage be so methodical? I had been called to help those two people get some justice; who was I to turn it down because I might be uncomfortable?

So, in the end, there was only duty: duty to the prosecutors' office, to the families of the victims, and even to the black community.

That night, a reporter friend stopped by my house and we sat on the couch, watching television and talking about my decision.

"What's to think about?" she asked. "When is the last time you've been in a trial where you really worked hard, where you've really been into it?"

I listened quietly and admitted that I was leaning toward taking the case. I stared straight ahead through the TV, without seeing the picture, not realizing that it would be a year before I again spent a whole night like this, relaxing in front of the television, flipping through the channels.

"This is a no-brainer." My friend laughed. "There are lawyers who would give their right arm to be on this case."

I nodded, knowing I might be asked to give a hell of a lot more than that.

I remember one night, after the trial was over, Marcia and I went to dinner with another lawyer, covering up with tough talk and gallows humor how deeply it had affected us. Everyone got up to go home, to be alone with our thoughts and regrets, when Marcia suddenly put her hand on top of mine. "If I had known what you were going to go through in all of this," she said, "I never would've asked you."

I needed to see exactly what I was facing. I was quite familiar with the prosecution case, since I had worked on Cowlings, but I wanted to look once more at the evidence, while there was still time to turn back. I didn't tell anyone in the office, but if I was going to put my reputation on the line, I had to make sure I was on the right side.

So I reviewed some of the witness interviews and the evidence, looking for holes, for any reason to reject this case. My reputation in the D.A.'s office was that I was someone who would go to the wall for a case I believed in—often to the displeasure of the police and even the other D.A.'s—but also someone who would drop a case if I didn't believe in it. It wasn't a matter of pride or a game for me. It was insane to concentrate on winning and losing when we were playing with people's lives. This had to be about justice or why were we even bothering?

It didn't take long to convince me. The blood evidence alone was overwhelming. His blood was at Nicole's condo, and the blood of both victims was in his Bronco, which had been missing—along with Simpson—for more than an hour around the time of the killing. There was a bloody glove at his house and its mate was at Nicole's condo, and we knew they were his gloves. There were also bloody shoeprints, exactly his size and the kind of shoe he wore—$160 treads, not the kind that robbers or burglars could afford. It went on and on and on.

And there was no way Fuhrman or any other officer could have planted the blood either; too many people had seen it and it had been discovered and filed before a drop of Simpson's blood was ever taken, before police knew if he had an alibi or even if he was in town. Dozens of people would have to be involved if this were a conspiracy. Ten racist cops couldn't have pulled this one off. And that was just the blood evidence. There was so much more circumstantial evidence, it was overwhelming. It was the strongest murder case I'd ever seen. The prisons were full of people convicted on half the evidence we had against Simpson.

The case had already been moving along slowly, toward trial, without me, and by the time I joined the prosecution, the first twelve jurors had already been selected. While I was assessing the strength of the case, I also decided to take a look at the jury. We were still choosing the alternates, but as soon as I saw the first-teamers, I could tell it was one of the worst juries—from a prosecutor's standpoint—that I'd ever seen. And I'm not talking about race. These were simply not happy-looking, motivated, or successful people. From the first day, I sensed that many of them were angry at the system for various insults and injuries—twelve people lined up at the grinder with big axes.

Any trial lawyer will tell you that it is impossible to underestimate the importance of jury selection. Most jurors have already developed conclusions about the defendant, the lawyers, even the evidence, sometimes. It can be the difference between starting on level ground and starting in a six-foot hole. Jury selection is also the time when lawyers can do damage control, letting the jurors know there are weaknesses in your case and offering them a way to believe your version of events anyway.

A few years earlier, I had selected some of the fastest juries in the history of the CCB. I would sit quietly as the defense attorney droned on for hours, prying into each juror's private life, trying to condition the jurors before they'd heard a stitch of evidence. Then it would be my turn and I would stand and address the court: "The prosecution has no questions for the jury." I would smile at them and it would be clear the defense attorney was a nosy ass who was looking to hide something when I said, plainly, "They look OK to us." It wouldn't have worked in this case.

As soon as I became a member of the Simpson team, I immediately read each of the first twelve jurors' questionnaires and the transcripts of their voir dire, the in-court questioning by the lawyers. I didn't like what I saw. Certainly, I was concerned about the racial makeup of the jury, but not because of my father's prediction that blacks wouldn't convict Simpson. I was still clinging to my belief that blacks had such a strong sense of morality and justice that they would convict once they saw the overwhelming evidence against Simpson.

No, I was more concerned by the rumor that Johnnie Cochran had said, "Just give me one black on that jury." It was clear that their jury consultant had pushed for the kind of panel that we ended up with, mostly black, with little education beyond high school. It wasn't that I didn't want black jurors. But Cochran had made it clear that this was going to be a case based on the fact that O. J. Simpson was black. I was offended by that from the beginning and I could see how destructive this case could be. Anyone who has truly fought for racial equity in the justice system hated to see those issues manipulated to fit an accused double murderer who—for years—had done everything he could to remove himself from the black community and had actually received *coddling* from the LAPD. They had practically looked the other way while the man beat his wife! And now, Cochran and the rest of Simpson's lawyers were going to say that O. J. had been framed? They were going to claim that this was about racial prejudice? That's what a predominantly black jury meant; more encouragement for Cochran to take this case away from the two slaughtered victims, to cry wolf with every civil rights issue and turn a murder case into a bogus retribution for past injustices.

But race wasn't the only problem with this panel. Only a couple of jurors had college degrees, even though we were planning to rely heavily on a relatively new, incredibly complex kind of forensics—DNA. One juror was an employee of the Hertz Corporation, the company Simpson had shilled for during the last decade. I couldn't believe some of these people had slipped through voir dire.

When I brought up my questions about the jury to Bill and Marcia, they were understandably defensive.

"They were the best of the lot," Bill said, rubbing his close-cropped beard. "If you think they're bad, you ought to see the ones who were coming up." So I read the questionnaires of the juror candidates who were to be questioned next. They were incredible. One prospective juror said she wasn't surprised Simpson had been arrested because "it just seems like black men get picked on quite a bit." She went on to say she didn't know *anyone* who'd had a pleasant encounter with police.

Another potential juror was the focus of a narcotics search warrant, in which the police didn't find any dope, but they found $50,000 beneath his bed. Twice he'd been arrested for possession of cocaine; how was a guy like that going to respond to police testimony? One candidate said the justice system had cheated his brother after he was arrested for a carjacking in which he'd killed someone. We later found that the juror's brother pleaded guilty to murder! It was incredible. The guy admitted being a murderer and his brother still thought the system had cheated him! Another said "a lot of innocent people are convicted of things they didn't do."

Time after time, jurors wrote that they read tabloids, *People* magazine, and the *L.A. Times*, yet knew nothing of the case. They were so clearly lying, it was ridiculous. But the alternative was someone who really *didn't* know about the case, someone who didn't read and was so out of touch with society that he didn't know O. J. Simpson was a suspect in a double murder. There was no way to win with this group.

Some jurors seemed to go out of their way to get a good look at Simpson, so they could smile at him. They repeatedly expressed shock that he was a suspect. One jury candidate said Simpson had "a friendly image" and that it was hard to believe he would kill his ex-wife. After hearing of the awful 911 tape of Nicole Brown Simpson calling for help in 1993, another said the years of systematic spousal abuse was "just like other couples having problems." Domestic violence was an appropriate response "any time," one prospective juror answered. Another said "family violence should be handled in the family." Was domestic violence sometimes warranted? "Hell yes," one prospective juror said.

One prospective juror said that she wanted F. Lee Bailey, who was on Simpson's defense team, as her personal attorney. Another tried to speak to Cochran in the hallway and then smiled admiringly at Shapiro. They seemed to hate the prosecutors as much as they liked the defense. "You're pumping me as if I'm on trial or something!" one seventy-one-year-old man said to Hodgman, who was conveniently accused by the defense of questioning the black jurors more harshly than others.

The jury candidates wrote of being the last ones served in a restaurant, of being stopped by the LAPD for no reason, sometimes even of being beaten. A couple of jurors said outright that police officers lie on the stand. It was a nightmare jury pool, a stagnant, shallow pool of bitterness and anger, and I couldn't say that I was the least bit surprised. The system itself had forged this jury in Simi Valley and in the molten anger of a million indignities and injustices, some collective and historical, some deeply personal. I knew where this jury pool came from, but why did we have to have them on this case?

A prosecutor has a picture in his mind of an ideal juror: an upper-middle-class, college-educated Republican, living in the suburbs because he had to get out of the crime-ridden city; a law-and-justice type, a person who had no use for criminals or those charged with a crime. And not just white people. Despite the media's insistence otherwise, there is a healthy black middle class and there are many conservative, tough-on-crime blacks.

Not here. This was a downtown jury, a CCB jury, notorious for screwing up cases with outrageous verdicts, for having more sympathy for the gangsters than for the cops. "You never know what a downtown jury will do," was the cry of disappointed prosecutors. We heard about cases secondhand: the acquittal of a defendant even after the jury heard his audiotaped confession; the guy whose conviction was reduced from a capital murder to second-degree for shooting a cop during a jewelry store robbery—practically the definition of a first-degree death penalty case.

That was classic downtown L.A., where the rules of prosecution were often turned on their ear. Prosecution rule: The testimony of a police officer will have more credibility with jurors than will the testimony of other people. CCB rule: Jurors will assume the cops are lying.

But that was the jury we were given, the one we helped select, and as October faded into November and the trial loomed around the corner, there wasn't time to bemoan the fact that we were going to have to convince jurors who probably didn't like us and already discounted our case.

I have heard pundits and others say that the Simpson case was lost as soon as we allowed it to be tried downtown, that we should have tried the Simpson case at the Santa Monica courthouse.

I strongly disagree. According to policy and practice, such huge cases would always be tried in the downtown courts building because no other courthouse was big enough or even remotely prepared for such a behemoth. The case belonged downtown. To move it would have been unethical and manipulative.

It is hard to stomach the hypocrisy of those people who criticize Johnnie Cochran for "playing the race card," yet would have had us move the trial to the suburbs to avoid black jurors. That is just another version of the same card game Cochran played. I understand the frustration about the verdict, yet I feel sorry for people who are so cynical about our criminal justice system.

Yes, I recognized that black jurors were likely to see Simpson differently, see our case differently, even see me differently. But these were Americans, these were Angelinos, and they had every right and every duty to serve on this jury. We can't have a system that creates the prejudices and beliefs of those jurors—emotions that run much deeper than just the Simpson jury pool—and then hope they won't show up when we call for a jury of peers.

It was our responsibility to try to appeal to this group of people, no matter how suspicious and bitter they were. And we failed. But I would rather fail than win by perverting and twisting the justice system—as I believe the defense team did.

If the prosecutors had moved the Simpson case out of downtown to avoid black jurors, I would not have worked on it.

* * *

We leaned forward on Judge Lance Ito's couch like an awkward double date, Marcia Clark and I on one side, Johnnie Cochran and his protégé Carl Douglas on the other.

Ito sat on the other side of his desk, which was covered with so many random stacks of paper that I wondered to myself: How is this guy going to control this case when he can't even control his desk? File cabinets and tables were also stacked with documents, so that you might think someone was moving in or out. Instead, it was just Ito.

Douglas and I were arguing one of the many discovery issues in the case, when it seemed to dawn on Ito that I was arguing a point on the Simpson case and not the Cowlings case. My addition to the prosecution team hadn't yet been announced, and Ito looked confused.

"But you're not working on the case, right?" he asked, staring at me through his owly glasses. I exchanged a glance with Marcia and she quickly jumped in. "No, actually, Your Honor, he is on the case. And he'll be presenting evidence."

Cochran and Douglas leaned forward on their side of the couch and cocked their heads to look at me. It gave me a bad feeling, like a dying man being eyed by vultures. The defense was notorious for its discussions with the media of in-camera conversations—off-the-record meetings with the judge. This was not the way we wanted my role in the case publicized, before the Cowlings investigation was officially closed. I was no sooner at my desk than the telephone began ringing with reporters wanting to know if I was on the case. I had been case manager for two weeks, but now it was clear I would be in the courtroom as well. I decided to call my parents and tell them before Dan Rather did.

"I'm so proud of you," my mother said. Pops was a bit more reserved, and at first, he was uncomfortably quiet. When he feels something is wrong, he has a habit of rolling his eyes, blowing air out of his cheeks, and then sighing, "Uh, boy." I could just see him doing that. "Just keep your head down," he said. "Try not to get involved in any of that racial stuff. Just do your job like a professional and go on about your business."

I promised I would.

A few days later, an L.A. newspaper reporter sidled up to me in the hallway. "Johnnie Cochran is saying the only reason you're on this case is because you're black."

I recoiled. "What?"

He repeated it, and I shifted the files in my arms and took another step toward my office. "Johnnie wouldn't say something like that."

The reporter asked for a comment but I said no.

"Until I hear Johnnie say it, I'm not going to comment." I walked past him. Bullshit, I figured. Cochran was low, but not that low.

A little while later the reporter showed up with a tape player and held it out. "Here. You want to hear it? I got it right here."

"I don't want to hear it." The anger rose in my throat and I clenched my teeth. "I don't want to hear that."

That night, it was on most of the 11 P.M. television news shows, which I arrived home in time to watch for the first time in weeks.

"All of a sudden, he shows up here," Cochran said of me. "Now why is that, after we have eight African Americans [on the jury]? We're concerned about it. Why now?"

I watched in disbelief. This was a man I considered a colleague. We had worked separately on many of the same cases—him from the civil side, me from the criminal—battles against racist cops and unnecessary police violence. Now he was accusing me of being a sellout. I understood that he had a job to do, to protect his client. But this had nothing to do with that. This was a private message between Cochran and me, a message meant to be overheard by anyone who had ever been pulled over by a police officer because he looked suspicious in his dark skin. Blacks could hear what he was saying between the lines: *This brother is being used by the Man. This brother is an Uncle Tom.* It was the most offensive thing a black could be called by another black, and hearing it repeated on television and in the newspapers was the equivalent of publicly being called a nigger by a white lawyer.

"Under the guise of looking at A. C. Cowlings, either all along he was planning on working on the O. J. Simpson case—we don't think that's fair—or he's over here because of the makeup of our jury, which I think is wrong," Cochran said. "Christopher Darden is a fine lawyer, but I don't think he should be on this case."

There have been many long nights after that one. There have been death threats and racist letters from whites and blacks. There have been nights when I couldn't believe the pain this case was causing my family. Yet I will never forget how I felt that first night, watching Johnnie

Cochran make it painfully clear that there were going to be two sides in this case, not prosecution and defense, but black and white. And I was welcome on neither. I will never forget watching Cochran draw a line in the sand. I will never forget watching him choose that butcher over me.

Black professionals always have to justify their existence. We go to work and face stares that insinuate we have only achieved because of quotas and affirmative action, not because of ability. We are always having to justify our presence in the boardroom, the operating room, and, unfortunately, the courtroom. But I didn't expect it from another black lawyer. I didn't expect it from Cochran.

The fallout was immediate. On talk radio and in newspapers, in barbershops and restaurants, I was branded an Uncle Tom, a sellout, a house Negro. I couldn't understand how they could attack me when they didn't know me. Other black "experts" stepped forward, such as a lawyer named Leo Terrell, who was suddenly on every television show that would have him, saying that I had a responsibility to the community and to my "blackness" to reject the case.

I waited for prominent blacks to come to my defense, to say that Cochran was wrong to question my ethics and my reasons for being on the case. I waited for prominent blacks to say they were proud that we had black prosecutors as well as black defense attorneys, that it was bigoted and small-minded to expect only one philosophy and one position from African Americans. I waited. But they were silent.

All I heard was Cochran's message to me, echoing in the deafening lack of support. *Dear Chris,* the message said, *we are playing for keeps.*

The next day, I went to Gil Garcetti and his director of communications, Suzanne Childs, to talk about my addition to the case.

"Your life won't ever be the same," Suzanne said, smiling.

"That's what I'm afraid of." I explained Cochran's attack on me and how it would certainly play in the black community. "I'd like to do a few interviews with the black press." I was thinking of Black Entertainment Television and the *Sentinel,* a local black-owned, black-run, black-written newspaper.

Garcetti seemed uncomfortable. "Why?"

"Because I think it's important that people understand who I am and what my role is in this case." I wanted to tell black people about the other cases I'd prosecuted and the reasons I took this case. I wanted people to understand that I had a job to do and that I wouldn't take this case if it wasn't aboveboard, if my addition to the prosecution team wasn't ethical and necessary.

"The prosecution team hasn't done any interviews to this point," Garcetti said. This was an incredibly sensitive case, politically and socially, and Gil wanted one cohesive voice from the D.A.'s office, one united front.

I understood, but I needed to respond in some way. "My position is different from Bill's or Marcia's," I said.

"People will understand," Suzanne said. "If you start doing interviews, you'll do more harm by drawing attention to yourself."

People in the mainstream of white society don't always realize there are other streams, some just as deep and fast-moving, rivers of thought that aren't often reflected in *Time* magazine and on the *CBS Evening News*. In black barbershops, black taverns, and black Baptist churches, there were people very much in their own mainstream who didn't believe for a minute that O. J. Simpson was guilty. These weren't criminals or uneducated people. These were people who wondered why successful black men were so often targeted by law enforcement. They didn't wonder why Washington, D.C., mayor Marion Barry would smoke crack while in office; they wondered why agents would set up a sting to catch him. They didn't wonder about all the evidence gathered against Simpson; they wondered why police were so eager to suspect him. And those same people were going to wonder who that black man was trying to convict O. J.

But Gil was adamant and Suzanne backed him up with a smiling nod. They would handle it with a simple press conference and news release.

For months afterward, I would wish I had talked to the black press. Maybe it wouldn't have made any difference. But maybe it would've kept me from being alienated from my community, from being stranded in this inhospitable borderland where I've found myself, smack between black anger and white anger, between retribution and condescension, between two very different kinds of fear. In the coming months, I would find myself miles from either place. Alone.

ELEVEN

I have A piece of information that could prove critical to your case."
How many phone conversations had begun that way recently? Yet I
took note this time because I immediately recognized the voice on
the other end of the line. He was a man I had spoken to before, who had
proved to have some involvement in the case. He was a very good source.

"What does it have to do with?"

The man paused, then went on. "O. J.'s blood and a preservative
called EDTA."

I scribbled notes and waved with my other hand for the chattering
law clerks to be quiet. "What about them?"

"The defense is going to claim that the bloodstain on the gate was
taken from O. J.'s blood afterwards and planted and that this preservative is proof of that."

"That's ridiculous," I said. "Where did they come up with that bullshit?"

"It wasn't on their own," said the source. "Somebody else thought it
up for them. And a woman in the police lab is assisting them. She claims
to have been ordered by a supervisor to put O. J.'s blood from a vial onto
a clean swatch."

I wrote down the woman's name; it was familiar. I began to have a
bad feeling about all of this.

"But the idea is actually coming from an author of a book proposal
who claims to have talked to the woman. A guy named Stephen Singular."

"You're serious?"

"Yeah. I'm serious."

I hung up the phone and stared at Runyon, who shrugged his bony shoulders. "What is it?"

"Oh, it's probably nothing."

I had been deluged with such telephone calls since taking over as Simpson case manager. In my first weeks on the case, I noticed that there was no one coordinating the investigation and so it was one of the first tasks I gave myself—assigning out good tips, making sure the police provided us with what we needed, and overseeing the D.A.'s own investigators. And so I screened many of the tips myself. Most went nowhere, but this one was intriguing.

Each evening, Marcia, Bill, and I would get together and talk about the case and that day's developments. At five o'clock that day in early November 1994, I made my way over to Marcia's office with my notes on the conversation about Singular. I had tried briefly to run down the book proposal, but hadn't been able to find it.

"Bullshit," Marcia said when I told her about the supposed book proposal. There was no way the evidence could've been planted, she said.

"Of course not," I said. "But does that mean the defense won't argue it anyway? No."

Marcia was hot, especially about the idea that Fuhrman had planted blood at Nicole Brown's condominium. "Nothing but bullshit," she repeated. "That blood was seen by officers Rossi, Lange, Vannatter, and Riske long before Simpson's blood sample was ever taken."

Hodgman, always thoughtful and professorial, nodded his agreement.

Sure, it sounded very much like bullshit. But if we'd learned anything in the early stages of the case, it was that we shouldn't discount anything. "Just let me see if I can get a copy of the proposal before we go crazy over this."

I left Marcia's office and went down to the war room, where the motions and orders were filed. Our DNA experts had been pounded with discovery requests to test our blood evidence, and I had been so busy in my first two weeks as case manager that I hadn't kept up with what the defense was asking for. As I went over their motions and requests ("Two empty test tubes, tops and seals used by the nurse who drew blood from defendant O. J. Simpson on June 13, 1994 . . . thirty unused clean swatches from the same batch the Singular book proposal began to concern me more and more.

One of the D.A. investigators, Steve Oppler, went looking for the manuscript, and I turned my attention to the defense. This was Brady material—named after the landmark case that governed discovery rules—and we were required to turn it over to the defense because the manuscript (if it existed) might contain information that could conceivably exonerate their client. A few days later, I appeared in Judge Lance Ito's chambers, on the record, to tell the defense about the Singular manuscript.

Cochran and Carl Douglas hemmed and hawed and caught each other's eyes a couple of times. Carl said that he'd met Singular once briefly and that the guy couldn't be taken seriously. He was a nut, they said nervously.

"We have no interest in obtaining that document," Cochran said. Marcia and I said that we didn't either.

As we walked out of Ito's chambers, down a twelve-foot-long hallway barely wide enough for my shoulders, I asked Marcia, "Believe any of that?"

"Nope."

On November 7, Oppler got a copy of Stephen Singular's book proposal and plunked it down on my desk.

Strictly Confidential: Do Not Duplicate
Untitled on the O. J. Simpson Case

How many documents that looked like this one were being spread around Los Angeles? There had to be dozens. Anyone with any connection to the case, it seemed, was working on a proposal, a treatment, or a manuscript. I recall a newspaper cartoon that showed two lawyers in front of Judge Ito, one saying, "Your Honor, we're having trouble finding twelve jurors who haven't written a book about the case."

Singular, as it turned out, was a true-crime writer from Colorado, who had been nosing around L.A., saying that he was working for the defense team and trying to sell a manuscript on the side. I flipped through the twenty-two-page draft.

His book treatment began with a meeting between himself, Cochran, and Douglas.

"We're fucked man," [Douglas] tells me. "We need help. Do you understand what I'm saying? We need a break."

I nod, but keep my silence. When Carl gets angry, he can be nasty, and all morning I've sensed that his underlying mood is bad. It's bad because I haven't been able to give him what he wants. Of course, what he wants is . . . basically impossible, but he still wants it.

What Douglas and Cochran wanted, according to Singular's book proposal, was information about the LAPD crime lab. Singular claimed that he'd given Cochran and Douglas "everything they needed to free O. J. Simpson and to uncover the greatest scandal in the history of the LAPD."

I turned the pages. Singular wrote that he gave the defense four pieces of information back in August, just a couple of months after the murders. First, according to his book proposal, Singular told them that Detective Mark Fuhrman had known Nicole Simpson since 1985 and had been her "special cop." Second, he said that Fuhrman used a stick to pick up one of the two bloody gloves lying next to Goldman at the murder scene. Third, Singular told the defense, Fuhrman put the glove in a small, blue plastic evidence bag, drove over to Simpson's, jumped his fence, dropped the bloody glove, and hid the stick and evidence bag nearby. Fourth, he told Cochran, Fuhrman briefly had access to the blood sample drawn from Simpson the day he returned from Chicago and had dropped the blood on the sidewalk and on the gate at Nicole Brown's condominium.

The proof of that, Singular wrote, was that a police lab preservative, EDTA, would be found in the last blood sample, proving that it had been stored at the crime lab for a time. Singular wrote about approaching Cochran and Douglas with his theories. They wanted more, according to Singular. They wanted a way to propose that all the blood was planted. But Singular didn't know about other bloodstains.

"Here they are," and [Douglas] opened the book, showing me photos of the interior of O. J.'s Ford Bronco. I saw large red smears on both the driver's and passenger's seat. "Do you know what those are?"

"No."

"They are Nicole Simpson's and Ron Goldman's blood."

I looked up at Carl, not quite able to absorb all at once what he was telling and showing me.

"This is Ron Goldman's blood?" I said.

"Yes. Now do you see why I'm fucked?"

I was basically looking at a blueprint of O. J. Simpson's defense, months before it became operational. Clearly the guy had spent more than a brief moment with Cochran and Douglas. Singular was writing about information that hadn't been made public at the time he wrote his treatment.

Later, as the defense team argued their impossible conspiracy theory, and reporters wrote about the Dream Team as if it were the 1927 New York Yankees, I would wonder how much Simpson had paid for a defense that really came from a true-crime writer that Simpson's lawyers had dismissed as "a nut." As for the Dream Team, I doubt they had an original idea the entire trial.

"Managing" the Simpson case, it turned out, was a little like being social director at a prison riot. Runyon and I had set up shop in the war room, a large conference room on the eighteenth floor of the CCB, split into cubicles in which a couple dozen prosecutors, clerks, cops, investigators, secretaries, and random visitors ran day and night like lab rats in a maze. I took the only cubicle with a door, which really didn't filter the noise from the frenzy; paper flew around the war room as if it were caught in a New York City windstorm.

My cubicle quickly became the center of activity, as I tried desperately to keep track of all the information coming in, tried to assign all the tasks that weren't getting done, and tried—usually in vain—to control the daily crises.

The sun was just coming up when I arrived at the CCB, twenty-two ounces of Styrofoam and coffee in my left hand, the work I'd taken home eight hours earlier in my right. I had no time to read the newspaper anymore and so one of the people in media relations clipped everything I needed to read and videotaped everything I needed to see. By the time I left at night, it was long past dark again, usually around 10 P.M. For months, I had no idea what the weather was like outside.

The elevator chugged up to eighteen and a big elevator bay, which led in four different directions to coded doors and the D.A.'s offices. I punched in the code and made my way to the war room.

Patti Jo always seemed to be there, monitoring the front of the war room like a pit bull in a wrecking yard. In every office, there is a Patti Jo—demanding and demonstrative. Ignore titles and salaries, the Patti Jos of the world are truly in charge, the career office assistants who know everything: from where the felt pens are stored to where the bodies are buried. In my first thirteen years as a deputy D.A., Patti Jo hadn't said a word to me, even though I'd seen her in the elevators almost daily. There was no reason for her to talk to me. Until Cowlings, and eventually Simpson, I was unnecessary.

But when I became case manager, she took me aside right away and ran through the team. It was a talented and hard-working group; I could see that right away. But, compared to the defense team, we were understaffed. And we were disorganized.

"We are floundering a little bit," confided a deputy D.A. named Cheri Lewis. Cheri was forty-two, pert and professional, a Grade 2 lawyer who'd been brought on board because of her talent for writing legal briefs and responses to the flock of defense motions that seemed to fly into our offices every day. Cheri said the Simpson case was the most exciting thing that had happened to her and she shared none of my reservations about joining the prosecution.

"You're gonna give up your life," Hodgman had advised her.

Cheri, divorced with no kids, shot back, "That's OK. I don't have one."

The other senior lawyer was Hank Goldberg, a careful, smart Grade 3 who worked with Cheri behind the scenes, helping Marcia and Bill ward off the defense tactics and prepare for the trial. But Hank and Cheri couldn't keep up with the increasing flow of paper from Camp Cochran, which seemed increasingly frivolous and designed simply to keep us busy.

We had a handful of clerks and Grade 1 lawyers—baby-cake deputy D.A.'s, as we called them. Our clerks were all senior law clerks, though, mostly young men who had finished law school, taken the bar, and were just waiting for notification that they'd passed. So when the results came, those young lawyers would also be reassigned and we'd be staring at a huge trial, trying to retrain a whole new group of clerks.

I realized that what we needed were junior law clerks, the bottom of the bottom, the people who made it through six or seven years of school for the honor of making sure I had a teaspoon of nondairy creamer and a third of a packet of Sweet'N Low in my coffee. Of course, they had other duties—typing, making telephone calls, running errands, doing some interviews, writing first-draft briefs and arguments, and, especially, doing all levels of research.

We also needed clerks for security reasons. It was better to have law students with some sense of ethics than some county employee who was there because it was his or her job. So I did the math. I needed five clerks. We already had five men, so I began looking for talented young women.

I hired one woman, Susan Dozier, a confident Korean-American woman nicknamed D.J., on the advice of Runyon and Scott Gordon, the conservative SID prosecutor who was teaching part-time at South-western University. Dozier was helping Scott prepare a D.A.'s domestic violence handbook. He recommended another bright woman, Kathy Behfarin, and so I took her too. Lisa Fox was in the top 10 percent of her class and, while she seemed conservative and quiet, she turned out to be a ball of energy. She was an easy choice. Another woman had called me—seven hundred times, it seemed—and I finally agreed to interview her. Tracy Miller was charming and serious and I couldn't get her to stop talking long enough to ask a question. It was almost by accident that I found out she had been student body vice president of Loyola Mary-mount College. Tracy made four. I needed one more.

Melissa Decker was slightly older than some of the others, a twenty-eight-year-old black woman who had gone back to law school after a brief career in business. I had initially hired her as a clerk for the Special Investigations Division, which suffered a chronic shortage of black lawyers and clerks. I quickly realized that we needed someone as idealistic and smart as Melissa on Simpson as well. So I called her and told her that when she reported to work, she should come to the Simpson investigation rather than SID. She remained on the books in SID until March when Allen Field received a letter from the administrative offices saying it was time to evaluate her job performance in his department. I imagine it wasn't easy to do, since she hadn't worked a day for him.

The new group of clerks—which Judge Ito would nickname "the minions"—was set to start in January. In the meantime, I supervised the rest of the staff of Fort Simpson, and I still wasn't happy with what I saw. We were being buried in defense motions and investigative tips, and while I was assigning most of that work out, many of the important issues still required too much attention from Bill and Marcia.

We were stuck. I could see that our top litigators shouldn't be battling specific motions over topics like DNA and domestic violence, yet we needed experienced lawyers to work on those issues, certainly not the baby cakes. So my idea was to bring in specialists from all over the office to handle each motion, the way Lisa Kahn was serving as our expert on DNA. So, if search warrant issues came up, I would call the drug unit prosecutors, who dealt every day with searches; and if domestic violence issues came up, the D.V. lawyers would be brought aboard. It was an expensive, involved process, but I firmly believed that the D.A.'s office should not be outspent and outresearched; I was not going to lose the case because we couldn't afford to keep up with a wealthy defendant's lawyers.

Some lawyers didn't need more than one invitation to become involved. Since moving into administration, Scott Gordon—the former cop—had been named a special assistant to Sandy Buttitta, the number-two person beneath Garcetti. Scott's duty was to write, push, and monitor the legislative crime bills sponsored by the office. Scott's latest project had been a domestic violence handbook, and from the beginning of Simpson, he'd been hanging around Marcia, Bill, and—soon—me, like an insurance agent, trying to convince us that we needed to pay more attention to the patterns of spousal abuse and control in this case.

"It's not just about motive," Scott said in his earnest-cop voice, the one they usually use to explain the traffic laws as they're writing you a ticket. He was silver-haired and plug-chested and a dead ringer for Newt Gingrich.

"It's about how the jury is going to see Simpson," Scott said. "We have an image of what a criminal should look like. Murderers, robbers, you expect them to look like crooks. People who commit crimes against women don't look like that. They're intimates. In every house where spousal abuse has occurred, there is a wedding photo of the killer and his victim; that's a hard image for a jury to get past."

I knew he was right, but I was strictly in the middle of triage, trying to coordinate *all* the evidence and make sure we got everything into trial. And here was Gordon, talking like a psychologist. He explained Simpson's obsessiveness and feelings of inferiority, the pattern of obsession, abuse, and apology, and it was fascinating. But very little of it seemed admissible. And, with alternate jury selection moving along almost too quickly, I didn't have time to spend on theories and psychoanalysis unless it was going to help us convict that butcher.

So I would half-listen to Gordon's ideas, while I held a phone at my ear, browsed over an investigative report, and gave hand signals to the clerks. "That's interesting, Scott, but write it into a brief that will somehow get it in front of the jury and I'll really be impressed."

Scott was bugging me every day about domestic violence. I knew much of what he talked about could prove helpful to our case: like Simpson's beating of Nicole in 1989 and her frantic 911 call in 1993. I had seen relationship violence before and had successfully prosecuted three such murders to juries. But much of what Scott was talking about was tangential and inadmissible.

"You guys are making a critical mistake," Scott said, following me through the packed war room and stooping to pick up the file folder I dropped. "You aren't using all the evidence at your disposal."

"That's fine, Scott." I dropped a handful of papers on Runyon's desk, waved off a phone call from Patti Jo, and hurried back into my cubicle. "Is there some reason you can't put this in writing? Because I'm dying here and I don't have time to shoot the shit."

"I submitted it to Bill and Marcia a long time ago, last July, and I never got a response."

"Well, get me a copy and let me take a look at it."

But Gordon just kept coming back without paper, bugging the hell out of me. Throughout, I had encouraged Scott to gather all the research he could find and so I guess it was my fault.

And, ultimately, I suppose it was my fault that there were two frustrated domestic violence experts sitting on the floor in my cubicle one Saturday afternoon in December, huddling with Scott while I ignored them. They sat there amid boxes and stacks of paperwork all afternoon, while Runyon and I battled whatever wildfires were overtaking us that week.

"I'll be with you in a minute," I said. And even though I really didn't have time to meet with them, by then I knew how critical their information could be.

The defense had filed a motion seeking to preclude us from introducing any evidence of what they called "domestic discord." That really pissed me off, pissed us all off, really. Domestic discord? Anyone who'd seen the pictures and reports from the 1989 beating would've been offended by that term. Domestic discord. This wasn't a disagreement over which drapes to buy. He had beaten her, bruised her, and chased her from their home half-naked. According to her friends, the 1989 beating wasn't out of the ordinary either, wasn't even the worst of it. I met with Marcia and we talked about the motion the defense had filed.

Our opinion was the same. First, we weren't going to have the defense dictate to us what evidence we might admit. We would fight the motion on strategy first. But there were deeper issues. What else were they hiding? Why were they so afraid of the domestic violence evidence?

And so I talked with Scott Gordon about it. I decided that Marcia and Bill were too busy to fight this motion and so I assigned it to Scott. But he needed help too. There was another deputy D.A. named Lydia Bodin who had been a domestic violence expert, but, for some reason, she had been transferred to an outlying office. We desperately needed Lydia back. So I talked to management, pulled some strings, and she was back, ready to help Gordon fight the domestic violence motion.

"Let's keep this in the real world," I said to Gordon. "Ask yourself, 'How does this help or hurt our case?' Let's go easy on the hearsay and pop psychology."

We had already noticed that any mention of domestic violence caused Simpson to become agitated in court, and I remembered his interview with the cops ("She battered *me* . . .") and stories that he'd felt battered by his first wife, Marguerite, as well. This guy blamed the women in his life so completely for his violence, he'd convinced himself that they were beating the shit out of him. I thought of him squirming over the evidence of domestic violence and knew we had to poke and prod as much as the law would allow. As much as it bugged me to say so, that pain-in-the-ass Gordon was close to being right on this one.

"We need a strong response," I said. "We need one that will have them pulling O. J.'s ass off the ceiling. State-of-the-art."

In the next few days, I read as many journals and articles about domestic violence as I could get my hands on, and the pieces fell into place.

We had the "who" and we had the "how." The physical evidence would establish that. What we didn't have—without domestic violence—was the "why." *Why would a rich, successful guy like O. J. Simpson kill his ex-wife?* The research on the issue made it clear. He was obsessed with her, obsessed with controlling her. He had raised her from her youth and she owed everything to him. He couldn't stand losing her, losing control of her. He had warned her so many times that he would kill her, and the first time she had laughed at him. At *him!* She had even told him once that he was too old, that she was thirty-five, in her prime, and she couldn't imagine spending the rest of her life with a man in his sexual decline—practically a cripple. You could just see this insecure, frightened beast inside this guy, hurt, vengeful, and dangerous.

Domestic violence explained why. And it gave us the opportunity to present the real O. J., the one capable of this brutal murder, the one whose voice was captured on the 911 tape, the one Nicole described to her friends, wrote about in her diary, and dragged to a therapist. Not the public face the jury had seen on television, but the other face, the possessive and controlling, immature, insecure, obsessive, and compulsive face. The stalker.

And so Gordon and Lydia brought in these two experts, Donald Dutton and Angela Brown. They arrived that Saturday in December at 10 A.M., and by noon they were still waiting to see Marcia and me about how domestic violence fit into our case. I told a frustrated Gordon to take them to lunch, after which they continued to wait.

"Yeah, just a sec." I held up my hand and nodded to the doctors, who shook their heads and continued to wait. For Christ's sake, I wondered, couldn't they just do this in writing? This was Gordon's M.O., demanding a meeting when a report would suffice. Couldn't the guy write? Perhaps, I thought, I should glue his fingers to a computer keyboard until he had written me just one report on domestic violence, instead of always insisting on telling me in person.

By late afternoon, Scott and his experts were parked on the floor in my cubicle, waiting.

"Easy D!" Runyon stuck his head in the cubicle.

"I'm sorry," I said to the domestic violence experts, and then turned to Runyon. "What is it?"

"Another tip on a juror."

"OK. Give me just a second."

"Da-a-a-a-ar-de-e-e-en!" Patti Jo's foghorn of a voice cut through even the din of the war room. The telephone was a fairly reliable means of communication by that point in Western civilization, yet Patti Jo preferred to scream across sixty feet of office. "You got a phone call! Woman says A. C. told her O. J. did it!"

I smiled at Gordon and his experts and then took the call. When I hung up that call, the phone rang again. It was LAPD detectives wondering whether to investigate a certain tip; and then it was the crime lab calling to ask whether it should ship evidence samples; and then it was a reporter. "Any comment on what Cochran said today?"

"What'd he say?" Someone from media relations dumped a handful of news stories on my desk and a clerk came in with the results of some random research I'd assigned out. I smiled at the two doctors. Just a few more minutes. Finally, at 8 P.M., after ten hours of waiting, the domestic violence experts got their chance to talk.

But somehow, pinning Marcia down was even more difficult. She wasn't free until nine-thirty. Luckily, it was a Saturday or it would've been closer to midnight.

The doctors were only a few minutes into their presentation when Marcia interrupted them. "Can we talk about this over a drink?"

We drove to the Intercontinental Hotel, and as we entered the bar, the patrons turned their heads and began whispering. It was Marcia. They were gawking at Marcia. I was still in the background of this case, but it was my first indication of how many people were watching the case and its players.

I had never had much confidence in expert witnesses, especially shrinks. It seemed as if you could find a psychologist to say anything, and whatever your shrink said, their shrink would say just the opposite.

But Don and Angela were OK and their knowledge of domestic violence was impressive. When we'd gone over their advice, I asked what they had been whispering about on the floor of my office earlier in the day.

They laughed and then began talking about the prosecutors on the case and their observations of the day.

"You can't keep working at this pace," Dr. Dutton said to me. "Sooner or later, there's going to be a major meltdown." He diagnosed me as "shy and sensitive" and said that he was concerned that I had too much going on and that I was missing some of what was being said to me.

"I'm sorry," I deadpanned. "What was that?"

As for Marcia, he wondered, "How could any one person have that much energy?"

And then came the diagnosis. "There's some electricity between the two of you."

We both laughed uncomfortably.

"There's some sexual tension here."

He was out of his mind.

"Before this thing is over, you two are going to end up sleeping together."

I almost swallowed my beer bottle. Marcia and I both laughed it off and then stared at each other, probably for too long. "So much for our experts," I said quietly.

It was another Saturday and I walked into the conference room somewhat anxiously, aware that I was assuming an ever-expanding role in the Simpson prosecution, that I was being drawn deeper and deeper into the presentation of evidence and other controversies I couldn't control.

This was not going to be an ordinary murder trial. It couldn't. Weeks earlier, the *National Law Journal* had commissioned a survey of lawyers in which only 27 percent had said that Simpson would be found guilty. Twenty-seven percent!

"We have found the unconvictable client," famed lawyer William Kunstler told *USA Today*, one of hundreds of pessimistic legal voices making predictions that we would lose. "The best the prosecution can hope for is a hung jury. You couldn't find twelve people anywhere in this country who would all vote to convict."

With all the evidence we had, a month before trial, we were still prohibitive underdogs. On those mornings when I was alert enough, I would ask myself: What the hell have I gotten into?

It was time to find out. Marcia convened a meeting in mid-December to discuss the evidence and witnesses, to split responsibilities. The senior lawyers were all assembled: Bill, Marcia, and me; Hank Goldberg; and the two deputy D.A.'s brought in from elsewhere in the state, Rockne Harmon and Woody Clarke.

I looked around the room and it was like a prosecutor's meeting from some cheap murder mystery.

Sitting at my left was Bill Hodgman, balding and bearded, a serious and mannered lawyer, a star in Los Angeles County. He'd run a string of murder convictions in the Long Beach office and had been promoted from a Grade 4 to director of central operations, completely bypassing Grade 5 and assistant director. Nobody wears a whiter shirt than Bill Hodgman, and he was so controlled and professional, it was hard to imagine sweat stains or rings around any of his collars.

"Bill," Marcia said, "you've got the coroner."

Next to Hodgman was Hank Goldberg, who looked like the Big Boy hamburger guy with his curly-top hair. Hank was a waifish thirty-one, an eight-year veteran of the D.A.'s office who had been racking up convictions in the Santa Monica office. Hank was extremely intelligent and wrote complex legal briefs suitable for the *Law Review.*

"Hank has Fung, Mazzola, and the other crime lab witnesses."

I had never met Woody Clarke before. He was a conservative San Diego boy, neat and tidy in his $69 Florsheim shoes and C&R off-the-rack suit, like some deputy D.A. poster boy. Rock Harmon was in his fifties. A former riverboat pilot on the Mekong Delta in Vietnam, Rock had a thin, severe face, like that of an Old West hanging judge. A prominent defense attorney in San Francisco had called and said that Rock was an asshole and was "entirely unpredictable." I watched these two out-of-towners with some suspicion. I wasn't convinced that we needed to go out of town for talent; we had some incredible lawyers in our office whom we could've called in. And they just didn't fit. This was L.A., Tombstone Territory. It didn't matter what they'd done in their own jurisdictions. Here, a jury might just agree that if someone scratched your car, you ought to shoot him. I'd seen prosecutors run a string of convictions in outlying areas, then come downtown and lose five in a row. I was waiting to see how these guys would handle their first taste of downtown justice.

"Woody, Rock. Of course you have DNA evidence."

That left Marcia and me. She looked down and scratched above one of her big, round blue eyes. Marcia wore a serious business suit with slightly less skirt than you might want to wear to a board meeting. She wasn't within fifty pounds of any of the men at this meeting, and yet here was this tiny, curly-headed thing, completely in charge. She barked orders with no misgivings about how these men might feel about being ordered around by a woman. Those feelings were dealt with and discarded. We were moving steadily toward trial and Marcia Clark was leading us.

"I'll take the dog bark witnesses and the cops at the crime scene."

That left me. I looked around the room and realized how white they looked. All these white people and me. How would that look to the homies in South Central: one brother surrounded by all this whiteness, sticking out like a scratch on a new Mercedes? Damn, I thought, I really am going to pay hell for this.

"Chris, you have Fuhrman and Vannatter."

Damn. We had talked about this, but to hear it was like getting kicked. Those two were the most controversial witnesses in the case, the two who could turn the case, lose it for us. This wasn't putting witnesses on the stand, it was taking cattle to the butcher. Vannatter was going to be drilled by the defense for statements he made applying for a search warrant, and—worse—there were reports Fuhrman had gone through some psychological tests that uncovered deep racist sentiments.

The other lawyers seemed to freeze, maybe expecting me to throw up or let loose with a wild string of expletives. They waited. Only Marcia didn't look up at me. She continued to stare at the pages in front of her.

"Yeah," I said. "No problem."

On the way out the door, I passed Dana Escobar, one of the brand-new baby-cake deputy D.A.'s we had on the case.

"So?" I asked him. "What do you think of the way the witnesses were split?"

"I think it's fucked-up," he said. "I feel sorry for you."

One of the other clerks suggested that Marcia was dumping the worst witnesses and taking only the clean ones for herself. I didn't think so. I watched how hard she worked, and knew she wouldn't back down from any witness.

I drove home with one hand on my mouth and my brow rippled, lost in thought. Did Bill and Marcia think that hearing about a once-racist cop from a black lawyer would somehow defuse the awful beliefs? I had insisted that my addition to this case had nothing to do with my race, but now I wondered if my colleagues thought they could "sneak" Fuhrman and Vannatter through by giving them to the black guy.

Did they think black jurors were so stupid that they would believe any witnesses I presented just because I was black too? It was ludicrous. Black jurors would do what any black person would do, what any person would do. They would evaluate the testimony and—if they didn't believe a witness—it wouldn't matter if Martin Luther King put him on the stand. The only thing that having me "sneak" these witnesses would accomplish is that the jury would decide I was being used and I would lose any credibility I had in front of them.

If my fellow prosecutors wanted me to coddle these witnesses and were somehow trying to show the jury that I was vouching for them, they were beating at the wrong door. From the beginning, I had said that I wouldn't allow my race to be used in this case and I still wouldn't. I would put the witnesses on, because that is my job and my talent, but I would question them the way I thought best.

There was no ethical dilemma here, no moral conundrum. I am a lawyer. My law school diploma wasn't a black Juris Doctorate. My bar card said nothing about being a black lawyer, just as Marcia's didn't say woman lawyer and Hank Goldberg's didn't say Jewish lawyer. I am a lawyer.

And I am black. In fact, I love the color of my skin. It is dark and perfect. When you look at me, you don't see the remnants of slavery—light skin, thin lips, pinched nose. You see an African face. I am proud of that.

But there is no dichotomy, no division between the color of my skin and the demands of my profession. We all bring our heritage, backgrounds, and beliefs to whatever case we take. And we all end up with witnesses we would rather not associate with. As a prosecutor, I have had to put thieves on the stand to testify against rapists. I have put drug dealers on the stand to testify against burglars. Even if Mark Fuhrman was a racist, I would put him on the stand to testify that O. J. Simpson was a murderer. Yet if I was going to be saddled with a bad witness, I was going to damned well do it my way.

I was going to do what a prosecutor should do: find the truth. If Mark Fuhrman was a racist and the judge decided it had anything to do with this case, I would show the jury his beliefs. I would tell them why and how and let them know that it had nothing whatsoever to do with this case. I would grill him about the evidence so that the jury saw that he couldn't possibly have planted it. I wasn't going to leave any land mines for the defense. I was going to take Fuhrman for a stroll through the minefield and, between the two of us, blow them all up, even if it meant blowing up the entire prosecution case. My direct questioning would be harsher than anything the defense could throw at Fuhrman because it was the only way Fuhrman was of any use to us. And it was the only way to get to the truth.

In the coming weeks, Johnnie Cochran would invent the conflict of interest between being black and being a prosecutor. He would say that I was an "apologist" for a racist. It was a preposterous and offensive claim. If I put a convicted drug dealer on the stand to convict a serial rapist, would he say that I was an apologist for drug dealing? It was an outrageous thing for another lawyer to say.

Every day, I watched Cochran embrace and hug O. J. Simpson; every day, I watched him fight to keep evidence of Simpson's guilt out of the courtroom; every day, I watched him stand up for his client. Yet, no matter what I believed personally, I would never stand up publicly and say that Cochran was an apologist for a murderer.

He was a lawyer. We were advocates for the relative sides we represented, and I respected his duty as an attorney, even though I found his side to be untenable.

All I demanded was the same respect, no matter what he thought of my side of the case.

Because my side was simple: If your blood is tracked all over the scene and the victim's blood is all over your vehicle, if you have motive and opportunity, if there is no way you could have been set up, you are a murderer. All the racists in Los Angeles couldn't change that.

TWELVE

There is nothing subtle about tequila. It is pure throat-constricting, sinus-clearing, brain-killing poison, the kind of booze your mama warned you about. Or should have warned you about. People who drink tequila remember those occasions differently than they remember beer or wine or even whiskey. Those drinks, you remember as fond relationships: "I'm a wine drinker" or "I love beer." Tequila, you remember as a series of one-night stands. Nobody who is sane loves tequila. For most people, it resides in embarrassing anecdotes—stories that often begin, "God, I can barely remember . . ." and end, ". . . I have never been so sick." Yet there are a few connoisseurs, people who can appreciate and control a straight shot of tequila now and then. Like me. Since college, I have thrown back tequila on occasion, usually when I needed a drink as hard and unforgiving as my thoughts.

"Mark Fuhrman." I read the name on the file aloud as I reached for the bottle of Sauza Commemorative tequila I stowed in my top drawer. One bottle a year in the office, one swig now and then, that's all I allowed myself. I would offer shots to people who came into my office, but I warned them first: "I pull straight from that bottle."

Mark Fuhrman. The file just felt bad. I was going to the wall for this guy? The tequila went down the way tequila always goes down. Unrepentant.

I had asked Cheri Lewis for Fuhrman's file. She was the deputy D.A. tracking the issue of whether his alleged racism was going to make it into the trial and she was preparing to argue that it shouldn't. Cheri had collected everything that came in, including letters from the public,

Internal Affairs documents, correspondence from his attorney, and press coverage of him.

When I asked her for the file, she was hesitant at first. Fuhrman was a personable guy, and Cheri had grown fond of him, saying he was an intelligent, careful cop. It was the opinion most people seemed to have of him. How could this guy be connected to the things that were being said about him? It is so much easier to think of racists as ignorant fools. There is nothing more unsettling than a smart racist.

I had read—like everyone else—*The New Yorker*'s story about Fuhrman and the defense team's plan to shift attention away from the murders and convince the jury that O. J. Simpson was being framed by the racist cop. Now I opened the files to see how much truth there was to the article.

I started in the present, with Fuhrman's careful notes the night of the murders. Unlike some of the other police officers on the case, Fuhrman kept specific, detailed notes that backed up his assertions. If this was only about his performance that night, at Nicole Brown's condo on Bundy, Fuhrman would have been an excellent witness, perhaps the best of all the cops in the case:

> At scene 0210 hours . . .
>
> Item 13) At rear gate on N/S of residence: two blood [stains] at bottom inside of gate. This area might have been where the dog was kept. Susp. ran through this area. Susp possibly bitten by dog? . . .
>
> Item 15) Rear gate, inside dead bolt (turn knob type) poss blood smudge and visible fingerprint . . .
>
> Item 17) Ski mask, one glove by feet of male victim.

But as I went deeper into the file—and back in time—it was easy to see where the problems were going to be.

Mark Fuhrman was forty-three, raised in Washington State by an overprotective mother and a father he described as an "irresponsible, insensitive bullshitter." He went to a military academy in fifth and sixth grades, was big and athletic, but actually wanted to be an artist. When he graduated from high school, he wanted to go to art school but joined the marines instead. He was trained as a machine gunner at Camp Pend-leton in San Diego and went to Vietnam in 1973, as the fighting was winding down. Fuhrman liked the military because it was "black and white. . . . You get rewarded for what you are supposed to do."

A private, first class, named Michael Landa—a friend of Fuhr-man's—remembered his buddy saying that he "hated fucking niggers." Fuhrman denied it. But he left the marines, he said later, because "I was tired of having a bunch of niggers and Mexicans that should be in prison telling me they weren't going to do something."

It was outrageous. It was also twenty-one years ago. That was a long time. However, there was a more recent incident involving the Marine Corps too. A woman named Kathleen Bell alleged that, in 1985, she met Fuhrman inside a Marine Corps recruitment station when he was considering reenlisting. During a conversation inside the station, Bell alleged, Fuhrman said he would pull over any car that contained a black man and a white woman.

> I then asked him, "What if you don't have a good reason to pull them over?"
> Mr. Fuhrman stated, "I'd make one up."
> I then asked Fuhrman, "What if the two people are in love?"
> Fuhrman then appeared to get disgusted with me and stated, "If I had my way, they would take all the niggers, put them together in a big group and burn them."

Genocide.
Jesus. What was I getting into?
Of course, Fuhrman denied it. Bell said there were other marines in the office when Fuhrman said those things. The file also included inter-views with those marines. They said they hadn't heard any of the slurs that Kathleen Bell was talking about. I turned first to the interview with a marine named Maximo Cordoba. He was a black man, a bodybuilder, completely ripped, who would've laid Fuhrman out if he'd heard him make racial slurs. He hadn't heard Fuhrman say anything and he hadn't heard anyone even talk about it. "No, I have never heard of anything on that level from [Kathleen Bell] or any other marines in that office."

Someone was lying. I guessed the truth lay somewhere between Kathleen Bell, Fuhrman, and the marines.

Next was Fuhrman's LAPD personnel file. I turned to a psychologist's reports from 1981 and 1982, when Fuhrman was trying to get off the force on a disability retirement. He was claiming that he was afraid he might kill someone because of posttraumatic stress disorder, which had him flashing back to his days in Vietnam. His burnout had begun, Fuhrman said, when he was assigned to a Mexican gang unit where he worked sixty to eighty hours a week. When he talked about it, Fuhrman seemed to include his years as a marine in his frustration over public service.

> I've given eleven years of my life for this fucking public that doesn't give a shit if I live or die. I've had it . . . I'm really capable of violent things. I feel like I'm out on a limb and somebody's sawing it off. I have this urge to kill people that upset me.
>
> If you only knew what it feels like when some guy's doin' something, acting cool, thinking no one sees him and you come up and put a shotgun to his head. [Laughs] . . . Some assholes, I'll break every bone in their body.

I had to set the file down for a moment. According to Cheri, the defense had all this information, even the personnel file, which, according to California law, was supposed to be kept confidential. Rumor had it that an attorney in another case had paid an L.A. cop to steal it. *They* had gotten the personnel file before *we* had.

It was completely fucked-up. I picked the file back up and noticed that these psychiatric reports were coming at a time when Fuhrman was going through his second divorce, a messy split that began with his wife's affair. She left him in March 1980, telling him that he had "'changed' since she first met him, becoming more hateful and distrustful of people." I turned to the psychiatrist's analysis of Fuhrman.

> His career in the police was similar to his career in the Marines. In both instances, he became bored after five years and wanted out. In the Marines, also, he has fond memories of killing and

> beating up on people without any remorse. . . . He brags about his use of excessive force and goes on at great length about how much fun he had breaking the arms and legs of suspects when they gave him a hard time.
>
> . . . this patient is narcissistic, self-indulgent and somewhat emotionally unstable. . . . Just as he is exaggerating his conscious feelings of violence, he is exaggerating the violence in his dreams. . . . There is no work-related psychiatric disability. This man has not changed significantly since his Marine days. He has personality problems, but they are long-standing.

Yes, he did have personality problems. Big ones. And he was my witness. Here I was, as black as black could be, fresh from the Special Investigations Division, where other deputy D.A.'s thought I was too tough on the cops. I had seen it as one of my duties to ferret out racist officers like Fuhrman and now I had to put him in front of a jury and question him.

How do you prove a man is a racist? How do you quantify hate? With Fuhrman, it seemed, the defense was going to focus on racial epithets. Did he use the word "nigger," and, if so, how often? I would have to argue that the epithet was inadmissible, that its relevance—its probative value—wasn't worth the anguish it caused those jurors—its prejudicial value.

Thankfully, I didn't have to argue that Fuhrman wasn't a racist. I was going to argue that Fuhrman's beliefs had nothing to do with the deaths of Nicole Brown Simpson and Ronald Goldman. This was the difference between words and action; nothing could compare to the brutality of those two murders. How many times must Fuhrman say "nigger" before his transgression was the moral equivalent of two homicides?

I believe that any defendant has the right to question police officers about racial bias, assuming there was some possibility that the bias had a connection to the case. In this case, it didn't. Fuhrman had made no racist statements or actions in this case and had no opportunity to plant evidence or somehow violate Simpson's civil rights. He was just one of fourteen detectives at the scene, and even if they'd all conspired to frame Simpson, they still couldn't have done it. It was physically impossible. Mark Fuhrman had not killed those two people with his bigotry and small-mindedness. O. J. Simpson, the evidence demonstrated, had killed them with a knife that he drew viciously across their throats.

Still, I was troubled. I set the Fuhrman file back on my desk and thought about running. Just walking away from the case. Let the white lawyers deal with it. It was a joke I made sometimes, that I was just a black guy caught up in some white folks' shit. Perhaps this was not an issue for a black attorney. Maybe I should let Cheri argue that the N-word shouldn't be allowed into testimony. Or Marcia.

I couldn't fool myself, though. It would have been hypocritical and would have violated the rules I had set a long time ago: Give the same treatment to all defendants, regardless of race or anything else. That was Darden's Law. When I was challenged the most, was I going to run away from the rules I'd established? Because of fear? Or political correctness?

I was a full partner in this thing, whether I liked it or not. I did not want to be limited. I would carry myself with dignity and purpose, and I would argue what I believed: that Mark Fuhrman's racism had nothing to do with this case.

I looked up at the clock in my office. It was after midnight.

Ron Phillips was known as a real straight shooter, an honest, sincere detective. He was over six feet tall and 220 pounds, in the last stages of male pattern baldness, with thick, tinted glasses that he might've gotten from a car dealer. He had helped Fuhrman out a few years back and had been his partner the night of the murders.

I called and explained that I was trying to find out about Fuhrman. Phillips told me that Fuhrman really hadn't been able to work since the Simpson case because of all the publicity. He was taking it hard, Phillips said.

I got right to it. "So, you're his partner. If anyone knows about this guy, it's you: Is he a racist?"

"No," Phillips answered right away. "He's not a racist. He voices his opinion." I heard the chair whine beneath his weight and I imagined him leaning forward on his desk. "Let me tell you about Mark. Mark really dislikes criminals. And he doesn't care who you are or what color you are. He just hates criminals.

"If Mark made statements back then, ten, fifteen years ago, it was a time when Mark was a lot more immature than he is now. I mean, he's matured so much in the last three years."

Great, I thought. The jury is going to be so pleased to hear about Mark Fuhrman's personal growth.

Phillips asked if I knew Danette Meyers, a black female deputy district attorney in West L.A. and Santa Monica. Sure, I said. She was tall, dark, and lanky. I had offended her one time by calling her "girlfriend," a common greeting among black women.

"I am not a girl," she had said. "I am a woman."

Phillips said Danette and Fuhrman were friends and that they ate lunch twice a week and that she even baby-sat his kids. "Plus he plays basketball three times a week over at the YMCA with a bunch of brothers."

Great. I knew it wouldn't take long for basketball to come up as a defense against his racism. How would the jury respond to those character witnesses? It was the old cliché that each of them had heard a million times: "Some of my best friends are black . . .," "Hey, I play basketball. . . ."

I asked Phillips about a 1985 report that Fuhrman had gotten into trouble for battling the department's affirmative action policy.

Yeah, Phillips acknowledged. But Fuhrman had gotten that off his official record.

What about rumors that he collected white separatist literature and Nazi paraphernalia?

Just rumors, Phillips said. All of them untrue.

What about his plans to retire and move to Sandpoint, Idaho, near Hayden Lake, home of the Aryan Nations, a white supremacist haven?

Coincidence, Phillips said. Fuhrman was moving to Idaho for the hunting and fishing.

Hunting and fishing wouldn't necessarily play with a South Central jury any better than racism, I mused.

Phillips said that his divorce had been tough on Fuhrman, that perhaps it had brought out the worst in him during his psychological evaluations. "Look," he said, "Mark is a hot dog and has always been one. He's not a racist."

I tried to call Danette Meyers, thinking I still might call her as a witness later. But she was on a long vacation in Mexico.

Then I called some of the black police officers I knew, and asked if they could put out the word, quietly. Were there any recent stories about Fuhrman? There is a black cop network that provides support and help for officers in the face of institutional racism and individual problems. Those officers know who is racist.

I heard back that Fuhrman was an unrepentant asshole, uptight and arrogant. Hell, he was a cop. To some cops, "asshole" is a compliment. Nobody had anything *bad* to say about him. The black cops who worked with him now couldn't believe he was a racist. They had never seen any indication of that.

If he was that way ten, eleven, twelve years ago, the black officers said, he'd gone through a transformation since then. A drastic change. He was a good man now, they said.

A drastic change. Could a man like Fuhrman change? Could an outright racist see the light?

Malcolm X had. At home, I reached for a worn paperback copy of Malcolm's autobiography. When he made his pilgrimage to Mecca, Malcolm X discovered that there were all types of Muslims, black, brown, and white. He discovered that the white devils, whom he blamed for the world's evil, could also be worthy servants of Allah.

"Since I have learned the truth in Mecca, my dearest friends have come to include all kinds—some Christians, Jews, Buddhists, Hindus, agnostics, and even atheists! I have friends who are called capitalists, Socialists, and Communists! Some of my friends are moderates, conservatives, extremists—some are even Uncle Toms! My friends today are black, brown, red, yellow, and white!"

But that was Malcolm X, one of the most respected men of his time and one of my teenage heroes. His racism had been forged by generations of oppression and bigotry. His change was testimony to his own forgiving nature and grace, as if he were saying to whites, "I no longer hate you for *what you've done.*"

But could someone like Mark Fuhrman change? And even if he did, wasn't the result different because the source of his racism was different? One was reactive, the other proactive. Effect and cause. Fuhrman's change would be like saying: "I no longer hate you for *what you are.*"

Could Mark Fuhrman change? I sure as hell hoped so. Because in a couple of days, I was going to be forever connected to him.

* * *

I didn't like him from the first time I saw him. I looked at him sitting in Scott Gordon's office, waiting for me, and I had the urge to run again. We were set to meet at one-thirty that afternoon, but as usual, there were a million brushfires.

"Apparently," I said to Runyon, "I'm the only one with a hose long enough to put them out."

And so Mark Fuhrman had to wait, until about 3 P.M., when I came into Gordon's office and introduced myself. Fuhrman didn't like to wait and he was in a lousy mood. I didn't give a shit. On this case, everyone waited.

Gordon seemed to like Fuhrman. Scott was an ex-cop himself, and his office was filled with police mementos, especially from the Royal Canadian Mounted Police. Scott loved all things Canadian, especially his wife, Lisa.

I didn't screw around. "What will you tell the jury if the defense asks if you used the N-word?"

Mark Fuhrman was huge, over six feet, two inches and 200 pounds, a onetime bodybuilder with shoulders that easily covered the back of his chair. "I'm not gonna say that I never used a racial slur," he said.

"Under what circumstances have you used them?"

"I don't know," he said. "I guess when I'm incensed about something."

"Like what?"

"Like traffic, I guess. Never on the job."

I asked about his sports heroes, and he listed George Foreman, Magic Johnson, and Larry Bird. He knew some interracial couples and had black friends, he said. It was a short interview, and he seemed glad when it was over. I said I would talk to him again when I had more time. But I had one more question.

"Any skeletons that we don't know about? Anything that's going to bite us in the ass?" He talked about the things we knew, which were bad enough, but assured us that was it.

Afterward, Scott was pleased. See, he said, the guy wasn't so bad. I disagreed. I felt completely uncomfortable with him. There was something eerie about the guy. It was as if he'd been playing with me, coy on some answers, evasive on others. I watched all the other deputy D.A.'s smile and agree that he would make a very good witness. But I was sick. There was something about this guy . . .

I still planned to go right at him in direct examination, to almost treat him as a hostile witness. But first, I had to deal with the issues of admissibility of his racist slurs. I had to deal with the N-word.

It was January 12 and my new batch of clerks had just recently joined the team. I quickly called Melissa Decker, the only other African American working on the case at the time, now that another clerk, David Wooden, was off studying for the bar. Melissa was in her third and final year at Southwestern University School of Law. I reached her about ten o'clock, Wednesday night. She answered on the third ring.

"Hello?" Her voice was sleepy, drained.

"Decker?"

"Yeah." A cat moaned in the background. Decker was a strange one, twenty-eight and beautiful, and yet she lived alone with a cat, rejecting any number of lawyers from any number of nationalities and background, all variety of heights and weights, all manner of wealth, every stage of baldness. "Not until I've passed the bar," she'd say.

"I need some information, sociological and psychological studies that address the effects of the word 'nigger' when heard by black people. I don't need a whole lot. Just two or three."

Decker seemed stunned and she fumbled for words. It was essentially her first assignment. "B-b-but . . . Wha . . . "

"Don't ask a bunch of questions. Do you understand what I'm looking for?"

"Yes."

"And you can handle it?"

"I'll have to go to the library at UCLA."

"How long will it take?"

"Tomorrow. Five o'clock?"

"OK. Keep me updated."

I hung up the phone and blew air out of my mouth. With the trial about to start any day, this might be the case right here. If we lost here, we wouldn't be able to keep the race card out of this trial. I thought of Ron Goldman and Nicole Brown Simpson, as I often did when things got tough.

The only way to get justice for Ron and Nicole was to keep this from becoming a case about race. And the only way to do that was to keep the defense from beating the jury over the head with that word. How could I impress upon the judge just how deeply the word "nigger" affected African Americans? Where could I begin?

Johnnie Cochran and I sat on the back bench in Ito's courtroom, facing forward and small-talking about the funeral Cochran was to attend that day, for a man shot to death outside his Pacific Palisades home. The man had several civil suits pending against him, suits alleging that he ripped off old and financially strapped people, that he stole their homes out from under them. And Cochran was speaking at the man's funeral.

When Judge Lance Ito came in, Cochran and I stood up.

"You don't need to turn this into a race case," I said to Cochran as we moved toward our respective positions. "Don't do this. There are other ways to defend this guy."

He didn't say anything. He just stared straight ahead.

"Well," I said. "Let's make this one for the ages."

"Yeah," he said. "Let's."

Cheri Lewis argued first that Fuhrman's past shouldn't be part of the case. And then it was my turn. I stepped up to the podium, spread out my notes, and pushed my glasses up on my nose. I said that the best indication of the power of that word was that Cochran and I were the two stuck arguing it. White lawyers couldn't get away with using it, I said. And neither could white witnesses.

"It is a dirty, filthy word," I said. "It is not a word that I allow people to use in my household. I'm sure Mr. Cochran doesn't, either. And the reason we don't is because it is an extremely derogatory and denigrating term, because it is so prejudicial and extremely inflammatory."

As I spoke, Simpson stared at the ceiling.

"Why should we allow that word in this courtroom? Especially in a case like this where it has no probative value. It is completely irrelevant. It was created and designed to do one thing and that is to demean people, to strip them of their humanity, to evoke an emotional response.

"Your Honor, when you use that word, you are using fighting words. When you use that word in the presence of an African American, you are asking that African American for a reaction. It is a call to arms. . . .

Because when that word is used in the presence of an African American, an African American has an obligation to do something about it, to say something. An African American has a duty, in most situations, to confront . . . to confront the declarant.

"It will do nothing to further the court's attempt at seeking the truth in this case. It will do one thing. It will upset black jurors. It will upset the black jurors; . . . it will issue a test . . . and the test will be: Whose side are you on? The side of the white policemen or the side of the black defendant and his very prominent and black lawyer? That is what it is going to do. Either you are with the Man or you are with the brothers. That is what it does. That is exactly what it does.

"No one, no African American, can hear that word without getting upset. You hear it in the movies, it upsets you. People don't listen to rap music, some black people, because they don't like that word. . . . And if you search black literature today, black magazines, you will see letters and articles from people asking why that word is used. Why does that word exist? Why would anybody want to use it? Why would anybody want to rap about it? Why would anybody want to repeat it or say it?

"The word has no place in the English language. It has no place in the courtroom. You shouldn't let them use it."

Shapiro and Cochran leaned forward and talked to each other, and Johnnie looked back at Carl Douglas. You could feel the tension in the courtroom. There was no murmuring in the back today.

"Detective Fuhrman is going to play a very, very small role in this case. This wasn't his case. He was not the investigating officer in this case. He went to Rockingham with four other or three other detectives and he just happened to find an item. . . . The man finds one item amongst six or seven or eight hundred other items collected by the police in this case and now when the man is called to the witness stand, we are going back fifteen years . . . and ask if he ever made a racial slur, repeated a racial epithet? Why?

"There is no legal purpose. There is no valid or legitimate purpose. But Mr. Cochran and the defense, they have a purpose in going into that area and the purpose is to inflame the passions of the jury and to ask them to pick sides, not on the basis of the evidence in this case. [Because] the evidence in this case against this defendant is overwhelming. There is a mountain of evidence pointing to this defendant's guilt.

"But when you mention that word to this jury or to any African American, it blinds people. It will blind this jury. It will blind them to the truth. They won't be able to discern what is true and what is not. It will affect their judgment. It will impair their ability to be fair and impartial. It will cause extreme prejudice to the prosecution's case.

"This isn't a race case. . . . Mr. Cochran wants to play the ace of spades and play the race card, but this isn't a race case and we shouldn't allow him to play that card . . . if what we are really interested in is playing by the rules, finding out just what happened at Bundy and if we are really interested in searching for the truth."

And then I read a quote from *Two Nations*, a book by Andrew Hacker:

> When a white person voices [the N-word], it becomes a knife with a whetted edge. No black person can hear it with equanimity or ignore it as simply a word. This word has the force to pierce, to wound, to penetrate as no other has . . . the N-word stands alone with this power to tear at one's insides. It will reveal that whites have never created so wrenching an epithet for even the most benighted members of their own race. It is a persistent reminder that you are still perceived as a degraded species of humanity, a level to which whites can never descend.

"I remember the first time I was ever called that word. . . . I'm sure Mr. Cochran remembers the first time. And whenever I reflect back on that experience, I find it extremely upsetting and I probably appear to be getting a little upset right now. It is probably the most negative experience I have ever had in my life.

"If we really want the jury's attention focused on the evidence and on the legal and factual issues . . . we shouldn't let them hear this word, because if they hear this word, they are going to focus their attention on the issue of race. They are going to be more concerned with whether Mark Fuhrman is a racist than they are with whether there was any way, any possibility, any chance, any theory offered by the defense to establish that Mark Fuhrman planted evidence.

"That's what Mr. Cochran wants the jury to do, to skip the evidence . . . to find this case on the basis of race."

I reiterated my legal point. It was a simple one. The incredible prejudicial value of the 1981 and 1982 psychological reports wasn't worth their probative value.

"In this situation, the prejudice that will flow to the people's case because of the inflammatory nature of that word is beyond substantial prejudice. It is extreme prejudice. . . . We can't win, no matter what, because we are trying a race case. We are not trying O. J. Simpson and we are not trying the issue of whether he killed two people on Bundy on June 12. We are trying a race case.

"And everything, every piece of evidence, every witness, everything that happens in this case beyond that is going to somehow be affected by the jury's perceptions of that witness's ethnicity and color and the real issues in this case are going to be painted, glossed over, missed by the jury and completely ignored.

"All the prosecution\wants in this case is a fair shot, a fair trial. . . . And we strongly urge the court, and respectfully so, that the court not allow that word, that it is not uttered in this courtroom."

"I have a funeral to attend today," Cochran said, his lips rigid and tight, his voice growing louder as he went on. "But I would be remiss were I not at this time to take this opportunity to respond to my good friend, Mr. Chris Darden.

"His remarks this morning are perhaps the most incredible remarks I've heard in a court of law in the thirty-two years I've been practicing law. His remarks are demeaning to African Americans as a group. . . . And so I want to apologize to African Americans across this country."

He was apologizing for me?

"It is demeaning to our jurors to say that African Americans who have lived under oppression for two hundred plus years in this country cannot work within the mainstream, cannot hear these offensive words."

I was dumbfounded. Nowhere in my argument did I say that. I simply made a legal argument, one that is made every day in America, that some evidence was too prejudicial to be used. Did Cochran realize what he was doing?

"I am ashamed that Mr. Darden would allow himself to become an apologist for this man, to justify the fact that he is a police officer."

That was all I could take. Apologist! I stood to say something and looked around the courtroom. Simpson had that same smug look on his face. Carl Douglas was rocking back and forth in his chair. And the judge just let Cochran roll on about me. He was using all the buzzwords: "demeaning," "offensive," "ashamed," "apologist," "used." I would be the first to acknowledge that my argument was emotional, but it was not vindictive and it was not personal. Cochran was talking to all the brothers out there, pulling back the curtain, pointing at me, and calling "Traitor!"

I knew how it would be received in the 'hood. I asked myself: Is he doing this on purpose? Is he trying to strip me of my identity, to put my life at risk? He said that we wanted to keep them from cross-examining Fuhrman, but that wasn't true. I realized the Kathleen Bell incident was fair game. I was just arguing that the 1981 and 1982 reports were too old and that the word itself, the awful word "nigger," had no place in this case. I sat down again and faced the back of the courtroom, enraged. At that moment, I hated Johnnie Cochran. And it pained me to hate another man, especially a black man I had considered a colleague.

Perhaps I really had offended Cochran. But more likely, I realized later, I also cut too close to the only case he had to present. When I said he only wanted to turn this into a race case, I didn't realize to what extent I was correct. Or the depths to which he and the other defense lawyers would go.

Everyone else was still looking at the evidence and the legal foreplay, but I had cut right to it, and Cochran was threatened. This was going to be a case about race and only about race. And since I was the only person who could see that, I was the enemy.

"I am a lawyer who happens to be an African American," Cochran continued. "But I would not allow myself to be used under these circumstances to become an apologist for people who used racist statements in the past, to malign other African Americans."

And then we broke for the noon recess. Douglas came up to Cochran, grinning, patting his back. Shapiro put his hands on Cochran's shoulders and complimented him. Marcia and Cheri tried to compliment me on my argument, but I walked past them, out of the courtroom, and took the elevator up to the war room. The phones were jumping off the hook. I was drained and bitterly angry at the same time.

"What do you think of Cochran?"

I spun around to see who had said it. It was a clerk. I just kept walking. Runyon was pacing around, pissed. Melissa Decker was sitting in a chair, frowning. In my cubicle, the telephone rang.

"Darden."

"You fucking sellout motherfucker!"

I slammed the phone down and it rang again.

"Uncle Tom."

And again.

"You are a disgrace to your race."

Again.

"Don't ever refer to yourself as black, 'cause you ain't."

Again.

"How could you allow yourself to be used like that?"

Some of the voices sounded like white people.

"You and your family are all apes."

Somewhere in there, Marcia called to say that court was back in session and that Judge Ito wanted me back in there. I told her to go on without me. But Ito joked that it wouldn't be as interesting until I returned.

In the courtroom, Cochran, Ito, and the rest laughed and joked. The Court TV commentators told their viewers that we were doing what lawyers did; we were acting. "It's all part of the game."

It wasn't a game for me. In my little, soft-walled office, the telephone just kept ringing and I answered each call: "Darden."

"If I ever see you on the streets of Los Angeles, you're one dead nigger."

I winced and stared at the random collection of notes that I'd used in court that day. What had I said? I had said that the first time you hear that word, you never forget. Even that day, the word hurt as badly as it had the first time.

I remember it clearly. It was warm and sunny, the summer of 1966, and a bay breeze tooled down Macdonald Street, dusting us all with ocean air. I was riding my bicycle up Macdonald, the main drag in Richmond, a busy strip of every kind of business and a few homes, a four-lane street running between the black and white neighborhoods. Music blared from car windows and open doors, and people smiled as I rode past, leaning forward in their lawn chairs or nodding from open doors.

I was ten.

My bike was well used and rickety, the kind of bike you got when you had seven brothers and sisters. Still, I was proud of it. It was a Schwinn Stingray knockoff, shiny green, pea-colored, with an imitation leather banana seat and a sissy bar. I stood on the pedals and cranked, rolling down Macdonald, looking for a hamburger, with a sweaty handful of change.

I pedaled carelessly, the way kids do, without thinking for a moment that I was alone. I pedaled across San Pablo, the unofficial border between black and white in Richmond. Maybe I was blind with hunger, or maybe I was just too trusting, but I didn't notice the eight white kids riding toward the same burger stand on their new, rust-free bicycles. I laid my bike on the curb and walked toward the door, but before I could get there, those white boys surrounded me, with their upturned noses and angry freckles.

"Hey, nigger. Don't park that raggedy bike next to ours."

"You better get out of here, nigger, or we're gonna kick your ass."

You never forget the first time. It is the most inflammatory word in the English language, and as soon as I heard it, I filed it away. I put it in this place inside myself, a place where I have corralled and harnessed the energy and anger. I found this place—as all black people do—inside myself, and as the years went on I filled it with all the wrongs that were told to me by Nanny and Grandpop, by Mama and Daddy, and by Gloria Alibaruho. I put in there all the indignities that I saw and all the injustices I read about.

I was surprised that the place was even there, and that it was already so full when I discovered it. It was full of things that happened before I was born. It was the place where I had been stripped of my identity, taken from my home, and sold like a possession, forced to work until I could work no more, and it was the place where I was tossed aside like a broken plow, to await my death. It was a place as cold and constricting as the hold of a ship, the barracks of a slave quarters, the floor of a jail cell, the grave of a sharecropper. It was the place where I wasn't allowed to read, where I wasn't allowed to vote, where I wasn't allowed to own land.

It was the place, too, where I learned to hate those people who did this to me and my ancestors, to hate the institutions that allowed this to happen, to hate the laws that encouraged it.

I looked around and saw black people suppressing that place, hiding the pain, repressing the anger. It was possible, I found, to do that, to hold it in check until somebody triggered it, resurrected the hate and unleashed the power. It was triggered for me and for many blacks, any time they heard a white person say the word "nigger." It didn't matter who said it. It could be my best friend, but as soon as he said that word, it opened up that place and it didn't matter how deeply the anger was stored. It came raging to the surface. That's where black power comes from, really, from that place of injustice and anger. For hundreds of years, that place was the only thing that kept us alive. It alerted us to danger, let us know when to keep our mouths shut, and told us when to go out the back way. It interpreted gestures and body language and let us know where we stood, separated for us right and wrong. It helped us escape and survive and fight for justice.

But it posed dangers of its own. Like most power, it could be misused in the wrong hands, simply because it could blind us to reason. It had the power to make the implausible highly likely, the impossible probable. Our responsibility was to not waste the power on dishonesty.

It was irresponsible to tap the insecurities, to open the repository of black anger and action for the wrong reasons. It was wrong to use that power loosely. It made us no better than those who had oppressed us. It was wrong to use the power to defeat justice instead of to serve it.

"Come on, nigger! Get out of here."

I remember looking up at those white faces and wondering why the world had to be this way. They were boys on bikes. I was a boy on a bike.

"I'm gonna count to ten, nigger."

I was gone by the time they got to two, riding my bike back toward my house as fast as I could, my face grim and determined. I wasn't going to cry for those bastards, wasn't going to give them the satisfaction. They threw rocks at my back, but I didn't turn around.

When I got home, I didn't tell anyone. I couldn't tell Michael that I had run away. When a white person called you nigger, you were supposed to whup his ass. I didn't and so I was ashamed. And after what those boys did to me, that I should feel shame was perhaps the worst part of what happened. I have never forgotten that day.

THIRTEEN

There was this uptight brother on the front page of the *Los Angeles Times*, his palms facing up like he was singing a hymn, his mouth pursed like someone about to spit. The caption said "Christopher Darden," but I didn't recognize him.

"Lawyers Bitterly Debate Race in Simpson Case," the headline read. The story called the proceedings from the day before "the most highly charged courtroom episode of the trial." I dropped the paper on my desk and went back to preparing my opening statement.

"Nice picture," Runyon said, his arms full of documents.

"Yeah, right," I said. "Out of the frying pan . . ." Runyon, Decker, and I were working on my portion of the opening—which was to be about domestic violence. In some ways, this was the most inflammatory evidence against Simpson, partly because he just hated it so much; in another way, it was the most tenuous.

Everything had changed the day before. Any respect I'd had for Cochran was pretty much gone, and it was becoming clear that this case was to be fought bitterly, with Cochran blatantly using race as a weapon. "As much as I don't want to see race brought into this case," he told one interviewer, "I think you'll see the defense really seek to exploit it." I could see it in the faces of the minions and the other prosecutors. We were at war. The usual rules of courtroom decorum no longer applied.

On my waist, my pager buzzed over and over. It was Andrea Ford, a reporter with the *L.A. Times*. I reached her at her home.

"Hi, Chris." She sounded nervous. "The reason I'm calling you is because of a story we're going to be running in tomorrow's paper. It's kind of a man-on-the-street thing, reporters asking blacks what they think about you." She paused. "Some people may be referring to you as an Uncle Tom."

I had gotten into an argument with Andrea the day before, when she'd accused me of showing favoritism to the *Los Angeles Daily News*. It was ridiculous, since I could barely stand to be in the same room with the *Daily News* reporter covering the trial. I thought of that argument now.

"What is this, a hit piece?" I yelled. Runyon and Decker peered around the doorway of my cubicle, curious. "That's what this is, isn't it?"

"No," she said, "it's news."

"How the hell is it news for people to call me an Uncle Tom?"

Andrea explained that they'd sent black reporters to malls, barbershops, and restaurants in the black community, asking what people thought of me. They got what they were looking for. And it wasn't just people on the street, she said. They had some experts, like a UCLA English professor named Richard Yarborough, who said, "To suggest black people are so sensitive to the term they are disabled is extraordinary."

Yes. That was extraordinary. And it wasn't what I'd said. I had argued that the jurors would lose focus, that the case would turn into a race case, that the entire trial would be diverted from Simpson to Fuhrman. As far as I could tell, that was exactly what happened. Yet people weren't responding to what I said. They were responding to Cochran's version of what I said. He was being allowed to frame the argument and to define me. One person told the *Times* that I was put on the case to hide police racism.

I grew angrier and angrier. "I spent six years fighting racism in the LAPD. Damn it, Andrea! That's not what this should be about!" I stood up and paced, rubbing my head. Runyon was staring at his shoes. Decker had found a chair and was near tears, distraught that her research had led to this.

The *Times* story was keyed to Martin Luther King Jr. Day, which was the next day. That was the perfect day to announce to Southern California that I was reviled in the black community, that I was an Uncle Tom. It seemed like the natural day to complete the stripping of my identity that had begun when Cochran attacked me for taking the Simpson case.

"Look, Andrea, I am one of the principals in this trial! Don't do this! You fucking do this and I won't say word one to the *L.A. Times.*"

"It's not my story," Andrea said. "I can't stop it."

I called Pathenia in Oakland and asked that she not let Jenee see the newspapers on Sunday and Monday. "If she hears about it at school or something, let me know, so I can talk to her about it."

I pleaded my case again with Andrea, to no avail. I talked to our director of communications, Suzanne Childs, and she tried to talk the *Times* out of running the story. Again, no luck.

Finally, I convinced them to at least interview some supportive voices. Fine, the *Times* said, but I had to provide sources before their deadline, in one hour. I gave them Gloria Alibaruho. She was quoted briefly, deep in the story, after the piece had already jumped twice, landing on page A-28. "He has honor," Gloria said of me. "He has courage. He has dignity. It is true that when you dangle the N-word in front of African Americans and you put it in the context of white versus black, then you're going to get a very strong reaction."

"It is true . . ." I was, as always, happy to have Gloria's support. Unfortunately, truth was no defense for me. In this case, truth was why I was in trouble. There are some things that are *too* true. Some things that we wish so badly weren't true that we don't want to hear about them.

I had truth on my side, all right. That's why the defense had to come after me. I was standing up alone, screaming, "This is going to be a race case!"

In bed that night, I lay on my back, staring at the ceiling. Car headlights explored the front of my house and then kept moving. With my bedroom window twenty feet from the curb, I heard every engine and every creak in my house. Would someone try a drive-by shooting?

But it wasn't fear that kept me awake. It was bitterness, a venom that churned my insides like an old washing machine.

Was I doing the right thing? I had heard countless black people say the same things I'd argued ("I hear a white person say nigger, it just sets me off!"), and yet now, I was under attack. I replayed each word in my mind, sorry I had said some things, shocked that others had become controversial.

I thought about what the defense was trying to do, and was baffled that I was the one whose ethics and morals were being challenged. They

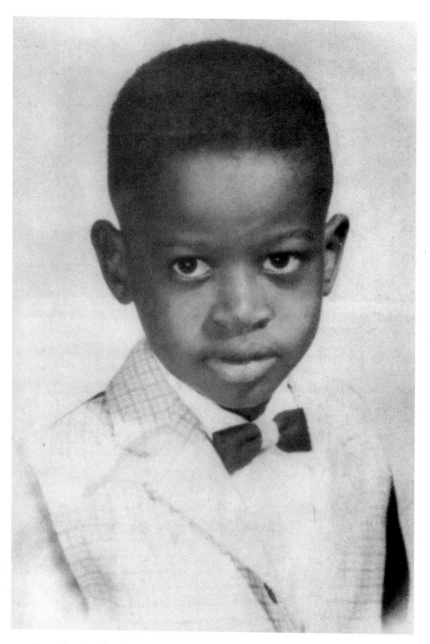

I was the fourth of eight children raised in a working-class neighborhood in Richmond, California. Here, in my first grade photo (1962), I work on my intimidation stare. *Courtesy of the Author*

My big brother, U.S. Airman Michael Darden (1976), never backed away from anything, especially trouble. *Courtesy of the Author*

I have remained a part of my daughter's life, and she has taught me so much about love. *Courtesy of the Author*

A whole flock of Dardens: I'm in the front wearing the tie. My brother
Michael and his wife, Carolyn *(far left)*; my brother Larry behind a mess
of uncles and cousins *(far back)*; my mother, Jean *(far right)*, holding my
nephew Doyle, and my sister Angie *(second from right)*. *Courtesy of the Author*

When you grow up without money, you imagine yourself someday leaning
on your own Mercedes-Benz. On a prosecutor's salary, as you might guess,
this one was used. *Courtesy of the Author*

In every spousal killing there are photographs of the couple in happier times. But this photo will always be haunted by Nicole's words to her friends, "He's going to kill me and get away with it." *Robin Platzer/Twin Images/The LIFE Images Collection/Getty Images*

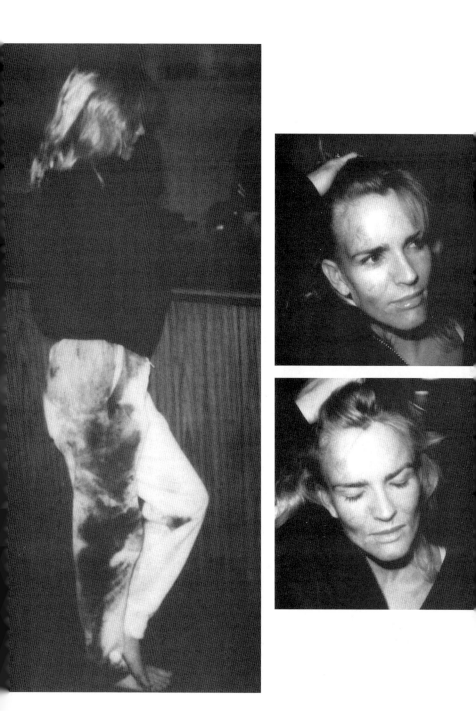

LAPD photos show Nicole Brown Simpson after being beaten by her husband in 1989. Simpson suggested in February 1996 that Nicole caused these injuries herself by picking at acne on her face. *Case file, The People* v. *O. J. Simpson*

My first involvement in the Simpson case was the investigation of Simpson's friend Al Cowlings, seen here during a hearing on July 29, 1994. A porn actress later testified that Cowlings thought Simpson was guilty. *AP Photo/Reed Saxon*

Denise Brown presented a sad, stirring picture of the relationship between O. J. and her sister, Nicole. But it was stunning how perceptions of her testimony—shown here on February 3, 1995—were divided along racial lines. *Pool/AFP/Getty Images*

During closing arguments, September 26, 1995, I tried in vain to remind the jury of the only N-word that should have meant anything in this case—Nicole. Here, I show a photograph of Nicole Brown Simpson and detail her fifteen years of abuse at the hands of O. J. Simpson. *Myung J. Chun/AFP/Getty Images*

On September 12, 1995, we tried to repair the damage from the glove demonstration. We'd showed that Nicole Simpson bought the gloves and that Simpson wore the same unique style. Here, witness Richard Rubin testifies that he is "100 percent certain" the crime scene gloves would fit Simpson's hands. *Pool/AFP/Getty Images*

From the beginning, Cochran publicly accused me of being a traitor to my race; although we were civil to each other during the trial, hard feelings ran deep. "Let these white people get up there and argue about Fuhrman," he told me one day. *Pool/AFP/Getty Images*

I have tremendous respect for Judge Lance Ito, but in my opinion he was too impressed with celebrity and lost control of this case the moment the lawyers stepped into the courtroom. *Pool/AFP/Getty Images)*

Marcia Clark and I had a passing friendship before the trial, but by the time I presented our rebuttal case on September 29, 1995, we had become close friends and confidants, bonded by the pressure of the Simpson case. Throughout the trial, we passed notes back and forth, writing about testimony, our personal lives, and our relationship. "I am honored that you are my friend," I wrote to her. *Lee Celano/WireImage*

At the end of the defense case, Judge Lance Ito allowed O. J. Simpson to stand and announce that he "would not and could not" have murdered his ex-wife. We were furious, and, like the pundits watching the case, we wondered, "What was Judge Ito thinking?" *AP Photo/Reed Saxon, Pool*

From the very beginning, I had misgivings about LAPD detective Mark Fuhrman—seen here testifying on March 10, 1995—yet his racist beliefs should have had nothing to do with the Simpson case, as we proved conclusively that he couldn't have planted evidence. *AP Photo/File*

When the trial began, I respected Johnnie Cochran for cases he'd taken that sought justice for people abused by the system. But his actions at the Simpson trial undermined much of that. *AP Photo/Nick Ut*

By the time we heard Laura Hart McKinny's testimony on August 29, 1995, Marcia and I feared that the evidence in the case no longer mattered, because it had degenerated into a case divided along racial lines. *Myung J. Chun/AFP/Getty Images*

During closing, I referred the jury to the Bible, Proverbs 6:16–17, "These . . . things doth the Lord hate: a proud look, a lying tongue and hands that shed innocent blood." *Pool/AFP/Getty Images*

O. J. Simpson's legal team—Barry Scheck, Peter Neufeld, Johnnie Cochran, and Robert Shapiro—won his acquittal through a slick blend of distraction and distortion. *Reed Saxon/AFP/Getty Images*

The scene I dreaded, the scene I feared one day I would turn around to see: Kim, Fred, and Patti Goldman react to the "Not guilty" verdict on October 3, 1995, while Detective Tom Lange stares forward. *AP Photo/Pool, Myung J. Chun*

With Juditha and Denise Brown after closing arguments. I grew
to respect their dignity as they came to court every day and were
bombarded with gruesome crime scene photos, intrusive reporters,
and cynical legal ploys. *Courtesy of the Author*

Fred Goldman addresses prosecutors after closing arguments,
while Gil Garcetti looks on and I comfort Kim Goldman.
The Goldman family railed against the defense team's tricks
and Simpson's arrogance. *Courtesy of the Author*

The only real hero in the case of *The People* v. *O. J. Simpson*, Ronald Goldman was a waiter and an aspiring actor who was killed trying to save the life of Nicole Brown. *Lee Celano/WireImage*

wanted to use the hatred of some whites to free a killer! They wanted to transform a double murderer into some kind of political prisoner! This "black man" who did not date black women, who rarely socialized with blacks, who turned his back on anything black, was being drawn back into the fold as I was being turned out.

It was the middle of January and I had worked at least twelve hours a day for seventy-nine of the last eighty days. The only day I took off was Christmas. Now I stared at the clock: 5 A.M. I gave up on sleep.

And then, out of my fatigue and anger came prayer. It was all I could do. It was as if God Himself placed His hand on my heart, calmed me, and allowed me to rid myself of the hatred and free my spirit from the burden that weighed on me.

I was doing the right thing. I was standing up for two defenseless victims and challenging the hypocrisy of 1990s America. I was being true to myself, to my heritage, and to God. The rest was in His hands. All I could do was keep getting up, going to work, and doing the best I could do.

And when I woke up that Sunday morning, the sun was out and it was 10 o'clock, the latest I'd slept in three months.

"You're gonna have to do more in this case."

The almost nightly phone conversations between Marcia and me had taken on a strange familiarity, like the intimate conversations you have with friends, soft-voiced and funny, with long, thoughtful pauses.

I shifted the phone to my other ear. This damned case was like quicksand. The more I struggled with it, the deeper I went. "What do you mean, more?"

I could hear some sort of scratching or grinding in the background as Marcia listed the witnesses she wanted me to take over from Bill.

It was far too many witnesses. Any anonymity I had left would be gone if I was in the courtroom that much. It would be just as my father had warned me. "I don't know, Marcia."

"You have to."

"Why? What's wrong with Hodgman?" At his core, Bill was a gentleman—proper and gentle. This trial was quickly turning into a street fight and it grated on him. He was tired and pale, lagging where he was once energetic.

"Bill's fine," Marcia said flatly.

I could still hear that rustle in the background, like a rat on a treadmill. "What the hell is that? A hamster?"

Every once in a while, I got a glimpse of Marcia's incredible energy. Like now. Marcia laughed. "No, it's my exercise bike." Twelve hours in the office and she had enough juice left to ride an exercise bike.

A few days later, we met with Bill in Marcia's office. She seemed awkward and she abruptly excused herself, leaving just Hodgman and me.

He didn't waste time. "I want you to assume a larger role in this case."

"Why? What's going on?"

He insisted there was nothing going on. He just thought I was better suited for this trial. But I was confused: Hodgman had prosecuted hundreds of cases. Was there some problem between him and Marcia?

"This case . . ." He hesitated. "We both know how it's going to be. And I'm not talking about race. I'm just talking about the strategy. It's going to be trench warfare. I just think you're better suited for that than me right now."

Early on, press reports had depicted Hodgman and Cochran as the respectful, well-mannered combatants in the trial, the adults shaking their heads while Marcia battled Shapiro, and their DNA expert, Barry Scheck, bitterly argued with our DNA expert, Lisa Kahn. Hodgman and Cochran had a good working relationship before this, but now Bill was drained by all the rancor. During voir dire, a black juror had become combative with Hodgman and he'd been hurt when the defense had accused him of questioning black jurors differently than he had questioned white jurors. Usually confident and smooth, for the first time Hodgman seemed unsure of himself.

Looking back, I think Bill was right. This wasn't a case for him. It wasn't a case for any of us. "OK," I told Hodgman. He seemed strangely relieved, and when Marcia came back, I was coprosecutor.

I had gotten a sense of our roles earlier, when I went to a meeting called by Ito to set a few ground rules before opening statements. When I arrived at Ito's chambers, his clerk told me the lawyers were all in the jury room.

That was odd. Conferences were usually held in Ito's chambers. It wasn't until I got there that I figured out why this one had been moved.

The whole Dream Team was there, seated gleefully around the room. Nine very expensive suits. As I looked around the room, I wondered what the criteria could be for admittance to this team. Among the frontline attorneys, the only thing they seemed to have in common was their penchant for defending spoiled, nasty rich people and their ability to attract and create publicity:

- Johnnie Cochran sat there facing sideways, legs crossed, picking lint off one of his shimmery, Buck-and-the-Preacher suits, trying to contain his smile—the arrogant grin of a guy dealt two aces, who always carries two others in his sock. For Cochran, there were two defense strategies: Sew up witnesses and deny everything (the Michael Jackson child molestation case); or cry "Racism!" (every other case). This was his dream assignment. He could do both.

- Robert Shapiro, the "quarterback," as he called himself, smiled without really smiling, constantly straddling the border where friendly ended and slick began. His reputation was that of a plea bargainer and of someone whose client list was filled with celebrities like Johnny Carson, Linda Lovelace, and Christian Brando, and bad-boy athletes like Darryl Strawberry and Jose Canseco. Simpson was both, the dream defendant.

- F. Lee Bailey looked jowly and uncomfortable, as if he were about to cough up a cocktail onion. A Boston boy, Bailey made his career by successfully defending Sam Sheppard, the Cleveland doctor accused of murder. He had also represented Patty Hearst and the Boston Strangler. He had been called the best defense lawyer in America, but, to be honest, I hadn't even known he was still practicing. I had, however, heard about his drinking. Shapiro had gotten Bailey off on a charge of driving under the influence several years earlier by employing a brilliant defense strategy: Accuse the arresting officer of racism.

- Gerald Uelmen sat in the corner like somebody's grandfather, talking in his cracked, Wilford Brimley voice about case law that no one else had even *heard of*, let alone memorized, as he had. The outgoing dean of Santa Clara University Law

School, the scholarly Uelmen seemed as out of place with these media hounds as a nun on a chorus line.

- Alan Dershowitz anchored the front line. A Harvard law professor and author, Dershowitz had defended or filed appeals for the wealthy accused murderer Claus Von Bulow, the wealthy accused rapist Mike Tyson, and the wealthy accused tax evader Leona Helmsley. From what I could understand, he was being paid to monitor by television the case of the wealthy accused murderer in Boston. Good work if you could get it. Before joining the Dream Team, Dershowitz had suggested that Simpson should plead insanity.

- The DNA twins, New Yorkers Peter Neufeld and Barry Scheck, deferred to their famous counterparts and sat there fidgeting, about to burst with all their scientific knowledge. They had been busy springing convicted murderers and rapists based on DNA evidence. "If O. J. Simpson is not the murderer," Scheck had said before joining the Dream Team, "then DNA will tell us who the real killer is." Oops! Apparently it was someone with Simpson's blood.

- The benchwarmers, Carl Douglas and Sara Caplan, sat behind their bosses, Cochran and Shapiro, respectively. They were just two of the countless other lawyers working on the case, doing research, writing briefs, burying us in motions and discovery requests and carrying the stars' briefcases.

Later, it would amuse me to hear about this fight or that fight among the members of the Dream Team, and I would take some joy in court, watching them sit as far apart as they could. Early on, Bailey and Shapiro were the worst—arguing over control of the case and press leaks. The rumor was that Bailey was leaking confidential information to the press. "It's very painful," Shapiro told reporters. "We can't have snakes in the bed trying to sleep with us." As I looked over the defense lawyers, I wondered what they expected. If you don't want to sleep with snakes, don't crawl into bed with them.

I sat down next to my team, Bill and Marcia, and realized that they had become relatively famous as well. It was funny; I was probably the only lawyer in the room who wasn't famous.

Judge Ito talked about courtroom hours and other issues that seemed completely trivial to me. With all the preparations we were making for opening statements, it was ridiculous that he thought we needed to have both teams here for a big meeting over issues that could've been handled with a conference call between Marcia and Shapiro. I sensed that Ito craved the ceremony of this trial. He seemed infatuated with the idea of being the judge in the "trial of the century." It was a show to him, and he was acting unlike any judge I'd ever seen. An hour into the meeting, he dismissed us.

He may as well have had us arm wrestle and said, "May the best side win." It's no wonder the justice system has become a game when judges treat pretrial meetings like pregame coin tosses.

She didn't look much older than a child. Nicole Brown was perhaps eighteen or nineteen in the photograph—which eerily foreshadowed the pictures that police would take of Nicole in 1989. Her angular face bruised, her left eye swollen in a sad half-wink. Her eyes looked directly into the camera—directly at me. It was a photograph she had painstakingly locked away for me to find, to make sure she didn't die in vain. It was gut-wrenching.

We'd found the safe-deposit box in December. It included a will (how many thirty-two-year-olds make out a will?), a diary, news clippings about the 1989 beating, and Simpson's pathetic letters of apology. Any self-doubt about my involvement faded before this sad collection of evidence that Nicole had left us, before the picture of a beaten teenager and stark descriptions of a marriage punctuated with beatings and humiliation: "He continued to beat me for hours as I kept crawling for the door," she wrote. "O. J. hit me while he fucked me." Another time, she wrote that he took her outside and slapped her for talking to a man. Sometimes the abuse was psychological. Once she wrote about trying to convince Simpson to be with the family when he wanted to go out with his friends. When he came home, Simpson decided to unload on Nicole how unhappy he was that she was pregnant at the time.

Simpson "was telling A. C.— 'My wife's a fat ass— . . . a liar . . . I stopped fucking other girls and now I jack off' . . . He locked me out of our room and I buzzed him . . . 'Get out of my house, you fat ass liar . . . I want you to have an abortion with the baby.' So I packed a few things together. He locked the door again. I buzzed—'Do I really have to go tonight? Sydney's sleeping—It's late.'

"'Let me tell you how serious I am . . . I have a gun in my hand right now. Get the fuck out of here!'"Our court battles over domestic violence evidence were coming to a head, and based on the information in Nicole's safe-deposit box and interviews with friends like Faye Resnick, we compiled a list of Simpson's abusive behavior, everything from slapping her to stalking her. On January 11, the court unsealed our motion on domestic violence, which contained sixty-two separate incidents of abuse, manipulation, and threats by Simpson.

They began in 1977 (". . . threw her into a wall . . . beat Nicole Simpson on a corner and in a hotel . . . 'He continued to beat me as I crawled for the door'"), continued some time around 1982 (". . . said she was hit by Simpson . . . locked her in a wine closet and watched television while she begged . . . backhanded Nicole Simpson across the head, forced her out of a car") and 1986 (". . . beat Nicole Simpson . . . causing . . . a bruise to the head. Simpson . . . told a doctor she was hurt in a bicycle accident").

The 1989 beating, in which she finally called the police, was included, as were several incidents when she told friends that Simpson beat her ("'I really think he's going to kill me,' 1993"). There were examples of stalking (". . . Simpson peered through window . . . watching her have sex with another man, April 1992. . . . Nicole Simpson told her mother, 'He is following me again, Mommy. I'm scared,' May 1993") and examples of incriminating behavior (". . . Simpson told friend Bill Thibodeau he knew of a secret way to Nicole Simpson's house through a back alley and 'sometimes she doesn't even know I'm here,' March 1994. . . . Simpson warned Faye Resnick that he would kill Nicole Simpson if she saw any other man. . . . At Nicole Simpson's funeral, Simpson stood over her coffin and muttered such statements as 'I'm sorry,' and 'I loved you too much'").

The incidents built to a crescendo. Just months before she was killed, Nicole told her mother Simpson was stalking her. "I'm scared," she said. "I go to the gas station, he's there. I go to the Payless shoe store, and he's there. I'm driving and he's behind me."

And then, *four days* before Nicole Brown was murdered, a woman named Nicole called a battered women's shelter in Santa Monica, the Sojourn shelter, distraught and scared, saying that she was being stalked by her ex-husband, a celebrity to whom she'd been married eight years and with whom she had two children.

As Lydia Bodin read the incidents, one after the other, Simpson rolled his eyes and complained so loudly to his lawyers, Lydia had to ask Judge Ito to order him to be quiet. Simpson just couldn't stand for the world to know the truth about him. Once, during Lydia's presentation, he got that dazed, faraway look, his eyebrows arched, his eyes not seeming to focus on anything. In such moments, I guessed that he couldn't occupy himself with courtroom strategy and he was alone with his memories of drawing that knife across his ex-wife's throat.

I wanted to make sure Ito knew about the attempts Nicole had made to protect herself. I wanted to make sure they were on the record somewhere. "What you've heard so far in this case is nothing more than O. J. Simpson's life," I told reporters. "This is his character, his behavior, and it has come back to haunt him."

Ito ordered us to pare back our list of incidents by eighteen, but much of the evidence, it appeared, would make it to the jury. The defense accused us of using "a tabloid prosecution" and said we were engaged in a "smear campaign." But we were going ahead full steam with the domestic violence evidence. It would be the motive for our case against Simpson, the "why." And it would be my job to present it to the jury in opening statements.

Newspapers ran lineups of the two teams, as if the World Series were starting in the next few days. The Dream Team was all there. Marcia and Hodgman were there. Even Cheri Lewis was there. But I wasn't. We hadn't announced that I was going to be anything more than case manager, and so everyone expected Hodgman to make the opening statement.

Instead, I worked with Runyon, Decker, and the other minions, with Gordon, Lydia Bodin, and anyone else who had an idea, putting together a simple road map to the domestic violence evidence. On Saturday, January 21, two days before I was supposed to begin, I showed my rough outline to a friend—a speechwriter with a master's in journalism.

"Where is the passion?" she chided me.

"I'm the passion," I said. "Trust me. It won't lack passion." We bantered back and forth until I finally threw her out of my house. I didn't change a thing.

Sunday night, Marcia called me from the office. We hadn't spoken in a week while we prepared our openings separately, I in my cubicle and in my small house in Carson, she locked in that smoky office.

"I need to see your opening," Marcia said.

"OK. Got a pen? I'll give you directions."

She read it on the laptop computer I'd borrowed from Scott Gordon. She said it looked good. I offered her a glass of Scotch; in fact, I'd gone to the liquor store and gotten a special bottle of single malt stuff, with the kind of Scottish name I knew she liked. The Glenfiddich.

"I drink Glenlivet," she said. Marcia and I talked about the N-word argument and how I was still smarting from the things that had been said about me. I told her that Gil had asked me not to talk to the press, but I was frustrated because, to that point, I had been defined by Johnnie Cochran and not by myself. I had to speak to someone. Marcia talked me into calling one of the reporters who had been pestering me the last week. I wasn't going to call the *L.A. Times,* after what they'd done to me, so I called David Margolick, a reporter for the *New York Times,* and gave a short interview.

I sat around sipping tea and talking to a few people that I trusted. Pat Ector, a friend and fellow prosecutor in the Bay Area, offered to come down so I could practice my opening. I thanked her and said no. I lay awake all night, playing back scenes in my head: Jenee as a baby, Mama, Nanny, Michael.

I was worried about him and his depleted immune system. I had tried to call him, but the telephone just kept ringing and there was no answer. Sometimes, Mama said, Michael slept so soundly, he couldn't hear the telephone. A dead sleep. Other times, he didn't have the energy to answer the phone. He had a cat who'd given birth to kittens underneath his bed, and Michael had been too exhausted to do anything. He was upset a few days later, when he found out some of the kittens had died.

Late that night, he called me back.

"Hey," he said, his voice hollow and scratchy. "Don't let that Cochran guy tweak you. You know he's going to try to provoke you."

"He doesn't have to try and provoke me. After that shit he said last week, I just have to look at him and I'm provoked."

Michael wished me good luck with my opening statement.

"The hell with that," I said. "How are you?"

"I'm OK. I'd be a lot better if I could just catch my breath." He had hepatitis and some form of emphysema. One of his lungs was blackened and on the brink of collapse.

"Is there anything I can do? Do you need money? Food?"

"I'm fine, Chris."

"What, are you too good to accept my help?" I teased him. "It's good for me to help, Michael, it keeps everything in perspective. You must be craving something, some food you haven't eaten in years, maybe?" I thought about a dinner we'd had a few years back, one of the rare times all the Darden children and their spouses went out for dinner. Michael's wife, Carolyn, had ordered a lobster and, trying to get the meat out of the tail, accidentally sent it flying over our table. "How about an aquarium full of fresh lobsters?"

Michael laughed. "You know what I have been craving? Those Fritos corn chips. Thin ones." That was Michael, never one to ask for more than he needed.

"They're on the way," I said.

The next morning, I put on a new black suit and a red tie and left for the CCB. The war room was buzzing. The Goldmans and Browns were there, gracious and brave as always. I looked around at the lawyers and clerks, whom I'd seen late at night and on weekends dressed like a softball team. Today, they were in their best. It looked as if we were going to church. There was a cake. On it was written, "Let's kick some rich lawyer's ass." The looks were confident, serious.

I went back to my office for a moment and then one of the clerks came in. "They're calling for you." I stood, walked over to the coatrack, and grabbed my jacket. Then I went back to my desk and made a phone call to a friend. "Hey," I said, "help me send some Fritos to my brother."

When I stepped out of my cubicle, the clerks and lawyers were lined against the walls and desks of the war room, almost at attention, as if they were waiting for inspection. I stood there for a brief moment. We had been working together for three months, nonstop, and I was proud of all of them.

Department 103 was a standard CCB courtroom—thirty-five feet by thirty-five feet—wood-paneled, partially carpeted, and much smaller than it looked on television. There were four rows of seats for spectators, six to ten given out in a random drawing every morning. The rest of the sixty-three seats went to a selection of reporters, families of Simpson and the victims, and the lawyers who didn't fit at the respective tables. I'd never seen a courtroom so crowded.

Through the double half-doors, the defense and prosecution tables were right on top of each other, separated only by the small, cheap lectern. Behind those two tables were the "little kids' tables," like the ones that children are assigned to for Thanksgiving and Christmas dinner. Supporting lawyers and clerks sat at the little kids' tables, which were spiderwebbed with telephone lines and computer cords. The jury—twenty-two people in padded, executive chairs—spilled out of the jury box and waited for us to begin. Above the jury box, the twin television cameras emitted their electronic whir, and it was impossible not to realize sometimes that the whole world was watching.

I looked over to Simpson's side of the table. It looked like a legal convention over there. Cochran, Shapiro, Bailey, Douglas, and Uelmen sat with O. J. curling around the end of the defense table toward Judge Ito. Another lawyer, Robert Blasier, was hanging off the edge like the last guy to show up at a poker game. At least five other defense lawyers, including Robert Kardashian, sat at the kids' table or in the gallery. The Simpson defense team was larger than most law firms in Los Angeles.

And then it began. I stood, greeted the jury, and set out trying to explain to them why this man killed his wife, why he'd risk everything because of his obsession.

"You think, 'Why would he do it? Not the O. J. Simpson we've all known for years.' But that leads to another question: do you really know O. J. Simpson? Because what we've been seeing is the public face, the public persona, the athlete, the actor.

"But like many men, he has a private face as well, the face that Nicole Brown saw every day and the same face that Nicole Brown and Ronald Goldman faced in the last moments of their lives, the face of a batterer, a wife-beater, abuser, controller.

"He killed Nicole for a single reason—one as old as man himself—jealousy. . . . He could not stand losing her and so he murdered her. In his mind, she belonged to him. And if he couldn't have her, no one could."

I spoke for an hour.

Marcia went next, carefully detailing the enormous amount of physical evidence in the case. His blood was at the scene, confirmed by both DNA and conventional serology. "Matches the defendant," Marcia intoned, flipping from photograph to photograph of blood drops outside Nicole Brown's condominium. "Matches the defendant." Click. "Matches the defendant." Click. "Matches the defendant." Click . . .

There was a cut on the middle finger on his left hand, consistent with the blood drops at the scene. There were bloody footprints at the scene: size 12. His size. Bruno Maglis, $160 loafers. His shoes. There was one bloody glove at the scene of the murder. His glove. Another bloody glove at his house. His glove. There was blood in his bathroom, in his foyer, in his Bronco. The blood in his Bronco came from three different people and two of them were lying dead in front of Nicole Brown's condo. Nicole's blood was mingled with Ron Goldman's on Goldman's boot.

"Blood is where blood should not be," Marcia said in that voice which fascinated me—firm and feminine at the same time. There was hair and fiber evidence, she said, including a hair on Ronald Goldman that matched Simpson's, a man he'd never met before the murder.

Simpson had no alibi. And there was proof that he was on the road just before the murders. Cellular phone records showed calls from Simpson at 10:02 and 10:03 P.M. to his girlfriend, Paula Barbieri. He was driving around in the Bronco, trying to reach Paula ten or fifteen minutes before the murder. It was an incredible case—motive, physical evidence, opportunity.

Later, I read what the pundits had to say. It was one of the few times I paid attention to those armchair quarterbacks—book lawyers who'd spent no more than a few hours in the courtroom themselves, if that much. At times, it seemed as if we were the only lawyers in the country who weren't offering analysis on television or in the newspaper.

Marcia got good reviews as the pundits discussed the overwhelming physical evidence that she'd presented. Yet the same pundits spent almost no time talking about the substance of what I'd said. It was a sad indication of what I knew about this case. No one, it seemed, could see past race.

". . . Chris Darden is not a master orator, but what far outweighs that factor is having a male African-American prosecutor making the case of domestic violence against a male African-American defendant. . . . The symbolism of that is very important." "It's evident why the prosecution would want to diffuse the race issue by having a black prosecutor begin its opening statement." "Perhaps the prosecution—with all their protestations to the contrary and acknowledging that Darden is an excellent prosecutor, liked the idea of having an African-American lawyer argue part of its case."

So I was a black prosecutor, nothing more. Cochran had decided that everything in this case would be racial strategy and the pundits were playing right along, buying into that hype. Everything I did, it seemed, would be preceded by the modifier, "African American prosecutor," as if it explained everything I did and said. None of these armchair lawyers paid attention to the content of what I said, only the pigmentation of my skin, the breadth of my nose, thickness of my lips. "Yep, he's black, all right. That must be why he's up there." Everything in this case was sifted through a filter of bigoted expectations, like the pressure Jackie Robinson faced when he broke the color barrier in baseball. "Pretty good hitter for a darkie." It was bad for our case, but it was worse for the country. We were being ratcheted back fifty years because of a lying, murdering ex-jock and his unprincipled legal team. And the media, the pundits, and the starstruck judge played gleefully along.

Sometimes, when I'm teaching law courses now, I'll look up at my students and wonder what we are teaching them. Am I instilling the respect and responsibility they should have for the law? Because it should be the most important thing for them about being a lawyer—more important than trial technique or billable hours.

I try to instill in my students the idea that justice needs tending. It will not survive in the face of cynical manipulation and distortion, any more than a garden will survive being constantly trampled.

Bill Hodgman genuinely liked Johnnie Cochran. He'd lost to Cochran in the assault trial of Todd Bridges—a child actor gone bad—but Hodgman considered Cochran a friend of sorts and they had a mutual respect. In fact, Cochran was well liked throughout the D.A.'s office. During the late 1970s, Cochran had been assistant district attorney, the number-three position in the entire office. He'd managed most of the special prosecuting units, including SID and the gang unit, and he'd worked alongside many of the current supervisors. Even after he left in the 1980s, Cochran was treated like one of the family. He had access to files that other defense lawyers didn't and was given the best deals and plea bargains. He had a direct line to Hodgman himself and could work deals that other defense attorneys only dreamed about.

Even though Cochran was known for his outrageous openings, speeches that drew objecting prosecutors out of their seats like fans at a good ball game, I don't think the other prosecutors expected the argument he made on January 25.

He began by quoting Martin Luther King Jr. "Injustice anywhere is a threat to justice everywhere." I could see where he was going. This is about injustice *elsewhere*, he was telling the jury, about Rodney King, and Thirty-ninth and Dalton, and racist white cops. That injustice allowed them to ignore the facts and concentrate their anger on what has been done to African Americans.

"You jurors are the conscience of the community. . . ." Which community? The black community where some polls showed 80 percent of African Americans believed Simpson was innocent. ". . . the most important decision of your lives." You have to go home to that community when this is over.

But as much as his opening was directed toward blacks on the jury, it was also directed toward me. In the morning portion of his opening, he talked about Marcia three times: ". . . the very able discussion of Miss Marcia Clark . . ." He talked about me over and over, twenty-one times in a little over an hour: "Mr. Darden was . . . offensive to women."

Other black lawyers told me it seemed as if Cochran was coming after me again, constantly challenging me and eroding my reputation in front of the jury.

In the law, there are rules known as reciprocal discovery. The prosecution is required to turn over to the defense just about everything in our files, while the defense is required to turn over everything related to the witnesses they intend to call. The punishment for ignoring or breaking discovery rules ranges from the exclusion of witnesses to holding the lawyers in contempt.

With the experienced lawyers on the defense team, it is fair to assume they knew the rules. And it is easy to see why they decided to flout them. They were trying to make the prosecution appear afraid of the defense case. When they spring a new witness on us and we object, it gives the jury the impression that we have been surprised by their information and that we want to keep it out of the case because it is so damaging to our case.

It is a stupid and manipulative trick that the best defense lawyers outgrow and would be embarrassed to use. Cochran's, opening was full of what the pundits called surprises, what we later argued to Judge Ito were blatant violations of the rules of professional conduct and discovery. The pundits didn't get it. He *never* would have called these witnesses. Half of them were credibility nightmares, people who called in tips on every well-publicized case or who had obvious reasons to lie. The other half were actually damaging to his case.

Cochran had only two goals: (1) get us to object furiously and make it look as if we were afraid of his side of the case, and (2) plant in the jury the idea that it would be OK to let Simpson go, that there was all this nebulous information out there that, taken as a whole, could pass for doubt. He knew those jurors wanted to let O. J. go. They just wanted permission.

He began with Rosa Lopez and Mary Ann Gerchas, two witnesses they hadn't disclosed earlier, two people with fatal credibility flaws. Gerchas was a con woman and a crook with thirty lawsuits pending against her, most for fraud. The most recent case alleged that she stole a customer's credit card, checked into a hotel, and ran up $20,000 in charges. This was the woman who claimed to see four Hispanic and white men leaving Nicole Brown's house at 10:45 P.M.

"And that is what this lady was trying to tell the police, trying to tell the district attorney," Cochran said of Gerchas. "But they didn't want to listen . . . in this rush to judgment." Gerchas was never called.

Lopez, on the other hand, was apparently the victim of her own greed and the interview tactics of a private investigator named Bill Pavelic, a former LAPD officer. Lopez claimed to see Simpson's Bronco parked in the same place throughout the night, but would later fold like a cheap tent under our questioning.

"They failed to go next door," Cochran said, "and talk to a woman who provided [Simpson] with an alibi." The defense never called Lopez.

Cochran talked about Dr. Ron Fischman, the man who was seen talking to Simpson as Nicole Brown drove away from the piano recital the day she was killed. Again, we had been provided no statement or report about him. Had the defense done so, we could have reminded them that Fischman had told one of Nicole's friends that O. J. said he wasn't finished with Nicole yet. There were other problems with Fischman. He was being investigated by the L.A. County Sheriff's Department for criminal sexual misconduct—a case that was never filed—and his mother's name was on a bottle of Xanax—a prescription antianxiety drug—that Simpson was carrying the day he was finally arrested. If Fischman had given him the drug, it was a possible violation of the California Business and Professions Code and could lead to the termination of his medical license.

Fischman was never called.

Next, Cochran said he would call Michelle Abdurahm, the maid who said Nicole Brown slapped her. If they called her, she would also have to talk about the 1989 incident in which Simpson beat Nicole. She was never called.

When his opening was done, we counted twenty-six separate discovery violations, and Judge Ito penalized the defense for fourteen surprise witnesses. These were the people I described as "heroin addicts, thieves, felons and a court-certified, pathological liar." Ito ruled that the defense couldn't call them until the end of the trial. Yeah, I thought, if they aren't in jail.

By the time Johnnie Cochran was done with his opening statement, there was so much smoke in that courtroom, you couldn't see his mirrors.

Typical of Cochran's opening was his promise of an expert named Dr. Lenore Walker. First, he said, she had watched my opening statement and "has some feelings about this case and about Mr. Darden's remarks." He then went on to say that Walker, and others, felt I offended women when I said that Nicole Brown hadn't worked outside the home. He said that Walker would testify that the level of violence in this case was atypical. "And so, when Walker testifies," Cochran said, "she will talk about the fact that life-threatening violence usually precedes a homicide incident and she does not find that in this case."

Lenore Walker was called the "mother of the battered women's syndrome." By taking the Simpson case, domestic violence advocates said, she had betrayed all the work she'd done earlier. Advocates everywhere denounced her participation in the trial. In October 1994, at a conference at USC, Walker told the audience that "Simpson fits the classic profile of a batterer." She told another psychologist that she wouldn't touch the Simpson case for less than $250,000. After my opening statement, she faxed her notes to Cochran, ending with a personal note: "Smile and tell O. J. he is doing great."

After Cochran's opening, the National Coalition Against Domestic Violence issued a statement saying that Walker's assessment was "a mystery," and that the Simpson relationship was "incredibly typical" of battering relationships. "If Dr. Walker's testimony was accurately represented by Johnnie Cochran," the statement read, "her assessment is absolutely the opposite of the assessment of most battered women's advocates in this country."

We were salivating for the chance to question Walker. Apparently, she had given Simpson a number of tests, and if she was called, the information in those tests would be fair game for us to question her about. And so evidence that might otherwise be lost as hearsay—for instance, Nicole Brown's diary and her frantic telephone call to the Sojourn shelter—would be opened up for questioning.

But the defense never called her either. And the only thing the jury knew about her would come from Cochran's wild opening.

Cochran talked about what a wonderful guy Simpson was, how he helped support Nicole Brown's family and donated money to charity. He called it Simpson's "circle of benevolence." But I'd seen Simpson's tax records for 1991, when he didn't contribute one percent of his million-dollar salary to charity.

"They don't know this man," he said, nodding at our table. "We do."

Yes, I thought, you certainly do.

We sat at the prosecution table, fuming over each slippery word that came out of his mouth and weighing the strategic value of objecting and drawing the jury's attention to what he was saying. Since Hodgman had a smaller role in the case, we decided that he should be the one to handle most of the objections. That way, if he pissed the jury off, they might not hold it against Marcia and me.

Time and time again, Hodgman rose to interrupt Cochran, lodging objections to hearsay, speculation, conjecture, and—primarily—violation of discovery rules. I could see how it wore on him. He wasn't looking well. So Marcia and I began lodging objections as well. By the end of Cochran's rambling speech, we'd lodged about twenty complaints, mostly by Hodgman. He pleaded with Judge Ito to stop what Cochran was doing, this "trial by ambush." A few days later, Ito would give us the chance to rebut many of these "alibi witnesses."

But that day, Judge Ito simply sat there, letting Cochran roll over the bench, the jury, and the system. Great, I thought. With all the inherent problems of a circuslike trial, the last thing we needed was a weak judge.

As we left the courtroom, we received a note from upstairs. Garcetti wanted to see us immediately in his conference room. When we arrived, the entire executive staff was there, seated around Gil's large marble conference table. They were amazed at what Cochran had done. He was their pal, the guy who'd been given more freedom around the office than any other lawyer. They couldn't believe that he'd been so unethical, right there on national television.

Hodgman looked especially upset. He was pale and seemed to be sucking air, as if he'd just finished running a mile. He sat down, stood, sat down, left the room, came back, left, and came back again, red-faced and dizzy.

"I'm not feeling too well," he said. "I'm gonna get some air for a minute." One of the investigators volunteered to go with him.

We were only a few minutes back into the meeting when we heard someone yell, "Come quick! It's Bill!" We jumped from our seats and followed one of the minions down the hall to Cheri Lewis's office.

Hodgman was lying on the floor, disoriented, the color completely gone from his face. It looked as if he was having a heart attack. We cleared some space for him, loosened his collar, and got him into a chair. We made contact with the paramedics, bypassing the 911 frequency so that reporters wouldn't come crawling all over the office. The paramedics took one look at Hodgman and whisked him off to the hospital.

As they raised him up, his eyes caught mine and I smiled grimly. I just knew he was gone from the case. Now it seemed like Marcia and me against that team of nine prominent, ruthless lawyers. The minions stood alongside the wall, watching Hodgman go. They looked as if they were going to cry and I had the sensation of losing a comrade on the battlefield. What were we going to do without Bill's steady and honorable leadership?

Hodgman and I hadn't known each other before this case. We'd occupied many of the same spaces since law school, running alongside each other like parallel lines, but never intersecting. In just a couple of months, I had grown to respect him as much as I did any lawyer I knew. Just a few days earlier, I had teased him that one day he would take a seat as a federal judge because that's where the "proper lawyers" belonged. Now, we watched the elevator doors close and I just hoped that he wasn't dying.

The next morning, Marcia and I went into chambers to tell Ito about Hodgman's condition. It turned out that the stress from the trial and the eighteen-hour days had been wearing on him for some time. The defense lawyers were delighted that he was out of the picture. As we left chambers, Cochran, Douglas, and the others could barely contain themselves.

"We almost killed Hodgman," they joked.

"I guess he couldn't handle your opening statement," Douglas said. They laughed like children, the cold, insensitive bastards.

I walked back into the courtroom as the lawyers milled around, settling before we went back on the record. I saw Cochran sitting there smugly, walked over to his side of the table, leaned down, and spoke clearly and matter-of-factly.

"Just so you assholes understand, no matter what else happens, whether we win or lose, however long this takes, I'm gonna be standing here at the end. I'm gonna be here."

Cochran looked up at me and smiled, his lips peeling back to reveal those bared teeth. "I'm sure you will, my brother."

FOURTEEN

Traffic lurched and surged along the 110 Freeway into the 10 and a few cars broke with me at the Broadway exit, where I curled south at Spring Street. There were people everywhere on the downtown streets. Across Temple, I entered the driveway leading to the courthouse service entrance, below the street level, where deliveries were made each day, where O. J. Simpson arrived each day. Marcia and I were allowed to park in the basement because of the regular death threats and constant media attention. Each car would have to stop at the guard station before being allowed down the service driveway, and so I sat there one day, my car in the middle of the sidewalk, parked behind a truck. I went over, in my mind, the first witnesses we were going to call.

That's when, in my peripheral vision, I saw this brother moving quickly in my direction, bearing down on the driver's side of my car, his eyes locked onto mine. I glanced up at the rearview mirror. There was a car behind me too; I wasn't going anywhere. I thought about rolling up my window but decided against it. We made eye contact again as he arrived at the side of my car.

"Somebody is going to get all of you lying motherfuckers for what you're doing to O. J., you sellout!"

As he gathered himself, I hit the button and the window began humming upward. His head moved back and then forward and then he spat at me, spittle smearing on the window, the side of my face, and all over my suit. In front of me, the truck pulled forward. Disgusted and angry, I wiped at my face with a tissue and drove ahead, easing my car under the Criminal Courts Building.

The threatening telephone calls were still coming in, as were the glares on the freeway and the frothing letters. But whatever was happening outside the courtroom, inside it, we were finally up and moving, presenting our case, one witness, one piece of evidence at a time. As January became February—for one wonderful week—this wasn't a trial about race; it was a murder trial. I could handle the taunts and stares as long as we kept some illusion of justice inside those paneled walls. But that illusion didn't last long; the various perceptions of race were always nearby, ready at any moment to rear back and spit in our faces.

My responsibility was domestic violence, presenting evidence to prove that Simpson was a batterer, to strip away some of the armor that came with his celebrity. This was motive and it was the trickiest part of the case. We just hoped the women on the jury would understand the terror that Nicole Simpson had been put through. We started with the 1989 beating and called the 911 operator, followed by the officer who responded.

Simpson was still angry when Detective John Edwards had arrived in 1989. According to Edwards's testimony, Simpson said, "I don't want that woman in my bed anymore. I've got two other women. . . . You've been here eight times before and now you're going to arrest me?" Edwards testified that Nicole ran out of the bushes, screaming, "He's going to kill me!"

Next, I called Ron Shipp, and when the defense was done with him, race was very much back in this case, shadowing everything it touched.

Shipp was honest and forthright, a friendly, freckled black man who smiled a lot and who worried himself sick over whether to testify against his good friend, O. J. Simpson. "It was eating me up," Shipp said from the stand. "I knew I didn't want to tell you guys and be in this position."

They'd known each other twenty-six years, since someone introduced the starstruck Shipp to O. J. after Simpson won the Heisman Trophy. After Shipp became a cop, he stayed close to Simpson, running errands for him and "doing cop stuff" like researching license plate numbers. After Nicole's 1989 beating, Shipp tried to counsel Simpson, showing him a list of abusive traits. O. J. pointed to a column that read "pathological jealousy" and admitted that he might suffer from that. Shipp and Simpson remained friends, but during that time, Shipp also became Nicole's friend.

During direct examination, I was tough with Shipp about the fact that he brought so many police officers over to meet Simpson, some forty by his own accounting. To me, it showed just how helpless Nicole Brown felt. It must've seemed to her that the entire LAPD was on O. J.'s side.

The night after the murders, Shipp followed Simpson up to O. J.'s bedroom to talk. Simpson asked how long it took for DNA to come back from the lab. A couple of months, Shipp said.

On the stand, the earnest Shipp seemed sorry to repeat what his friend said next. "He kind of jokingly just said, 'You know, to be honest, Shipp, I've had some dreams of killing her.'" We couldn't tell the jury what preceded the dream comment. Simpson had confided to Shipp that the police wanted him to take a lie detector test. In California, such tests are inadmissible, as is any testimony about the tests. The comment was eerily similar to statements Simpson made to LAPD detectives Lange and Vannatter during his initial interview. When they asked him to take a lie detector test, he said that eventually he would. "But it's like, hey, I've got some weird thoughts now. And I've had some weird thoughts—you know, you've been with a person for seventeen years, you think everything."

It was an old ploy for people who feared they were going to flunk a lie detector test—blaming it on "weird thoughts" or dreams, and Simpson was already preparing to send the polygraph needle into spasms.

When I hear people say that Shipp was lying, I want to remind them that he recounted his conversation with Simpson *before* the content of the police interview with Simpson was made public. And more to the point, why would Shipp lie? He made no money on his version of the story; he had no disagreements with Simpson, no angle. He worshipped the man.

I thanked Shipp, left the podium, and sat down at the prosecution table. Marcia's hand rested on my forearm, and she looked up at me and nodded. I nodded back. Ron Shipp had been a strong witness.

But Carl Douglas came after Shipp with the kind of vigor the defense team reserved for blacks in this case, for people who went against what they had decided should be the proper point of view.

"You're not really this man's friend, are you, sir?" Douglas vibrated at the podium, screwing up his face and biting off the end of each word like a kid chewing tart candy. Upstairs, the minions were having a contest to see who could do the best Carl Douglas impersonation—complete with the pools of spit in the corners of their mouths.

In Department 103, Shipp was facing the real thing. Douglas started out with the worst of it. Hadn't Shipp—who was married—been in Simpson's Jacuzzi *with a blond-haired white woman*? I winced. If they could ruin his marriage or his reputation, they were going to do it.

"Did you lie about that, Mr. Shipp?" Douglas asked, with manufactured, Perry Mason inflection.

"This is sad, O. J.," Shipp said at one point, looking at his old friend. "This is really sad."

"You drink a lot, don't you?" Douglas spit.

"I used to," Shipp acknowledged.

Then Douglas repeatedly asked if Shipp was testifying to get attention, perhaps to jump-start a slow acting career.

Shipp scoffed at such ridiculous notions. How would testifying against a friend get him acting jobs? How would it do anything but make him miserable? "There is no way . . . I would sit here, go through all this for an acting career," Shipp snapped. "I could care less about acting!"

The pundits lauded Shipp's testimony and dismissed Douglas as wholly ineffective. (His cross-examination "should be taped and shown in law schools as an example of how not to cross a witness," one professor said.) But the pundits rarely saw this case the way the black community did, the way the jury did. Ron Shipp's credibility was split along racial lines. When we broke for the day, with Shipp still on the stand, I returned to my office and the phone was ringing. It was a black reporter, saying that Shipp was a sellout, a snitch. On the front page of its next issue, the black-owned L.A. newspaper, the *Sentinel*, ran a story about Shipp and Nicole Brown's sister Denise—who had cried as she testified about Simpson brutally beating her sister and who said that O. J. looked "spooky" the day of the murders. Denise also admitted having a drinking problem at one time. "Two Drunks Join O. J.'s Cast of 'Addicts, Liars,'" the *Sentinel's* headline blared.

This was the part of the case that made me crazy, the times when it seemed we were operating under two different sets of values. Black people have always had a strong sense of loyalty and friendship. For people who wanted to believe Simpson was being framed, Shipp made a perfect villain, just as Al Cowlings had made a perfect hero.

"Shipp was also Nicole's friend," I pleaded to people who criticized him. "Doesn't he have a responsibility to her, too? And what about himself? Doesn't he have a responsibility to follow his conscience?"

Shipp's phone was ringing too. Over and over, he fielded calls from angry men who threatened to come over and kill Ron, his wife, and their children. The threats continued for weeks, until Shipp—weary, afraid, and alone—considered moving his family away from L.A.

"You can't let them get to you," I said to him in my office. If anyone could understand what he was going through, it was me. There is nothing more demoralizing than being afraid of your own people, being an outcast in your own community.

"I'm still glad I testified." Shipp shrugged. "But what I don't understand is why people hate me so much for telling the truth."

I had stayed up many nights wondering that. I had wondered it in traffic almost every day, when people glared at me and sometimes followed me. I had wondered every day when the mail came, with more threats, more denigrations of me and my heritage. I took no solace in having Ron's company in this.

"The world is different for us now," I told him. "Things are never going to be the same."

Shipp just nodded and looked away. As they'd done with me, the defense had loaded up on Ron with buzzwords and innuendo. During the N-word argument I had used Simpson's "fetish for blond-haired white women" as an example of the kind of racial tactic that was unethical and shouldn't be used. I had said it with the jury out of the room and still I regretted saying it. During his rebuttal, Cochran had pounced on that phrase as offensive and, in that one instance, he was right. But now, Douglas unapologetically said that Shipp was in a Jacuzzi not just with a woman, but with a *white, blond-haired woman.* And Douglas said it with Shipp's wife watching and the mostly black jury sitting there watching.

These things were like a coded message to the blacks watching the trial. More to the point, it was a warning to anyone courageous enough to testify against O. J. Simpson. They would come after you with everything they had. Circle of benevolence? Hell. It was a circle, all right, and Simpson and his lawyers wanted to make sure it stayed closed, surrounding and insulating O. J. If you broke the circle, if you testified, then any secret he knew about you, any dirt (among a group of people who had their fair share) would be dragged to the surface. They would ruin your marriage and your career, and put your life in danger if it meant helping their case. They would dig at your deepest insecurities and pick off scabs that covered deep wounds.

On February 2, after two days on the stand, Ron Shipp finished testifying and walked wearily out of the courtroom. After he was gone, I remained motivated by his courage and by his words, which cut through Douglas's theatrics and hung in the air like an echoing rifle shot, reminding us why we were supposed to be there.

"I'm doing this for my conscience, my peace of mind," he said. "I will not have the blood of Nicole on Ron Shipp. I can sleep at night—unlike a lot of others."

Faye Resnick wore a shimmery, off-white suit and shoes made to match, tied with a sort of macramé shoestring. She had it going—that distinctive Southern California knack of looking posed at every moment, with her perfect square jaw, perfect full lips, and perfect blown hair.

The woman knew her way around a mirror.

Early in our case, as we put on witnesses of domestic violence, Faye Resnick was the kind of witness we should've been able to put on the stand. Attractive and intelligent, she had been Nicole's confidante and had heard not only stories of abuse from Nicole, but threats from O. J.

In some ways, Faye would have been a problematic witness no matter what (because of her admitted drug use), but it wasn't until she wrote a book that she became completely useless to the prosecution. There are few witnesses worse than someone who has profited because of her testimony.

Faye came in to talk to us in December, after hiding out for a couple of months in Vermont, writing *Nicole Brown Simpson: The Private Diary of a Life Interrupted* with a cowriter from the *National Enquirer*. Faye and her boyfriend—a chiropractor named Christian Reichardt—had planned from the beginning to keep their inside information and bikini-rich photographs from the prosecution until after they'd made some money. In the end, she went on without Reichardt, writing a 244-page book full of juicy dish ("O. J. . . . was one of the fastest cocksmen in town") and insights into Faye's and Nicole's West Hollywood/Beverly Hills set ("Breast implants have come a long way").

Much of what was in the book would have been hearsay (inadmissible, secondhand conversations) but Faye had heard and seen things herself that would've been useful on the stand. In any other case—say, if O. J. was a car salesman or a roofer—Faye might have been up there, telling us about the Simpsons' stormy relationship. She would have testified that not only did O. J. tell Nicole he was going to kill her, he told Faye the same thing, during a telephone conversation in April, weeks before the murders. From her book:

He cut me off. "If she's really serious about this, and I find her with another man before August, *I'll kill her.*"
"Whoa, O. J., what are you saying?"
 "I can't take this, Faye, I can't take this. I mean it. *I'll kill that bitch.*"

In that instance, Faye's version of events was backed up by her ex-boyfriend, Reichardt. Even though he remained loyal to Simpson, he corroborated Faye's story; she had told him that Simpson had threatened to kill Nicole days before the murders.

There were several other witnesses like Resnick, people who had been paid for their stories, like the friend of Ron Goldman who sold this story to the tabloids: He and Goldman had been at a Starbucks coffeehouse with Nicole a few weeks before the murders, when Simpson drove up and saw them. It would have been an important prosecution point, to show that Simpson knew both the victims and had seen them together before. But that too was lost.

It was especially painful to turn on the television and see someone like Jill Shively, the woman who said she saw Simpson run a red light near Nicole's house, just minutes after the murders. We could put her on the stand, but the defense had only to ask one question: "Is it true that you were paid $5,000 by a tabloid television program to say that you saw Mr. Simpson that night?" Worse, she'd denied being paid for her story earlier. Our case was being sold out from under us, a C-note at a time. I can imagine no case has ever lost as much testimony that way.

It is virtually impossible to compete with the media in a case like this. They were offering thousands of dollars; we were offering the chance to be humiliated as Shipp and Denise Brown had been humiliated, to be carved up by ruthless defense lawyers while Ito looked on.

Already, we were fighting Simpson's close circle of friends, people like Robert Kardashian, who protected and shielded him. Those people weren't about to testify, especially after Shipp had been made into an example. The words that had almost kept Shipp off the stand—"I didn't want to be known as the one who nailed O. J."—reverberated throughout Simpson's circle. Even someone on the fringe of the circle, like Jennifer Peace—the porn actress whom Cowlings told that Simpson was guilty—said she didn't want to be *the one* to tip the scales against Simpson.

Even Simpson's ex-wife Marguerite remained loyal to him. We hoped to call her about incidents in the 1970s in which two police officers recalled her telling them that Simpson had beaten her, once leaving marks on her neck. She seemed to be in hiding for weeks, moving without a forwarding address, lying as low as she could. It took us weeks to find her, living in a Fullerton apartment with her new husband, who was driving a BMW apparently leased to Simpson's daughter Arnelle. A D.A.'s investigator came up with a plan to serve Marguerite with a subpoena while Marcia and I tried to convince her to talk to us. He knocked on her door and told her husband that someone might have burglarized his car. While he was gone, the investigator served her with a subpoena and Marcia and I appeared at their door and asked Marguerite if she would talk to us.

"This is chickenshit," she said. "I would've talked to you." But she didn't. Her attorney tried to quash the subpoena, saying that our conduct had been outrageous. And Marguerite went public and claimed that O. J. Simpson had never abused her. The circle was drawing closer and tighter.

Even with all the obstacles, we still had a strong case. But it was weakened more when Judge Lance Ito penalized us for our own discovery violations. In December, when we'd presented our groundbreaking domestic violence motion, it had included witnesses that the defense said were surprises. Still more than a month before trial, and two, three, or four months before those witnesses were to be called, we didn't see it as a violation. They had plenty of time to investigate those people. To me, it was completely different from the defense team's blatant discovery violation. They intentionally hid witnesses from us until the day before opening statements. We were giving them witnesses just as quickly as we developed them.

But Ito penalized us anyway, in a form that was unprecedented. He decided that these "new" witnesses couldn't be called until the end of the trial, effectively breaking up our domestic violence evidence and our attempt to painstakingly paint the abusive nature of the Simpsons' relationship. Of course, by the time we got to the end of our case, it had dragged on and it would have been torture to submit the jury to more domestic violence evidence. And it was clear the jurors hadn't been convinced the first time around. In effect, those witnesses were lost to us. He delayed the surprise defense witnesses until later in the trial, but the defense wasn't even putting on a case until later in the trial!

I have prosecuted a lot of cases and I fully understand the flow of judicial decisions—some for you, some against. Admittedly, many rulings went our way early on, such as the admissibility of domestic violence evidence and the dream Simpson confided to Shipp. Yet the decision to force some of our witnesses to the end of our case was incredible. It was too severe and it undermined our ability to put on a case. Given the problems with witnesses who sold their stories to the media and with witnesses who refused to "betray" O. J., it was just one more erosion of a case that was in danger of sliding downhill, away from us.

The Akita's bark was strange that June night—sharp and persistent, faster and louder than usual, a "plaintive wail" to the screenwriter Pablo Fenjves who heard it. He recalled hearing the dog about fifteen minutes into the ten o'clock news, the same time another woman heard it from her bed. Across the street, Elsie Tistaert looked out her window and saw the Akita pacing back and forth in front of Nicole Brown's gate. She called the police, but they weren't interested in a loose, noisy dog. A few minutes before eleven, Steven Schwab was walking his own dog when he came across the Akita, still barking and pacing nervously. The dog edged along with Schwab, barking and pointing his nose down alleys and corridors, as if he had been looking for something in the shadows. It wasn't until Schwab got the dog home that he noticed the dog's white belly was matted with red and his paws were also dipped in blood.

Schwab asked his neighbor, Sukru Boztepe, to keep the dog overnight, but the Akita sniffed and scratched at the door, as if he wanted out. And so Boztepe decided to take the dog for a walk to calm him down. The dog pulled and tugged him down the street and Boztepe followed, down Bundy to a white gate, propped open and revealing a dark tile walkway. Boztepe looked at the dog's eyes and then followed the dog's gaze ten feet along the walkway, to an open gate and, finally, to a woman's body, seemingly floating in that slick of deep, pooled blood.

"Is that what you saw?" Marcia Clark asked, as a photograph of Nicole Brown's body—prostrate at the base of the stairs, drained of her life—flashed on the seven-foot screen in the courtroom.

O. J. Simpson turned away. Denise Brown wiped her eyes; Tanya Brown covered hers. Kim Goldman began crying. The jurors looked on impassively.

Yes, Sukru Boztepe said on the witness stand, that's what he'd seen, the dog's owner, Nicole Brown, cut and slashed to death. "I saw a lady, laying down," he said, "full of blood."

When Boztepe ran next door to get help, Elsie Tistaert saw him outside and called the police again. She said there was an intruder in the neighborhood.

West L.A. Division police officer Ron Riske showed up, looking for an intruder. Instead, the neighbors showed him Nicole Brown's body. It was so dark in the walkway, it took him a few seconds to notice Ron Goldman's body, lying just a few feet from Nicole. One of Goldman's eyes was open and so Riske checked him for a pulse, but found none. He found Goldman's pager near his body, along with an envelope containing the glasses of Juditha Brown—Nicole's mother. There was blood everywhere, drops along the walkway, smears near the steps, pools at the base, bloody shoeprints leading away. Near Goldman's body, Riske also saw a knit cap and one bloody leather glove. He was careful not to disturb anything. He and his partner called for backup and then stepped gingerly over Nicole's body and up the stairs.

The door to the three-story condo was open. Riske and his partner "cleared the house," carefully searching each room. On one wall, they noticed photos of O. J. Simpson. The workout room and the hallway were lit; the other rooms were dark. The young officer stuck his head into the bathroom, which flickered with candles that had been lit next to a drawn bath. Nicole's two children were in bed, safe. Riske woke them and took them out the garage door and through the back gate, where he noticed more blood drops.

He also noticed a cup of melting ice cream: Ben & Jerry's Chocolate Chip Cookie Dough, sitting on a banister.

"Did any police officer take photographs of the melting ice cream?" Cochran asked, looking down his nose at Riske.

No, the police officer said. He didn't think so.

And so came the introduction of the "ice cream defense," in which the Dream Team purported that the ice cream hadn't melted enough for the murders to have occurred more than two hours before police arrived. The LAPD, the theory went, hadn't taken any pictures of the ice cream because of its "rush to judgment." It was a ridiculous theory, but on February 9, after a string of what Marcia and I called "dog bark witnesses," it was the defense team's best shot at suggesting that the murders were committed later than 10:30 P.M. Cochran contended that the still somewhat-frozen ice cream proved that Nicole was still snacking after 11 P.M., while Simpson was already on the way to the airport.

That day, we were bombarded with faxes, letters, and diagrams, perhaps a hundred in all, just about the ice cream defense. It was the kind of thing that happened every day, correspondence from all over the country—crackpots, lawyers, celebrities, and just common folks trying to help us out. The ice cream defense was one of those topics that brought out all sorts of legal advisers.

There were tips that the chocolate chip cookie dough ice cream was actually her son Justin's flavor and that Nicole had actually ordered *rain forest crunch*. A guy in Illinois conducted an experiment ("I chose the wavy gravy flavor. . . . Note firmly supported pencil after five hours melt time at 70 degrees Fahrenheit") and included photos of his work: two tubs of ice cream on either side of a stopwatch hanging from a thermostat. A local newspaper conducted a similar experiment.

"I couldn't sleep," one letter began. "This 'ice cream testimony' is really bothering me." A woman from Ontario, Canada, told us about her husband accidentally leaving an ice cream cake in an unplugged freezer and about many parties when she served ice cream. A Colorado lawyer faxed "sequential photos . . . taken during testing of Ben & Jerry's Ice Cream for melting time" and an Oceanside, California, attorney wrote how his stepson microwaved ice cream.

"In the event you plan to conduct any tests of melting ice cream," another man wrote, "please consider that the contents of the ice cream cup could have been yogurt, which may have a longer melting time."

"The chemical composition of modern ice creme [sic] has a much slower melt," another woman wrote. "A few days ago, I suggested you hire a dog expert. . . . Today, I suggest you get a home economics expert who knows about ice creme [sic]. These kinds of experts would impress the jury."

"If Nicole was like I am, after a big meal, I couldn't eat an entire bowl of ice cream right away," wrote one woman, who suggested that Nicole put the stuff in the freezer and then got it out again later. "I know that I . . . would refreeze it until I could enjoy it when everything had calmed down."

It was times like that I realized I had no idea where this trial had come from. It was so far removed from reality—even in Los Angeles— that it was all I could do to come to work every day. There is so much to think about during a trial, without imagining the whole world watching over your shoulder, shaking their heads when you misspoke, cursing when you screwed up. The defense was hurling out bizarre theories like conspiracy buffs at a UFO gathering. They had a defense that claimed Simpson was hitting golf balls at ten-thirty at night! That he bled all over his own house and Bronco because of golf injuries! That the entire LAPD framed an innocent man! That Central American drug dealers were on the loose in Brentwood, cutting the throats of innocent people! That a cup of ice cream proved Simpson couldn't be the murderer! Maybe it was a sign of real trouble; with all the evidence and motive, with two butchered young people, the world was concerned about ice cream.

Eleven cars, two vans, and one bus—each with a number taped to the passenger-side window—caterpillared through Brentwood, on the official O. J. Simpson crime scene tour. The jurors were on the bus, the legal teams in separate vans, and most of the cars were filled with cops, including the one that carried O. J. Simpson. Twenty additional motor-cycle cops escorted the caravan, while four police helicopters flitted over-head. Two hundred police officers were combing Brentwood, as well as one bomb-sniffing dog. Hundreds of curious people craned their necks at each stop, hoping to get a look at Simpson or at one of the lawyers. They jammed the streets with their cars, leaned out over patios, and cov-ered every sidewalk.

It was Sunday morning, February 12, one of those incredible, sunny Southern California days, and we were taking the unusual step of giving the jurors a walk-through of the crime scene. The deal had been made days earlier and our way had been prepared in true trial-of-the-century fashion. The day before, the freeways had been cleared and cops had gone through Brentwood, preparing the neighborhood for takeover.

The bus stopped for a couple of minutes outside Ron Goldman's apartment, on Gorham Avenue and San Vicente, then drove two blocks to Mezzaluna, the restaurant where Goldman worked and where Nicole Brown ate her last meal.

A little after ten, we inched our way down the gently curved Bundy Drive and stopped in front of Nicole Brown's condominium. The jurors climbed off the bus like tourists, dressed in casual, weekend clothes. One man wore a San Francisco 49ers cap—one of the teams Simpson had played for before his retirement. We took them through the Bundy crime scene in groups of four jurors and a lawyer from each side. The rules were simple: We couldn't talk, they couldn't talk as we led them past important spots marked with signs showing where the bodies had been found, where Simpson's blood drops were found.

Simpson declined the opportunity to revisit the scene of the mur-ders and he sat outside in a police car.

I followed a group of jurors single-file through the six-foot white iron gate to the landing beneath the cement steps where Nicole Brown's body had been found. Pinched in by the foliage on one side, the steps on another, and the iron bars on two sides—we called it the cage—the area wasn't big enough for more than one killer, as the defense contended, and we hoped the jurors would understand that. But the jurors didn't take many notes and simply looked around matter-of-factly. They peeked inside the condo—which was empty and for sale—and then they were ready to move on. To O. J. Simpson's house on Rockingham Avenue.

Cheri Lewis had already argued in court that some things in Simpson's house would be prejudicial to jurors, and we all worried that they would be unduly impressed by Simpson's wealth and achievements; for instance, by his huge trophy room. Besides, what relevance could a trophy room have to a murder case? The jurors needed to see relevant places: where the chauffeur was sitting when he saw Simpson, where the glove was found. Instead, Ito took them on a tour.

The legal rule was that both locations remain as close to their condition on June 12 as possible. But when we got to 360 North Rockingham Avenue, it was incredible. Paula Barbieri's photo was prominently displayed in the foyer, near Simpson's mom's picture and other family photographs. In the bedroom, a new Bible had been placed on the table next to the bed. There were books over the fireplace in Simpson's bedroom, including Scott Turow's *Presumed Innocent.*

"Nice touch," I said quietly. I was surprised they hadn't put on some subtle subliminal background music—perhaps NWA's "Fuck Tha Police." We complained to Ito about the changes in the house, but the tour went on.

O. J. Simpson's house had four television sets, a bar, and a game room. Over the bar were pictures of Simpson with a buffet of celebrities and prominent people, from Bing Crosby to J. Edgar Hoover. The grounds were immaculate, like a park, and I doubt if there was a gram of dust in the whole house. I watched my group of jurors closely. Were they getting it? Were they seeing how easy it would've been for Simpson to drop that glove on the walkway? Were they seeing how easy it would have been for the limousine driver, Allan Park, to see Simpson moving mysteriously outside his house? Could they envision him racing around, trying to wash the blood off?

No. They were sightseeing—a bunch of middle-class people looking at the Ferrari, the Jacuzzi, the pool, the maid, and the cook. And they were probably thinking, "No one would piss all this away by murdering his ex-wife."

All afternoon, O. J. Simpson had been standing on the grounds, proudly pointing out features of his house to polite cops. For a while, he stood in the front yard, where his lawyers claimed he'd been "hitting golf balls" as the murders occurred. We had been told that he would be wearing restraints and an electronic device on this trip, which would allow the deputies to give him an electric shock if he tried to run away. But he wasn't wearing anything like that.

I sat down on a bench just outside his front door, and Simpson leaned forward and pointed at me. "Get off my bench!" he began yelling. "I don't want you on my bench or in my house!"

I turned to Cochran, who stood nearby. "Johnnie, you better restrain your client before I have him muzzled."

As evening approached and the viewing ended, all the lawyers gathered in a circle outside, in the garden. Marcia was trying to lodge objections on the record. But Ito was becoming irritated—as he did often with Marcia—because he couldn't hear her soft voice. We all gathered around, trying to hear, pulling closer and closer. I leaned forward, into the circle, to hear what she was saying.

And then I felt a nudge. I looked up. Simpson was standing next to me, his hands in his pants pockets. He bumped me again.

Asshole! I nudged him back. Then we sort of locked shoulders and bumped each other back and forth, leaning on each other like horned sheep. No one else seemed to notice. I got the message. I could see right through him, right to the evil, and he didn't like it. The battle was just beginning.

Marcia was rolling—her wide-set, bullet eyes trained on the witness, Officer Riske. Tell us about your training at the police academy in crime scenes, she said.

"They kind of gloss over it," said Riske, suddenly making his name seem all too fitting. "They don't really train you."

For a defense based on corrupt and sloppy police work, it must've looked like a ten-mile-an-hour fastball, fat over the plate. Two weeks into testimony, the police were playing into the Dream Team's hands.

Cochran didn't disappoint. His entire cross-examination was funneled through that one answer. Riske admitted using the phone in the kitchen, thereby losing the chance to hit the redial button and find out the last person Nicole had called. He fumbled over the ice cream and the candles and testified that he had no training regarding DNA sensitivity.

By that point, February 14, our case was probably as strong as it would get—at least until the scientific evidence was presented. Through domestic violence witnesses, we'd shown that Simpson was controlling and violent; that he beat Nicole in 1989 and stalked her afterward; that on the day she was killed, he was frightening and moody. We'd given them the dream conversation of Ron Shipp and the poignant tears of Denise Brown. We'd successfully pinpointed the time of the murders to around ten-fifteen, giving Simpson more than enough time to catch his flight. We had foreshadowed the blood and fiber evidence.

The defense had picked at our witnesses, trying to soften the focus of their memories or to discredit them completely. But they held up well.

But now came the critical point in the trial. The police. From Riske to the crime lab workers to the lead detectives, Tom Lange and Phil Vannatter, all defense roads led through Mark Fuhrman.

Cochran had shown where he was headed with Riske. His cross had been long-winded and beside the point, asking Riske questions that he knew—and Judge Ito should have known—weren't relevant for a patrol officer with no homicide training. It was like putting a high school science teacher on the stand and grilling him about nuclear fusion reactors to show how ill-trained he was. Cochran's voice dripped with sarcasm and condescension. The end result was that officers like Riske were on the stand for five or six days, carefully answering questions they should have just dismissed.

Just once I wished one of the cops would roll his eyes and say, "That's the dumbest question I've ever heard." But the defense team had the LAPD so uptight, they marched in like lambs to the slaughter. I couldn't believe it. These were tough, capable cops. Why were they letting the defense do this?

Tom Lange was the twenty-sixth witness to take the stand. Tom was an interesting guy. He had one speed: slow. It was impossible to shake the guy. As in most good detective teams I'd seen, Lange really complemented his partner, Phil Vannatter. Lange was serious and honest, a family man who didn't get lost in his job. Marcia and I were relieved when he took the stand.

He and Vannatter had shown up at the murder scene about two-twenty in the morning and he described the conclusions he reached from the positions of the bodies. For instance, since there was no blood on Nicole Brown's feet, he deduced that she'd been disabled before she was killed. A dug-out area in the dirt made Lange believe that Ron Goldman had stood his ground there and fought his attacker.

Marcia and I differed on our direct examination style. Sometimes I believed she took too long, setting up tedious bits of foundation when jurors—like everyone else—were ready to move along. But she did a great job with Lange, showing him to be the consummate professional, a veteran of 250 murder investigations.

And then we turned him over to Cochran, who didn't ask questions, really. He accused.

I thought Lange should react with outrage to the allegations of planting evidence, that he should point out how impossible it would have been to plant blood and a glove. When Cochran suggested the victim's hands should have been individually bagged by the coroner, I hoped he would have let the jury know how ridiculous that was. But he didn't. Like the cops who had gone before him, Lange answered in that monotone that lent credence to the ridiculous line of questioning.

Later, when Cochran began tossing out questions about "Colombian neckties"—brutal throat-slashing murders practiced by drug dealers—it was too much for me. Lange answered carefully, as if there really was some chance Colombian drug lords had ordered Nicole and Ron killed. Early in Lange's testimony, on February 22, I sat in my office with Runyon, complaining that the police officers weren't standing up for themselves. They hadn't done anything wrong and yet they were coming off looking guilty. These guys were my friends and I couldn't stand to see them pounded every day like this.

"Yeah," Runyon said, "but what can you do?"

I had been getting telephone calls from every television show on the dial, it seemed, but I had turned them all down. Geraldo Rivera had a nighttime cable talk show devoted exclusively to the trial, and I recently had called Rivera's producer, asking about a tape I wanted. I looked down at my desk and saw the producer's number.

When someone answered, I introduced myself and asked to talk to Rivera. He was on the air, filming his live show.

"Hello, hello," I said. "Is this the Arsenio Hall show?"

Rivera couldn't believe his journalistic scoop: the moody, reserved, black prosecutor, only on *Geraldo!*

"I would like the officers to be a bit more aggressive," I said. "They're answering the questions being put to them by the defense and some of the questions, I think, are a bit ridiculous. And I just wish they'd point that out to the jury sometimes."

Runyon laughed and stared at me as if I were crazy. I was going to catch hell for this, telling our witnesses on live TV to toughen up. But I was tired of this case being run by the aggressive defense lawyers. Judge Ito had proved to be no help and so I was ready to stand up to them myself. We needed to fight these bastards, to let the world know that they were trying to confuse and befuddle this case, to win by distracting the jury away from the truth. Their case was a wild spaghetti of theories and racial insinuations thrown against the wall, and some of it was bound to stick.

The trial was dragging weeks behind schedule, with the jury out of the room for days at a time while we argued ridiculous motions. Months of preparation, motions, and arguments had already taken their toll. While the rest of the world thought the Simpson trial began January 24, Marcia, I, and the other lawyers and clerks had been working nonstop for six, seven, eight months. By February, we spent fewer and fewer hours at home, usually just enough to get five or six hours' sleep.

I hadn't been to a grocery store since November and there were only stale coffee and bottled water in my refrigerator. A mountain of mail sat unopened on my dining room table, atop newspapers still folded crisply. Phone messages were backed up like L.A. traffic, old friends stuck behind Hollywood agents offering to sign me up and cranks threatening to kill me.

Sometimes, I just ran out of gas and overslept—a fitful, edgy sleep. That's what happened the day after I called Geraldo Rivera. I woke up late. Fortunately, Lange was still on the stand and he was Marcia's witness. I flipped on the nine-inch television in time to see Gil Garcetti on the *CBS Morning Show.*

"If we wind up with a hung jury in this case," he said, "I'll tell you right now, if the case is eleven to one in favor of acquittal—which would be a shock to me, if that happens—we will retry the case."

Oh boy! I knew immediately how that would play. The press would take it as a sign that we were already whipped, that we couldn't get a conviction, even before our strong physical evidence was presented. As I dressed for work, I could feel the pressure building, the noose tightening even as I pulled a tie into a knot around my throat.

I pulled my coat on and stared at the telephone. I dialed Jenee's number up in Oakland. I knew she'd already left for school, but sometimes it just felt good to dial that number, to hear her voice on her answering machine. I laughed as I heard the corny message she'd recorded, with some awful rap song in the background. I didn't leave a message. I just smiled, hung up, and drove to work.

Tom Lange was on day five of his testimony. I had tried entire murder cases that didn't last five days. Cochran asked ridiculous questions, fishing for information about whether Faye Resnick had ever lived at the condo, what nine-year-old Sydney had said to officers, questions that were hearsay or otherwise improper. I sat there, thinking about judges like Andy Weiss, who would've had a foot-dragging, manipulative lawyer like Cochran for lunch. Ito just sat there, perhaps admiring the collection of hourglasses his "fans" had sent him.

Marcia objected several times, but Cochran just kept going, the way he had with all the cops, asking ridiculous questions. Finally, we ended up at one of the endless sidebars, where Marcia complained about Cochran's questioning.

"They obviously haven't tried any cases in a long time," Cochran said, "and obviously don't know how, but this is cross-examination."

For weeks, Cochran had been making such demeaning remarks about us, while Ito sat there, entranced by Johnnie. I didn't blame Cochran. He was a defense attorney; it was his job to get away with as much as he could. But it was Ito's job to admonish Cochran, to instill order in the trial instead of allowing it to veer like a runaway bus. A competent judge would've controlled the case.

I asked Ito, "Who is he talking about, doesn't know how to try a case?"

Then I said, "Is he the only lawyer who knows how to try a case?" just as Ito simultaneously said, "Wait, Mr. Darden."

And then Judge Ito snapped. "I'm going to hold you in contempt!"

"I should be held in contempt," I shot back. "I have sat here and listened to this four weeks of aimless, inappropriate questioning."

"Mr. Darden, I'm warning you."

"This cross-examination is out of order," I said. "We will be here until September."

And then Ito angrily ordered the jury out of the courtroom and ran up the stairs to his bench like a sulking child. I respect Lance Ito. He is a nice man and a caring individual. But he surrendered the gavel to the defense in this case, perhaps out of fear that—as a former prosecutor—he would be open to criticism after the case. I don't know why, I only know he allowed a three-month trial to turn into a year-long joke.

When we all had returned to our seats, Judge Ito addressed me. He had threatened me with contempt, and even he knew that he'd gone too far. But, if he backed down, it would be yet another challenge to his authority.

"Mr. Darden," he said, "let me give you a piece of advice. Take about three deep breaths, as I'm going to do, and then contemplate what you're going to say next. You want to take a recess now for a moment?"

He was offering me a way out, but I wasn't about to turn back to the trial we'd been having, in which we put witnesses on for two hours and Cochran badgered them for two days. "I don't require a recess, Your Honor."

His lips tightened. I was calling his bluff. Now we moved on to the process that every lawyer knew in the back of his mind, the dance of contempt, in which a lawyer was tried, usually for some violation of trial ethics or protocol. But, as far as I was concerned, there were no ethics or protocol in this case. It was a travesty, and I was willing to pay a fine or go to jail to make my point.

"I'll hear your comment at this point," Judge Ito said. "I've cited you. Do you have any response?"

I said I wanted a lawyer.

Behind me, I heard the church-deep voice of Wyoming lawyer Gerry Spence, one of the many lawyers making a small fortune analyzing this case. I'd had a few conversations with Spence, and he was one of the few pundits I actually liked. He slammed his notebook down and muttered something under his breath, and it was clear he didn't like what I was doing.

"Mr. Spence," Ito said, "we don't need your comments."

Ito looked as if he'd swallowed a lemon. I wasn't going to back down. "You can have counsel," he said. "Do you want to have somebody from your appellate division come down?"

Next to me, Marcia stood up. The prosecution's concern was that the jury was being allowed to hear "slop," she said. I watched her and realized that, as she talked, she was taking off her jewelry.

It was a subtle move, letting Judge Ito know that if I went to jail, she was going with me. I watched her admiringly. "Cool," I said under my breath. It was the kind of thing you did for a partner and, at that moment, we were full partners.

Ito gave us ten minutes to go upstairs and confer with management. Gil was visibly upset. He thought I'd used profanity or something. I hadn't. I hadn't even raised my voice. We knew that Ito wanted a graceful way out of the mess he'd made, an apology probably, but I wasn't about to apologize. I had done nothing wrong. Maybe he had to punish me to realize that Cochran had been out of control for weeks.

Someone from media relations told me how the reporters and pundits were playing the argument at the bench, saying that I was losing my composure, buckling under pressure. They connected the contempt to my call to Geraldo Rivera and Garcetti's public statements that we would retry Simpson if the jury hung as signs that the stress was getting to the prosecution team.

"Screw 'em," I said. They had no idea what had happened at the sidebar. Ito was the one who had snapped. Somewhere, even Judge Ito knew this trial was spinning out of control and he just lost it.

Judge Ito's clerk said the judge demanded our presence. "Now." When we returned, Ito was already on the bench. "You seem to have two options," the judge said. "Either you offer an apology to the court and we proceed or we proceed to a contempt hearing. Those are your choices." He offered us a chance to look at the transcript. The things Ito and I had said simultaneously had been separated, so that it appeared as if he'd warned me first.

Marcia pulled me aside. "Apologize."

"Hell no."

"He's got you cold. This makes it look like he warned you. It ain't worth it, G." I'd been teaching Marcia some common phrases from the 'hood, like G, shorthand for gangster.

"I'm telling you," she said, pulling at my sleeve. "Apologize. That's all you can do." Otherwise, she said, it would be on my state bar record. Besides, I'd made my point. Her eyes softened and she cocked her head the way she did when she needed to convince me of something.

I looked back up at the judge. "I don't know."

At the bench, Ito pleaded with me. "Look, I'll tell you what: You apologize to me and I'll apologize to you and then we can move on. It's the best I can do. It's up to you."

Upstairs, the minions were splayed about the television set, ponying up cash for my bail. "Don't do it!" they said to the TV. "Don't apologize!"

I apologized. Then he apologized and, like a couple of third-graders, we went back out to the playground.

In the gallery, Gerry Spence smiled and gave me the thumbs-up. I had made my point. And while the pundits and armchair lawyers called me immature and petty, I had made an important stand. That night, I slept well for the first time in weeks. Finally, we were fighting back. And Marcia was there at my side. If Judge Ito felt compelled to hand the courtroom over to the defense team, so be it. But I wasn't about to hand our case over with it.

Since my early days as a lawyer, I had been advised to keep my emotions in check. Well, that wasn't me. And it never had been. I was outraged by the murders of Ron and Nicole. I was outraged by the cynical games the defense played and by the smug, circular denials of O. J. Simpson. I was outraged by police officers who allowed the Dream Team to walk over them and by a judge who refused to hold order in his courtroom.

A cruel, double murderer was on the verge of going free and I wasn't about to hide my disgust, my humanity, behind a law degree. I was going to keep fighting.

FIFTEEN

It was a relationship by Post-it note, two overworked lawyers exchanging strategy, support, and sarcasm on legal pads that we slid back and forth across the prosecution table. Pressed into an impossible case with unbearable scrutiny, Marcia Clark and I quickly moved from professional respect to deep friendship. Beneath cameras that never blinked, with millions of people watching, we kept a running log of our impressions of the trial and of each other.

"Too complicated," I wrote during some defense testimony about blood found under Nicole Brown's fingernails. "Even [Juror] 1233 stopped writing."

Marcia answered underneath my note. "I don't know if that's good or bad news—i.e., they already believe the evidence is all fucked-up."

I scribbled back on the lined, yellow page. "Note: The glass is half full. Plus, we gotta clean up with DNA. You know that."

Our trial methods differed. I was more direct and relied more on emotion and improvisation. Marcia's strength was preparation: When she drafted questions for a witness, she sometimes wrote down the answer she expected too. Her notes looked like movie scripts, mine like shopping lists.

"Pick it up," I wrote to her. "Slow Down!" she carved into a Post-it note, so that the next twenty notes were embossed with the same message. "Asked and answered!" we wrote when a defense lawyer was rambling.

Prosecutors develop a cynical shorthand with each other during trial. In our correspondence, we called Cochran "JC." F. Lee Bailey was "Flea," and Simpson was, simply, "Asshole."

While we were waiting to start or just sitting during tangential testimony, the notes between Marcia and me became more personal: "Do
you have to make me laugh when the cameras are on us?" Marcia asked
once. "Do you wish to have another baby?" she wrote another time.
"Were you in Richmond when [Jenee] was a baby?" I wrote yes to all
those questions.

We were working ourselves sick and no one else could really understand. When you're laboring eighty hours a week on national television,
second-guessed by every pin-striped suit in the country, there are few
people who can really sympathize. Two people exposed to that pressure
are going to become close friends, and we did almost immediately.

"I have been awake since 4:30 A.M., approx.," I scratched one day,
after she asked what was wrong.

"Why? What's going on?"

"I think about the case all the time."

"You should call me," Marcia wrote back, "so at least we can talk and
use the time wisely."

Marcia had the reputation as the toughest woman in the CCB and
she could use her 100 pounds to unleash a string of profanities that
would quiet a dock full of longshoremen. But after a few months on the
Simpson case, I began to see something few people ever saw: the vulnerable side of Marcia Clark.

Once while questioning a witness, I looked up to see her body
turned completely so that her back was to the jury, so that she was facing Scott Gordon. It seemed rude of her to check out while I questioned a witness. After all, I paid attention to her interminably long
direct examinations. When Judge Ito called that day for his favorite pas-
time, a sidebar, I noticed that Marcia wasn't budging. I leaned over. "Are
you coming or what?"

That's when she looked up at me and I could see that she was crying.
She got up and left the courtroom, still shielding her hollow, triangular
face. When I came back from the sidebar, Scott was sitting there alone,
and I asked him what had happened.

"It's complicated," Scott said. But after court that day, I saw what
she was crying about. At first, I had been oblivious to the tabloids' coverage of the trial. But I'd watched during the last few months as they
created scandals out of her two divorces, splitting her life open for the

world to see. "Marcia Clark's Suicide Ordeal!" "Marcia's Dirty Divorce!" "Marcia Clark's Wild Private Life and the Men She's Left Behind!"

Marcia's last husband, Gordon, seemed to have fueled many of the stories. A square-faced computer operator, Gordon seemed to be on every checkout stand, describing Marcia with words like "depressed" and "suicidal." But that was just the preview of what he had in mind: allegations that Marcia wasn't paying attention to her children anymore because of the trial. On February 27, 1995, in the heart of the trial, during the most stressful time in Marcia Clark's life, her ex-husband sued for custody of their two sons.

As a tabloid television reporter said of Gordon, "Keeping those feelings private has been a challenge, when your wife is in the trial of the century."

It's especially challenging when tabloids are willing to pay $50,000 for a good scandal, as in Gordon's case. He pushed for a quick hearing on the custody issue, likely hoping that Marcia would pay him a settlement rather than have her past dredged up by a bitter ex-husband. Eight months of constant work and worry were bad enough without having Marcia's scorned ex-husband spreading nasty gossip about her to anyone with a corporate checkbook. He hinted in stories that if Marcia received a big payoff from the trial, he ought to be entitled to some of it.

In late February, while we were arguing over Simpson's disastrous alibi witness, Rosa Lopez, Marcia insisted that she had to leave court one Friday afternoon to be with her children. Cochran accused her of using her children as an excuse because she wasn't ready to deal with Lopez in court that day.

Later, Marcia's ex-husband told reporters that Cochran was right and that he had the children that night.

Marcia couldn't believe it. Yes, Gordon was supposed to have the children, and that was precisely why she needed to leave early, because she'd promised her boys that she would see them before they went away for the weekend. She had warned the judge earlier that day that she couldn't work late, and Ito seemed sensitive to her need to leave at five-thirty. Marcia lashed out at Cochran for accusing her of lying about her desire to see her children: "I'm offended as a woman, as a single mother and a prosecutor."

I was more disgusted with Gordon Clark. What kind of person would torture someone he'd once loved that way? What kind of person would leave a tabloid record like that for his children to read? He seemed to be taking complete advantage of the situation, hoping that, to avoid embarrassment during the trial, Marcia would pay him off *and* give him custody of the children.

There seemed to be no limits on the coverage of Marcia's private life. After court that day, when she left crying, I stood in the hallway, looking at a tabloid that had published fifteen-year-old topless photographs of Marcia with her first husband on a nude beach in France.

"Hey." I stuck my head in her office. She sat with her head on her hands, her legs curled beneath her in that big chair, that life-sized poster of Jim Morrison looming above her, indifferent.

"I can't believe it," Marcia sniffed. She naturally thought that photographs like that would remain private. I didn't know about her first husband and so she told me about him, a professional backgammon player in Israel who had been paralyzed in an accidental shooting after they split up.

Marcia wept intermittently and wiped at her eyes. She said she felt badly for her first husband's misfortune, but I told her that it wasn't her fault.

She said she couldn't help feeling somewhat responsible. "So, what did you think of the photos?" Marcia asked.

I paused as if to carefully consider what effect these scandals might have on our case.

"Just be honest," she said.

"Personally, I thought they looked pretty good."

She looked up from the tissue, smiled for a second, and then burst into laughter. "Some therapist you'd make, Darden."

It was good to joke about the tabloids, because they caused us both tremendous stress. I have been told that we should have expected such coverage, that it was the price of fame. Perhaps. But fame has always been an alien concept to me. All fame brought me in the early months of the trial was angry telephone calls, death threats, and a man who spit on me. I know there is another side to celebrity. But trust me: Getting a good table at a restaurant is not a fair trade for your dignity and the privacy of your family.

* * *

"O. J. prosecutor's secret heartache!"

"O. J. Prosecutor Chris Darden has a secret heartbreak—the older brother he loves is a thief and a drug addict!"

The March 1 *National Enquirer* carried a thumb-sized photograph of my parents' house, a picture of me, and a horrible snapshot of a skeletal Michael—all drawn cheeks and hollow eyes, "trapped in a living hell of drugs and despair!" It had been several days since I'd seen Michael, and now, in this picture, I could see death in his eyes. I guess the tabloid photographer could see it too.

The reporters had begun going to my parents' house that February, trying to get a story out of them. Sometimes they showed up with photographers hiding at the base of the stairs. They had been doing the same thing to me, rooting through my garbage can, following me home, taking photographs of women they suspected I dated.

"Ignore them," I advised my parents. "Hang up the phone if they call and don't even stop to tell them you don't want to talk."

So the reporters went to my parents' neighbors. And then they went to Michael's apartment.

"I'm sorry," Michael told me the day the story came out. "It's my fault." I was going to call him as soon as I saw the story, but Michael called me first. He said he had refused to talk, but one reporter threatened to write a story about Mama and to say that she fed him on the porch like a dog.

"Write anything you want about me," Michael said he told the man. "But please don't write that about my mother." And so Michael sat and talked with them and, to show their thanks, they destroyed him with their story:

> While Chris made the heroic climb from the ghetto streets to become a top Los Angeles prosecutor, his brother Michael sank into a life of drugs and despair.
>
> Michael has been convicted of burglary five times. He lives in a tiny, shabby apartment and sometimes eats in a soup kitchen. His own parents don't trust him enough to let him in their house.
>
> "Who can blame them?" Michael sadly told *The ENQUIRER*. "Drug people have a tendency to steal stuff and I'm addicted to crack. I want to stop doing it, but I can't."

The reporter kept harping on Michael's health, asking if he had AIDS, but Michael insisted that, no, he had tuberculosis.

"You're lying," the reporter said. "We can get your medical records." But Michael wouldn't confirm it.

The whole thing tore at my insides. Why couldn't they just let him live his last days in peace? Michael wasn't part of the O. J. Simpson case. I had volunteered for this; if they wanted to write about my sloppy housekeeping or the fact that I cuss more than I should or that I drink tequila, or that I had stolen an umbrella in college—fine. Hell, they could make something up about me if they wanted to! But Michael? Did they need to draw him into this?

"I didn't mean to embarrass you," he said quietly.

"You don't owe me an apology," I said. "And you don't owe Mama one. You haven't embarrassed me. There's nothing you could do, there's nothing you've ever done that has embarrassed me."

That story seemed to open the floodgates. Soon, other reporters—tabloid and mainstream—began seeking out Michael at his apartment and at the mission where he often ate.

Who else could I talk to about the intrusion into my family's life? As we sat in court, I wrote Marcia a note about a message I'd just received on my pager from my sister. An L.A. news crew, KCBS, had gone to the mission and sent in a note offering Michael a sandwich if he'd come out and talk to them. It was so pitiful. "They waited—four and a half hours—despite the fact that my brother sent word that he wasn't coming outside," I wrote. "So, as they say in the 'hood, 'Once again, it's on.' But I talked to my bro. and he's doing OK."

"Thank God," Marcia wrote. "Those sleezy [*sic*] pieces of shit are fucking immoral, irresponsible, scumsucking [*sic*] pigs. There is simply no valid reason for this. Kind of similar to publishing one half of a custody case, don't you think?"

That was my Marcia Clark, tough, loyal, and unapologetic.

"I am honored that you are my friend," I wrote to her.

Sometimes, I marvel at the pressure that woman was under. She carried a burden in the courtroom that the rest of us didn't. It was clear from the words the defense used to describe her, words like "shrill" and "hysterical." Every day, she had to battle not only the other lawyers, but the world's preconceived notions of how a woman should behave.

Not that those notions meant anything to Marcia Clark. She is a strange blend of Type A personality and retro-hippie, an anything-goes, tough-on-crime Republican always ready to fight for what she believes in and always ready to drop to the floor and play dinosaurs with her three- and five-year-old sons.

One morning, the hip-hop radio station that I listened to—92.3, "The Beat"—had a contest it called "Marcia Clark, Babe or Bitch?" Everyone wanted to put her in one of those boxes. There was nothing I could do but call in and vote for the former. We joked sometimes about my traditional view of women: "You can't cook," I said. "As smart as you are, what good are you to me?"

"Oh, I can cook," she said. "I don't need to."

Judge Ito seemed to enjoy the sparring between the male attorneys, sometimes letting it go on too long. But when Marcia got into it, he was short with her. During court, he called the male attorneys by their formal names: "Mr. Darden," "Dean Uelmen," "Mr. Shapiro." But he often called her "Marcia"—completely inappropriate during a trial. Judge Ito joked and was playful with Cochran—who constantly challenged the judge's authority. But Ito was sharp with Marcia and didn't seem to like it when she challenged him. Even the Los Angeles chapter of the National Organization of Women criticized Ito's behavior.

Admittedly, Department 103 could be testosterone-driven, like most courtrooms, a decidedly unfriendly place for a female lawyer, even one as tough as Marcia. One day in court, for instance, Simpson's maid testified that she did the laundry before she left for the weekend. Since there were clothes in the washing machine, we were trying to show that Simpson may have washed the murder clothes that weekend. We displayed an enlarged photograph of Simpson's laundry room and it became apparent that a pair of women's underpants was on the washing machine.

"Those are panties," I heard Simpson say.

Everyone was somewhat amused and I certainly joked along. Later, as Cochran and I walked toward Ito's bench for a sidebar, I asked him, "Why didn't you guys tell me there were panties in that picture?"

Laughing like one of the guys, Judge Ito said, "Well, you couldn't ask Marcia because she doesn't wear any." I guess Ito thought he was playing along with Cochran and me, but it was completely inappropriate from the judge hearing this case, and I made it known that I didn't appreciate it. That was the atmosphere in which Marcia sometimes had to work.

But Marcia could always handle the men in court. It was the boys at home who occupied most of her thoughts.

She would charge through the hallways, her sinewy arms full of documents, a cellular telephone crooked in her neck as she spoke Spanish to her nanny about her sons. I was always getting Post-it notes with Marcia's schedule sketched on them: "Next Monday, May 8, I have to leave by 3:15."

"Why?"

"Travis—it's Mother's Day at his preschool."

Marcia was sick during much of the winter and spring and when I finally visited her house, I could see why. It was raining and her roof was so leaky, water was running down the walls in her bedroom, puddling up in the carpet. She had neither the time nor the money to have it fixed. Some D.A. investigators chipped in to cover her roof with a tarp. But they could do nothing about the other pressures in her life; Marcia was being flooded from all sides: from the trial; from being a single, working mom; and from her ex-husband, who stepped up the pressure in their custody case, calling her to be deposed during some of the most crucial testimony in the Simpson case.

"I'm sorry if I'm acting weird," she wrote one day. "I'm very sick, depressed and stressed-out—running between court, hair & trace [evidence], the kids and multiple depositions. I can't take this any more."

I tried to help her. I even went to a deposition with her, giving her advice and offering a shoulder when she needed it.

Incredibly, I never saw Marcia break down. She is great with her kids and I marveled that, after long days in court, she was still attentive and loving to her two boys. Anyone who has had a relationship dissolve or knows the pain of a divorce can appreciate some of what she was going through. Add to that two energetic boys, a vindictive ex-husband, and a position as lead attorney in the largest, most outlandish criminal trial in history—one the experts said we had lost from the beginning—and it becomes almost unimaginable, the pressure that Marcia Clark was under.

"For 13 years, [Gordon] always got what he wanted," she wrote on my legal pad one day, during some inevitable delay. "Even if I initially objected, I always wound up caving in, whether he did it by talking or demanding. But since I had children I have discovered I can be strong when their welfare is at issue, even if I can still be pushed around when it comes to myself. Gordon's problem is that he doesn't think that way—and all he knows is that, based on past history, if he pushes hard enough, I'll give in."

I set the pad down and turned toward her. "Not this time."

Two thousand reporters covered some part of O. J. Simpson's murder trial. They represented one hundred accredited news organizations and several less official outlets. There were 121 video feeds coming out of the Criminal Courts Building, eighty miles of cable. Nineteen television stations, eight radio stations, and twenty-three newspapers and magazines had space in the twelfth-floor press room, where there were 250 telephones.

There were another 650 telephones in "Camp O. J.," the nearby parking lot that looked something like a media shantytown: the Fourth Estate Trailer Park. CBS had five trailers, CNN four, NBC three, and ABC four. There were ten portable toilets and three Dumpster bins. Network scaffolding rose from every corner of the lot as if on some epic movie set. It took only weeks for the first reporter to do a story on all the reporters. A few months later, reporters were doing stories on other reporters doing stories on all the reporters.

Lance Ito's worst decision might have been to allow cameras in the courtroom. They shouldn't have been there. Cameras caused all the lawyers to change our approach and our style. Everyone became long-winded and abrasive. Often without meaning to, we tailored our arguments to the millions of people watching and the experts second-guessing our every move. Newspapers rated our performances and talked about "points" that we supposedly scored, giving everything the feeling of a game and causing lawyers to be more combative. That style of lawyering never helps achieve justice. It only tarnishes it.

This was a case in which justice was going to be almost impossible to achieve because of the defendant's wealth, his celebrity, and the racial divisions the case caused. Cameras only exacerbated those things, blurring the official courtroom actions with the hype, which followed every court session like a comet's tail.

I hoped that Judge Ito would yank the cameras, but he never had the courage to do it. "Go ahead," I dared him once, "take them out." It would have cut the length of the trial by at least 40 percent. But this was the judge who invited actors Richard Dreyfuss and James Woods back to his chambers, who gave network anchors and authors the best seats in the courtroom. This was L.A., and Ito was drunk with media attention. He was becoming one of those people so famous they need only one name: Madonna. Prince. Ito. He would no more have shut the cameras off than he would have recused himself from the case.

Sure, he made threats to snuff the cameras, but he never followed through. Once, after throwing a fit about the cameras, he posed for pictures with twenty-one boxes of mail, from letter writers who agreed that he should turn the cameras off. It was a strange response for someone supposedly concerned about the media to then pose for the media with fan mail. After he sat for a five-part interview with a Los Angeles television station (promoted with daily full-page ads in the *L.A. Times*), it was difficult to believe any of Ito's admonitions about not releasing information to the press or his threats of turning off the cameras. It seemed clear he would do whatever he could to stay in the spotlight.

It was a shame.

I tried to ignore the cameras; I didn't watch TV and tried to shut out what the pundits and experts were saying. But it was like walking past a funhouse mirror, over and over, a mirror that distorts your appearance so that you look taller and fatter than you really are. It isn't long before your very identity is in doubt: "Is that really how I am?"

We were on television at least five or six hours during weekdays on three national cable channels, as well as cut-ins on the networks. With the talk shows and news programs, the daily wrap-ups and weekend reviews, the news magazines and tabloid shows, the Simpson case had to average sixty hours a week on television—and that's a conservative estimate—for a year straight. There were days when you could watch the Simpson case all day.

Assuming he took no vacations, Jay Leno would have to work twelve years to match the television time of the lawyers on the case. Dan Rather would need twenty-four years, and your average sitcom star would have to be on the air for 120 years. It was insane!

Spy magazine reported that one poll showed that more Americans could identify Lance Ito (64 percent) than Newt Gingrich (52 percent). In another poll, Kato Kaelin was recognizable to 75 percent of those who responded, while Vice President Al Gore was identified by only 25 percent.

Certainly no lawyer has ever been put in the situation we were in; I doubt any professional has ever been followed to work by a couple million people every day. No lawyer should ever have the pressure of giving closing arguments in prime time.

Pundits interpreted every shudder and smirk. If you scowled one day, you were surly. If you frowned, the prosecution case was in trouble. If you objected too harshly, the strain was wearing on you. They chased you all day with microphones, harassed your family, second-guessed every move you made, and then marveled that you were worn down by the stress of it all. Many days, there wasn't much difference between the stories the tabloids covered and those reported by the "legitimate press." For instance, there were the "Marcia makeovers."

One Friday, in early April, I was supposed to meet Marcia at her house. I was in a slow burn waiting outside her house because she was already twenty minutes late. It was my birthday and she had promised me dinner. We had so little free time, I didn't have the time or the energy to sit around waiting for her.

She drove up finally and we walked into the house, standing face-to-face while I ripped her for being late. After about fifteen minutes, she ran a finger through her hair.

"What do you think?"

"What do I think? I just told you what I think!"

She laughed. "I mean, what do you think of my new hairstyle? You didn't notice?"

The fact was, I didn't. Unlike the rest of the country, I missed it completely. "It looks really good," I said. I had teased Marcia about her tight, curly hair and short skirts, but for some reason, I was the only person in the world who didn't seem to notice her incredibly publicized makeovers.

Lawyers often change their appearance. Part of our job is appealing to a jury, and part of that will always involve the way we look. Yet the media interest in Marcia's new look was unbelievable. I can't imagine any other circumstance in the world in which a haircut and a shopping trip become front-page news, along with analysis of what it all means. After her haircut, she received a standing ovation outside the courtroom!

Celebrity is such a valued commodity in our society, but it affects people differently. I felt more infamous than famous. Especially in the first few months after the N-word argument, I felt as if my constituents had voted me out of the 'hood, revoked my ghetto pass.

But Marcia's people idolized her. In Beverly Hills, at malls and restaurants, she was treated as a movie star, of sorts.

"All across the country, women are naming their newborn babies Marcia," I teased her. "Millions of little Marcias going around kicking ass in tight little skirts."

I guess the first time I had any sense of my own notoriety was in early December, when I got a call from Norma Johnson, the president of Loved Ones of Homicide Victims. Norma wanted me to come to an LOHV fund-raiser and auction at a house in Ladera Heights.

"I've got work to do," I said. It was my standard answer, my mantra.

But LOHV was a tribute to Norma's persistence and she wouldn't give up. She said that, as a past president of the victims' group, I had to be there. Finally, I relented.

I drove through Crenshaw, one of the neighborhoods I'd lived in, the heart of the 'hood, one of the centers of black consciousness in Southern California. If there was a community where I was despised, this was it. Farther on was Ladera Heights, where I pulled in front of a nice, big split-level house, set back from the street.

There were about fifty people, prominent African Americans mostly, milling around the cold cuts. I met a few of them, but I'm not big on socializing. I'm bad with names, worthless at small talk, and not really a cocktail party guy. When the auction started, I bid $150 for five CDs—four of which I already had—and then sneaked off toward the stairwell, to hide out for the rest of the evening.

"Now for the grand prizes," Norma said. "Who's gonna have dinner with Johnnie Cochran and Chris Darden?"

Nobody had told me I was going to be auctioned. I wouldn't have come if I'd known. It all happened very quickly. I went for $200; Cochran—who wasn't even there—went for $250.

This was before the N-word argument and I wasn't well known, but being outsold by Cochran still stirred something in me. "Whoever won me is going to have one hell of a nicer time than Cochran's date," I vowed.

Norma introduced me to my bidder, a tall, attractive, and confident woman named Loreli. I took her telephone number in December but we didn't go out until early March, when I asked her to go with the prosecution team to the House of Blues, a trendy West L.A. nightclub owned and frequented by movie stars. The entire team was planning to go; it was the first time we'd gone anywhere but the Saratoga—the smoky, red-boothed cop bar near the CCB.

They put us all in the VIP room and we went nuts, drinking and eating and having a wonderful time, cutting loose for the first time in months. We squeezed out of the VIP room and into the main part of the bar, overlooking a dance floor packed with fit people—white mostly—in jeans and tans; local Hollywood waiters and state university graduates. I was nervous to see how I'd be perceived, and I inched closer and closer to the crowded part of the club.

"You and Marcia," a security guard yelled in my ear, "are the two most famous people in the house tonight!" I couldn't understand what he meant. This was L.A. and it didn't register that we were "celebrities." It still doesn't. We were lawyers, not movie stars. I felt out of place and I shrank back behind a divider, away from the crowd.

Loreli—dressed in classy white—wasn't sure what to make of the raucous D.A. staff and especially the familiarity with which Marcia and I spoke. We joked with each other and Loreli just sat back and watched. We all had plenty to drink.

My clerk, Melissa Decker, scolded me: "Would you pay attention to your date!"

I was worried about Marcia driving and so I asked her if she needed a ride. She shot right back with a grin, "Fuck you, Darden! I can get home." It was the boisterous way we talked around the office. But when I looked up, Loreli was fuming. Her face tightened and her lips pursed and it was clear that she was offended.

"What?" I asked.

She was angry that Marcia spoke to me in the manner she did, and she was angry that I hadn't corrected her. We had ventured into that

confusing place where racial and sexual politics connect—crossing and
cutting like a bunch of melting phone lines, mixing conversations about
slavery, single parents, loyalty, and feminism into a mess, a din of confusion and misunderstanding.

It was disrespectful for a white woman to speak that way in public to
a black man, Loreli finally told me, grudgingly. It was especially insensitive, Loreli said, since Marcia should be aware of the fact that I had been
criticized as someone who was a dupe for whites in this case. And there
were other racial and sexual issues, she said patiently.

Many of my ex-girlfriends have remained friends and most of them
are black. Of course, my sisters also are black. And many of my closest
friends are black women. Each time the media connected Marcia Clark
and me in any way, the idea was wildly unpopular with the many black
women whom I knew.

I was aware that some people would call me a hypocrite if I dated a
white woman, because of my remark about Simpson's fetish for blond,
white women. The case was fraught with these issues—race and sex—so
that people were, at once, keenly aware of it and bitterly afraid to talk
about it.

It was a minefield. The defendant in this case was a black man who
had left his first, black wife for a white woman and had cheated on her
with other white women, and then had killed his white wife and her
young white, male friend. The jury was mainly black women. And here
I was, a black man working in a subordinate role to a white woman, connected romantically to her by the tabloids.

A friend from the Bay Area tried to explain her adverse reaction to
the rumors about Marcia and me.

It's always been different for black women, she said. During slavery, it was considered the right of the white plantation owner to rape
his slave women, who were seen as mere animals. From that time, black
men had a responsibility to protect their women, to promulgate their
race and keep them empowered.

In the late twentieth century, blacks were finally emerging from
poverty, but black women still lacked power. Too often, successful black
men "rewarded" themselves with a white woman, and black women
were left behind. Sex is about power, my friend said, and black women

had the least power: physically, economically, and socially. There is only one true underclass: single black mothers.

My friend acknowledged that it wasn't completely reasonable, but she said there will always be strong resentment for a white woman who "takes one of our men."

For decades, the ideals of beauty were all white. And even black women who crossed over into entertainment and modeling had distinctly Anglo looks, like Lena Horne and Dorothy Dandridge. Black men owed it to their daughters, my friend said, to encourage and appreciate another kind of beauty.

I told her she had every right to feel that way. She was right.

Yet that was just one side of the argument. I had dated a few non-black women over the years and held firm to my belief that it was the person who mattered and not the color. I would never see a white woman as "status" or "achievement," and when someone says "beautiful woman," I see a black woman in my mind.

Still, why not have a relationship with Marcia? She was attractive and I was impressed by her intelligence and toughness, intrigued by her vulnerability. We were working together as many as fifteen or sixteen hours a day, watching each other's backs in court and commiserating over the media and other things that no one else understood.

There is a balance, I know, a way to be respectful of the things that your heritage demands and to be true to your own emotions. It was something I struggled with as I thought about the possibilities with Marcia Clark. But could a romantic relationship survive the social pressures put upon each of us? Both Marcia Clark and I believed that race shouldn't keep two people apart, but we were faced every day with letters weighted with bigotry, from people who said that Nicole "got what she deserved" for messing with a black man. That was something I was especially aware of, given a jury with so many African-American women. Throughout, we read in their faces a lack of sympathy for Nicole Brown. We were reminded every day that idealism and tolerance aren't always welcome in the real world.

Dennis Schatzman was a reporter with a newspaper called the *Sentinel,* which served the black community in Los Angeles with the news and opinions as decided by Dennis Schatzman. His coverage of the Simpson case was decidedly different from that of the mainstream press. He believed strongly that Simpson was innocent, and his coverage reflected that. I have never believed that one person should represent himself as the voice of African Americans. Black media, like all media, should be unbiased and should reflect the diversity of their audience. For instance, I respect the work that Black Entertainment Television does and I have seen other publications that acknowledge diverse experiences and opinions among African Americans.

But the *Sentinel* saw this as a case in which blacks had to make a choice: the Man or the Juice. And to them, I was clearly on the wrong side. I was rarely mentioned in that newspaper and when I was, it was usually unflattering.

"Hey, Dennis," I said to him, half-jokingly, in the elevator one day. "How come you've never written anything good about me in the *Sentinel*? You've even had Shapiro on the front page, above the fold, but not me."

A few weeks later, in early May, I was honored at a small gathering sponsored by the National Black Prosecutors Association. It was one of the few attempts I made at public speaking, and the media covered it heavily. When I was done, Marcia—who'd asked if it was OK to attend—came up with her arms extended and embraced me.

And so I finally made the front page of the *Sentinel*. The photo showed Marcia coming toward me, about to hug me. There was no story, just the photo and a caption that said I was being congratulated by fellow prosecutor Marcia Clark.

The picture sparked a new wave of criticism, threats, and angry letters—"You couldn't wait to get what O. J. had!" one woman wrote. All that over a hug.

"It just amazes me that people can be so unfair," I wrote to Marcia a few days later.

"I guess I shouldn't have hugged you," she wrote back. "It was just a spontaneous, natural feeling. I'm sorry."

"Pleeez! That is not the issue," I scrawled. "I am not the least bit bothered by that. I'm not upset at the picture, but at the use being made of it."

"True," she wrote. "But maybe I should be more guarded right now. It's hard not to act the way you feel. But every move has consequences right now and I definitely don't want to be a source of problems for you."

"You are not. I don't mind the photo, just the spin they are putting on it."

What relationship could we possibly have built amid all that pressure, wondering whether a picture of us hugging would get back to the jury and what effect it would have, wondering how the world's view of Marcia would change if we began seeing each other?

For some reason, interracial dating still brings out the deepest, most destructive bigotry in some people. And Marcia Clark and I were not in the position to ignore that. Still, our friendship deepened and we began leaning on each other more and more for encouragement and comfort. And for fun.

The limousine pulled up to Marcia's house and I could just see the eyes and hair of her younger boy, Kyle—three and crazy about cars, barely able to peer over the windowsill.

He came running out like it was some sort of prison break.

"Wow, Uncle Chris! Is that your car?"

"Yep."

He dove into the backseat and seemed in danger of going completely nuts. Travis, who was five, climbed in as well, looking around the big backseats, which faced each other behind the partitioned driver's seat. Marcia came out in something black and we drove the boys to the baby-sitter in the limo, playing *The Lion King* for them on the car's VCR and television. They stretched out on the seats and floorboard as if they were at home in their living room.

"That was really nice of you," Marcia said.

"Don't mention it. Happy birthday."

We went to the House of Blues again for Marcia's birthday party, where we met some of the other prosecutors. The Ohio Players were the band that night, and Marcia and I went backstage to meet two of the originals—Sugarfoot and Diamond. I was impressed that Marcia was a fan. The Ohio Players were one of my all-time favorite bands. As long as I'd owned my own stereo, there had been an Ohio Players' album on it.

At the end of the night, we each carried a sleeping boy as Marcia fumbled with her keys. We carried them into the house and tucked them in and then I headed for my limo ride home.

"Thanks for everything," she said.

"Any time." I hugged her at her front door—no photographers to catch this one—and rode home to Carson.

Usually, our evenings together didn't start until 10 P.M. or so and consisted of a few drinks after long days in court and in our offices. We'd stay up late, drinking wine, and a couple of times, I pitched off to sleep on her couch, my suit coat bunched up in my arms. Once, when I awakened, I looked outside in time to see a private detective, who, I found out later, was employed by the tabloids. He was writing down my license plate number.

Our recent courtroom notes had taken on the topic of 1960s Motown and current rap music, and one night—when her children were at their father's house—Marcia invited me to bring some of my CD collection. I brought Tower of Power's *East Bay Grease*. I played "Sparkling in the Sand" and some of the Dramatics' better stuff, like "Me and Mrs. Jones." I threw in the Dells; the Delphonics; the Isley Brothers; Earth, Wind and Fire; and the Ohio Players, and we sat there in front of her stereo, squinting with laughter. She especially liked the rap song "Keep Their Heads Ringing," by Dr. Dre, which, I have to admit, impressed me.

She played some of her old 1960s rock, and you've never heard anything until you've heard Marcia Clark sing Janis Joplin. But if you haven't heard that, consider yourself lucky.

"As much as I love your speaking voice," I said, "you cannot sing." And that got us laughing again. We danced a little, drank some wine, and talked seriously about the case and what it was doing to our families and to her kids. There were other people in our lives, but it was as if they were at the top of some deep hole and we were at the bottom. They couldn't reach us, couldn't relate to the part of us that was trapped in this trial. The pressure intensified every day and that hole seemed to get deeper and deeper. For instance, we were always fatigued, we were eating poorly, and the teeth-grinding stress left us both with serious dental problems. Who else was going to understand that? Who else could we talk to? Who else would comfort us?

By the time I lay down on the couch that night, it was only hours before the trial started again. For an hour or so, I lay awake, staring at the ceiling. And then I fell asleep.

I am amazed and troubled by the media's fascination over whether Marcia Clark and I had a romantic relationship. After the trial, with the injustice still bitter in my mouth, the question most often put to me was about Marcia. I have spent far too much time walking through airports, denying that Marcia and I are getting married.

She and I were two passionate people thrown together in a trial that left us exhausted and lonely. She was willing to take off her jewelry and go to jail with me over a ridiculous contempt ruling. I was willing to be at her side during her child custody deposition. We sat up listening to hip-hop and R&B. We danced a few times and drank a few bottles of wine. We still call each other late at night with issues no one else can understand and stories no one else can appreciate. In my mind, that is a relationship.

Of course, the question the media ask is more base. It is a locker-room question, but also a question weighted with the kinds of social and racial implications that should never be put on the shoulders of two lonesome people. You know the question.

My parents taught me that locker-room talk isn't at all gentlemanly. I refuse to surrender the last posts of privacy that we have left, simply because the media in this country have lost their shame and their sense of propriety and dignity. I have not lost those things.

I will say this. As spring melted into summer, I began to wonder what might happen away from the flash of tabloid photographers and television cameras. The glare from the people who wanted to know if we were together may have been one of the things that ultimately kept us apart.

As it is, I will always care for and respect Marcia Clark, and I will always remember the times we made each other feel less alone. I will always be her friend. And that is enough.

SIXTEEN

Cochran, Shapiro, Bailey, and Douglas were already at the defense table, huddled together as if they were looking at a dirty magazine. I walked past them quietly, as I did every day, my eyes locked on our side of the podium.

Unlike other trials I'd prosecuted, there was almost no camaraderie between their camp and ours; the stakes were too high for that, the tactics too low. Marcia followed me inside. "Good morning," she said, and then the deputies let the reporters come in. While the trial watchers settled into their seats in the gallery, I sat still in my chair reading a memo. Suddenly, I felt two hands on my shoulders.

From behind, Cochran embraced me and put his mouth near my ear.

"Listen." He said something about the way we'd argued the N-word. "We can't ever do that kind of thing again," he said. "This shouldn't be your issue. Let these white people get up there and argue about Fuhrman. OK?"

"I can't do that," I said, staring forward.

"Why not?"

I wasn't going to be limited by my race and I told him so.

"Just don't put him on," Cochran said.

I watched him walk back to his side of the courtroom, that chamber-of-commerce smile back at full wattage as he sat next to O. J. Simpson. Since then, I've thought a lot about what he said, looked at it from all sides. I've wondered if he was setting me up or perhaps taunting me, or if he was trying to limit Fuhrman's effectiveness and impact. While I don't put any of those things past him, I think it was something else. I think Cochran knew from the beginning about the racist tapes Fuhrman made with a North Carolina screenwriter, and I think he was honestly trying to warn me away. Perhaps he felt badly over what he'd done to my reputation during the N-word argument; I don't know. But I believe Cochran was serious about his warning.

I was just as serious; I wasn't going to be limited by my race. And I wasn't going to leave Marcia in a position like that. She was preparing forty witnesses. That's forty people to interview, research, and prepare for testimony. I had roughly fifteen. I couldn't give Fuhrman to her and I couldn't give him to one of the DNA prosecutors, Rock Harmon or Woody Clarke. Hank Goldberg was a possibility, but he had Dennis Fung—another troublesome witness.

No, I had signed on as a full partner and I intended to live up to my oath as a prosecutor.

I had prepared a tough direct examination, and in early February, I met with Fuhrman again in my office to go over some questions. Scott Gordon and Cheri Lewis had been assigned to baby-sit the guy. Later, I would read about Mark Fuhrman—this big, scary racist—and I would laugh a little. Around the D.A.'s office, he was a big baby, whining when no one was paying attention to him, always accusing prosecutors of not believing in him. He was the only witness to whom we had to assign someone full-time whenever he was in the office. Otherwise, he'd just sit and sulk, afraid the whole world was plotting against him.

In November, the defense had begun making noise about Peggy York, Judge Ito's wife, who was a captain in the LAPD and had been Fuhrman's supervisor for a short time. The rumor was that York had been assigned to the West L.A. Division to investigate a police group called MAW—Men Against Women—and that Fuhrman might have some involvement in the group.

If that were true, it might mean that York would be called as a witness, and—according to the rules of judicial conduct—Ito would be required to remove himself from the case. But with Judge Ego, as some people called him, proudly collecting his hourglasses and sitting for five-part interviews, it wasn't likely that he'd allow himself to be removed.

It turned out that York hadn't investigated MAW, but she raised a few eyebrows when she stated in a written declaration: "I have no recollection of the nature of any interactions between then-officer Fuhrman and me."

Fuhrman was in a lousy mood in my office that day in early February, grumbling that York was lying and her husband knew it. "If Ito fucks with me, he goes down with me," Fuhrman said. Cheri Lewis took me aside and said Fuhrman had been saying the same thing all day.

Fuhrman was adamant that Ito's wife had lied when she recalled no interaction between the two of them. "How could she possibly forget me?" Fuhrman asked.

It was New Year's Eve a few years back, when York was in charge of the West L.A. patrol unit where Fuhrman was stationed. On the calendar, someone had written "KKK" across Martin Luther King Jr.'s birthday, and York was furious, demanding to know who had done it.

Fuhrman smirked and grunted and she ordered him to her office, where they argued and Fuhrman teased her, saying that she knew nothing about patrol. On other occasions, Fuhrman openly challenged York's authority, calling her names and yelling at her loudly enough that everyone in the station could hear.

"We stood there nose to nose, yelling at each other for fifteen minutes," Fuhrman bragged. He wanted Ito to keep the defense lawyers from humiliating him. "She's lying and Ito knows it. If he doesn't take care of me, I'm telling everything I know."

Every time I talked to Fuhrman, I wanted less and less to do with him. We went over some questions, but he was coy and short with me. I asked Cheri Lewis if he'd said anything about me. She said no.

"Look," Cochran said to me a few days later. "Just don't put him on. OK? You don't know what you're messing with. You don't know everything that I do. I'm just trying to do you a favor."

"A favor?" I asked, turning to face him. "What favor would that be? The kind of favors you've already done for me?"

Cochran warned me three or four times. I knew they must have something on Fuhrman, but what could it be? That he had been a racist? A Nazi? Unfortunately that wasn't enough to keep him off the stand.

Did Cochran think I liked putting Fuhrman up there? I didn't. But both Cochran and I knew that, whatever his beliefs, they had nothing to do with whether or not O. J. Simpson was a murderer. If we'd put a thief on the stand, that wouldn't have affected what Simpson did either. As long as Fuhrman told the truth, I would do my job: put him on the stand.

The next time I met with Fuhrman, to go over some of the questions the defense might ask, I was firm with him. "Is there anything that you're hiding? Anything at all?"

"No!"

"I want you to understand this," I said. "By putting you on the stand I'm risking my own life too. I just want to know if there's anything that will come back to haunt us. Because if you go down, I go down."

I took a breath. "So, one more time, is there anything we need to be aware of?"

"There's nothing else."

We stared at each other. Mark Fuhrman was smart and he was smooth, but there was something about him that was keeping me up at night, making me wonder if I was doing the right thing. There were so many things racing through my mind. He was hiding something. I wondered if the jury would see the same thing.

I had chosen to be in this position, but my family hadn't. I thought about what my parents would go through if Fuhrman turned out to have some awful racist actions in his past and their son was the one who had to present this guy.

But it was strange. The other prosecutors, from Marcia to Scott to Cheri, all seemed to think that Fuhrman would be OK on the stand; in fact, that he was an exemplary witness. Maybe my sense of the guy was skewed by the language in his old psych reports, or by all the media attention. I decided to gather some people I trusted, to get their opinions of Fuhrman. And so I drove to work one day in mid-February pondering a question that I still can't answer: Is it possible to look at someone and see inside his heart?

It was Presidents' Day weekend, 1995, and the eighteenth floor of the CCB was empty except for the clerks and lawyers working on Simpson and a small group of people I had called together: my friend Elka Woerner; Deputy D.A.'s Alan Yochelson, Scott Gordon, and Cheri Lewis; my clerks, Melissa Decker and Michael Runyon; and Mark Fuhrman.

I'd also asked my friend Terry White, the black prosecutor who had worked with Yochelson on the Simi Valley trial of the officers who beat Rodney King and the legal advisor to the Los Angeles County Grand Jury. He and Alan were tough trial lawyers, and I trusted their sense of people.

We assembled about one o'clock in the afternoon, my team and Fuhrman with two huge Metro Division police bodyguards who accompanied him everywhere because of the death threats he'd received. Since it was a holiday weekend the county had shut off the air-conditioning. The air in the war room was stale and we were on top of one another, so we moved to a small conference room on the seventeenth floor. Still no air. Finally, we moved down to the thirteenth floor, where Terry White worked. Air! Terry opened the grand jury room and we all went inside and got comfortable. Terry and I sat in the front row, four chairs apart, looking at Fuhrman. The others sat behind us.

I left the room to take a telephone call, and when I came back, everyone was laughing and talking to one another. Fuhrman seemed comfortable. People came and left and we talked casually for several minutes. Fuhrman's bodyguards brought him a sandwich and some chips.

One by one, I took people into the hallway and asked for their quick impressions of Fuhrman. Woerner was adamant. He was a racist.

Back in the grand jury room after most of the people had left, I asked Fuhrman what he was going to do if he was asked whether he had ever used the N-word.

"What does that have to do with anything?" He tensed. "I thought the judge ruled they could only ask me about Kathleen Bell."

"Well," I said, "this judge tends to rule and refuse to enforce his own ruling. So, if he allows it, what will you say? Have you ever used it in the last ten years?"

He hesitated for just a brief moment. "No."

I asked about interracial couples, and he assured me that he has friends who have interracial marriages and that they went to one another's houses.

"What are your hobbies?" I asked.

"I like to collect World War II memorabilia."

"What kind of memorabilia?" I asked.

"Well, medals."

"Any particular kind?"

He shifted in his chair. "Well, don't take this the wrong way, but I collect German medals."

Swastikas!

"The craftsmanship is incredible," Mark Fuhrman said. "None of them are the same. Each of them are works of art. I also collect memorabilia from the other countries, from France, England, and the United States."

And that was it. After forty minutes or so, perhaps ten or fifteen actual questions, I broke up the meeting that the defense would later claim was a "mock cross-examination." It was mock, all right. Mark Fuhrman was mocking our intelligence.

I'd seen enough. I knew all I needed to know and more, actually. Maybe we shouldn't put this guy on. I *couldn't* put this guy on. I couldn't accept his answer that he hadn't used the N-word in the last ten years. A cop like Fuhrman—who showed in his 1980 and 1981 shrink reports that he was well versed in racial epithets—couldn't know with such precision that he hadn't used that word in ten years. It made no sense. Who would keep count of something like that? Who would date it? If only he had said, "I don't recall the last time I used the word." Once I even suggested to him that most people would have trouble remembering every word they'd used in the last ten years, but Fuhrman wouldn't take the hint. And ethically, a lawyer can't advise a witness to change his testimony.

I walked into Marcia's office. She was puffing away on a long, filtered cigarette, reading a stack of loose pages. When she wasn't in court, Marcia wore black leggings, black sweat socks, black sneakers, and a sweatshirt or T-shirt.

I sat down, but she barely looked up at me.

"I'm not going to say that we shouldn't call Fuhrman—"

That caused her to look up.

"—because if we don't, they will, and it will look like we were trying to hide him." I took my glasses off and rubbed the bridge of my nose. "But I'm going to ask you a favor. One that I've given a lot of thought.

"I know you're busy. But I need you to take Fuhrman. I'll take any of your witnesses, but I just can't put this guy on. Have Hank or Cheri do it, but I can't."

Marcia blew up. "Why?"

"It would be bad for our case for me to put this guy on," I said. "It will be clear that I don't believe in him, that I don't like him." And there was something else. "Putting this guy on will get me killed. I can't. I won't."

I stood to leave the room, expecting to hear Marcia say that she understood and that it was OK. But she didn't. I closed the door on my way out and walked slowly back to my office, twisted in knots.

I told Cheri that I had decided not to put Fuhrman on, and she said, "That's probably best."

"Why? What has he been saying about me?"

She looked at her feet. I hadn't liked Cheri much when I first joined the case. She always seemed secretive and ran interference for Marcia. She was also pro-cop and had disagreed with some of my actions in SID. She was one of those deputy D.A.'s who felt I was too hard on the police. But lately, I had grown to trust her and to rely on her straightforward intelligence.

"Fuhrman doesn't think you support him," Cheri said, shrugging. "He doesn't think you're confident putting him on. It seemed like he'd rather have someone else put him on too."

Between February 23 and March 7, the jury heard *four hours* of testimony.

Most of that time was spent in hearings outside the jury's presence, mostly over whether Rosa Lopez should be allowed to testify.

Lopez was Simpson's vaunted alibi, the one Cochran had promised during his ridiculous opening statement. A Salvadoran maid who worked for Simpson's Rockingham neighbors, Lopez wasn't supposed to testify until the defense presented its case, but they went in front of Ito, claiming she might flee the country if she wasn't allowed to testify out of order.

She appeared in court—away from the jury—on Friday, February 24, in a velour sweat suit, fidgeting and claiming that, yes, she was ready to leave Los Angeles and move back to El Salvador.

The following Monday, a new Rosa Lopez showed up, wearing a deep blue dress with a beaded collar. She was calm and had clearly been coached over the weekend.

"*Esa mujer es mala*," she said, looking at Marcia.

I had asked a friend who speaks fluent Spanish to come to court that day, to make sure the translations were accurate. "What does that mean?" I asked her.

"It means, That woman is evil," she said.

During her first interview, the day after the murders, Lopez said nothing to investigators about seeing Simpson's Bronco at the time of the murders. In a second interview, with defense investigators on July 29, she still said nothing about seeing the Bronco. Finally, on August 18, she said in Spanish that she'd seen the "Bronco *bianco*" at 10:15 P.M., about the time of the murders.

We asked for tapes or transcripts of the July 29 defense interview.

"There are no tape-recorded statements of Ms. Lopez," Carl Douglas told Ito on February 27. "There are no tape recordings of Ms. Lopez by any of our investigators." Yet later that day, defense investigator Bill Pavelic testified that he had tape-recorded the interview in question. Neither the tapes nor the transcripts of that interview had been given to us, a huge discovery violation.

"I'll do my best" to bring the tape the next day, Pavelic said.

But that was a blatant violation, too much for even Judge Ito to overlook.

"No, don't do your best," he snapped. "Have them here tomorrow."

As he had done with the discovery violations before opening statements, Douglas took the blame—fell on his sword. The defense seemed to be following strict strategy. Mislead, and if you're caught, blame the young guy.

Judge Ito fined Cochran and Douglas $950 each, a significant amount because if the fine were fifty bucks more, the violation would have to be reported to the state bar. To the end, Ito treated the defense lawyers with a deference that we didn't receive and didn't understand.

Finally, Ito sorted through the arguments and decided that Lopez could testify out of order, but only on tape, to be shown to the jury later.

So Cochran put her on and Lopez testified through an interpreter that she went out several times on the night of June 12 and saw Simpson's Bronco parked outside. She went out about 10 P.M., she testified, and it was there again.

"What car did you see parked out there?" Cochran asked.

"The Bronco," she said.

And then it was my turn with Rosa Lopez.

Unlike what happens in television shows about lawyers, most testimony in real trials isn't confrontational and doesn't result in bombshell revelations. Most testimony is elicited slowly and painstakingly, building a foundation by moving from one point to the next. Usually witnesses have been coached and recoached. It is incredibly rare that a lawyer can actually shred a witness's story. Yet every once in a while, you get a chance to really draw the rhetorical sword.

Rosa Lopez had testified earlier that she was leaving the country and already had her airline ticket. I asked her then, if she was leaving the country, why had she filled out application forms for unemployment insurance? In earlier testimony, she had denied filling out the forms.

"I was given the forms but I haven't filled them out," she said through an interpreter.

I presented her with the completed forms. "When you told us last Friday that you hadn't filled out your employment forms, that wasn't true, was it?"

Cochran objected, but Ito shut him down. Yes, she said, it was true.

I pressed her. "That was a lie, correct?" Yes, she admitted, she had filed for unemployment. She intended to receive her unemployment check in California while living in El Salvador.

I moved to the topic of airline tickets. Lopez had testified that she had already bought a ticket to fly home to El Salvador. Now she admitted that she hadn't purchased a ticket.

The questions alternated between challenging and gentle, and the inconsistencies piled up. I asked if investigator Bill Pavelic suggested to Lopez the times when she saw the Bronco. The tapes—which Douglas had said didn't exist—showed Pavelic suggesting what they wanted from the housekeeper:

> PAVELIC: So you take your dog for a walk about 10:15?
> LOPEZ: Ten-fifteen.
> PAVELIC: Ten-fifteen, ten-twenty, ten-thirty, OK.
> LOPEZ: Yeah.
> PAVELIC: Now, when you took your dog for a walk, could you still see the Bronco outside?
> LOPEZ: Yes.

The defense was blatantly leading Lopez. "All I said was that it was after ten," Lopez said to me in court on March 2.

"So you don't know how long after ten?"

"No, sir," she responded.

I asked if she remembered telling a former employer that "O. J. Simpson is a good guy and I'll testify to anything, any time."

"*No me recuerdo*," she said. I don't remember.

Did she tell someone else that Simpson wouldn't kill Nicole himself, that he'd have someone else do it?

"*No me recuerdo.*"

Over and over, Lopez gave the same answer: "I don't remember." One pundit stopped counting the "I don't remember"s at ninety-five. The woman couldn't remember what had happened two days earlier, and the defense wanted us to believe something she had remembered back in July, after she'd failed to mention it twice before?

I leaned on the podium and asked if Pavelic had coached her to say "I don't remember" to any difficult questions. No, she said. She'd only been advised to tell the truth. When I laughed, Judge Ito admonished me.

Lopez reverently called Cochran "Mr. Johnnie," and I asked several questions about how "Mr. Johnnie" and the other lawyers had convinced her to testify.

Cochran repeatedly objected and appeared to coach Lopez with hand signals from the defense table. When I called him on one gesture—his hands spreading both ways in a calming motion—he said, "That's ludicrous!" He said that he was gesturing to the court reporter, not Lopez. I didn't bother to ask why he would possibly be gesturing to the court reporter.

Later, when Cochran objected to the form of one of my questions and Ito suggested a way to rephrase it, a frustrated Cochran snapped, "He went to law school, your honor."

There were more contradictions: Lopez gave the wrong date of birth on her driver's license; she couldn't explain why Simpson's secretary Cathy Randa, surreptitiously met her on a neighboring street and drove her to a meeting at Simpson's office; she said she hadn't heard any voices the night of the killing, even though she said earlier that she had; she didn't recall in what month or even in what season she'd given her first statement to police.

I asked if she had trouble with dates and times.

"If I don't have it written down, how can I remember?" she responded. I paused and leafed through my notes. An alibi witness who needed to write things down to remember them. I could feel Cochran deflating nearby.

Lopez hadn't even given her real name. "Why do you want my correct name?" she asked.

I asked if she hated Nicole because Nicole had once slapped her maid, a friend of Lopez.

"I didn't say I hated her," she responded. "I said I didn't like her."

And then I paved the way for a slew of rebuttal witnesses, including a police officer who interviewed Lopez, someone she claimed never to have met.

I asked if she recalled telling a friend she could make $5,000 by testifying for Simpson.

"No me recuerdo."

Then I asked if she recalled talking to the *National Enquirer*. Again, she couldn't remember. In both cases, I had witnesses who would challenge her.

When Lopez was done testifying, on March 3, she was essentially useless as a witness. Hoping to save face, the defense lawyers insisted they would call her anyway, but I doubted it.

The pundits praised my work and agreed that Lopez had been a defense disaster. I rarely was mindful of the New York media, but the *Post* caught my eye with its headline: "Bye Bye Alibi: Prosecutor Destroys O. J.'s Key Witness." The only other *Post* story that grabbed my attention was an embarrassing headline that called me "Mr. Prosecutie." Upstairs, the minions celebrated and high-fived after the Lopez cross.

But I took no joy in watching Rosa Lopez limp off the stand. We'd caught the defense at its ethical lowest and I was curious to see how Cochran explained to the jury what had happened to the alibi he'd promised them. But I felt badly that an immigrant housekeeper had been caught up in the defense shenanigans.

"Her lack of credibility was so apparent," Marcia told the *New York Times*, "we could never have imagined the defense would hinge their whole case on this witness."

But Cochran didn't seem worried. He told the same reporter: "If she thinks that our whole case hinges on this witness, then she, like so many people who write about this case, don't know what she's talking about."

I knew he knew what *he* was talking about. Johnnie always had the race card.

Everything else to him was just so much noise. When the Rosa Lopez intermission was over, it was back to the LAPD. Tom Lange was on the stand (he would stay up there almost eight days), and Cochran wasted no time playing his hand. Grilling Lange over some minor piece of evidence, he suddenly asked if Lange had taken it "to your home in Simi Valley?"

Simi Valley. Where an all-white jury had acquitted the cops who beat Rodney King, triggering the 1992 riots. Maybe I wasn't admitting to myself just how low Cochran would sink. As the trial progressed, he showed no intention of allowing this to be a straight murder case. From the middle of March on, it was essentially a race case and the rules were completely different. Who needs a case when you have conspiracy? Who needs an alibi when you have cops who live in Simi Valley? Who needs evidence when you have Mark Fuhrman?

He was driving us all crazy.

We weren't preparing him to testify, just holding his hand. He seemed to care nothing about the case, about justice, about the victims. He was just worried what was going to happen to him. He grew more and more testy during preparation sessions, and so we tried to think of someone we could bring down to keep him calm.

Fuhrman's partner, the respected detective Ron Phillips, came up with the answer. "Higbee!"

Lieutenant Charles Higbee, LAPD, was retired, but we had all heard stories about him. He was a legend, a cop's cop—in charge of the police department's officer-involved-shooting teams. The D.A.'s office at the time had a roll-out program, sending its deputies out with the police investigators on officer-involved shootings. As one might guess, it wasn't a popular program with the cops.

"Don't worry about it," cops would say to one another when they were in trouble. "Higbee will know what to do."

According to Higbee lore, one time, a deputy D.A. and his investigator arrived at a shooting scene and were forced to wait a half-block from the scene. When the deputy complained that he was supposed to observe the investigation and collection of evidence, Higbee brought them to the shooting scene.

"Can you see everything from here?"

"Yeah, thanks," the deputy D.A. said.

"OK. Good." Higbee took a piece of chalk and drew a circle around the prosecutor and his investigator. "If you move an inch out of this circle, I'm throwing your asses out of here."

Fuhrman relaxed as soon as Higbee joined him. Finally, on March 9, the defense ran out of ridiculous questions for Lange and he was excused. Now it was Fuhrman's turn.

Ron Goldman's mother, Patti, and sister Kim stopped by my office, as they did whenever they were confused about a procedure or worried about some new rumor. They always carried their grief with dignity, but that day, I could clearly see they were troubled.

"What's gonna happen with Fuhrman?" Kim asked. "I mean, how is it gonna affect the case?"

"That's hard to say," I said. "The jury probably thinks he's a racist already. As long as he's honest, things should work out fine. They can't prove that he planted evidence. Because he didn't."

"But, Chris . . ." Kim was uncomfortable, like everyone else. "What about all the racism?"

"Well, the jury isn't going to like it. They're going to be pissed. We'll do what we can, but we're going to have a couple of bad days."

The courtroom was packed that day. It was quiet and tense as Fuhrman walked through, in a navy blue suit and red tie, his hair perfectly parted and combed, that serene, tough look on his face.

"Detective Fuhrman, can you tell us how you feel about testifying today?" Marcia rested against the podium in her own blue suit.

"Nervous. Reluctant."

"Can you tell us why?"

"Since June thirteenth, I've seen a lot of evidence ignored and a lot of the personal issues come to the forefront. I think that's too bad."

"Heard a lot about yourself in the press, have you?"

"Daily."

And so it began. Marcia set off on one of her detailed, structured direct examinations. We'd done all we could to keep out the nasty baggage that he carried, to allow the jury to focus on the murder and not Fuhrman's past. We'd managed to keep out of the trial: a political cartoon from Fuhrman's desk showing a swastika rising from the ashes; unfounded allegations that he'd planted evidence; the 1980 and 1981 psychiatric reports; and a rumor that he had made a comment to a colleague about seeing Nicole Brown's augmented breasts before she was killed.

That first day, March 9, Marcia went straight to the Kathleen Bell letter, in which Bell claimed Fuhrman wanted "nothing more than to see all niggers gathered together and killed."

"Did the conversation that Kathleen Bell describes in this letter occur?" Marcia asked.

"No."

Next, Marcia moved to the crime scene, carefully showing that everything Fuhrman did was in the presence of other officers and that he couldn't have planted evidence if he'd wanted to. He and Phillips were the tenth and eleventh police officers to arrive.

Marcia was masterful with him, gentle enough to calm him down when he was jittery early in his testimony, firm enough on the details to leave no room for the defense to claim he planted evidence. It was a sharp contrast to the mistrust and discomfort with which I would have questioned Fuhrman. The following day, Friday, they picked up where they'd left off, Fuhrman explaining that it was not his idea alone to climb over the wall surrounding Simpson's Rockingham estate.

The angular detective described how blood spots led him to Simpson's Ford Bronco. All that was left for Monday was Fuhrman's discovery of the second bloody glove in the walkway between Simpson's mansion and the fence. Again, Marcia pulled Fuhrman along perfectly, showing how impossible it would have been for Fuhrman to have planted the glove. He testified that he had no idea where Simpson was or whether he had an alibi.

Upstairs that Friday afternoon, there were flowers everywhere, at least fifty bouquets and arrangements sent to Fuhrman, some from old married couples, some from admiring women, others from cops from all over the country.

Later, Marcia sat in her office with a glass of Scotch, reading through a stack of faxes and reports. I told her how well she'd done with Fuhrman.

"You know," she said, "I'm sorry I got so upset when you asked me to take Fuhrman. You were right to be concerned. I should have realized earlier the pressures you were under."

"No problem," I said.

"We're going to kick your asses."

I turned to see F. Lee Bailey grinning at me. "Pardon me?"

"We're going to kick your asses."

"You mean figuratively, I hope."

He just stood there, that smug look on his jowly face.

"Well," I said. "Be sure and bring some help, asshole."

That was the F. Lee Bailey I had come to know. Flea. A foul-mouthed, arrogant SOB, nothing but an attack dog—waiting—ignoring the rest of the trial, taking sips from a tiny thermos. Some days he wouldn't appear in court at all and we'd get telephone tips from people letting us know where he'd hung out the night before, in case we wanted to check it out. We didn't.

Bailey hated me. One day, while Marcia was arguing a motion at the podium, Bailey—seated just to her immediate left—had become entranced, staring at Marcia's butt, a lecherous look on his face. For fifteen minutes he stared at her, as if he were in the room by himself.

At the break, I pulled Cochran aside and told him to take Flea for walks more often and explained that it wasn't appropriate for him to be leering at my cocounsel. Cochran laughed and said he'd talk to Bailey about it. After that, the tension between Bailey and me was palpable.

The distaste between Bailey and Fuhrman was just as thick. The detective sipped from a cup of water and answered nervously as Bailey started out slowly, asking over and over if Fuhrman knew Kathleen Bell.

"I do not recognize this woman as anyone I've ever met," Fuhrman said, looking at a photograph of Bell.

Bailey's style—if you could call it that—was nothing but badgering, asking questions over and over, testifying with his descriptive questions, raising his voice: a caricature of the tough defense lawyer he was supposed to be.

"How about a couple of gloves?" he asked. "Did you see a couple of gloves?"

"No," Fuhrman said repeatedly. "I found one."

The next day, March 14, Bailey was on the attack immediately, implying that Fuhrman planted the glove so that he could remain on the case. He was bitterly sarcastic, asking questions that were in fact testimony, questions that Judge Ito should never have allowed. "Was it not your purpose to be in the area along the south wall [where Fuhrman found the glove] alone?" Bailey asked.

"No, it wasn't."

"It just worked out that way," Bailey said derisively. "Is that it?"

"I didn't even know the south wall was accessible," Fuhrman answered calmly.

"It just worked out that you left the house and made your investigation for fifteen minutes or more, *alone?*"

"That's how it worked out," Fuhrman said.

Bailey rambled, made inappropriate statements, and offered up theories with no support. Judge Ito had, once again, changed his mind, allowing the defense to probe more deeply into Fuhrman's alleged racial bias.

So Bailey brought up marine sergeant Max Cordoba, who had changed his story at least twice about what, if anything, he'd heard Fuhrman say. Early on, he'd said that he hadn't heard Fuhrman say anything. But the black bodybuilder and aspiring actor (who wasn't in this case?) changed his mind and decided that Fuhrman had once called him "boy." It came to him, he said, in a dream.

Now Bailey told the court that he'd talked to Cordoba—"marine to marine"—and that Cordoba would come into court and, in fact, testify that Fuhrman had called him a nigger. But that night, on NBC's *Dateline,* Cordoba said that he'd never even talked to Bailey.

The next morning, March 15, Marcia dragged in a little bit late. I sat in the courtroom, eager to see Bailey beaten senseless with his own flaky witness and apparent lie to the court.

"What the hell's wrong with you?" I asked Marcia. This had the potential to be a great day.

"The kids don't feel well," she said. "They slept in my bed all night, a foot in this side, a knee in the other. I didn't sleep."

"Well, you gotta do Bailey."

"No," she said. "You do it."

"Hey, Bailey's yours. You earned it. Besides, you're a lot better suited for this." And she was. Marcia, like a lot of animals, is most dangerous when she's hungry or tired. I didn't know about her appetite, but she was plenty tired that day.

"I feel like shit," she said.

"So what's new. Come on, baby, get up there and break off a piece for daddy."

She laughed and Ito came out to the bench as Marcia rose to the podium. She played a portion of Cordoba's interview the night before and then reminded the judge of Bailey's contention that Cordoba had told him that Fuhrman called him a nigger. "This is the kind of nonsense that gives lawyers a bad name," Marcia said. She pointed at Bailey. "As an officer of this court, he has lied. He was impeached by his own witness."

Bailey jumped to his feet, wagging a stubby finger. "I object, Your Honor! I ask you to put a stop to it."

Marcia barely looked over her shoulder. "Excuse me, Mr. Bailey. Stand up and speak when it's your turn."

Bailey shook with anger. He hadn't expected a band of amateurs— civil servants—to cut holes in his highly anticipated cross-examination, to accuse him of lying. Although Cordoba changed his story again and said he had in fact spoken with Bailey, it was a good-sized helping of Southern California law.

Later that day, Bailey tried to use another glove to show how Fuhrman might have transported a glove to Rockingham—never mind that there was no evidence supporting it. Marcia objected, turned the leather glove over in her hand, and smirked. "Size small. I guess it's Mr. Bailey's." Judge Ito refused to allow Bailey to use the glove in front of the jury.

Outside the courtroom, Bailey sputtered, "Whoever has a witness has Marcia Clark in his face. And the worse she's faring, the more shrill she gets."

Later, on television, some of the experts too were hard on Marcia, calling the display "embarrassing." Others chided Ito for losing control of the courtroom. But most of the criticism was for Bailey. "Bailey didn't lay a glove on Fuhrman," said Laurie Levenson, a Loyola Law School professor. In the courtroom, the words were harsher: "washed-up," "one-note," "a bully."

The next morning, Ito was flustered by the show and he brokered one of his trademark playground solutions, asking the lawyers to apologize.

Marcia slipped me a note. "Speak up for me," it read. She stared straight ahead, tight-lipped.

"Judge," I said, "if their fighter will apologize, then so will mine." Marcia looked as if she were choking on a chunk of pot roast. She and Bailey apologized to each other, full of insincerity. Marcia followed me closely out of the courtroom and I was surprised she didn't kick me in the ass.

"You motherfucker!" she said outside. "I ask you for help and what do you do? You rolled over on me!"

"Look, Marcia. I did it for your own good. You're getting blasted on TV. You made your point; don't tarnish your image now on the likes of Bailey. Just trust me on this one."

We all felt great. The day was almost over and Fuhrman was handling Bailey easily. And the detective said that he enjoyed the way Marcia had trashed Bailey. As Fuhrman sat leaning against the jury box during a recess, I whispered to Marcia, "Follow my lead." I put my arm around her shoulder and pulled her head to rest on my chest, and we walked in Fuhrman's direction. His face turned bright red and he stared at us.

"What are you doing having that guy hanging all over you like a cheap suit?" Fuhrman asked Marcia after I'd left. I took it very seriously; perhaps Mark Fuhrman hadn't changed after all.

I've never heard one man use the word "nigger" so many times. By the end of Flea's cross-examination, I was as tense and sweaty as if I had been on the stand myself. I couldn't imagine how the jury was taking it. Bailey spat the word in just the way that I remembered hearing it the first time, bitterly and cruelly.

I watched Cochran, who sat there with his hands folded, his index fingers pointed to his lips, leaning forward. He had put Bailey up to this, had unleashed this man on the case and decided that we'd have no semblance of a fair trial. "Let the white people fight over Fuhrman," Cochran had said to me. Well, that didn't change his complicity in all this. He had given Bailey license to say that word over and over, fully aware of the guttural way in which Bailey used it and the effect on that jury. He allowed Bailey to put on a show for the white people. Bailey was speaking, but Cochran was a full partner in this.

Bailey made a big deal over our "mock cross-examination," alleging that we'd prepared Fuhrman for his testimony about the word. A vivid description of that meeting had been published in *Newsweek* magazine, and I'd gone in search of the leaks, finding them in the D.A.'s office.

Everything else Bailey had done failed, and so he went after Fuhrman indirectly, by throwing out racial epithets all over the courtroom, hoping the jury would later connect them to Fuhrman's testimony, hoping some of it stuck. "Did you tell the lawyers in that room that you never used the word 'nigger'?"

"It was never asked," Fuhrman said. Each time we objected, but Ito let the ridiculous questioning continue.

"Do you use the word 'nigger' in describing people?" Bailey asked.

"No, sir."

I clenched my teeth, wondering what this could possibly have to do with the deaths of Ron Goldman and Nicole Brown.

And then Bailey asked the question that I'd posed to Fuhrman, the one that had convinced me I couldn't put him on the stand. "Have you used that word in the past ten years?"

I leaned toward Marcia and whispered, "Object. Object. Object. Object!" This was the trap they'd been waiting to spring for nine months. How hard would it be to find some witness to come in and corroborate the defense claim that Fuhrman had used the word in the past ten years? If they could lead Rosa Lopez into saying that she saw a Bronco where there was none, how hard would it be to find someone to testify against the most reviled police officer in L.A.? "Object," I said.

But Marcia didn't object.

"Have you used that word in the past ten years?"

I wanted to scream: No! If he answered with that same arrogance, our case was, in essence, over.

"Not that I recall, no."

"I want you to assume that perhaps at some time since 1985 or '86, you addressed a member of the African-American race as a nigger," Bailey said. "Is it possible that you have forgotten that act on your part?"

Yes! Yes! I hoped he would take the escape route.

"No. It is not possible."

"Are you therefore saying that you have not used that word in the past ten years, Detective Fuhrman?"

"Yes, that is what I'm saying."

It was just as I had argued months earlier, when I tried to exclude the word that Bailey now threw around with such glee. I had argued that this would be nothing but a race case, that this word would be used to bludgeon justice right out of this courtroom. After the cross-examination was over, the other prosecutors would believe that Fuhrman had withstood the defense's hardest hits, but I knew better. With each answer, our hope for a conviction slipped away.

Even Bailey knew what he had in front of him: "And you say under oath that you have not addressed any black person as 'nigger' or spoken about black people as niggers in the past ten years, Detective Fuhrman?"

Mark Fuhrman looked out with those BB eyes, dead and soulless. "That's what I'm saying, sir."

SEVENTEEN

I eased out of the car and into the gloomy, commercial street, walking toward what looked like an old dairy or a meat-packing plant—chipped brick and industrial—set back from the street in an eighty-year-old neighborhood in Venice. It was dark, after 10 P.M., and the building appeared empty. With all that was going on in this case, it wouldn't have been too much of a stretch to suspect this was a setup.

"So, this is it?" Runyon asked.

"This is it," said Craig Richman, the deputy district attorney who had come up with this lead. It was December 6, 1994, and we were checking out one of the many telephone tips that came in about the Simpson jury. I've never seen anything like it. Friends and relatives were constantly calling in with allegations that jurors had made up their minds, had lied, had gotten information from the outside, had begun writing books, or had criminal records.

We knocked at the front door and a man answered. Inside, the building was home to a fully modern business, the brick walls brightly painted, the space filled with telephones, fax machines, and a glass table and four chairs. After a moment, an attorney named Felipa Richland came out to see us.

"You should know, my client is having second thoughts about all of this," Felipa said. Then she left for a moment and returned with a woman who was startlingly uncomfortable. She appeared to be Mediterranean, about five feet, seven inches tall, with dark hair and a face that came to a point at her protruding lips and nose.

"Hi, I'm Deputy D.A. Christopher Darden." She turned and walked right through my handshake. A cigarette hung from her right hand, and her right elbow was planted in her left palm. She blew smoke out the side of her mouth.

"She really didn't want to talk," Richland said. "But she felt she should."

"What do you mean?"

This time the woman answered for herself: "Well, I gave the same information to Judge Ito and nothing has happened with it. I don't know why."

She said that two weeks earlier she'd called Ito's clerk, Deirdre Robertson, and told her that one of the jurors knew O. J. Simpson and had worked with his daughter Arnelle. It was the juror who worked for Hertz. This woman had even passed on to the judge a handbook from a 1982 Hertz cocktail party for which the juror had been on a planning committee and Simpson was a celebrity guest.

The Hertz juror had bothered me from the beginning, when I asked Hodgman and Marcia why they had allowed him to remain on the jury. I recalled a conversation in which the juror had talked to Ito about the apparent conflict.

> POTENTIAL JUROR 228: I believe I heard someone say that if I get called for this case, I wouldn't be chosen because I work . . . for the Hertz Corporation.
> COURT: What did you think of that?
> POTENTIAL JUROR 228: Well, I didn't think it had no bearing because . . . *I haven't formerly met the defendant.* [Italics added.]

But this woman insisted they had met. Not only that, but Juror 228 worked with Simpson's daughter Arnelle at the Hertz VIP services unit at Los Angeles International Airport, the woman said. At a 1982 reception, she claimed, Simpson walked down a line of people and shook hands with Juror 228.

"Is there anyone who can corroborate this?" I asked.

She gave me the name of a former Hertz employee. We called her the next day. Yeah, she agreed, Juror 228 knew Simpson.

When Ito heard that I'd investigated one of the jurors, he was livid. It seemed, before I was added to the case, the attorneys had agreed not to investigate jurors, but nobody ever told me.

Of all the overblown and destructive aspects of this case, perhaps none was as bizarre as the battles inside and over the jury. From our standpoint, of course, this was a bad jury. Our own consultant had said that—based on jury questionnaires—there were jurors and alternates who would *never* convict O. J. Simpson of murder.

Marcia had remarked once that she wished she could give polygraph tests to the jurors and alternates, so certain was she that they had lied to get on the case. There were football fans claiming they were "shocked" to find out O. J. Simpson was charged in his wife's murder, people who claimed not to have heard of Simpson, and people who claimed to know nothing about the Bronco chase. Who in Los Angeles knew nothing about the Bronco chase?

By the time I joined the prosecution team, the only thing we could do with this jury was root out those who lied about their pasts and about their knowledge of the case. And so we followed through with several leads. But our inquiries were nothing compared to the skullduggery going on in Simpson's camp.

One man who claimed to be a reporter covering the case repeatedly tried to pass me information that he'd "uncovered" about a juror. I declined, but the man continued to pester me. It was strange. The man said he was from the *"Post Gazette Chronicle,"* but, pushed on it, admitted he didn't have a paper yet, that he was thinking of starting one. Finally, the man "published" his story, photocopying it and handing it out to reporters at the trial. It was a collection of allegations about a white juror who would later be dismissed. The "reporter" was often seen talking to the defense team, and I received unconfirmed reports that he was a defense plant.

It wouldn't have surprised me. There was a whole web of investigators working for the defense team, led by Bill Pavelic and Pat McKenna, two well-known private investigators.

In June, another defense investigator, Scott Barnes, filed a strange lawsuit—ostensibly charging Judge Ito with jury tampering—but, if you believed him, also offering a rare glimpse into the defense camp, which seemed from the outside like a bunch of squabbling wannabe Humphrey Bogarts, skulking around like spies, feeding information to tabloid reporters and trying to get rid of jurors they believed were favorable to the prosecution. Barnes, in his lawsuit—since dismissed—said he'd had conversations with Pavelic "concerning being able to make it appear a conspiracy exists in the LAPD to frame Mr. Simpson . . ." Pavelic and McKenna didn't trust each other, according to the suit, accusing each other of creating false leads and leaking information to the tabloids. "Pavelic told me he knew their client was Guilty but that he wanted to help create an environment that 'The Juice' would at least get a Mistrial the first time around and Pavelic would look like the best investigator for doing so . . ."

The suit was a run-on description of "setting up" people, tailing vehicles, monitoring cellular telephones, and—most disturbing—trying to get nonblack jurors tossed off the case. Barnes accused the defense of engaging ". . . in a Conspiracy to alter evidence, create a False and Groundless environment in [an] attempt to convince the Judge to remove certain jurors from the panel that they felt were pro-Prosecution. . . . [F]alse letters and anonymous phone 'TIPS' were created to cause jurors to be removed . . ."

It was crazy stuff and I probably would've just dismissed it if it weren't for what was happening to a juror named Francine Florio-Bunten. She was a white woman, an experienced juror, well-read—the only juror who volunteered that DNA stood for deoxyribonucleic acid. The defense hated her. In fact, she was the juror who had been the subject of the story by the reporter without a paper.

Late in the spring, after seven other jurors had already been dismissed, an anonymous letter surfaced, allegedly from the secretary at a literary agency. The letter was clearly a setup, written to convince us that Florio-Bunten was writing a book called *Standing Alone for Nicole*.

Florio-Bunten vehemently denied the allegations. Given the reporter without a paper and Barnes's allegations ("[F]alse letters . . . were created to cause jurors to be removed . . ."), I believed the letter was a fake.

However, before calling Florio-Bunten in, Judge Ito had questioned another juror, and when she left, she passed Florio-Bunten a note, saying the judge wanted to question her next, about a book. The judge had admonished the jury not to talk about in-camera discussions. Another juror reported the note to Ito, but when Ito asked Florio-Bunten about it, she denied receiving a note.

Later, it was reported that Florio-Bunten was kicked off the jury for writing a book, but in the end, she was dismissed for lying about the note she'd apparently received. After that, we couldn't argue that she should stay on the panel. We agreed that she should go.

Meanwhile, with a straight face, Cochran continued to claim that we were "targeting" black jurors. It was a ridiculous contention, since we started out with eight black jurors and ended with nine. And it was disingenuous given the fact that the defense was investigating jurors and Cochran assented to the removal of every white juror and fought the dismissal of every black juror but one—a woman who asked to leave the jury and was later hospitalized for stress.

In fact, Cochran gloated when nonblack jurors were dismissed. After Francine Florio-Bunten was dismissed amid rumors that she was writing a book—a book that doesn't exist—Cochran gushed to a *USA Today* reporter, "You'll notice I'm smiling. That's all I'm going to say."

For eight days, the defense accused Tom Lange of every conspiracy this side of the grassy knoll. For six more days, they tried to convince Mark Fuhrman that he'd planted evidence. By the end of March, as I tried to prepare Lange's partner, Phil Vannatter, you couldn't blame him for not being eager to testify in this case. It was torture for a senior detective with Vannatter's credentials and integrity to have his credibility challenged.

There was no mystery about where they were going to attack Vannatter. He had written the search warrant the morning of June 13, writing in the supporting affidavit that Simpson's trip to Chicago was unplanned and that blood observed on the Bronco that morning was tested and determined to be human. To me, the conclusions Vannatter had reached were natural, based on the best knowledge he had at the time. But the defense went after Vannatter as a liar, and Ito went along, ruling that Phil wrote the warrant with a "reckless disregard for the truth."

Phil Vannatter was an Indiana boy, already a year late for retirement, counting the days till he could return to his family farm. I watched his hound-dog face as we sat at the Saratoga, avoiding the case over two bottles of beer.

"I've been a cop twenty-six years," Vannatter said ruefully. "Twenty-six years and no one has ever accused me of lying."

Vannatter and Lange were the I/Os—the investigating officers—in this case. In the best circumstances, I/Os and prosecutors make a strong team, combining the cop's knowledge of the streets with the lawyer's knowledge of the courtroom. I'd gotten close to a few I/Os in the past, like Arce and Stephens, and I put the two lead Simpson investigators in the same category. Of course, I had a reputation in SID as being tough on cops, but I had the deepest respect for good cops—like Phil and Tom—guys who took it seriously, guys who were fair and courageous.

In the office before his testimony, Vannatter was visibly nervous. I grabbed him by the arm and gave him the same advice I'd passed along earlier on the Geraldo Rivera show.

"Hey, whatever happens up there, remember, you're a good cop," I said. "Don't let those bastards mess with you."

Phil testified strongly and reasonably, settling in as comfortably as an Indiana farm boy in a feed store. He'd never met Fuhrman before this case, he said, showing that it would make no sense for these two suddenly to enter into a conspiracy together. He also made it clear that he was in charge, that Fuhrman was just a junior detective and wouldn't have done anything without some guidance from him or Lange. We talked about the blood trail from the bodies down the walkway, ending in Nicole's driveway and picking up at Simpson's house, on his Bronco and in his bathroom.

We played a tape of Vannatter driving back and forth from Simpson's house to Nicole's condo, a trip that took about five minutes each way—plenty of time for Simpson to get there, kill Nicole and Ron, and get back home. We showed pictures of Simpson's finger, the one he told police he cut twice, in exactly the same place. Before the murders, he said, he cut the finger on some paper, and he claimed he often cut his fingers "playing golf." After the murders, of course, he cut the finger on a shard of glass.

"You've heard Mr. Cochran use the term 'rush to judgment'?" I asked.

"Yes, I've heard that," Vannatter said.

"Did you 'rush to judgment' in this case?"

"No," he said.

Robert Shapiro handled the cross-examination. Without the histrionics of Bailey and Cochran, he showed that there was no cut on the left glove to match the cut on Simpson's hand and pointed out that Simpson had agreed to be interviewed by police. But Vannatter

destroyed Shapiro on most points and I was glad to see him stand up to
the ridiculous, minute scrutiny over meaningless items.

So, when Shapiro brought up the famous ice cream defense and
asked if Vannatter wished he would've taken the ice cream cup as evidence, the detective did what they all should've done.

"Gee. Monday morning quarterbacking is wonderful," he said. "I
still, to this day, don't believe that the ice cream is connected to the crime
scene."

From the prosecution table, I nodded. No matter what happened, it
was good for the cops on this case to be up and fighting.

Marcia had the next witness after Vannatter: Brian "Kato" Kaelin,
Nicole Brown's former friend and the Fabio-haired freeloader who lived
in Simpson's guest house. Kato said he'd gone to get a hamburger with
Simpson around 9 P.M., and an hour after returning from McDonald's,
he'd heard three loud thumps outside Simpson's house in the walkway
where the bloody glove was later found. That hour in between—during
which Simpson was unaccounted for—was when Nicole Brown and
Ronald Goldman were murdered.

The day after the killings, as he was making telephone calls to
Cathy Randa, the Brown family, and others, O. J. made several calls to
Kaelin—strange, because he and Kato weren't that close. But the reason
became apparent when one of Kaelin's friends told us that Simpson had
said to Kaelin, "Thank God, you can tell them I was home all the time."
O. J. was fishing for an alibi.

Kato wasn't willing to go that far for Simpson, but he wasn't much
help to investigators either. At first, in the days following the murders,
he was coy, refusing to answer questions. We received tips that he'd told
friends he had crucial information. But by the time he testified, in late
March, he was as helpful as a pile of hair. I've rarely seen a witness work
so hard to be vague and inconclusive on the stand. He denied that Simpson had asked him to be his alibi. Kato later recalled Simpson as being
animated and upset about Nicole, even though, on the stand, he said
Simpson didn't seem particularly angry the night of the murders. Only
after treating him as a hostile witness did Marcia finally get Kaelin to
admit—in Kato-speak—that "there was some upsetness." Throughout
his testimony, Kato played dumb. It was the perfect role for him; he was
a natural.

In some ways, Kato was the perfect mascot of this trial, a stereotypical, vacuous Southern Californian. He personified the way people tried to cash in on the crime (if you don't think this case was blown out of proportion, just remember: Kato Kaelin got his own radio show).

More to the point, Kato was representative of the way Simpson's friends protected him at all costs. As he testified, I thought of all the people who were withholding critical information, people like Paula Barbieri, who neglected to tell us she'd broken up with Simpson that day, like Simpson's friends, who knew that he'd beaten Nicole but wouldn't talk.

All over Brentwood and Beverly Hills, people held their one puzzle piece tightly in their hands, thinking to themselves, "I don't want to be the one to convict the guy." Throughout the spring, we tried to show the jury the complete picture, but sometimes I wonder how the puzzle might have turned out with whatever pieces someone like Kato Kaelin withheld from the world.

Conversely, Allan Park, the limousine driver who showed up at Simpson's estate to take him to the airport, was one of the most believable and honest witnesses in the case. He had no agent, no book deals, and no axe to grind. Park's testimony was simple: The Ford Bronco was not at the front of the estate when he pulled up at 10:22 P.M. Park repeatedly checked his watch and rang Simpson's buzzer, but got no answer. He drove around to another gate. Then, about 10:55 P.M., a black man, about six feet tall and 200 pounds, entered Simpson's house through the front door.

Marcia had Simpson stand up.

"Yes," Park said, "around that size." When Simpson finally showed up that night, he told Park that he'd "overslept," even though later O. J. would deny sleeping and would say that he was outside, hitting golf balls, and inside, sitting on his bed.

Even Cochran admitted to reporters that Park was "a wonderful witness."

By the end of March, we'd established much of our case. The first half of our domestic violence evidence had shown a jealous, violent ex-husband. Witnesses like Kato Kaelin and Allan Park showed that Simpson wasn't home during the time in which his wife was killed and that he had no explanation for a seventy-eight-minute gap and no alibi. He had motive; he had opportunity. Now we moved to the strongest leg of our case, the overwhelming physical evidence.

But we were also moving into the teeth of the defense, the allegation that Simpson had been framed by a combination of racist cops and incompetent lab technicians. The defense had given racism a face: Mark Fuhrman. Now, they would try to introduce the jury to the face of incompetence: Dennis Fung.

Every once in a while, when we were bogged down with work, I would wonder why we couldn't use Hank Goldberg, who had proved himself to be a smart and energetic lawyer.

Marcia would answer me with one word: "Fung."

Dennis Fung was a good criminalist—the person assigned to catalogue and collect evidence from a crime scene. He'd been doing the job for eleven years, working five hundred crime scenes. But he'd botched this one, plain and simple, collecting some of the bloodstains weeks after he should have, assigning an inexperienced assistant to the case, and keeping sloppy records. None of his mistakes was critical, but the defense had shown that it didn't need much to blow everything out of proportion and connect the witness to their mushrooming conspiracy. We knew Fung was in for tough cross-examination.

Some people just aren't cut out to be witnesses in criminal cases. It is a tremendous amount of pressure and no place for people who are scatter-brained or indecisive. Sometimes, just being too earnest can make someone a troublesome witness. Goldberg spent weeks preparing Fung, going over his testimony, familiarizing him with the issues. It didn't matter.

Later, Hank would be roundly criticized for not preparing Fung, but nothing could be further from the truth.

Fung and Goldberg started out well, with a tight, methodical direct examination. Fung smoothly handled the mistake of assigning the Simpson investigation to his young assistant, Andrea Mazzola. "When I found out it was a high-profile case and it was going to be a complicated crime scene, I decided that she should, in a sense, take the back seat."

Hank did very well with Fung, getting the criminalist to admit his mistakes and to explain his complex methods. But then it was Barry Scheck's turn. And he carved Fung like an over-cooked turkey.

He showed a video of Andrea Mazzola handling evidence without changing gloves, highlighted Fung's failure to recall whether there was

blood on the gate at Nicole Brown's home, and accused him of lying to
the grand jury. Fung had told the grand jury that he'd put the bloody
glove at Bundy into an evidence bag. But the defense showed a videotape
of Mazzola putting the glove in the bag. It was a tiny misstatement, but
Scheck leaped at it.

"That testimony wasn't accurate, was it?" Scheck asked.

"That I personally did that stuff? No."

"And that testimony you gave the grand jury was under oath?"

"Yes."

They showed a photo of the gate and asked Fung where the bloodstain was. It wasn't evident in the picture they used.

"Where is it, Mr. Fung?" Scheck asked accusingly.

"I can't see it in that photograph."

Scheck played every tiny concession with a flourish and mocking
disdain for Fung. Next to me, Marcia fidgeted, sliding her legal pad in
front of me. "This is so painful," she wrote. "We need to help Hank set
up a short, but powerful re-direct to resurrect Fung a little. I think things
look bad at the moment."

But the defense offered a little bit of help in bringing Fung back.
Like sharks, they were so taken with the scent of blood, they got greedy
and mean-spirited.

Cochran told reporters that Fung was "the worst witness I've seen in
thirty-three years of practicing law."

Before one of Fung's daily adventures on the stand, Shapiro came
into the courtroom with a bag of fortune cookies, giving them to reporters and others. He offered one to me. "These are from Hang Fung
restaurant," he said, chuckling with other members of the defense team.
I stared at him and just walked away.

During one of the breaks, I sat alongside Fung, who was upset about
Shapiro's joke and considered it racist.

"What do I do if he tries to apologize?" Fung asked.

"Well, do you believe that an apology fairly resolves the matter?"

"No."

"Then don't accept it."

And so, when Shapiro came over and apologized, Fung told him he
wouldn't accept it. Later, during a break, Shapiro had to go downstairs to
apologize at a press conference with representatives from various Asian-

lawyer organizations. As he walked toward the door, Cochran caught his attention.

"Hey, be sure to tell them I had nothing to do with it."

Shapiro looked back at him sheepishly.

"I'm serious."

The defense team's zeal cost them in the courtroom too. A cross-examination that should've lasted two days stretched to five, as Scheck tried to squeeze a little more juice from Fung. The press loved Scheck, as did the jury. It is easy to become taken with the accolades, and every day, Scheck hammered harder at Fung, getting further and further afield. Near the end, he accused Fung of altering the form on which he recorded evidence collection. The form consisted of four pages, three of which had writing on them. One did not. The three pages with writing had tiny holes in the upper left-hand corner—staple holes. The fourth page didn't have staple holes.

"One of those pages doesn't have staple holes in it, Mr. Fung," Scheck accused.

"That's correct."

"That's because you got rid of the original page four. Isn't that true, Mr. Fung?"

"That's not true," Fung countered. But Scheck kept at him, asking those wonderful Perry Mason questions about this huge staple conspiracy. He alleged that Fung had switched pages because there was something damaging on the missing page. Later, Fung and Goldberg found the harmless page, and Hank came to Marcia and me with it.

"Should I tell Barry?" Hank asked.

No way. Scheck had badgered our witness, shouted and sneered at the man, argued with him and called him a liar when he knew that Fung was trying to answer the best that he could. Scheck knew Fung wasn't part of some conspiracy. Let him find out the hard way that there was nothing suspicious on the "missing page."

During his redirect, Goldberg presented the newly discovered sheet to Fung, and Scheck went ballistic. He asked Judge Ito to tell the jury that the prosecution was being deliberately deceptive. It was a bitter, ninety-minute debate. Goldberg told the judge that was what Scheck got for basing a conspiracy on a couple of missing staple holes. It was the way the defense fought their case, looking for any tiny discrepancies that they could spend hours talking about, until they'd completely distracted the jury from the issue at hand: the brutal murders of two people.

As he'd done once earlier with Goldberg, Ito advised the jury that we had behaved unethically. The first time had occurred after Hank accidentally showed the jury a luggage tag that Ito had ruled shouldn't be shown. I have never met a lawyer as honest as Hank Goldberg and I know those admonitions to the jury had to hurt him.

But all in all, Hank did a good job rehabilitating Fung. Fung denied being a coconspirator, said he'd never met Fuhrman before and barely knew Lange and Vannatter. He showed—as we had with other witnesses—that logistics and timing made it impossible for someone to have planted evidence. Finally, on April 18, Fung was allowed to leave.

After nine days of testimony, Dennis Fung walked over to the defense table and shook hands with Simpson and the men who had destroyed him. Perhaps he was like a hostage who develops sympathy for his captors. Strangely, he didn't shake hands with Goldberg, the man who spent four months preparing him and the man whose reputation suffered because of Fung's bumbling. He did, however, shake hands with Shapiro and Scheck.

A graduate of Yale and Cal Berkeley Law School, Barry Scheck is clearly an intelligent man and a talented defense lawyer. But I could only shake my head as pundits buzzed over his "brilliant" cross-examination skills. It was like praising a big-game hunter for bagging a lion at a zoo. The ability to dismantle a confused and earnest witness like Dennis Fung no more makes him a great lawyer than my destruction of a bad witness like Rosa Lopez makes me a great lawyer. That's one of the things wrong with this system and, especially, this trial. The focus is so heavily placed upon competition and confrontation that it distorts our true duties and responsibilities. Our system will rarely result in justice as long as the only measure of a great lawyer is *winning*.

By the middle of April, the *Los Angeles Times* reported, there had already been 430 sidebars. The jury had seen only 41 percent of the court proceedings. We were averaging two hours of jury presentation per day.

On that front, the defense was winning; they knew the longer the trial dragged on, the less likely we would be to have twelve people left alive, let alone agreeable enough to return a verdict.

I thought a retired superior court judge named George Dell was correct when he wrote, on April 16, that the case was out of control: "There are people on death row with far less evidence than there is in this case," he wrote to one newspaper. "This is a case that demonstrates that if you have enough money . . . the trial will go differently. There is a fight every millimeter of the way. No one will stipulate to anything. The prosecution is having to prove every milli-fact. This is something you normally just don't see in a criminal case."

Bearing the strain was the jury. Paid $5 a day, sequestered at the Hotel Inter-Continental downtown, the jurors wore the pressure on their faces. The case had already lasted almost as long as Ito had warned them it would and we weren't half done with our case.

Around the same time the Hertz juror was dismissed, attention turned to a young Hispanic woman who came to court earlier with a mark on her face. I had hoped it was just a cold sore. However, on her questionnaire, it turned out that she'd written that she was the victim of domestic abuse. She was dismissed as well.

The attrition rate for jurors was almost one every two weeks. The seats changed, the people changed, but the faces never seemed to change. It was the most stone-faced group of people I've ever seen. Denise Brown cried and spoke powerfully about her sister's abusive relationship, and the jurors just sat there. We showed them crime scene photos that elicited gasps from grizzled prosecutors, and while a few jurors looked away, others sat dull-eyed, seemingly unmoved.

On February 7, a sixty-three-year-old white juror named Katherine Murdoch was removed after telling the judge that she was a patient of Simpson's arthritis doctor. Murdoch was replaced by a fifty-four-year-old postal manager named Willie Cravin, a stern-faced black man who seemed to fundamentally change the jury chemistry as soon as he joined it. Soon after Cravin's addition, it was apparent to us that the jury was racially polarized. One of the white women complained that Cravin was a bully. He accused her of bullying him. She bumped him once, Cravin said, and another time, she kicked his chair in the jury box. That big bear of a man claimed he was intimidated by a woman he outweighed by a hundred pounds. Cravin also complained that the deputies gave preferential treatment to the white jurors.

Cravin seemed to be the leader of a clique that had formed, four black jurors who smiled at everything the defense said and tried to run the panel behind the scenes. Did we target jurors? Absolutely not. Were we happy when Cravin's clique began to draw the attention of Judge Ito? Absolutely. To us, these were jurors who had made up their minds before they ever sat down.

The first of the clique to be dismissed from the case was Michael Knox, a forty-six-year-old courier who failed to disclose a 1984 arrest for kidnapping and assault, charges that the victim later dropped. Knox was dismissed in March and immediately set to work on a book. But he wasn't the only wannabe author. In March, another juror, Tracy Kennedy, came under suspicion for asking strange personal questions and—according to other jurors—listening in on telephone conversations and trying to stir up emotions. They also complained of other things, that he put his feet on the furniture and gargled at the dinner table.

"I think the evidence at this point," I said to Ito, "may establish that he is somewhat of a jerk. . . . But he's done nothing that constitutes misconduct."

However, on March 17, deputies found a laptop computer in his room, on which he'd typed the names of all the jurors and other notes that appeared to indicate he was writing a book. This time, we agreed that he should go.

By the middle of April, the remaining jurors were on the verge of imploding. The Cravin clique was alleging racial bias at every turn, and tips continued coming in about other panelists.

Jeanette Harris seemed to be a strong member of the pro-defense clique, chuckling at Cochran's sarcasm and rolling her eyes during Marcia's direct examinations. One day the court got a tip that Harris was a victim of spousal abuse and had failed to report it. She'd filed a petition for a restraining order in 1988, alleging that she'd been beaten by her husband and forced to have sex with him. Now she denied the whole thing.

Cochran fought Harris's removal, but Ito had no choice. Either she lied on her questionnaire or—if, as she claimed, the abuse had never happened—she lied in her petition for a restraining order. On April 6, Harris, the second member of the visibly pro-defense clique, was dismissed. Again, Cochran accused us of targeting Harris and other black jurors.

The next day, Jeanette Harris dropped a bomb. She sat for an interview with KCAL television in Los Angeles, saying that our case had amounted to "a whole lot of nothing," and that the domestic violence evidence "doesn't mean he's guilty of murder." She predicted a hung jury and depicted a panel polarized by race, divisions that extended to the mostly white deputies who guarded the jury. Off-camera, she told the reporter that she regularly talked about the case with a handful of other jurors, a violation of Judge Ito's stern daily admonitions.

The media went nuts. In a way, we did too. We weren't surprised that we hadn't reached a group of jurors, but we were plainly disappointed by Harris's reaction to the domestic violence evidence. This woman was a victim of spousal abuse herself and she couldn't see that this was a murder that was the culmination of years of battering? Would any jurors? First Scott Gordon and then I had pushed the domestic violence angle so strongly because we knew that it explained why Simpson had acted and that it showed who he really was. Now there were questions in the office about whether the strategy had been wise. I argued that Judge Ito had crippled the domestic violence evidence when he ruled that some of our witnesses had to be put on at the end of the case.

But at the rate we were going, the case would never end. Ito took time out of the proceedings to interview the jurors over the things Jeanette Harris had said. He spoke to each juror separately, with lawyers from each side in chambers too, trying to find out if the jurors were really talking to one another about the case and whether the racial tensions were as bad as Harris described.

Tracy Hampton was a twenty-five-year-old flight attendant, a petite, pretty black woman whom I had worried about from the beginning. She was young and nervous, cowering in the box and avoiding everyone's eyes. She couldn't have taken ten pages of notes throughout the entire trial. When she caught someone looking at her, she'd grasp the collar of her blouse as if she was trying to cover herself.

In chambers, we watched as she told Ito that she'd awakened one day to find a female deputy standing alone at the foot of her bed, staring at her. She said the deputy hadn't knocked.

I handed Marcia a note: "Sexual misconduct allegations?"

"No way," she wrote back. But I wasn't sure.

Another juror said that she'd seen the deputy knock before going in to wake Hampton up. According to the other juror, Hampton told her that she feared the mirror in her room was a two-way mirror and that there were people watching her dress and undress. She wanted off the case, but Ito talked her into staying.

A few other jurors ascribed racist motives to the deputies. "Those damn bastards have been controlling me all my life!" one juror raged. It was incredible. How were we supposed to get a fair trial from these people, from a group who believed they were being treated unfairly by so-called racist law enforcement officers?

So, trying to appease the remaining members of the Cravin clique, Judge Ito removed three deputies who were watching over the jurors. They denied the allegations in a brief hearing and then they were gone.

"This isn't fair to the deputies," Marcia said on the telephone that night.

"Maybe not," I agreed. I didn't think for a minute that the deputies were racist or were mistreating jurors. But if it meant we finished the case sooner and got a fair verdict, I was in favor of removing the deputies.

The next morning, I turned on the radio and couldn't believe what I was hearing. I dialed a number that had become more familiar than my own.

"Marcia? It's Chris. What's your ETA?" I asked from my car phone.

"I'm on my way to drop the kids off at school."

"Well, you'd better do it quickly. There's a jury protest. The radio is reporting that they won't go inside the courtroom."

On Friday, April 21, thirteen of the eighteen remaining jurors wore black clothing to court. They were protesting the removal of the deputies. They had prepared a document signed by all but four of the jurors, saying that the removal of the deputies was wrong. Jurors of all different races protested the move, and they had sent a clear signal—to us anyway—that this jury wasn't controlled by any clique. With Harris and Knox gone and Cravin under investigation for intimidating other jurors, we thought we might have a chance.

Ito set to work trying to soothe the jurors. Throughout the trial, he had to promise them things that he shouldn't have. He promised to pay money to one juror who said she was losing income from a rental property while she was sequestered. After the trial, she said that she had never received any money. At one point, a male juror complained that he wanted desperately to go to a football game. I couldn't believe what Judge Ito did next. He turned to Cochran, who was in the judge's chambers with me and the juror, and asked if Cochran could help him get the juror tickets for a UCLA game. Cochran jumped at the chance to help and promised the juror great seats. It was completely inappropriate. Ito was practically brokering a gift from the defense.

But in such ways, Judge Ito calmed the jury revolt, and we set back to work. But it was only a matter of days before another juror sent a note saying she needed to talk to the judge.

"I am a nervous wreck," a skittish Tracy Hampton told Judge Ito. She sat uncomfortably in his chambers for the second time in five days, insisting that someone was slamming doors and talking directly outside her room. She would be sleeping or reading and they would be out there, right by her door. "I'm a nervous wreck," she repeated. "I have had a nervous breakdown, I guess. I cannot concentrate."

Deputies were playing mind games, she said, making gestures toward her. "I do not really know what's going on with me. I am a mess now." Other jurors weren't happy with her "because I don't socialize with them."

During testimony, Hampton said, lawyers stared at her. Strange things were happening in court, she said. For instance, a couple of beepers went off.

I looked over at Marcia. This juror was losing it.

"This case has really stressed me out," Hampton said. "I think for my mental well-being . . ." She left the thought unfinished. And she left the case. A few days later, suffering from stress because of the packs of reporters who followed her, Hampton checked into a hospital for a few days. After the trial, with jurors writing books and going on talk shows, I found it somewhat ironic that Tracy Hampton showed up posing in *Playboy* magazine. This woman who was afraid people were watching her undress decided to undress for the world.

In early June, Willie Cravin was finally dismissed, along with another juror, the ninth and tenth to go down. We were left with twelve jurors and just two alternates.

After that, we watched jurors as if they were patients in an intensive care ward. "Juror #98 is watching 1386," Marcia wrote to me. "And #2457 has been consoling 1386. What do you think? What do you think about the jury interaction?"

"Nothing," I answered. "They are basically a cohesive group now."

And they were. Several times during testimony, I would drift away from whatever witness was on the stand and I would scan those faces—eight black women, two white women, a black man, and a Latino man—wondering what was going through their minds, curious about the social dynamics at work on them.

Despite my better instincts, I tried to convince myself that this jury was wise to Cochran's attempt to turn this into a race case.

I remembered how, early on, one juror had reported hearing another say, "This is payback time!" I went from face to face, wondering which jurors had that fire inside them, which were angry enough that they could find reasonable doubt in the diversions and defamations offered up by Simpson's lawyers.

We debated whether it was a bad sign that one of the jurors was often seen carrying *Makes Me Wanna Holler,* the stirring autobiography of Nathan McCall, a *Washington Post* reporter. In the end, the book was a vivid repudiation of the rage with which young black men fight the system, but the book's powerful scenes of racial violence and anger made some of our team nervous. After all, this was a book that began with the brutal beating of a white boy who happened to be riding through McCall's neighborhood.

> We called it "gettin' some get-back," securing revenge for all the shit they'd heaped on blacks all these years. They were still heaping hell on us, and especially on our parents. The difference was, cats in my generation weren't taking it lying down . . .
>
> Sometimes, when I think about all the crazy things the fellas and I did and I remember the hate and violence that we unleashed, it's hard to believe I was once a part of all that—I feel so removed from it now that I've left the streets. Yet when I consider white America and the way it's treated blacks, our random rage in the old days makes perfect sense to me.

I argued that the overall message of the book was a positive one. I hoped that this jury would realize that no matter what "shit they'd heaped on blacks all these years," freeing a murderer would provide no more relief than beating an innocent kid on a bike.

But there were signs that the jurors were deeply affected by race. By summer, Knox's book, *The Private Diary of an O. J. Juror,* hit the stands. Knox admitted that race had a huge effect on the jurors: "For the black jurors, Simpson was one of our own," Knox wrote. "He was a brother and he was in trouble."

In the face of Cochran's racial overtures, would this jury fail to understand that all evidence should not be given the same weight?

That Judge Ito allowed four days of defense cross-examination about some wild theories didn't mean the theories had merit. And the disproof of some small points didn't disprove our central argument. Mark Fuhrman may very well have despicable beliefs, and Dennis Fung may very well have sloppy work habits. But those things could not change the fact that O. J. Simpson killed two people.

No matter how much I wanted these jurors to look beyond race, I don't think they could. As we prepared our strongest evidence, the scientific and physical evidence—blood, DNA, hair, and fibers—we faced jurors who couldn't forgive, jurors whose subconscious anger had been pricked by Cochran's sly mention of a detective's "home in Simi Valley," and by F. Lee Bailey's vicious chorus of "nigger, nigger, nigger." We faced a jury looking for the tiniest justification for an acquittal, a jury willing to find reasonable doubt in the slimmest of margins: one in 170 million, one in 6.8 billion. They would take their chances with the 6.8 billion and ignore the one right in front of them.

We couldn't know it, but in their eyes, this case was already over.

EIGHTEEN

They wore their grief in vastly different fashions. The Goldman family winced and sobbed, stared at the sky, and shook their heads. They raged against the defense team's unprincipled games inside the courtroom and their public manipulation outside. Fred, Patti, and Kim Goldman came to court nearly every day, bearing witness to the fact that this case wasn't about the lawyers or the tabloids or the TV ratings, but about two very real victims. Incredibly, they were often the ones to offer *us* support, bringing us food, thanking us for our efforts. Sometimes, when a photograph would flash in court, or some testimony would bring Ron Goldman back for just a moment, the horror of it all seemed to hit the Goldmans again and you couldn't help but share their agony.

The Browns were, for the most part, stoic and silent, watching the proceedings with firm jaws, perhaps set against the awful pressure they faced, two people in their sixties, trying to raise two children whose father was on trial for murdering their mother. Juditha and Lou Brown, along with Nicole's sisters, sat in the courtroom with dignity and poise, and we drew a different kind of motivation from them, knowing by their faces that there was no way things could ever be made right again.

Both families sat through the tedious and the terrifying, through crime scene and autopsy photos that were unspeakably evil. When we made tactical errors, they were understanding; when the defense abused the system, they were outraged.

Some days, Patti and Kim would pass notes to the babycake D.A.'s in the back row, who would then pass them on to me. They gave us little bits of intelligence they'd picked up and tips and even questions for prospective witnesses—which I sometimes used. "Are you just humoring us, trying to make us feel better?" the Goldmans wrote one day. No, I told them. They were truly helping. We were a team, and they were a strong part of it.

It meant so much for Marcia, for me, and for the other lawyers and clerks to walk in and see the Goldmans and the Browns nearly every day. Because of them, we never lost sight of why we were getting up at 6 A.M. and going to bed after midnight every day, why we were fighting so hard.

Yet by spring, neither Marcia nor I knew how much longer we could go. We had girded for a six-month trial but as we approached month six, we weren't close to being finished. A person can work only so many straight sixteen-hour days before the tank hits empty. I rose in the mornings, but couldn't get my eyes to open for several minutes, sometimes feeling disoriented and fighting a wrenched back that had begun seizing up on me.

"How you doing?" Marcia jotted one day.

"Exhausted," I wrote back.

"I'm exhausted. Can't keep my eyes open."

"Go home," I wrote.

"Can't."

"Why?"

"Too much stuff to do."

Thankfully, in May, we moved to some of the scientific testimony, much of it evidence that Marcia and I would not be putting on.

And so, at just the right time, we handed the baton to other lawyers: Hank Goldberg; the out-of-town DNA experts, Rock Harmon and Woody Clarke; and Brian Kelberg, an animated lawyer who had attended three weeks of medical school before choosing a messier profession. A bit of a maverick in the office, the studious Kelberg came and went as he pleased, usually arriving at 5 A.M. to an office stacked with boxes and documents. He was the best and most intelligent medical cross-examiner I have ever seen.

My role diminished slightly as the scientific testimony began. Like Marcia, I was still in the office every day, still in court on most days, and still consumed by the trial. But now, for the first time in eight months, there was room to breathe.

Freedom sneaked up on me one afternoon as I was driving home from court, when I realized that something was different. But I couldn't put my finger on it until I drove up to my house, the two palm trees in my front yard waving slowly at me. It had been so long since I'd come home in the daytime. Now, I was only working sixty hours a week and I felt great, like a kid on spring break.

In the fall of 1994, I had taken a position as an adjunct professor at Southwestern University School of Law and had taught three hours a week throughout the trial. As summer semester started, I began teaching six hours a week, drawing a kind of satisfaction from the classroom that I was losing in the courtroom. That May, Jenee and her mom came to visit me. Jenee had been down to L.A. earlier in the trial, but this trip was special.

Southwestern was having its graduation, and U.S. Supreme Court Justice Sandra Day O'Connor was the commencement speaker. I have always made it a point to introduce Jenee to women I considered strong and intelligent, appropriate role models for a young woman. The night before graduation, I asked Justice O'Connor if I could introduce her to my daughter. She seemed delighted.

For a fifteen-year-old, Jenee Darden was incredibly poised. She worked the room the following day, engaging faculty members and trustees in adult conversations, leaning forward confidently, making eye contact with everyone she spoke to. I was so filled with pride, for her, but also—strangely—for myself. My daughter was growing into a bright, young woman—a feminist, no less—and it suddenly dawned on me that, along with Pathenia, I was partly responsible for the person she was becoming. Finally, she met Justice O'Connor and they talked like old friends. In the end, Justice O'Connor touched Jenee's arm and said she knew that Jenee would "go out into the world and do some good."

Jenee touched the justice's arm politely and said, "And you too." Later, as the graduates filed through the auditorium, Justice O'Connor turned to me and said, "I can see why you're proud of your daughter."

At the end of the weekend, when Jenee left, I felt as warm and happy as I could ever remember feeling.

Although Marcia and I were still spending nearly every day in court, we managed to catch up on our sleep, knowing we would be back on center stage soon.

"How do you feel these days?" I wrote one day.

"Better than before, but . . . freaked out about getting back up to speed. What about you?"

"Same," I answered. "I feel the pressure again."

"Hair and trace seems like a morass," Marcia wrote. "And adding science witnesses just doubles the pain. Also, I had thought we could stay in the office for this, but I can see clearly that we need to be here, both to learn and to give pointers."

Marcia and I were being recognized in more and more places. We were invited to parties where movie stars lined up to meet *us*. In May, Carrie Fisher hosted a benefit for victims of domestic violence, and I was shocked to see that Jack Nicholson, Warren Beatty, and Michelle Pfeiffer knew who I was. At times, I felt completely out of touch, even though I was right in the center of this thing. After all, the lawyers involved in the case were the only ones who didn't have time to watch the trial on television.

The recognition wore on both Marcia and me, though. Worried about our safety because of all the death threats, the D.A. investigators accompanied us almost everywhere, checking with us at home and following us when we had to go somewhere. At one point, a D.A. investigator lit into Marcia for driving too fast and losing the tail assigned to keep up with her.

She gave him a standard Marcia response, cussing and yelling until the man apologized. As she stormed out of her office, Marcia passed the parents of Susan Dozier, one of the clerks, who had come to meet the famous prosecutor and had been waiting outside when Mount Clark erupted. They looked as if they'd just seen an execution. I'd already met Susan's parents and I happened to be passing by when Marcia blew up, so I ran down the hall and grabbed her. Marcia turned right around and greeted them warmly.

One weekend, I just decided to get away. For me, the Bay Area had always been my refuge from the strain of Los Angeles, the place where I tapped my strengths, Jenee and my family. I'd been up there for a day a few weeks before, to see Michael, but now I made a clandestine trip to San Francisco, bailing out one day after court, driving north in my Toyota Camry. I didn't tell anyone where I was going. In the passenger seat, thumbing through my CD collection, was Marcia Clark, wearing a bulky coat with a hood.

A shaggy-haired attendant at a remote gas station in central California recognized me as I stopped to fill up. "Hey, Chris Darden," he said. "Where's Marcia Clark?"

"Who knows?" I shrugged, returning to my car and the woman who leaned against it, cigarette smoke coming from the dark hood that covered her face. We checked behind us; no one was following. We were giddy with freedom and we talked about anything we could think of, as long as it had nothing to do with Simpson. It was almost like being normal again.

At the Fairmont Hotel in San Francisco, I dropped Marcia off at a side door and checked into the neighboring rooms we'd reserved— under fictitious names. In jeans, a sweatshirt, and a baseball cap, I wasn't recognized. I was grinning like a kid as I met Marcia on the side of the building, where we unloaded the bags and went to our separate rooms.

We walked along Fisherman's Wharf, ate and drank and laughed. In the progressive city of San Francisco, no one stared at a black man walking with a white woman, and for a while we moved undetected through restaurants, clothing stores, and clubs. We couldn't even get a cab. It was great.

We made fun of each other's wardrobe, bought new clothes, and modeled for each other. We laughed about jokes that seemed, at the time, worth remembering. Back at the hotel, we dressed up and went out, walking into a packed, wide-open club, where people were drinking and dancing and laughing until we walked in.

"Hey, that's Marcia Clark and Christopher Darden." The bar went silent and people turned to see us. But it wasn't the reaction I often saw in L.A. on the rare occasions I went out; there were no glares or angry comments, no second-guessing, no resentment for a black man out with a white woman. People congratulated us and told us how well we were doing, how proud they were of us.

With that weird pronouncement, it was as if the entire city was in on our secret. Suddenly, we had more cabs than we needed. We were recognized everywhere after that, but it was OK because no one hassled us. When we came back to San Francisco a few months later, it was all different, photographers chasing us, tabloid reporters trying to buy our bedsheets. But our first trip to the Bay was perfect.

It was like the secret bus journey to San Francisco that Harold, Rusty, and I took with the rest of the gang, when we'd tumbled up and down San Francisco's rolling streets, captivated by an alien world. For Marcia and me, it was a world without jurors, experts, and television cameras, without sidebars, sanctions, and press conferences. There were no Ito, no Flea, no Asshole.

Much later, we paused at our separate doors, ten feet of papered wall between us. She faced her hotel room door in a trademark Marcia dress, short and black. She looked down toward her shoes.

"I'll see you in the morning," I said.

"Good night, Chris."

Through May and early June, the Los Angeles County District Attorney's Office presented perhaps the most impressive scientific evidence ever offered in a criminal trial. For six weeks, we presented a solid and high wall of physical evidence: blood, hair, and fiber evidence from *three* separate sites—and showed that it would be impossible to fabricate or plant.

In the second week of May, we called Robin Cotton, the director of Cellmark Diagnostics of Maryland, the preeminent DNA lab in the country. With Woody Clarke asking intelligent but understandable questions, Cotton spent three days explaining DNA and the tests used to identify it. We received much criticism for the exercise from experts who said that we didn't need to teach jurors about a combustion engine to teach them how to drive.

They were right that the science lesson—like much of our evidence—took too long to present. No matter how simple Cotton tried to make it—"DNA is that part of the chromosomes that carries the information that programs an organism from the point of conception"—the complex theories still seemed to bore the jurors, who could hardly be blamed for their impatience by that point. Throughout the trial, I was trying to speed up testimony, but in this case, Woody and Rockne Harmon hoped to teach the jury just how conclusive this evidence was and how impossible it would have been to fabricate.

By the time Cotton finally got around to tying the blood at the murder scene to Simpson, and the blood at his estate and in his Bronco to Ron and Nicole, the experts criticized us for "anticlimactic" and "undramatic" testimony. I couldn't believe it. These were numbers! How sexy can you make numbers? We gave them the murderer and the pundits wanted drama! The case's transformation was complete: This was no longer a murder trial, it was a TV movie. Now, the critics had spoken. The second act, they said, needed more drama.

Instead, we presented facts. After Cotton, we called Gary Sims, of the California Department of Justice, which had done DNA tests independent of Cellmark and had come to the same conclusions. When these two witnesses were done, we had presented a trail of evidence as conclusive as a videotape of Simpson committing the murders. More conclusive, in fact. It would have been more likely for a person who looked exactly like Simpson to show up on videotape than for the blood to have been from someone else.

It was the same evidence that had convinced me to take the case, that had convinced me that this wasn't a case about racial prejudice, but one about two brutal murders.

After cutting and slashing two people, O. J. Simpson left one of his gloves at the murder scene, along with his shoe prints, his hat, some of his blood and hair. At Nicole Brown's condo, three blood samples (at least eight separate drops of blood) matched Simpson's blood. One of the drops had a one in 170 million chance of being someone else's.

At Simpson's estate, O. J.'s blood was in his driveway and foyer, while Goldman's blood was on the glove alongside his house, and O. J.'s and Nicole's blood was on the socks in his bedroom. The blood was spattered on the socks—nineteen separate blood spots right around the ankles, where blood would likely splash as Simpson hacked at the victims and then walked through the pools of their blood. There were also blood smears at the tops of the socks, where he'd pulled them off his feet. The chance that the blood was someone else's besides Nicole's? One in 21 billion. Ron's? One in 41 billion. Pretty significant figures when there are only 5.5 billion people in the world.

In Simpson's Bronco, Nicole's blood was mixed with O. J.'s on the carpet. Goldman's blood was on the console, and a mixture of the blood of all three was elsewhere on the console.

Tests were done at two different labs. Contamination was impossible. And in all this testing, no other blood was found. In these lakes of blood, there were identifiable traces of only three people: Ron, Nicole, and O. J. Simpson.

Each time a defense attorney stood, his story became more absurd and contradictory. The attorneys argued vast incompetence and then argued a sophisticated conspiracy—all by the same people. If they couldn't find tiny mistakes in a witness's testimony—like missing staple holes—then the witness became part of a conspiracy that they insinuated spread even to the D.A.'s office, a huge plot apparently masterminded by one racist junior detective and carried out by people who had never met one another before.

During the science testimony, Scheck was the best at this duplicitous attack, asking hypothetical questions with no basis in fact and no evidence that anything he asked had ever happened. He attacked the numbers from Cellmark by bringing up mistakes made at the lab in 1989. He could find no errors in the analysis done on this case and so he had to go back six years and talk about problems that had already been addressed at the lab.

Rockne Harmon was Scheck's mortal opposite, a Vietnam vet who exuded military precision in the courtroom as he used DNA to convict criminals. Scheck was a Legal Aid–style lawyer who used the same technology to set them free. They had battled before, and once, while giving a slide presentation at a conference, Harmon had shown a photograph of Scheck and Neufeld and said "the princes of darkness."

Harmon went after some of Scheck's groundless theories, asking Sims—of the DOJ lab—if DNA could be contaminated by airborne particles, a theory Scheck had droned on about for hours.

"Now, can DNA fly?" Rock asked. "I mean, there are no scientific studies that have shown that, are there?"

"No," Sims said. "I don't think it has wings."

"How about if it's from a bird—can it fly? Does the DNA of an athletic person have any greater athletic prowess than that of a dead person?" Harmon asked. Scheck objected strenuously.

Like good seconds, Neufeld and Clarke argued as strongly as Scheck and Harmon, once getting into it over an unpublished letter by some experts questioning the value of forensic DNA. Neufeld wanted to introduce the letter as evidence and Woody argued that it had nothing to do with the case.

As they climbed all over each other, Ito snapped again. "Get your checkbooks out. Right now! I'm not going to tolerate this thing any more."

He fined them each $250, but Woody didn't have any money on him. Earlier, Marcia had paid me back some money she'd borrowed on our trip to San Francisco—a few hundred dollars in an envelope that I still carried in my pocket. I stood, reached inside my pocket, pulled out the envelope, and gave Woody $250.

It wasn't until I sat down that I heard the buzz in the courtroom. By the time the day was over, there was a rumor about a prosecution slush fund that I, apparently, controlled from my coat pocket. It was ridiculous, but I wasn't going to explain the truth, that the money was given to me by Marcia to pay her half of our weekend getaway.

As May turned into June, the defense stepped up its ridiculous claims—like the theory that the blood under Nicole's fingernails might point to another suspect. They spent days talking about it, and we spent days refuting it. In this case, DNA showed it was Nicole's own blood. But with these kinds of arguments, by the time we settled the issue, I was afraid that enough noise had been made to distract and confuse the jury.

With every witness in this case, the defense spent days on cross-examination, giving the appearance of inconsistencies by the mere volume of questions they asked. And I have to believe that we played into their hands in some respects, trying to anticipate their attacks, spending too long debunking ridiculous theories.

Still, the science was overwhelming. Experienced lawyers were amazed at the amount and the level of scientific evidence we had against Simpson. Vincent Bugliosi, who prosecuted the Charles Manson family, said we could throw away 80 percent of our evidence and still get a conviction. Never in our legal system has so much blood and DNA evidence been amassed against one defendant.

One in 6.8 billion! That blood in Simpson's socks was Nicole's blood; there was no other explanation. One in 170 million! That blood at the scene was Simpson's; no other explanation.

And yet, all along, we had a feeling that the science was coming up short with these jurors. They watched matter-of-factly, as if the positive identification of Simpson's blood at the murder scene had no more meaning than Kato Kaelin's recalling what they ate at McDonald's.

There was some vital connection between the physical evidence and Simpson that was escaping these jurors. The science was too ethereal. We needed something concrete and visual, something to give life and meaning to these astronomical numbers.

I remembered earlier, in the fall, soon after Marcia asked me to be on the case, sitting in her office: Marcia, her assistant Dana Escobar, and me, flipping through the crime scene photos and marveling at all the evidence. I turned to a photograph of a knit hat, stretched to the point of unraveling from a big head like the defendant's. The gloves fit, the shoes fit, the blood fit.

"This is our man," I said.

"And at some point," Marcia said to me, "I'm going to put that hat on his head and I'm going to put those damned gloves on his hands."

It sounded like such a good idea to me. "Bet your ass!" I said. And then we high-fived.

We called him Dr. Lucky—as ironic a nickname as you could ever give a coroner. Lakshmanan Sathyavagiswaran was representative of the kind of witness we called during the science portion of the case. Confident, intelligent, unmoved, they were a nice balance to the nervous cops and bumbling lab technicians who preceded them. In fact, we needed Lakshmanan to testify because his assistant, the attending autopsy surgeon, had made several errors and would have been destroyed on the stand. Questioned professionally and capably by Kelberg, Lakshmanan debunked one defense conspiracy after another.

Shapiro argued that Lakshmanan's assistant could have determined the precise time of Nicole's death if he'd preserved the contents of her stomach. First of all, Lakshmanan testified, precisely nailing the time of death was impossible. And second, if the coroner can visually identify the stomach contents, no preservation is needed. Rigatoni, spinach, and black olives, the coroner's assistant had recorded, all consistent with the meal the waitress and Denise Brown said that Nicole ordered. The best possible estimate, Dr. Lucky said, was that Nicole had been killed within two hours of her last meal—entirely consistent with our timeline.

But Kelberg and Lakshmanan were at their best when they acted out the murders for the jury, showing how one person could have killed both victims. Knifing at the air with a ruler, Kelberg showed simply and convincingly how the murders had likely happened. Then he allowed Lakshmanan to move in behind him and simulate cutting the smaller man's throat, his arm around Kelberg's chest, the ruler pulled across Kelberg's throat. Lakshmanan testified that the bodies indicated the killer may have paused while stabbing Brown, as if he'd been interrupted by Goldman. The defense lawyers could only sit there, watching as Lakshmanan and Kelberg brought the murders directly to the jury for the first time.

Earlier, Shapiro had asked whether Lakshmanan would stake his reputation on a minor conclusion about whether there was spinach in Nicole Brown's stomach. Now, Kelberg turned the question around.

He asked Lakshmanan if the evidence pointed to "a single killer of a height greater than Mr. Goldman, in a swift and violent assault on both these human beings[,] as the perpetrator."

Lakshmanan said yes and Kelberg put a point on it. "Doctor, would you be willing to stake your reputation . . . that all of the evidence is in fact consistent with one killer, 6 feet 2, 210 pounds, athletically built, with the element of surprise, with a six-inch single-edged knife killing Nicole Brown Simpson and Ronald Goldman?"

"Yes," he answered.

Lakshmanan's testimony was dragging to a close by the morning of June 15 and we were going to be moving on to what I guess could be called our accessory offense: the proof that the hat, gloves, and shoes belonged to Simpson.

I walked into court that morning and the defense was already there. I followed Robert Shapiro into chambers, where he suddenly asked Judge Ito, "Can we take the gloves into lockup?"

Ito refused. I stood there, wondering why Shapiro would make the request, especially in front of me. For days, as we approached testimony about the gloves, there had been a sense in the courtroom that we might make Simpson try on the gloves found at the murder scene. We worried the defense might practice with gloves in lock-up, showing Simpson how to struggle while putting them on. Were they planning to put the gloves on Simpson themselves, to show that they were very tight, like the ones in photos of Simpson that had recently appeared in tabloids? Or were they challenging me, daring me to put the gloves on Simpson? It was a weak attempt to set me up.

Upcoming testimony would be vital, we knew, tying the scientific evidence to what jurors could see in front of them: shoe prints, a hat, a pair of gloves.

The shoe prints outside Nicole Brown's condominium showed a distinctive traction pattern and were easily traced. They were from a pair of $160 Bruno Maglis, a style made in 1991 and 1992. Most stores carried only one pair of them. In all, only *three hundred pairs* of that particular shoe were sold in size 12.

O. J. Simpson wore size 12, but, as with the rest of the clothes used during the murders, we never recovered *his* size 12 Bruno Maglis.

We had better luck with the hat, showing it was Simpson's by pulling hair samples from the knit cap, which matched Simpson's hair.

That left the gloves.

Richard Rubin was an affable guy, charming and genuine, with no axe to grind in this case. The former vice president and general manager of Aris Gloves, he wasn't after publicity and he wasn't out to make money. He simply knew everything there was to know about the manufacture, marketing, and sale of gloves. The first time I'd met him, Rubin brought a few hundred samples of gloves with him, showing them to me, pointing out the different kinds of stitching, lining, and leathers.

I had read the report of his interview with the LAPD. Rubin had seen the glove on television and immediately recognized it as one of his, style 70263, Aris Leather Light. Rubin testified that the glove was sold exclusively at Bloomingdale's between 1989 and 1992.

There was no Bloomingdale's west of Chicago, so we narrowed our search. We knew that Simpson spent his winters, during football season, at his home in New York. Of course, that was the perfect time of year to buy gloves. So we had asked Bloomingdale's in New York to search its records for any glove purchases by Simpson or Nicole.

We had no illusions about our chances. The gloves could have been bought years before and, if it were a cash transaction, there might be no records. But we were pleased to find out that Bloomingdale's records went back to 1989, and ecstatic when word arrived that they'd found the receipt.

On December 18, 1990, Nicole Brown bought two pairs of Aris Light gloves. These gloves retailed at $55 a pair. These weren't the kind of gloves that a burglar or drug dealer would buy. Just like the Bruno Magli shoes, these were rich-guy accouterments.

On the receipt, the model number differed from the number Rubin had given us—70268 versus 70263. Brenda Vemich, a buyer of men's accessories for Bloomingdale's, testified that the store did not use bar codes in 1990 and so the numbers would have been typed by hand, and that a mistake was likely. After all, Rubin testified, style 70268 was never sold in the United States.

We had photos of Simpson in a pair of the same style of gloves, taken during a football game and shown in a tabloid. The tabloid photo made us uncomfortable, because we couldn't assume that the photo hadn't been altered. Strangely, in the picture, there seemed to be gaps between his fingers and one inch of space at the fingertips in those gloves, as if they weren't pulled on all the way or were a little bit too small. Unlike the murder gloves, which were brown, those gloves were black—likely the other pair Nicole bought that day.

I asked Rubin what size he thought Simpson wore. Rubin said that the gloves were made to be quite tight and that Simpson could likely pull on any glove from a medium to an extra large.

The tag on the gloves said "Extra Large." Three pairs of gloves in Simpson's golf bag were also extra large.

Rubin testified that the gloves were 20 percent lighter than any of the other Isotoners, had very fine and tight stitching and a distinctive V pattern in the palm. Quite identifiable, he said. Were the gloves found at Simpson's estate and Nicole Brown's condominium the same style purchased by Nicole Brown in 1990, the same kind manufactured between 1989 and 1992 and sold at only one store in the country?

"Oh, yes," Rubin said.

It was clear. Those were his gloves. But the jury sat there, stone-faced and unimpressed with everything. Were they going to buy the defense theory that Fuhrman had planted one of the gloves? I didn't want to lose the gloves; of all the physical evidence, the gloves were—in some ways—the most tangible.

They were also the most tragic. Nicole had bought and then given Simpson the gloves that he wore to kill her.

There was no way Cochran and the others should be able to disconnect those gloves from Simpson. All the racists in L.A. couldn't change the fact that we were staring at O. J. Simpson's gloves.

I'd been watching him, studying his hands. They were large,

certainly larger than mine. They were much larger than Cochran's, three times larger than Bailey's. That morning, I sat in my office, studying the diagram of the gloves done by the LAPD. From Rockingham: right glove, middle finger—9¼ inches. From Bundy: left glove, middle finger—9⅝ inches. A little stretched out, perhaps.

That afternoon, as Cochran cross-examined Rubin, I sat there wondering if we were coming up short with this jury.

Cochran repeatedly asked Rubin and Vemich what size the gloves were and seemed to refuse to believe they were extra larges. He pulled the right glove onto his hand and twisted his face a little bit.

"The extra large is kind of small."

"But they stretch," Vemich said.

Cochran held out his hand. "Is it too small?"

"It is too big," she answered.

"Since I'm wearing it, it seems too small for me," Cochran argued. "But we won't argue that."

He held up the other glove. "And is this—this is supposedly also an extra large glove?"

"Yes, it is."

I watched Cochran try to set the stage for jurors to believe the gloves were too small. While it seemed clear they were up to something, I felt a strong urge to act. Simply, I thought we had to put the gloves on Simpson ourselves.

I turned to Marcia. Skipping our usual legal pad communication, I said, "Let's put them on him now."

She shook her head.

"If we don't, they will," I said. Cochran knew we were going to put the gloves on Simpson, but he would rather do it himself, I told her, to give him a chance to practice and to make it appear as if the defense had brought to the jury's attention the fact that these gloves were tight. That morning, Shapiro had asked to borrow the gloves, probably to have Simpson practice with them. We should put them on before they had a chance to practice, I argued. No matter what happened we had to be the ones to put those gloves on him—symbolically at least.

She looked grim. "I don't need this shit right now, Chris." We talked some more and she said she would only consider it if someone with hands as big as Simpson's—someone like Phil Vannatter—tried one of the gloves on first. So Vannatter came up and easily slid his sausage fingers into a similar glove.

"OK," Marcia relented.

We asked for a sidebar and explained that we intended to put the gloves on Simpson. Ito had been ordering everyone to wear latex gloves while handling the evidence and Marcia said that was a problem. "They're going to alter the fit."

"We'll take that up when we get there," the judge said.

"We would like to have Mr. Simpson put on the original evidence items," I said, as calmly as I could.

"First of all, we've had no time to prepare for this," Cochran said. "He would have to have gloves on underneath. And we have one other item I would like to put on the record."

At the bench, Cochran was nervous, excited. "My client has no objection basically, but the problem is, he doesn't want to do it with the TV cameras trained on him, all that sort of thing.

"First of all, I don't want him to do it without having latex gloves on . . . [and] I would ask if the court insist that the camera be directed—he doesn't want this to seem like he's giving some kind of performance."

It was a strange choice of words. Just a few moments earlier, Cochran had said they hadn't prepared for it. Now, he insisted that Simpson wear latex gloves and expressed concern about "a performance." Sounded like they were prepared to me. I fought back the bad feeling that worked its way up in my throat.

They were his gloves, I told myself. We were just putting *his* gloves on *his* hands.

Cochran repeated his concern about "giving some kind of performance."

I countered, reminding Judge Ito that the defense had used Simpson in other demonstrations to show that he was incapable of the murders: "He was more than willing to walk over to the jury and show them his hand and show them his knees and everything else when it serves his purposes."

Then Cochran asked for "a wide shot, not a tight shot," from the camera.

Had they choreographed this? Were they afraid that, under tight scrutiny, people would see Simpson acting as if the gloves didn't fit? A wide shot? "This is a court of law," I said, "not 'A Night at the Improv.'" Back at the prosecution table, I asked Rubin a few more questions. Marcia wouldn't meet my eyes. "Your Honor, at this time, the people would ask that Mr. Simpson step forward and try on the glove recovered at Bundy as well as the glove recovered at Rockingham."

The tension was thick in the courtroom. You could see it like the heat on a desert highway. My heart was pounding and my mouth was dry, but someone had to do this. Someone had to stop the games these defense lawyers were playing and just put the damned gloves on his hands.

I gave him the left glove, the leather stiff and cold in my hand. Asshole was shaking. I watched his hands closely. His finger seemed cocked and it was apparent he wasn't really trying to pull it on.

"Your Honor," I said sarcastically, "apparently Mr. Simpson seems to be having a problem putting on his glove."

He was bullshitting and I hoped everyone could see that, hoped the jury could see it. But as I glanced quickly around the courtroom, I saw that everyone else was staring at his hands and not his face.

At first, his eyebrows were arched and his mouth set, nervous, like someone about to dive off a bridge. Then he broke into a weird, relieved smile, unlike any I'd seen in any of the old football footage or any of his movies, a smile that I think was as close to the real O. J. Simpson as I'd ever seen, as if he'd surprised even himself.

My God, I'm getting away with it.

He gestured at me, as if to ask if I wanted to try to push the gloves onto his hands, then he showed the gloves proudly to the jury, whose members scribbled furiously. "Mr. Simpson is indicating that his fingers aren't all the way into the gloves, your honor," I said. "Can we ask him to straighten his fingers and extend them into the glove as one normally might put a glove on?"

The courtroom swirled around me, wide-eyed faces staring, the room falling away. I said, flatly, "Mr. Simpson told the jury that the gloves are too small."

"If you didn't put them on him, someone else would have," Judge Ito said at the bench. I nodded weakly.

I also did everything I could think of to lessen the damage. I had Simpson make a fist and hold a pen before he took the gloves off, to show that he could've wielded a knife in the tight gloves. When Richard Rubin got back on the witness stand, I asked if the latex glove would've affected the fit of the leather gloves. I asked Rubin if the gloves should have fit Simpson's hands and he said yes.

"At one point in time," Rubin said, "those gloves would be actually, I think, large on Mr. Simpson's hand."

In the coming days, we brought in experts to testify that the gloves could've shrunk. We had Simpson try on another pair of the same kind of gloves, without latex underneath, and they fit fine.

Sixty-one percent of people polled said they thought the gloves had actually fit. More than even the ice cream defense, the glove experiment brought letters from people who offered explanations for what had happened. On his television program, Rush Limbaugh used a pointer to show that Simpson hadn't pulled the latex gloves all the way onto his hands, his knuckles showing up in the latex well below the fingers of the gloves and bunching up under the leather gloves.

But I knew what the damage truly was. People ask me now would I do it again. No. Of course not. I should have taken into account shrinkage and the defense team's trickery. But, while I wouldn't do it again, I know those are his gloves. I look at the photograph in the newspaper of him smiling in front of the jury and I see Marcia in the background, a look of disgust on her face. Not for him. For me.

That afternoon, I went upstairs and passed a clerk; he did not look at me. No one did. No one said a word. I passed my colleagues in the hallway and they were silent. They had nothing to say to me.

Back in my cold, cluttered office, the telephone was ringing. I let it ring several times, finally picking it up, expecting to hear a reporter's voice. It was Michael.

"I don't care what happened today," he said. "You're still the best lawyer in that courtroom."

I compounded my mistake by turning on the television. It looked wholly different on television, just like Cochran had predicted, a performance, much better than one might expect from a B-movie actor like O. J. Simpson. The experts were harsh: It was stupid, they said. The biggest blunder of the case. This could mean acquittal.

I hoped they weren't right. How many times did I tell my law school students that they should never ask a question they didn't know the answer to?

Gil Garcetti came by. "Whose idea was it to have him try on the gloves?" he asked grimly.

"Mine. I accept full responsibility."

We walked out of my office toward his door. "Gil, it's not over yet. We'll still get him. I promise." He walked toward his office without looking back at me.

"I know we will," he said.

I also tell my students that to be a prosecutor is to accept the responsibility of being the only thing standing between the defendant and the jailhouse door sometimes. We have the duty to make sure no one else can be victimized by the person we're prosecuting. That pressure, that fear, can choke you, I tell my students, and cause you to become too conservative. That fear has a face: the face of a child molested by someone you couldn't convict, the face of a person killed by a murderer you couldn't put away.

As I sat at my desk, staring at the ceiling, the senior lawyers convened a meeting to talk about the gloves. I wasn't invited, or even told about the meeting. Marcia didn't talk to me for a few days. For weeks after that, I was left out of major decisions involving the case. I rode the elevator alone to the basement, got in my car, and drove home, some light still left in the sky. It was gone by the time I reached my house.

I hate living alone. I like the freedom, but there are times when the loneliness is overwhelming and the idea of a cold, dark house is unbearable. My blinds are rarely open, the pots in my kitchen are used but a few times a year; it is a cold and uninspiring house, on a block of one-story Spanish-style stuccos filled with quiet people who mostly keep to themselves and don't go out much after dark.

Inside, I dropped my car keys on a table overflowing with unread newspapers and unopened mail. I sat quietly in the dark, ignoring the chirping telephone. After a time, I called my parents, and one of my sisters answered the phone. "We know one of those white people had you do the glove demonstration," she said.

"No." I sighed. "It was all my idea."

"Hey," my father said, "it's over with now. All you can do is try and repair the damage."

"Yeah," I said.

"It's obvious that he didn't want to get them on his hand, but whether the jury saw that or not, you probably know better than me.

"Just hang in there," Pops said. "And don't watch any TV."

"Too late for that."

But after I'd hung up the phone, I was alone again with my thoughts, my self-pity and hatred. God, what had I done?

Yes, it had been "some kind of performance." And it had been my fault. I ached with regret for what I might have done to the case, what I had done to the victims' families. I didn't have Juditha and Lou Brown's telephone number at home with me, so I called the Goldmans. The answering machine came on.

"About court today, I just want to say how sorry I am. I know they're saying a lot of stuff on TV and I just want you to know: We can still win. It isn't over." I could hear how flat my own voice sounded. "I'm sorry."

I sat up in bed that night, sipping a bottle of tequila, wondering if I had the nerve to go to court the next day It wasn't over yet. Not by a long shot. I had to get back up and walk through another gauntlet of reporters; I had to stand up in that courtroom and try again. I didn't know if I could do it.

I sat inside my cold, dark house all weekend. That Sunday night, while I was sleeping, I woke up short of breath, my chest pounding. I thought I could see it flailing away beneath my T-shirt. Was this a heart attack? I remembered what had happened to Hodgman and what the defense had said, my promise to Cochran: ". . . I'll still be standing . . ." I still felt empty, but I vowed to keep fighting. After all, nothing had changed: Come Monday, the murderer would still be sitting over there. The families of Ron and Nicole would still be sitting in the gallery. And I would be back at work, trying to minimize my mistake.

I called Marcia, who hadn't talked to me since Thursday. "I'm sorry that I screwed up your case," I said.

"Hey," she said quietly, "if this is all it takes to lose the case then we never really had a chance of winning it anyway." We were both silent for a moment, and then she asked, "How are you, anyway?"

"I'm having a heart attack, actually."
"Huh?"
"Never mind."

NINETEEN

A passport. A fake beard and mustache. Almost $9,000 in cash and an envelope reportedly filled with checks. Throughout the trial, the evidence from the slow-speed Bronco chase loomed in front of us—as tempting as a pair of O. J. Simpson's bloody gloves. But we just couldn't present it. It was clear to everyone on the prosecution team that Simpson had made an abortive attempt to escape that day. But it was also clear that, like everything else in this case, the chase would lead to a morass of misperception.

Every pundit with two credits in law school seemed to insist that we present the chase evidence. But we couldn't do it. The chase presented many of the same problems I had seen in my investigation of Al Cowlings (no intent, no way to prove where they were going). But most important, having watched the witnesses testify before the Cowlings grand jury, I knew that Simpson's state of mind would be called into question if we allowed testimony about the chase.

That meant the jury would hear about Simpson's sobbing telephone calls to his family, including his mother. The friends whom he called would parade up to the witness stand to testify that Simpson was suicidal, distraught about his ex-wife's death and the unjust police investigation of him. The joke during the Cowlings investigation was that no one left the grand jury room without crying. Did we want to put these emotional people on the stand and have them testify about how the police had nearly driven O. J. Simpson to blow his own head off? Cowlings—a neighborhood hero for his support of Simpson—would testify that Simpson had wanted to go to Nicole's grave to commit suicide. Of course, news footage would be shown, with crowds on the side of the road, cheering Simpson on. It would be a disaster for our case.

And there was the issue of the physical evidence. It was Cowlings and not Simpson who was actually in possession of the money. The excuse for the disguise was lame (a man in love with celebrity expects us to believe he needed a disguise to take his kids to Disneyland?), but it would likely have played well in front of jurors who idolized him. What about the three envelopes that Simpson had given to Cowlings, along with the money? The police had never opened those envelopes or booked them into evidence. It wouldn't take a Dream Team to ask the police why they hadn't done that—the cops didn't consider it evidence of a crime. If the cops didn't think he was escaping, would a jury believe that he was?

As with any case, prosecutors must leave some evidence on the cutting room floor, basing decisions on strategy and the overall good of the case.

For instance, I would've loved to introduce the contradictions and incriminating statements from Simpson's interview with detectives Lange and Vannatter, but that would have opened up his statements of innocence and would have allowed him to deny his guilt without having to testify, without being opened up for cross-examination. In this game, a prosecutor's best move is always to get the defendant to testify. We had no choice but to hold back his interview.

Among the other evidence I wanted to get into testimony—but which I knew would probably be ruled inadmissible by Ito—was the telephone call to Sojourn, a shelter for battered women. On the evening of June 8, 1994, a volunteer worker at Sojourn answered a frantic call from the wife of a prominent man in West Los Angeles.

"My name is Nicole," said the woman on the other line. Her voice was shaking and emotional, agitated. She spoke quickly, as if she was trying to get it all out before it was too late. Nicole said she just needed to talk to somebody.

The volunteer had been dealing with battered woman for a couple of years and she recognized all the signs in this caller. She said that she had been having problems and that her ex-husband was stalking her. He was calling and asking if they could get back together, Nicole said, and when she refused, he would become furious. He told her that if he caught her with another man, he would kill her.

The counselor offered Nicole a place to stay. But there was nowhere to go. He would find her.

Four days later, Nicole Brown was dead.

It was clear from the notes we saw from Sojourn that the call came from Nicole Brown: married eight years, two children and other pieces of information that tied her to Simpson. It also made sense that Nicole Brown would call Sojourn; O. J. had been ordered by the court to donate money to that very shelter after beating Nicole in 1989.

Judge Ito ruled that the telephone call to the shelter was inadmissible, because it was hearsay—a conversation or statement made outside of court that is offered in court as proof. Any case loses much of its evidence and testimony because of hearsay, and prosecutors are often hamstrung by the rules that govern it.

But, like everything about this case, there was an inordinate amount of hearsay evidence—stuff that the public heard about, but the jury didn't. It's difficult for a prosecutor when the media has a better case than you do.

We couldn't use mental health professionals like Dr. Susan Forward, the author of *Men Who Hate Women and the Women Who Love Them,* who saw Nicole briefly and said that Nicole had been beaten repeatedly by Simpson and that she feared for her life. There was also a mental health professional who claimed to have seen Ronald Goldman and who claimed to have pertinent information. But we discounted that lead anyway after she said that Goldman's files had been stolen during a break-in. Once we reviewed the police report and talked to detectives, it appeared the break-in was a hoax.

Also hearsay or irrelevant were the rumors of O. J. Simpson's drug usage—even though traces of marijuana showed up in his blood sample—and the fact that he knew Nicole was deathly afraid of knives.

"That was her greatest fear," said her cousin, Rolf Bauer. "She said, 'Anybody could grab me, shoot me with a bullet or a gun, no problem.' But a knife, that just tears her up."

The investigator who interviewed Bauer asked if Simpson knew about his wife's fear of knives.

"Oh, yeah," he said.

Nicole's conversations with friends like Faye Resnick and Cynthia Shahian were also inadmissible. And so the jury didn't hear about Nicole's relationship with the football star (and Simpson's friend) Marcus Allen, or the warnings her friends gave about Simpson's reaction to her affair with Allen.

"I would say to Nicole, 'If he finds you with [Allen], it's over. You know that?'" Shahian asked Nicole.

"Nicole knew her life would end," Shahian said. "She always knew her life would end. She told me repeatedly at various points . . . during their relationship . . . that he would kill her if he ever found her with another man."

Nicole saw Cynthia Shahian, whom she called Cici, two weeks before she was murdered. She told her friend that a set of keys was missing. "Cici," she said, "I'm afraid."

But we knew coming into the case that there was much we wouldn't be able to present to the jury. As June melted into July, we were still debating which evidence we *wanted* to put in front of the jury. Earlier, Judge Ito had severed half of our domestic violence evidence, requiring us to save many of those witnesses for the end of the trial. It was a terrible blow to the continuity of our case, but we were determined to complete the picture of Simpson as abuser and stalker.

However, the dismissed juror Jeanette Harris had gone on television news programs to say that she didn't see a connection between domestic violence and the murder. That opinion resonated with Marcia and with others.

I had coordinated that part of the case, but now—after the glove demonstration—it seemed as if my ideas were discounted. There was some strain between Marcia and me, and in late June, she was considering eliminating the final spousal abuse witnesses.

As we sat in court one day, she passed me a yellow legal pad. "What D.V. witnesses do you think are important to call?"

"Too late," I responded. "You already rejected my idea. And now I feel uncomfortable—very uncomfortable actually."

"I guess I do feel pretty strongly about this one," Marcia wrote back. "Sorry. But I also think that they'll scream character assassination no matter what we do. AND—I do believe they will blunder into opening the doors on some of it."

By the first week of July our case—already weakened by sloppy police work, by Mark Fuhrman, and by my glove demonstration— took another hit when a statistician named Bruce Weir testified that some errors had been made while figuring the DNA frequencies. The changes in the numbers were inconsequential—the blood trail was just as solid—but the mistakes blurred a prosecution case that had already been smeared with the impression of incompetence.

Finally, Douglas Deedrick, an FBI agent, testified that a single hair on Ron Goldman's shirt appeared to be just like Simpson's hair sample and that fibers from the Bronco were found on the knit cap next to the bodies. That was it.

Ninety-two days of testimony. Fifty-eight witnesses; 488 exhibits. A cost to taxpayers of nearly $6 million. As the prosecution case ended, television experts said we'd presented enough evidence to convict five murderers under normal circumstances. The rest of that analysis didn't need to be said. These weren't normal circumstances.

On July 6, Marcia rose from her chair, the circles drawn deeply beneath her sharp eyes. I stared at the jury. "At this time," she said crisply, "subject to receipt of the people's exhibits into evidence, the people rest."

Johnnie Cochran and I locked eyes in the cramped space behind the podium and edgily joked with each other, like two basketball players talking trash.

"You'd better watch out for the brothers," he said.

"You forget, I am a brother," I said back. "You'd better be watching out for the white supremacists."

Beneath our jokes were very real threats. One afternoon, Cochran asked to see Judge Ito and showed him a long, handwritten letter. Cochran was clearly bothered by the letter, and he demanded that Ito help him contact the FBI.

It was a death threat against his children. I felt badly for him and especially for his family, which shouldn't have been dragged into all this. I certainly could sympathize with Cochran.

By that time, threats of violence—from all races—were so common-place, I barely noticed them unless the author proposed some method of pain I hadn't thought of yet. The difference between the threats Cochran and I received was that I had done nothing to contribute to the danger he was in, while I blamed him for focusing much of the hatred against me.

Still, he and I joked about such things, taking little shots at each other—sometimes without even making eye contact—sarcastic barbs in passing, infused with too much threat to be entirely funny.

It happened again that summer, as we crossed in court while awaiting some testimony. "Keep your head down the rest of the way," Cochran said. "Stay out of the racial stuff and we'll see what we can do about getting you back in."

I said nothing.

". . . back in." I knew what he meant. He would see what he could do about getting me "back in" the black community. He'd insinuated the same thing earlier, shaking his head after a particularly bitter disagreement: "You're making it awful tough for us to get you back in."

From the moment we argued the N-word, Cochran had implied that I was turning my back on my heritage, on my people. Beneath the court case that everyone else saw, Cochran and I fought another battle, over the expectations and responsibilities of being a black man in America. He took shots at me, both subtle and not so subtle, and I listened with a clenched jaw. Later, I began to fire back, to show there were responsibilities as a human being that were just as important as the responsibilities of being an African American.

By the time the defense began presenting its case, the tension between Cochran and me was a heavy subtext to the rest of the trial. My family certainly felt the pressure. By telephone, my parents asked why Cochran was going after me that way. My mother worried after she heard a report that I had been booed in church one Sunday. I promised her that hadn't happened. At the mission in Richmond, Michael had nearly gotten into a fight defending his little brother, and the people there knew better than to talk about the case with him anymore.

The bitterness between Cochran and me was coming to a head as the defense team presented its case and we moved inexorably to the resolution of the Fuhrman issue, to the final play of their race card.

But first, there were other stages of the Simpson defense, topics to be covered for the sake of appearance, while the true defense surged and rose in the background, a great wave.

The first stage of the Simpson defense was the kind that courts traditionally discourage—a stream of evidence meant to unduly discredit one prosecution witness, Ron Shipp. Shipp was a devastating witness to their case and to Simpson personally. All his life, Simpson had been coddled and encouraged by his male friends, with whom he shared stories of womanizing and testosterone. It seemed to gnaw at him that this guy had come clean. Even after the trial, Simpson continued to attack Shipp for acting in a most un-Cowlings way. He criticized Shipp during interviews and challenged "investigative reporters" to find out who the blonde was in the hot tub.

In court, the defense also went after Shipp's marriage, calling a series of women to testify about the blond woman. Witnesses testified that Shipp was drinking the night Simpson told him about his dreams, and that Shipp appeared high, "muttering to himself and talking in circles," according to one of Simpson's sisters.

Before Simpson's mother, Eunice, testified, I asked Judge Ito to allow a break so she could take the stand before the jury came back in. But the judge refused and so the jury watched as Carl Douglas helped Mrs. Simpson ease out of her wheelchair and walk gingerly toward the witness stand. It seemed to take ten minutes, ten dramatic, sympathetic minutes. Once on the stand, even kindly old Eunice Simpson went after Shipp: "He appeared to be spaced."

Simpson's daughter Arnelle gave measured, sincere testimony and seemed reluctant—unlike the others—to accuse Shipp of being drunk.

Another stage of the defense focused on demeanor, showing that Simpson didn't act like a butcher after the murders, while at the airport and on the flight to Chicago. The people aboard the airplane said Simpson appeared normal, friendly even; the only somewhat odd behavior was that he didn't sleep and was staring out the window at 2:45 A.M., when the pilot came out to talk to him.

Hell, I would have stipulated that Simpson appeared normal after the murders; if nothing else, our case had shown that he was a cold, stone-faced bastard. A calm murderer was consistent with research into intimate killers and fit the crime scene evidence. The footprints that led away from the murder scene suggested a slow, patient walk back to the alley.

Next, the defense presented medical witnesses to show that O. J. Simpson was in no shape to commit two murders. Dr. Robert Huizenga, Simpson's internist, said that Simpson walked like "Tarzan's grandfather."

A quick walk or even a slow jog would have been "very difficult, if not impossible that day."

But waiting for their Harvard-trained doctor was our Southwestern University-trained lawyer. By the time Brian Kelberg finished his brilliant cross-examination of Huizenga, it was as if we'd called him to testify ourselves.

"O. J. has an above average, very well-muscled body," Huizenga admitted. A grip test on both hands was normal. Simpson could easily hold a knife in either hand. If Nicole were stationary, he could grab her hair with one hand and slit her throat while holding a knife in the other. After Huizenga said that Simpson had walked with a limp on June 15, Kelberg pointed out that an earlier witness had testified that, on the day of the murders—three days earlier—Simpson hadn't limped. Then we played an exercise video that showed O. J. displaying a wide range of motion and joking about spousal abuse. Huizenga acknowledged that there was nothing that prevented Simpson from being physically able to kill Brown and Goldman, especially if he was in the throes of an adrenaline rush.

Then Kelberg pointed to a report in which Huizenga noted that Simpson's arthritis "may have implications for the forensic pathologist." In a letter to Douglas, Huizenga asked if that was the report the defense wanted. It appeared the doctor worded his diagnosis to fit what the defense needed.

More important to the Simpson defense was the timeline testimony, meant to prove that the murders occurred later than we had argued. We had staked much of our case on the idea that the murders occurred at 10:15 P.M., yet I didn't think we should have allowed ourselves to be pinned down like that. To me, the murders could have occurred as late as 10:40 P.M., and Simpson would still have had time to drive five minutes back to his estate.

The defense started with a couple on a blind date—Danny Mandel and Ellen Aaronson—who testified that they passed Nicole Brown's condo and saw nothing unusual. At first, Aaronson had told police they'd passed by about 11 P.M., and Mandel had drawn a route that didn't take them past Nicole's condo at all. But later they talked it over and changed their stories; they decided they'd walked right past the condo at 10:30 P.M. Marcia hated these witnesses and I agreed.

Some people wanted to be involved in this case so badly, they seemed eager to adjust their memories. Certainly, we had been contacted by witnesses like that. But we didn't call them to testify.

Next was a woman named Francesca Harman who drove north on Bundy that night and had seen nothing unusual. But on cross-examination, I asked if her headlights had actually illuminated the dark condo walkway and she acknowledged that they hadn't. Of course she hadn't seen anything and she'd told the defense that. They called her anyway. Denise Pilnak was next, giving the most detailed itinerary I'd ever heard from a witness. I wondered if anyone really lived that way ("At 10:13, I went . . .") as she testified that she hadn't heard the "plaintive wail" of the dog when she stood on her porch at precisely 10:25 P.M. How important was time to this quirky witness? At one point, she pulled up her sleeve to show that she was wearing two watches.

That left Robert Heidstra, who testified that while walking his two decrepit dogs near the crime scene, he'd heard a dog bark and, five minutes later, heard a man yell, "Hey, hey hey!" followed by a second voice. He pegged the time at 10:40 P.M., which the defense argued was outside our timeline.

Heidstra was easy pickings. He softened immediately, saying he hadn't looked at his watch, that he might've heard the dog at 10:30 instead of 10:35. He acknowledged that he'd told police that he saw a white sport utility vehicle, possibly a Blazer—Chevrolet's answer to the Bronco. In fact, I had four witnesses who were willing to testify that Heidstra had told them he saw a Bronco, and Heidstra admitted it might have been a Bronco.

Heidstra also said he heard an iron gate slam shut, which helped him peg the time. He was sure it was Nicole's because it was the only iron gate in the neighborhood, he said. So I showed him pictures of twenty-one other iron gates in the neighborhood. I asked about his contacts with defense attorneys and his financial motive for testifying.

"Didn't you tell Patricia Baret [Heidstra's friend] that when this case is finished, you are going to make a lot of money?"

A small, weathered Frenchman, Heidstra became agitated, his hands shaking, feet twitching, eyelids fluttering. "I didn't say that."

"You never told her that?"

"Maybe something might come out of it. But I never said money."

"So, you think you might make some money as a result of testifying in this case?"

"Maybe." Like Huizenga before him, Heidstra was ours. The defense had given us this gift and I was determined to make the most of it. I asked about reports that the second voice he'd heard, the older one, he'd described as that of a black man.

Cochran practically leaped at the chance to play another race card. "Your Honor! This is offensive."

"Wait! Wait!" Ito fumed. "Ladies and gentlemen of the jury, please leave!"

They filed out, wide-eyed, and when they were gone, I explained carefully that Heidstra had told a witness that he heard a black man's voice. "That is the good-faith basis on which I am asking these questions, Your Honor."

"I resent that statement," Cochran clipped, leaning on the podium in his off-white, linen suit, like some angry plantation owner. "You can't tell by somebody's voice whether they sounded black."

His upper lip curled underneath his mustache and Cochran came after me again. "That's a racist statement!"

I am ashamed, but I had the urge to beat his ass right there in the courtroom. "That's what has created a lot of problems for my family and myself, statements that you make about me and race," I said, ignoring Judge Ito and talking to the man who really controlled this courtroom: Cochran.

It was a simple question for Judge Ito: Was this proper questioning, based on the law? Instead, he accepted a new kind of objection—"That's racist."

Seven months earlier, I had stood at that same podium and I had argued with all my heart that Judge Ito couldn't allow this to happen, that he couldn't allow the divisive face of racism to take over this courtroom. This was supposed to be a place of principles and ideals, but the specter of racism took no quarter for principles and ideals. It paid no respect to a system of laws, bullying it with irrelevance and emotion.

"I'm going to take a recess right now because I'm so mad at both you guys," Ito said. "I'm about to hold both of you in contempt."

"I'm sorry, Your Honor," I said.

But he stormed off the bench. "It'll take more than that."

After that, I vowed never to apologize to Lance Ito again. He deserved no more apologies. A lawyer looks to the bench for guidance and protection. Protection from inadmissible evidence and testimony that had no probative value. But we were prosecutors, civil servants, and not rich, powerful lawyers. We had no constituency, no one who voted, and we got no such protection. Cochran was clearly the only lawyer in contempt that day, interrupting our questioning, arguing far afield about some made-up racial slight. But Ito insisted on saying we would both be in contempt. And what, exactly, was I being tagged for? Trying to question a witness? Or was Ito so oversensitive about the charge of racism that he had once again turned the keys to the courtroom over to Cochran, deciding that something was racist because Johnnie Cochran said so?

That very month, in *The New Yorker* magazine, a leading black intellectual, Henry Louis Gates, wrote about retired General Colin Powell's place in the black and white communities and how his political career would be affected by his speech patterns—by the fact that he doesn't sound very black: "I speak reasonably well," Powell was quoted as saying in the article, "like a white person."

African-American singers, actors, and comedians have long fought for the opportunity to reflect genuine black voices—urban, hip, with traces of the South, of the West Indies, of Africa. Schools and colleges instill pride in the heritages of black speech. Who in America would deny that many black people have distinctive speech patterns and language? Who would equate saying that people are different with denigrating them?

I believe that the charge of "Racism!" is a delicate weapon. Use it carelessly and it loses its power. Use it unjustly and it disappears when someone actually needs it. Use it when it doesn't apply and it disrespects the people who have battled real racism—discrimination, segregation, slavery.

But Cochran's principles depended on how it affected an accused murderer. When it benefited Cochran's client, he wanted to live in the "real world," where black people hear the word "nigger" every day and steel themselves against it, unmoved by its hateful power. Yet, at other times, he feigned disgust at someone who asked simply if a voice sounded like that of a black man. How, I wondered, could a man who prodded F. Lee Bailey to serenade this jury with the word "nigger," be offended by anything?

Even seven months earlier, as I predicted where this case was going, I had no idea how far afield we would be. Nor how easily Judge Ito would go along.

I had watched him cozy up to the defense, winking at Cochran when his team scored some points, joking about Marcia's appearance or my moodiness. Over and over, he castigated us in front of the jury, admonishing them to disregard evidence and questions. He made sarcastic remarks to Hank Goldberg and Brian Kelberg in front of the jury for taking too long with their questioning. It was ridiculous! As defense attorneys spent two, three, four days asking about an imagined hit team of Colombian drug warriors, he singled us out for criticism. Perhaps, I thought, it was because of his own background as a prosecutor; maybe he couldn't separate our handling of the case from how he would've handled it.

For instance, later in the trial, after a particularly nasty off-the-record hearing between Cochran and me, Judge Ito criticized my approach with a certain witness.

"I could do it in three questions," Ito said.

I smiled. "It would be more dramatic if we did it in fifteen."

"But we're not here for drama, are we, Mr. Darden?"

"Not anymore."

Cochran piped in: "Not after the gloves."

Even Ito said it was "a cheap shot." I stood there, waiting for Cochran to apologize, knowing I had been threatened with contempt for much less.

"Did Mr. Cochran apologize?" I asked sarcastically.

"Not yet," Ito said. "But he will."

The defense case moved on, through more minor witnesses who offered more minor testimony about more minor points. Everyone knew where we were headed. July faded into August into September. As summer ended, the case of *The People v. Simpson* was headed for a showdown over racism, over Mark Fuhrman. Apparently, by that time, we had come too far for apologies.

* * *

Sometimes, it's a mistake to even answer the telephone.

"Hey, you know anything about some tapes Fuhrman made with a writer?" The caller was a very good source and had been right far too often to ignore in this instance. "Some tapes where he uses fifty epithets?"

"Sounds like bullshit to me."

"Maybe. I heard a rumor that the defense is trying to get the tapes."

I put my head in my hands. This was not what we needed. After handling Huizenga, Heidstra, and a slew of other defense witnesses, we were regaining some of the momentum we'd lost with Fuhrman, Fung, the gloves, and the DNA statistics. If this tape existed, it could be disastrous. "Where is this tape?"

"It's in L.A. That's all I know. I'll look around and get back to you."

I sat on it for a day, not wanting to start any rumors myself, and then I called a few reporters, asking if there was anything new, anything on the rumor mill about what the defense planned for Fuhrman. No one had any information.

We knew they would call witnesses to contradict Fuhrman's contention that he hadn't used the word "nigger" in the past ten years. They had worked hard to lay the trap; they would surely try to spring it. But the only witness we knew about was a guy named Hodge, a man detained about ten times by the West L.A. police in the early eighties. Hodge had since moved to Illinois, where he had been arrested and convicted for carrying a gun and possession of cocaine. If that was the best they could do on Fuhrman, fine. Perhaps then we could expose the Fuhrman strategy for what it was: a ridiculous, desperate ploy.

One day, earlier in the trial, while I was talking on the telephone to one of the defense lawyers about discovery material, the issue of Mark Fuhrman first came up, and I accused him of using racism out of desperation.

"Your entire defense is bullshit and you know it," I said. I said that he must know his client was guilty and that there was no evidence of police misconduct, no way evidence could have been planted.

"I'm not saying they did plant evidence," said the lawyer on Simpson's team. "And I know all the evidence points toward O. J. and that it looks bad, but that doesn't mean he's *guilty.*"

In lawyer-speak, that usually meant the client claimed to have suffered some sort of mental disorder or deficiency. In other words, my guy did it, but he's not guilty of murder in the legal sense. I figured that if the defense couldn't get the jury to bite on their crazy theory of one racist cop elaborately setting up a black icon, then they would have pleaded Simpson not guilty by reason of insanity.

But that summer, the telephone calls kept coming and the more I heard about the tapes Mark Fuhrman had made, the more I knew their desperate, cynical trick could work.

A few days later, another telephone call.

"The tapes exist, all right," the caller said. "A screenwriter in North Carolina, a woman named Laura Hart McKinny. Apparently, she made the tapes for a screenplay she was writing and Fuhrman was giving her research."

"Thanks."

It was mid-July and we were all exhausted again, our nerves close to the surface and raw. It was a struggle to come to court every day; the relationships between our lawyers and theirs were soured beyond repair. Marcia wasn't speaking to the defense DNA experts, Barry Scheck and Peter Neufeld, and they weren't speaking to her. Standing in chambers one day when the topic of the McKinny tapes came up, Scheck interrupted Marcia.

"Shut up!" she snapped. Scheck turned crimson and interrupted her again. We ended the meeting as if we were referees pulling two fighters apart.

The defense was putting on more science witnesses—an FBI blood analyst named Roger Martz and a forensic specialist, Dr. Herbert MacDonell—and I asked Marcia not to cross-examine them. Scheck would be handling MacDonell and the last thing Marcia needed, the last thing this case needed, was for the two of them to go at it again.

"Let one of the science guys do it," I suggested. Marcia had lost perhaps ten pounds and her face had become lined with stress and lack of sleep. She dismissed me with a wave. She would do the witnesses herself.

Through July and August, the defense presented experts who argued that the evidence *could be interpreted* to show tampering or incompetence on the part of the police. As a lawyer, you learn quickly that there are expert witnesses who will tailor their expertise to whatever a defense lawyer needs. Given an assignment (find out if blood could have been planted on the socks), they will set out to prove that, somehow, the blood could be explained as planted evidence. It may not be the most likely explanation, but that's not what they are paid to find out. And, make no mistake, they are paid very well.

We handled most of those witnesses, for instance, showing that the blood smear on the socks was as likely to have been placed there by Nicole, reaching out for the ankle of her killer, or by Simpson, bumping her body in the cramped walkway or later, when taking off his socks.

The expert testimony had an unearthly feel anyway, as if it didn't really matter because of what was happening on the other coast. First in a North Carolina trial court, then in an appellate court, Cochran was pushing to acquire the tapes that Fuhrman had made with Laura Hart McKinny. Even as we fought their experts' attempt to confuse the physical evidence, we kept one eye on the Fuhrman tape issue, knowing that it had the potential to undo all we had done.

Defense expert John Gerdes testified that the LAPD crime lab was "a cesspool of contamination." A private medical lab would be shut down for less, he said. As Gerdes testified about the possibility of cross-contamination—blood from one sample contaminating another—a few jurors nodded in agreement.

But there was no cross-contamination in this case. In the end, all Gerdes offered was conjecture. On cross-examination, Woody Clarke showed that Gerdes had no experience or expertise collecting or analyzing evidence. And he admitted to having no conclusive proof of cross-contamination. The defense had argued that DNA particles had flown through the air, contaminating other samples. But Woody showed that was impossible, since DNA was extracted from many of the samples at two independent labs—Cellmark and the California Department of Justice. Some samples were never touched by the LAPD lab technicians.

I watched the jury, wondering how this speculative science was playing with them. Would they allow weeks of meaningless testimony to somehow substitute for reasonable doubt? Later, one juror referred to "all the business about blood," and I wondered if all this wrangling over possibilities and theories would pool up in these jurors, giving them the impression that something of substance was actually behind the allegations.

On August 7, it ceased to matter. A North Carolina appellate court granted the defense motion for the McKinny tapes. The next day, the defense filed a motion asserting that Fuhrman perjured himself. They demanded a special prosecutor and all Internal Affairs investigative ties having to do with Fuhrman.

On the stand, Kelberg was getting under the skin of Dr. Michael Baden, jamming him about the time of death, which the former medical examiner tried to imply was later than we'd shown, by going back to that defense staple, the stomach contents. Kelberg kept at him, showing his leaps in logic until Baden seemed to give up.

"I cannot tell you," Baden said finally, "if you're asking me, I cannot tell you—from the stomach contents—the difference between being killed at 10:30 or 10:40 or 10:50. I have not said that I would make that claim."

The tapes arrived Friday, August 11. They were copied, and a plain brown box of seventeen cassette tapes arrived on my desk and sat there, untouched for days. We had them transcribed by a group of D.A. secretaries, but it wasn't a certified transcription and it was a disaster—inaccurate and difficult to follow.

I stood, looked at the first page of the transcript, and kicked my door shut. I pulled the nearly empty bottle of tequila from my bottom drawer and settled in, skimming the awful pages. It was worse than I had imagined. I didn't even understand what some of his language meant, for instance, that a "split-tail" was a woman. The racial epithets were everywhere ("Nigger driving a Porsche that doesn't look like he's got a $300 suit on, you always stop him. . . . How do you intellectualize when you punch a nigger? He either deserves it or he doesn't") along with something potentially worse, suggestions of planting evidence and lying about cases ("It's like my partner now. He's so hung up on the rules and stuff. . . . This job is not rules. . . . Fuck the rules; we'll make them up later").

I took a long drink and set the pages down. Many of the conversations were from as long ago as 1985, although others were more recent. I turned to the last transcript, of a tape made in July 1994, just a month after the murders. A story in *The New Yorker* had first floated the idea that a racist cop might have set Simpson up, and on tape, Fuhrman referred to the case and said something about keeping quiet about the screenplay. He was planning to sue Robert Shapiro.

Fuhrman used the N-word at least three dozen times during the taped conversations made over the past ten years; he bragged about beating suspects and suggested that evidence is often planted by male officers. He denied planting evidence in the Simpson case, but seemed to enjoy his role in the center of controversy.

"I'm the key witness in the biggest case of the century," he bragged to McKinny. "And if I go down, they lose the case. The glove is everything. Without the glove—bye, bye."

I didn't read any more.

In court, Marcia continued to scrap. Fredric Rieders testified that he had examined the FBI results of bloodstains and found EDTA, the chemical that the defense alleged pointed to planted blood. Our argument was that there was no EDTA in the blood but that trace amounts could occur naturally. Marcia thought Rieders's conclusions were outside the realm of conventional science, and she went after him with biting sarcasm and angry questions.

I pushed a Post-it note in front of her—"Calm down"—but she ignored me. She questioned Rieders about an older case in which she claimed he'd made a monumental error, saying there was poison in a tissue sample when there was none. She hammered him so much, even the jurors exchanged glances.

"Let's try the Simpson case today," Ito said, again interrupting us in front of the jury the way he rarely did with the defense.

But Marcia wasn't going to stop. She had sat through the defense team's questioning of our experts about mistakes at their labs four and five years earlier, and she continued to ask about the old poisoning case.

"This is the end of this inquiry," Ito said sternly. "It's completely irrelevant at this point. Move on!"

There was only one place to move on to. The tapes.

I hadn't read any more of the transcripts and hadn't listened to the tapes, which sat in that box on my desk. Cheri Lewis prepared a summary of the tapes and it became clear that one of the issues we would have to deal with was Judge Ito's wife, Peggy York, the West L.A. captain who denied remembering any confrontations with Fuhrman. On the tapes, the detective laid her out, making derogatory comments about her, statements that were likely to upset Ito.

Many of the prosecutors and senior lawyers on the trial team in our office were angry with Ito for the way he'd handled the case, allowing it to spin out of control, humiliating us in front of the jury and showing deference to the defense team. If there was a conflict, they argued, we should get rid of Ito immediately. But nobody wanted a mistrial.

To be honest, I wasn't interested in getting rid of him. The trial had dragged on too long already and, at some level, there were more important things than winning this case at all costs.

But I was the guy who had tried to put the gloves on Simpson and my opinions weren't exactly cherished.

That afternoon, we talked about the reference to Captain York. Surrounded by the trappings of the most famous judge in the world, Lance Ito wept.

"I love my wife dearly and I am wounded by criticism of her, as any spouse would be. I think it is reasonable to assume that could have some impact."

It was incredible. If there wasn't ammunition to have him removed before, his performance that day was all we would need.

There were meetings on top of meetings with the senior lawyers on the trial team in our office. In court that evening, Marcia told Judge Ito, "It would appear, based on consultation with everyone, that the only road to take is not to waive on any matters and to proceed with a complete recusal from this point forward."

"Are you sure you want to do that?" Ito asked.

Marcia asked for the evening to think about it.

The senior lawyers on the case drafted a letter for Ito, cold and direct, demanding he recuse himself from the case. I didn't like the language.

There was already so much that was disingenuous and mean-spirited about this case, from Johnnie Cochran to Mark Fuhrman. The idea that we were seeking justice for the families of two murdered people had been forgotten long before, and now we were operating in a cool pit of gamesmanship and I didn't like it. If we were going to lose, we should lose the way we came in, with the moral high ground and respect for the system we were serving.

Besides, what good would another trial do? The evidence was already in the public domain and, if it had been hard to find a jury this time, it would be impossible the next. We should let the case run its course, no matter the result.

I walked down the hall toward Marcia's office. She was the only person who could change the opinions of the deputy D.A.'s down the hall.

Outside the courtroom, Cochran was telling reporters that the whole thing was a ruse, that we were scared that we were going to lose. He was half-right. We were going to lose. But we weren't scared anymore. Marcia agreed with me. We should just keep fighting our case.

The letter was never sent. The next morning, we went into chambers and told Ito that we wouldn't ask for his recusal. His transcripts were stacked on his desk for delivery to a new judge. We sat down and joked a little bit, me, Marcia, Shapiro, and Cochran. And then we told Ito that we had some serious issues with the way he'd conducted the case so far, the way some of our attorneys were treated in front of the jury.

"I'm not going to sit here and listen to this," Cochran said.

Shapiro joined in. "You know what? This stinks."

We had no choice but to go out into the courtroom and have the discussion on the record. In court, Shapiro brought out several off-the-record and in-camera discussions we'd had, some no more than whining sessions. It was the behind-the-scenes squabbling that accompanied every trial and had no place on the official record.

We had come all the way to this—arguing in front of the world like a bunch of children. I regretted many of the things that happened during this trial, but none so much as the general rancor with which we dealt with one another. We heaped disrespect and dishonor upon the legal profession, and I was angry at the defense for creating that atmosphere and disappointed in myself for taking part.

I refused to speak at the same podium and accused the defense of trying to create a circus from these proceedings. "When this case is over," I said, "I will be referring defense attorneys to the United States Attorney's office."

But the worst behavior in this case was still going on—the complete and final transformation of this murder case into one long distraction about racism. "There has been a year-long extortion attempt by the defense to get you to allow as much racist and irrelevant and inflammatory incidents into this trial as possible," I said to Ito. "They have known about Fuhrman all the time."

* * *

When the defense filed a motion to introduce the Fuhrman tapes, Cochran said his office "accidentally" failed to file the motion under seal. It contained excerpts from the tapes, and when the media got hold of the motion, they went crazy. In his response that the defense motion was incoherent, Ito included more excerpts.

We had no illusions that sequestration had kept the jury from receiving information during conjugal visits or conversations with friends and family. To play the tapes in court served no purpose, we argued. We agreed to stipulate that it was Fuhrman's voice on the tape and that he had used the N-word in the past ten years. The tapes were reprehensible, but we pointed out that they offered no evidence to support their theory of planted evidence, that one racist cop could have set Simpson up.

But, on August 29—with the jury out of the room—Judge Ito allowed the defense to play the tapes for the world. And we knew full well that discussions of the tapes would make their way to the jury.

Later, we learned that a man had called a local radio station and given his first name. The man said his sister was on the jury and that he had visited her the Tuesday after the tapes were played, telling her everything he'd heard. Judge Ito checked, and a man by that name had visited his sister on the jury that day. The judge began an investigation, but never completed it. The juror remained.

On August 31, Ito ruled that two excerpts, far fewer than the defense had hoped, would played for the jury. That day, the defense team called a press conference and emerged—en masse—from around a corner, like a gang moving toward a fight. Cochran said he was "outraged" and "livid" and implied that Ito's decision was racist—"one of the crudest and unfair decisions ever rendered in a criminal court."

The next day, we waited for Ito to sanction Cochran for his outburst. Instead, the judge looked like a punished child. Even though he'd warned both sides about their statements to the press, now he only told Cochran that he was "hurt" by the defense press conference. He called Cochran's statements "contemptible," but didn't hold him in contempt. It made me sick. We had been held in contempt for interrupting the judge, sanctioned for showing up a few minutes late; they accused Ito of "the cruelest . . . decision ever rendered in a criminal court" and their punishment was finding out they'd "hurt" the judge.

Laura Hart McKinny was coquettish and breathless on the stand, swiping at her thick, dark hair and expressing newfound outrage at the language that Fuhrman had used. As the tapes were played behind her, McKinny's face twisted like that of an actress hearing bad news. I asked how she felt.

"I'm all right."

"Me too," I said quietly.

I had heard her voice on the tapes played in court, giggling at one of Fuhrman's tirades. As if it were funny, this heinous and disgusting rap about people of color and women. I have little patience for people who laugh at epithets and genocide, misogyny and racism. Anyone who stands by and allows this stuff to be said—in any context—is part of the problem.

In North Carolina, McKinny had testified that much of what Fuhrman said seemed to be in the context of a fictitious character. But by the time she testified, she distanced herself from Fuhrman—even though she had been the one to encourage him as he prattled on about "dumb niggers" and "Mexicans who can't even spell the name of the car they're driving."

In the foyer outside of Department 103, I ran into McKinny's husband, himself a film professor and aspiring screenwriter. The tapes had only been discovered because the couple had tried to shop their screenplay once Fuhrman became a player in the case.

"I'm just curious," I said. "What's your motive behind all this, I mean, getting involved? Why are you guys even here?"

Apparently, I had forgotten that I was in L.A. He looked at me as if I had asked a stupid question. "To sell a screenplay," he said.

In the war room, I saw the look of defeat finally on the faces of my colleagues, leaning on boxes of documents and reports that, finally, amounted to nothing. We had survived gloves and Gerdes, ice cream, and Colombian hit teams. But this was too much. It felt like purgatory in there, some lifeless place between heaven and hell, waiting for the end, for judgment.

Outside, Fred Goldman raged against what this trial had become. "Ron and Nicole were butchered by their client. This is not the Mark Fuhrman trial. This is a trial about the man who murdered my son!"

"I don't understand why the hell we had to listen to two hours of this hate!" Fred told reporters after hearing the Fuhrman tapes. "It's disgusting. My son, Nicole, our families have a right to a fair trial. And this is not fair!"

He was right. This was meant to distract and prejudice the jury, that's all. Mark Fuhrman didn't have the opportunity to take a glove from Nicole Brown's condo. Too many other officers had already seen the crime scene when he arrived. And there was so much incontrovertible evidence that Fuhrman could never have planted, that it was a ridiculous theory. On tapes in which he admitted the most heinous acts and views I'd ever heard, even Mark Fuhrman said that he hadn't planted evidence.

But he had lied. He had gotten up there and lied about his views and he had given Johnnie Cochran the final piece to a horrible puzzle he'd been assembling from the first day and that sat in front of us now, a conflation of much that is wrong about our country, that has always been wrong about our country.

I ached as I watched Fred Goldman try to wring some sense from what was happening around him. I felt partly responsible. Of course, I had known nothing about the Fuhrman tapes; none of us had. He had told us that he held no racist views, that he was a changed man.

But I had known that this day would come. I had a bad feeling about Fuhrman and I knew where Cochran was going, and even though there was nothing I could do, nothing I could have done, I felt badly, like someone who watches an accident unfold before him—mouth open in a half-uttered warning that no one could hear.

Nicole Brown and Ronald Goldman didn't deserve this.

On the streets, police officers would stop me and apologize for Fuhrman, clench-jawed with anger that he had defamed all police officers that way. There are so many good cops in Los Angeles, patrol officers and detectives who had worked so hard to restore some credibility in the black community after the riots. Some of the black officers who worked with Fuhrman in West Los Angeles sought me out to share my disappointment and assure me they had no idea about him. In the notes back and forth between Marcia and me, the standard code for Fuhrman, "MF," took on another meaning.

"Motherfucker," Marcia said. "Everything we worked for . . ."

She didn't need to finish the thought. Like me, the other lawyers, and the clerks, Marcia had labored to the point of exhaustion over this case. I had seen this woman—no thicker than a coatrack—stand up to everything the defense threw our way. But now, even Marcia Clark looked beaten.

On September 5, Judge Ito allowed the defense to play two excerpts from the tapes in front of the jurors, who sat there grim-faced and hardly seemed surprised by what they heard.

His voice seemed to come out of the paneled walls of Department 103, petulant and hateful, complaining about women officers: "They don't do anything. They don't go out and initiate contact with some six-foot, five-inch nigger that's been in prison for seven years, pumping weights."

I put my head down.

On the stand, McKinny said that Fuhrman used the epithet about forty-two times in the nine years they'd been making the tapes. "It was in a very casual, ordinary pattern of speech," she said.

Two other women, Kathleen Bell and Natalie Singer, testified about hearing Fuhrman make racist and genocidal statements, and Ito inexplicably allowed them to testify about how the slurs "made them feel."

"I kind of got teary-eyed and left," Bell said. Marcia and I went upstairs to our offices in silence. What was there to say?

The next morning, Mark Fuhrman returned. We had been warned that he was planning to plead the Fifth Amendment, refusing to testify on the grounds he might incriminate himself.

"Wooden, Decker, and I won't be in court when he comes in," I told Marcia. David Wooden and Melissa Decker were the only other black members of the prosecution team, and I had already told them that I didn't want them in court that day. Their lives—like mine—had been risked for this man, and now it was going to stop. Both David and Melissa had long careers ahead of them in the law and they shouldn't have to take with them the memory of Fuhrman's face, his betrayal of us all. He had looked directly into our eyes and promised that he wasn't a racist—all the while hating us and denigrating us in his mind.

Marcia had a sick look on her face—disapproval, maybe—but she didn't say anything. There was nothing she could say. I had seen enough. I wanted no more of this.

I waited in my office that morning when I heard that he was in the building. Outside my office, I saw Kim Goldman, her long angular face marked by tear-carved lines, haunting the hallways like a whispery ghost. Kim was only twenty-three. She must have felt beset on all sides by evil: by the man who killed her brother, the lawyers whose tricks defiled his memory, and the police officer who gave awful credence to their cruel defense. It is easier to think of the world as having two clearly divided sides —good and evil. Poor Kim Goldman was awfully young to find out that sometimes we encounter evil on all sides.

I pulled her close and squeezed her slack arms, told her it wasn't over yet: "We have a little fight left in us."

I spent some of the morning in court but left when I heard Fuhrman was on his way down. Back in my office, I waited for the telephone call that would tell me it was over, that I could return. When the word came that I was needed again, I took the elevator down nine floors and walked into the courtroom. I approached Marcia on our side of the table and, out of the corner of my eye, I saw him, sitting at the "little kids' table," waiting to testify.

I felt set up. I turned to face him and—for a split second—our eyes locked. Then we both looked away.

Judge Ito began the proceedings and I turned to leave. But I didn't walk out the doors. I couldn't. I sat in the back, his eyes still burning in mine. I wanted to see him, to watch him up there. His eyes were narrowed and drawn and his face seemed to have no detail, empty, drained of his cop arrogance. He looked to his attorney and answered each question with "On the advice of my attorney . . ."

I rose from my seat and walked through the double doors, wishing they led to someplace outdoors, someplace miles from here. Instead, I stood in the hallway, alone. He came out a few moments later with his contingent of bodyguards. I turned my back until he was gone.

I found Kim Goldman, who shook with anger, tears bubbling at the bottoms of her eyes. "I want to scream at him!"

"I know," I said. "Well, if that will make you feel better."

"I just want to go in there and ask him why he would do this."

"If you want to talk to him, I'll take you up there. If anybody is owed an explanation, it's you."

But Kim decided against it and we never went inside. Later, one of the men guarding him said Fuhrman had sat in that room, staring at the floor, saying nothing. "It was pretty pathetic."

The rumor was that, as he left the eighteenth floor, he mouthed to one of the prosecutors: "I'm sorry."

TWENTY

Sometimes, the view is best from the bottom. There are places that you can sink within yourself that are freeing and creative, where your perspective is of a world where there is only the possibility of improvement. It was out of such a hole inside myself that I began to imagine a closing argument for *People v. Simpson.*

It was mid-September of 1995. We were exhausted, and I think the senior prosecutors believed that the case was lost, though it remained unsaid. Moody and pessimistic myself, I put in my sixteen hours a day and wondered if the trial would somehow go on forever. All we could hope for was a few holdouts on the jury, "a couple of hangers" to give some other prosecutor a chance with the case.

I certainly wouldn't be back. I had no more energy for this circus, and I had nothing more to sacrifice.

That month, we presented our rebuttal witnesses (exclamation points on the physical evidence and more proof that they were Simpson's gloves); they put on their rebuttal witnesses (Mafia informants who spun more crazy conspiracies); but there was a sense that it was all perfunctory, that everything that could be said, had been said.

For closings, Marcia and I divided the case again. She took the physical evidence and I took the motive—premeditation and the domestic violence evidence. Then we retreated to our respective offices, and we didn't talk to each other for a while. All along, this had been Marcia's case and I respected her abilities and her position too much to challenge her authority. I had even altered my trial technique somewhat to fit Marcia's methodical style—quietly taking suggestions from her about how to question witnesses and draw out testimony.

But as I approached closing, I began to see the case through the eyes of Kim and Fred Goldman, through the eyes of Lou and Juditha Brown. They didn't see this case as a series of blood swatches, hair samples, and DNA strands to be compared, debated, and evaluated. They saw a smooth, violent celebrity who threatened to kill his wife and then did it, murdering her young friend as well. They saw a man with a motive and without an alibi, a man who left his own blood at the scene and dragged the blood of his victims back to his vehicle and his house.

My backyard is small but has neatly trimmed, five-foot bushes fencing it off from the clotheslined backyards of my neighbors. I almost never go into my yard, but that fall, I sat in a plastic lawn chair with a legal pad on my lap and field glasses around my neck, watching a couple of doves and a hawk jockey for positions on the electrical transformer rising above my neighborhood. "Ghetto wildlife," I said to nobody in particular.

I needed to bring this case back to the place we'd started, the murders of Ron Goldman and Nicole Brown. Someone just needed to point to O. J. Simpson and remind the jury that he was guilty, that no matter what they thought of him before, there was only one conclusion after looking at the evidence: O. J. Simpson was a murderer. Someone needed to just stand up and shout the things that we had been whispering to the jury with statistics, photographs, and testimony.

After his illness in January, Bill Hodgman had settled in as case manager, providing balance, perspective, and his vast experience to a trial team that ranged from manic to very manic. As soon as I had begun to frame a possible closing, Bill came to me with bad news. Marcia would argue the evidence of premeditation as well. I would handle only domestic violence, evidence that had been rejected, not only by some jurors, but by us too the day we decided against finishing that part of our case. In other words, Marcia would take the evidence that worked and I would argue the stuff that didn't. I was surprised they hadn't given me Fuhrman and Fung as well.

"What is this about?" I had given a year of my life to this case; I had given my very identity to this case. I blew up, the fatigue and passion roiling inside me like the basin of some deep falls. "Don't give me some token piece of a closing argument!"

I suppose I had felt the office's lack of confidence in me ever since the glove demonstration. It had become symbolic of our failures in this case, but it was hardly the only error. It wasn't even the worst. I hadn't chosen this jury or built a case that may have relied too heavily on Mark Fuhrman. I hadn't bored jurors with three-day classes on DNA or presented expert witnesses that fell like card houses before the defense lawyers. "Damn it, Bill!" I said. "No one in this office can argue this case the way I can." I told him that if they didn't think I was up to the premeditation evidence, perhaps I shouldn't argue any of the case. "In fact, I won't argue any of it."

I continued to stew about it and that's when Alan Yochelson came into my office, swept a mound of files off a chair, and sat down across from me. Yogi had been—along with Terry White—one of the prosecutors in the Simi Valley trial of the police officers who beat Rodney King. After a rough performance questioning one of the officers, Yochelson was relieved of some of his duties in the case. When it came time for closing arguments, he was not allowed to address the jury.

Of course, the D.A.'s office lost that case and, as the city was torn apart by riots, Yochelson sat in front of his television set, wondering if he could have made a difference. He was haunted by the closing argument he was never able to give.

"You know the Simpson case as well as anyone." He said that I owed it to the families of Ron and Nicole to argue as passionately and firmly as he'd seen me argue in cases about racist cops and gang murders. Yogi paused on his way out the door. "Don't let yourself feel the way I feel every day."

Alan was a good friend and had always been there for me. He was right about this. So I set to writing a closing argument that would untie all the emotional and logical knots that the defense team had tied. But, of course, they weren't done manipulating.

In court on Friday, September 22, both sides officially rested their cases and Johnnie Cochran told Judge Ito that Simpson wanted to address the court about his decision not to testify. Cochran said he had the right to stand and reject his right to testify. And that was it.

Marcia shot out of her chair, warning that this was another trick. "It is inappropriate, and it is done very deliberately by the defense for a clear purpose," she said. "Please don't do this, Your Honor. I beg you. I beg you."

Cochran shot back sarcastically, "This is still America and we can talk."

The jury was gone and the courtroom was dead quiet when O. J. Simpson stood and addressed the judge, the gallery, the television cameras, and—very conspicuously—the missing jury. "As much as I would like to address some of the misrepresentations made about myself and Nicole concerning our life together, I am mindful of the mood and the stamina of this jury," Simpson said. Cochran sat behind him in his God-father pose, elbows resting on his knees, hands coming to a point in front of his face. He could barely contain his smile. Marcia and I could barely keep from exploding.

"I have confidence," he said, "a lot more it seems than Miss Clark has, of their integrity, and that they will find—as the record stands now—that I did not, could not, and would not have committed this crime. I have four kids—two kids I haven't seen in a year. They ask me every week, 'Dad, how much longer?'" Simpson's eyes jerked around the courtroom like an auditioning actor checking the reaction to his performance, and I thought about some of Nicole's letters, in which she bemoaned the fact that Simpson never wanted to see his kids.

"All right," Ito said with a tinge of regret.

"I want this trial over," Simpson added. "Thank you."

Marcia shook with anger. She had warned Judge Ito, and he had allowed it to happen anyway. "Since he would like to make these statements to the court," she gritted, "I would like the opportunity to examine him about them. May he take a seat in the blue chair and we'll have a discussion?"

Deflated, Ito said only, "Thank you."

When he was done, Simpson frowned and sat down and Johnnie Cochran put his hand on his client's back, resting it there at the base of Simpson's neck. Cochran looked for all the world like a ventriloquist and I realized that—with his hands in front of his face while Simpson spoke—I hadn't seen Johnnie's lips move even once.

In front of reporters afterward, Cochran bragged that Simpson's remarks were "unscripted," even though a member of the defense team told the *L.A. Times* that they'd been working on the statement for two weeks, trying to find a way for Simpson to testify without having to submit to cross-examination. Apparently, in a practice session with a female lawyer simulating Marcia Clark, Simpson hadn't fared very well—his lack of respect for women quickly bubbled to the surface.

By that time, the defense knew what we had long suspected, that some jurors' conjugal visits were like little news programs, where they learned what was happening outside the courtroom.

For weeks, Fred Goldman had lashed out at the defense team's tactics, and this outburst put him over the edge. "I want this man convicted and in jail where he belongs. If he has a statement to make, he should have gotten on the damned stand and said something and not been a coward!"

Taking a break from grading the lawyers, the pundits went after the judge.

Peter Arenella, a UCLA law professor, said that Ito had allowed Simpson to informally testify in words that would surely make it back to the jury.

"Marcia Clark gave him fair warning as to what was about to happen," he said. "What is Judge Ito thinking about?"

Movie stars and other celebrities are, as a group, shorter than you'd think. Nicer too. After a while, their interest in this case seemed almost natural and we barely flinched when Jack Nicholson asked how things were going, when Carrie Fisher paged one of us, when Ed Begley Jr. listened in on our conversations, and when advice was faxed from Richard Dreyfuss or Dick Cavett—who suggested Simpson took his gloves off during the murders and then dropped one. "Haven't we all stuffed gloves in our pocket—we thought—and gotten home with one glove? Or none?"

For the most part, I eschewed the celebrity side of the trial and even turned down a date with a beautiful actress who inexplicably called me one day. I did have dinner with the singer Lionel Richie and told him I'd seen him with the Commodores at the San Jose Civic Auditorium in 1975. Another day, I was honored when Gregory Peck, at a dinner, talked with me about the lawyer he played in *To Kill a Mockingbird*.

I appreciated the support and the advice, although I was always surprised how intently the rich and famous followed the case. Perhaps celebrities and people on welfare were the only ones with the time to watch the whole trial.

Gavin de Becker—the stalking expert who provided security for celebrities and who had helped us with the Simpson case—offered his own theory about the Hollywood fascination with the trial.

"O. J. Simpson is an example of celebrity stripped bare," Gavin said. He said that most celebrities believe they are impostors and they wonder what it would be like to be exposed, to have it all taken away. "They want to see every detail of how it is to fall."

Gavin also believed that it was impossible to underestimate the power of celebrity in this case. Unfortunately for us, "O. J. Simpson is the biggest celebrity these jurors know now. That's a very powerful thing."

I spent more time thinking about the birds in my backyard than I did about celebrities, but in this case, you couldn't escape them. That weekend, I gathered a team of people—Scott Gordon, Cheri Lewis, Melissa Decker, David Wooden, and de Becker—to work on the closing. We had trouble getting started at first, because an actor kept calling with advice for the closing: "Three words," he said. "Just repeat three words: 'Two dead bodies! Two dead bodies!'" Still, it wasn't much worse than the stuff we were coming up with. On Sunday, I slumped in my office with Gordon and de Becker, whose computer sat open on his lap. Earlier versions filled the garbage cans like rejected love letters, and we struggled to find the right tone, the right inspiration, the right anything.

That night, I delivered the rough draft of my closing to a half-empty jury box of Gordon, de Becker, Hank Goldberg, Woody Clarke, Rock Harmon, Cheri Lewis, and a pack of minions. I hated it. In the dark courtroom where I'd spent the last year, I had trouble finding the passion that I knew this case needed. About 8 P.M., Gil Garcetti came in and sat quietly behind me; he left without saying a word.

Frustrated, I walked to the eighteenth-floor lunchroom to get some coffee. What was the problem? I'd lived with this damned case for a year! And now I was freezing up before my one chance to convince those jurors to do the right thing, to overlook the racist ploys of Cochran, to give those families justice—something they had stopped expecting months earlier, as the trial slipped further and further from them.

I sat down in the lunchroom—the kind every office has, nothing more than a coffee machine and a long table—and talked to a couple

of minions who also had retreated up there. In another room, Marcia
worked with her team on their closing. Surprisingly, we had almost no
coordination on our closings. I didn't know about Marcia, but I was brittle from the pressure from this thing.

"You OK?" Scott Gordon stuck his head into the lunchroom and
then came in with a cassette player in his thick hands.

"I'm fine."

He smiled somewhat coyly and hit the play button, and when the
bass line started in, a smile spread across my face. It was the Temptations'
"Ball of Confusion."

> *People movin' out; people movin' in;*
> *Why? Because of the color of their skin.*

The words started to come back to me and I stood up, dancing and
singing along. Gordon stood up too and danced next to me—like Newt
Gingrich and Louis Gossett Jr., singing some crazy duet.

Passing minions stuck their heads inside and howled with laughter,
and soon the room was full of lawyers and clerks, dancing and hooting
and cutting loose as if the cap had blown off a hot radiator, shaking and
gyrating, teary-eyed with laughter as the Temptations funked on a twenty-
year-old song that seemed to have been written just that day and just for
us, a song about segregation, integration, humiliation, and obligation.

The minions doubled over when I demonstrated the Hustle and
the Bus Stop—all the old school dances—and when the chorus came
around again, the whole room sang out like it was some ancient incan-
tation, a way out of this trial, the answer to some question we'd been
pondering for a year:

> *Ball of confusion!*
> *That's what the world is today.*

Marcia Clark stood up in a bone white dress that bunched up around
her thin arms. She greeted the jury and in a voice both patient and persistent, began to methodically lay out the evidence.

But first, there was some unfinished business. Mark Fuhrman.

"Did he lie when he testified here in this courtroom . . . that he did not use racial epithets in the last ten years? Yes. Is he a racist? Yes. Is he the worst the LAPD has to offer? Yes. Do we wish this person was never hired by the LAPD? Yes.

"But the fact that Mark Fuhrman is a racist and lied about it on the witness stand does not mean that we haven't proven the defendant guilty beyond a reasonable doubt, and it would be a tragedy if . . . you found the defendant not guilty . . . because of the racist attitudes of one police officer."

And then Marcia was off, doing what she did best, detailing the crime scene—her voice building along with her case—and the testimony of limo driver Allan Park, and of Kato Kaelin and his three bumps.

"Just think about that," she said. "Regardless of where or how they happened, just the fact that they happened shortly after the murders . . . and just before the defendant walked up his driveway in dark clothing like the dark blue or black sweat outfit that Kato described, you just put those facts together and you realize what has happened. The defendant has come back from Bundy in a hurry.

"He was moving quickly down a dark, narrow pathway overhung with trees, strewn with leaves, and in his haste, he ran right into that air conditioner that was hanging over that south pathway.

"You don't need science to tell you that. You just need reason and logic."

And then Marcia talked about the gloves and Simpson's weird demeanor when he tried them on in the courtroom. "If I were asked to try on the gloves that were worn by the murderer of the [mother] of my children, I would not be laughing. I would not be mugging. I would not think that was funny at all. Is that the attitude you expect, the laughing and the mugging, putting on the bloody gloves that were used to murder the mother of your children?"

Cochran objected for the first time that day.

The families of Ron and Nicole sobbed as Marcia showed the gruesome crime scene photos. "This is not the mark of a professional killer," she said. "These are not efficient murders. These are murders that are really slaughters, that are personal. And in that respect, they reveal a great deal about who did them. No stranger, no Colombian drug dealer."

She reconstructed the mountains of evidence, the blood, the hair and fiber evidence, and the DNA. She spoke of blood at the crime scene

that could be found in only one person in every 57 billion! O. J. Simpson's blood. "That's identity," she said. "That's his blood."

She worked to pull it all together—calling it a puzzle—and pointing
out that the defense hadn't been able to remove any important pieces.
She spoke all morning, all afternoon, and into the evening—six hours
in all—rarely saying Simpson's name. It appeared that would be left up
to me.

"You have a wealth of evidence," Marcia said, "all of it pointing to
one person: the defendant."

She sat down, heavy-lidded and tired, as if she'd been standing up
there for a year. Which, I guess, she had.

"That was brilliant," I told her. "I'm proud of you."

Earlier, defense attorneys had prompted Judge Ito to order Marcia
to remove an angel pin that symbolized Ron and Nicole. As I talked at
the bench with Judge Ito and with the defense lawyers before my closing,
Cochran suddenly demanded that I take off a ribbon that was pinned to
my lapel. It wasn't an angel pin.

It was a red AIDS ribbon. I knew Michael would be watching television that day, and I just wanted him to know—after all the support he'd
given me throughout the trial—that I was thinking about him. I looked
pleadingly at Judge Ito, but he was already ruling. He told Cochran that
there was nothing wrong with the ribbon. After all of Judge Ito's failings
in the case, I was grateful, at least, for that.

We weren't sure if I was going to start my closing that night, and
when I returned to my office, the telephone rang. It was a network news
official asking whether I was going to speak that night. Finally, I started
my argument about 7 P.M., just about the time the significance and pressure of the telephone call finally hit me: They needed to know when I
was speaking, because that night, I would be their prime-time program-
ming.

"I'm not afraid to point to him."

I turned and stared down my arm toward Simpson and then I
turned slowly back to stare each juror in the eyes, my hand still pointing
over my shoulder at him.

"Nobody pointed him out and said, 'He did it.' I'll point to him.
Why not? The evidence all points to him. Because, when you look at the

bloody ruthlessness of these murders . . . you see . . . that these killings were rage killings. Rage.

"You have to say to yourself, well, who in the past has ever raised a hand to this woman? And who in the days and the hours leading to her death was upset with her?

"The killing was personal. . . . The way it was done, this was personal.

"You look at the domestic violence, the manner of the killing, the physical evidence, the history of abuse and their relationship, the intimidation, the stalking. You look at it and it all points to him. It all points to him.

"Now, they may not think this evidence is important. But it was important to Nicole Brown."

I glanced down at my notes but I was already veering away from the outline Gordon, de Becker, and I had come up with. Jonathan Fairtlough, who was supposed to follow my script and display exhibits, was flustered, flipping through the pages, trying to find my cue for the exhibits. But I wasn't following any script. I was pulling from this idea and that idea—bits and pieces from everyone who had helped me—but I was also just talking, talking to the jury, telling them what we all knew, trying to shake free of the subterfuge and manipulation that had taken over this case.

"This relationship between this man and Nicole, you know, it is like a time bomb ticking away. Just a matter of time. Just a matter of time before something really bad happened. . . . There are people with short fuses. You know, they just go off. . . . This thing was like a fuse, a bomb with a long fuse.

"There were incidents along the way, and along the way, as each incident occurred, that fuse got shorter. . . . In 1985, that night when he took that baseball bat to her car . . . when you stop and look at it and you consider the conduct—he breaks the windshield, dents the car up, uses a baseball bat. . . . [His] wife is seated on top of the car crying, face covered, hair over her face. . . . What message does that send to Nicole?

"That fuse is burning. It's burning in 1985."

I tried to give some passion to the case, to show the outrage that these jurors should feel. I talked about other incidents of Simpson's obsession and violence, moving to the 1989 beating, when police arrived at the Rockingham estate after Nicole's 911 call. An officer knocked at the door, but Simpson's maid told him there was no problem. Fortunately, the police officer wouldn't leave.

"Someone ran from the bushes in the dark. It was a woman, a woman with blond hair. She was wearing a bra. She was wearing a bra and sweatpants. Do you remember what she was shouting?

"She was shouting 'He's going to kill me. He's going to kill me. He's going to kill me.' . . . And sure enough, he has.

"Officer Edwards said that she had a hand print—he saw a hand print on the left side of her neck, on the left side of her throat. A hand print. Someone had grabbed this woman . . . hard enough to leave an imprint around her neck, an imprint in the shape of his hand.

"Let me say this to you. We submit to you that the hand that left this imprint five years ago is the same hand that cut that same throat, that same neck, on June 12, 1994. It was the defendant. It was the defendant then. It's the defendant now.

"And she said to Officer Edwards . . . 'You never do anything about him. You come out here, you've been out here eight times and you never do anything about him.'

"They want to tell you that the police conspired against O. J. Simpson. Nicole says they had been out there eight times before and never did anything to him.

"Let me ask you this. How many times does it take?"

"And what does the defendant say? He says the same thing Nicole said, in a sense. He says . . . 'You've been up here eight times before, and now you're going to arrest me for this?'

"The fuse is burning. The fuse is burning. And at some point, this fuse is going to run out . . . it is going to get so short and so close to the bomb that, at some point, this bomb is going to explode."

I paused, pushed up my glasses, and was aware of myself for the first time since I'd begun speaking. I was standing in this crowded courtroom, lawyers leaning forward in their black-backed chairs, the victims' family members holding one another, the air charged with expectation and fear. This was why I had gone into the law, for those moments when compromise and confusion fell aside and I was left standing alone, fighting for the victims and speaking for their families, for people who looked to me for some help. We had allowed people like Johnnie Cochran to knock our legal system off course, but for just a moment, I could see again the course we had charted at the beginning. It was a thin line on the horizon, but I could see it.

And so I moved forward, to the letters that Simpson wrote to Nicole, the photographs of a beaten Nicole, and the other evidence recovered from Nicole's safe-deposit box.

"He wrote her some letters. He was trying to get back on her good side . . . trying to realize how he got so crazy. He had such emotional feelings toward her that were as high as any he ever felt.

"By April of 1992, this woman knew she was going to die. [Police] found that letter and they found two other letters from the defendant, from O. J. Simpson to Nicole, attempting to convince her to take him back, attempting to convince her that things would be better the next time.

"In that safe-deposit box, they found something else. They found a will. This woman's will. It had been executed during 1990, which means she must have been about thirty years old. You know many people who, at the age of thirty, execute wills? There were [also] some photographs . . . from when he beat her in 1989.

"She put those things there for a reason. . . . She is leaving you a road map to let you know who it is who will eventually kill her. She knew in 1989. She knew it and she wants you to know it.

"That fuse is burning."

And I broke until the next day. As I left the courtroom, Lou Brown stood suddenly, grabbed me, and gave me a hug. Marcia and I smiled at each other and took the elevator to the eighteenth floor, stepped off, and walked around a corner into a standing ovation of lawyers, law clerks, cops, and secretaries. They had chipped at our case, scratched it, and cracked it in places. But I believe that day, Marcia Clark and I presented it to the jury whole—a complete and vivid description of a gruesome double murder and an arrogant celebrity who was trying to get away with it.

"I told you it was a simmering relationship. It was a slow burn. It was a slow burn."

On Wednesday, I finished my closing argument, picking up where I'd left off the day before.

"Let's just cut right to the chase. Imagine the defendant in his Bronco. He is full of anger, and he is full of rage, and it is nighttime, and he is driving that Bronco, and he is full of jealousy, and the fuse continues to burn, and the focus of his anger is Nicole. For some reason, in his mind, she has done something he can't ignore, something that has set him off; he's jealous, he's raging, he's out of control, and he's in that Bronco, driving as fast as he can to Nicole's house. . . . He quickly parks the Bronco and gets out.

"But we're not talking about June 12, 1994. We're talking about October 25, 1993."

And then I played the 911 tape from that day, when Simpson had stormed over to her house, kicked in her door, and yelled about a man that Nicole had dated more than a year before. I stood up, sat down, paced, and watched the jury as Nicole's frightened voice washed over them, punctuated by the profanity-laced ravings of O. J. Simpson in the background. Did this sound like the voice of someone in a simple argument? If O. J. Simpson wasn't a violent person, why would she call the police during an argument? I watched the jury closely, hoping they realized they were listening to a woman foreshadowing her own death.

> Can you get someone over here now to 325 Gretna Green? He's back! He's O. J. Simpson. I think you know his record. Could you just send someone over here!
> He's in a white Bronco. First of all, he broke down the door to get in. . . . He's going nuts . . .

When the tape was done, I sighed and stood back at the podium. "We have suggested to you and proven that he is not the person you see on those TV commercials and at half-time of the football game. That is his public persona.

"I'm not suggesting to you that this man was angry and depressed and consumed with jealousy each and every moment of the day or each day he was with Nicole. I'm sure there were periods of calm, periods when they had a good time, when things worked out great for both of them. But always, beneath the surface, looms this jealousy and this anger and this passion and that rage, the rage you just heard on that tape."

And then we moved to June 12, 1994, and the dance recital where Simpson saw Nicole and her family. I explained that Paula wanted to go Sydney's recital, but O. J. said no and Paula left angry. I talked about Simpson's telephone call to Nicole that day and how she wouldn't talk to him. I recounted Kato Kaelin's testimony, that Simpson was angry about his wife's short skirt.

Nicole's friend Candace Garvey had testified that Simpson had a blank stare on his face and was distracted, as if he didn't recognize her. She and Denise Brown had both said that Simpson appeared angry. He sat behind the Browns, greeted everyone but Nicole, then got up, took his chair, and sat in a corner by himself. When Candace Garvey or Denise Brown turned to look at him, he wasn't watching the dance recital. He was watching Nicole's back. After dinner, the Browns made plans to go to dinner. Without him.

"He was in a slow burn and the fuse was getting shorter. Something set him off. There's going to be an explosion, folks, there's going to be an explosion."

That night, Simpson talked to Faye Resnick's boyfriend, Christian Reichardt, about 9 P.M. He seemed oddly happy and said he was packing for a red-eye flight, even though witnesses had paraded across the stand, saying that Simpson always packed late for trips.

"The next thing you know, he is in that Bronco. He is in that Bronco at 10 o'clock. . . . He is panicked and he is out of control and he needs someone or something to help calm him. And so what does he do? He calls Paula. [But] Paula is gone. Nicole is gone, and whose fault is all of this? . . . It isn't the defendant's fault; it's Nicole's fault.

"We know what kind of killing this is. This is a rage killing. He's using a knife because he's there to settle a personal score, a personal vendetta. He stabs this woman in the neck and he's right there, it's one on one and the rage that he has, the anger, the hate, he has for her that night, at that time, it flows out of him . . . into the knife and into her. And he kills Goldman in this rage.

"He killed her that way because he wanted to make a statement, he wanted to teach her a lesson. . . . He wanted to let her know. He wanted her to be there, face-to-face . . . to know just who was doing this to her.

"With each thrust of that knife into her body and into Ron's body, there is a release . . . a gradual release of that anger and that rage. And he stabs, and he cuts, and he slices until that rage is gone and these people are dead.

"And after that rage is gone, he's better. After he did this to these two people, he didn't run away, he didn't jog away. . . . He just walked away.

"He is a murderer. He was also one hell of a good football player, but he is a murderer.

"And so we've come full circle." I pulled out two photographs of Ron and Nicole, and the pictures froze me for a moment and I found myself talking to the pictures instead of the jury. "Ron, he was just at the wrong place at the wrong time. Nicole, she was in the wrong place for a long time.

"We began with them, two very much alive and vibrant human beings," I said. "We've come full circle. The only common element in all of this, the only direction in which all this points is to O. J. Simpson."

I finished by talking about the defense case.

"The defense got lost in minutiae in their attempt to confuse you," I said. "It's all about distracting you from the real evidence in this case. Well, the smoke is about to get heavier because they're about to talk to you."

Behind me, Cochran and Scheck scowled, looked at the judge and at each other, like a couple of kids holding a baseball bat, staring at a ball-sized hole in their neighbor's window.

I listed some of the many witnesses they had promised to call, like Rosa Lopez, Mary Ann Gerchas, and Dr. Lenore Walker.

"It wasn't the kind of defense where they showed you he wasn't there at the time of the murder," I said. "They never did that.

"What you really wanted to know was where was he at the time of the murders, right? Where was that Bronco?"

And then I talked about the ridiculous idea that police had worked to frame Simpson from the beginning. If this was a "rush to judgment," I said, why did the police go to Simpson's house eight times before citing him for the 1989 beating incident? Why did they wait outside his estate for detectives Lange and Vannatter to arrive? Why did they give him five days to turn himself in?

"Use your common sense," I said. "Take a look at the crime scene and follow that blood trail. Because when you do, you're gonna follow it right into his house, into his yard, into his bathroom, into his bedroom, right into his lap."

Then I asked the jury to "weigh the evidence . . . and do the right thing." And then I sat down. And Johnnie Cochran stood up.

He had arrived that day—and all of those last days of the trial— flanked by tall, bow-tied representatives of the Nation of Islam, a strong, proud, and worthy group, but also the very symbol of black separatism. Gradually, completely, Johnnie L. Cochran Jr. had transformed this case from a murder trial into a backhanded hearing about centuries of oppression and racism.

That is a trial that needs to be held, but not here. Not now. We have been giving testimony in that case for centuries, in Birmingham, Montgomery, and Selma; in Watts, Detroit, and Washington, D.C.; in Kenya, Zimbabwe, and the Sudan. O. J. Simpson belittles those struggles.

The revolution is over when the revolutionaries have nothing better to do than decry the treatment of a millionaire who was given every deference by the system. The movement will be a farce when young blacks are forced to storm the streets, yelling "Remember Brentwood!"

He said my name so many times, I wondered for a moment if I were the one on trial. Cochran showed a photograph of Simpson with his children and asked snidely, "Where is the fuse now, Mr. Darden?"

He said that our case was slipping away as soon as I had Simpson try on the gloves.

"You'll always remember those gloves, when Darden asked him to try it on, didn't fit. . . . No matter what they do, they can't make them fit." He said prosecutors would "do anything to contort, distort the facts." He repeated his themes, "If it doesn't fit, you must acquit," and "journey to justice."

He went after Fuhrman as "a genocidal racist," and said that, somehow, the detective had been waiting for an opportunity to frame Simpson *for nine years.* He said that we knew about Fuhrman's racism all along. He unveiled a graphic entitled "Fuhrman's Big Lie" and another one that infuriated me: "Vannatter's Big Lies." I couldn't believe they were painting Vannatter with the same brush they used on Fuhrman.

He hammered away at his ridiculous conspiracy—"Because of their vanity, they very soon pretended to solve this crime and, we think, implicated an innocent man"—ignoring the fact that police went out of their way to accommodate Simpson, in 1985, 1989, 1993, and who knows how many other times, all the way up to 1994.

But Cochran's objective was never the Simpson case.

"Your verdict in this case will go far beyond the walls of Department 103 because your verdict talks about justice in America and it talks about the police and whether they should be above the law," Cochran said.

The next day, he ratcheted up the rhetoric even further, talking about the "twins of deception"—Vannatter and Fuhrman. Later, they became the "twin demons," and by the time he called them the "twin *devils* of deception," he had tapped the very term used by Black Muslims like Malcolm X to describe whites—"devils."

"Maybe this is why you were selected," Cochran said to a jury with nine African Americans. "There's something in your background . . . that helps you understand that this is wrong.

"Maybe you're the right people, at the right time, at the right place to say, 'No more—we're not going to have this.'" Barry Scheck took on the real work, arguing the merits of their case, which he did strongly and effectively.

Cochran, meanwhile, dropped every pretense and played only the race card, appealing to jurors who knew of stories in which their relatives or friends—or even they themselves—were faced with police prejudice.

"Stop this cover-up!" he demanded. "If you don't stop it, then who? Do you think the Police Department is going to stop it? Do you think the D.A.'s office is going to stop it? Do you think we can stop it by ourselves? It has to be stopped by you."

But even I was surprised at how far he went when it came to Mark Fuhrman. "There was another man, not too long ago, who had those same views, who wanted to burn people," Cochran said. "This man, this scourge, became one of the worst people in the history of the world, Adolf Hitler."

"If you don't speak out, if you don't stand up, if you don't do what's right, this kind of conduct will continue on forever. And we'll never have an ideal society."

When he was done, there was an emptiness in that courtroom. Maybe it had been filled before with the potential for this. Now, it was completely empty. Later, in the face of sharp criticism from Fred Goldman and people of all races and religions, Cochran said, "I'm just here doing my job."

I was only supposed to talk once. But as we realized the scope of what Cochran was saying, it became clear I was the only person who could address it. During one of the breaks, we talked about giving two rebuttals, Marcia addressing Scheck and the Simpson case, me addressing Cochran and his twin devils.

If, early in the case, Marcia had been ignorant of the special pressures I faced, now she flattered and touched me with her sensitivity.

She slipped me a note saying I didn't have to give any rebuttal if I didn't want to. "I will never, ever hold it against you," she wrote.

I just smiled.

Marcia's teeth had been hurting and the pain became more intense. And so, when arguments were completed on Thursday, at 6:30 P.M., she went to an emergency dental appointment. There, the dentist found out she had an abscess. They used general anesthesia to knock her out and then they operated. Marcia never knew what hit her.

Back at the CCB, the rest of the lawyers crowded in a conference room, trying to figure out how to respond to the defense closing. With Hank Goldberg writing on a display board at the front of the room, the rest of the lawyers threw out suggestions. It was clear no one was in charge and that they lacked direction.

From the back of the conference room, Gavin de Becker, Scott Gordon, and I winced as Hank wrote down the ideas thrown out: dry, complex discussions of swatch numbers, alleles, and statistics. Gavin had complimented me, saying that I had "given the case a soul," and now he leaned over and said, "If I'm bored with the stuff, the jury's gonna be bored with this stuff."

At some point, exhausted after two days of arguments, I fell asleep. Finally, at 10 P.M., her mouth still somewhat numb, Marcia arrived, quickly dividing up the deceptions from the defense team and doling out assignments, me on one end, her on the other.

Marcia thanked me again for taking half of her rebuttal and asked if there was anything she could do to help me.

"You know that red dress you wear sometimes?" I asked.

She laughed. "Yeah."

"You could wear that for me."

And so I took my team and left, went to a hotel room, and began working on my rebuttal. It was the same team as before—Scott, Gavin, Cheri Lewis, Melissa Decker, and David Wooden. Gavin typed while the rest of us kicked around possible themes and metaphors. One thing that Cochran and I both realized, I think, was the power of religious allusion, and I turned quickly to the Bible for inspiration, looking for just the right reference.

"Does it really matter which part of the Bible you quote?" Gavin asked rhetorically.

"Oh," I said, "it matters to some of those jurors."

In the end, I settled on Proverbs 6:16-17: "These . . . things doth the Lord hate: . . . A proud look, a lying tongue, and hands that shed innocent blood." There was a description there of Cochran too, in verse 19: "A false witness that speaketh lies, and he that soweth discord among brethren."

We worked well past midnight, past 1 A.M. and 2 A.M. and 3 A.M., until, finally, we had a decent, workable draft.

"OK!" Scott said. And then he looked around. "Where's Darden?" He and Gavin walked into the bedroom and found me asleep, stretched out in the clothes I'd worn to court that day, my tie loosened.

"Well," Gavin said. "At least someone's not nervous."

Scott, Cheri and Gavin went down to the CCB to print out the argument. They got there at 3:45 A.M. Marcia had just left.

This was the end. I felt strangely calm as I arrived in court on Friday, September 29, 1995, a year since I'd been dragged into this mess. In the courtroom, Robert Shapiro grabbed me by the arm and complimented me on my arguments. "You've had it the worst of any lawyer in this courtroom," he said. "I admire you."

I thanked him. Cochran and Shapiro were no longer speaking, and Robert would soon criticize Cochran for "dealing the race card from the bottom of the deck."

As Shapiro returned to the defense table, Cochran nodded his head toward me. "What did that traitor tell you?"

The courtroom buzzed with anticipation and I was afraid some of the reporters would fall out of their seats. I smiled at the Goldmans and the Browns and conferred briefly with Marcia. She was wearing that red dress.

"Good luck." She smiled. And then I rose to speak for the last time in a court of law.

"You can't send a message to Fuhrman, you can't send a message to the LAPD, you can't eradicate racism within the LAPD or the L.A. community or within the nation as a whole by delivering a verdict of not guilty in a case like this.

"The evidence is there. You just have to find your way through the smoke. You just have to find your way through the smoke.

"In this case they have interjected this racism and now they want you to become impassioned, to be upset, and they want you to make quantum leaps in logic and in judgment.

"It is true that Fuhrman is a racist and it is also true that [Simpson] killed these two people, and that we proved that he killed these two people."

Cochran interrupted me several times and as Ito overruled one of his objections, I held up my hand. "This is my time to talk," I said. I talked about family, and suddenly Michael popped into my head. I'm not sure why, but I said, "My big brother would do anything for me."

I didn't go on for very long, though. My message was simple and I had delivered it to the jury in the same words I would use today or tomorrow or any time a double murderer was on the verge of getting away with it because of the color of his skin.

"I have been a prosecutor for almost fifteen years. And if there is one rule that I have lived by, if there is one rule that means a lot to me, it is this one: No one is above the law; not the police, not the rich, no one. And I hope you agree with that.

"O. J. Simpson isn't above the law."

PART 3

MICHAEL

And God shall wipe away all tears from their eyes;
and there shall be no more death, neither sorrow,
nor crying, neither shall there be any more pain:
for the former things are passed away
And he that sat upon the throne said, Behold,
I make all things new.

—Revelation 21:4–5

TWENTY-ONE

y Big Brother was dying. I spoke to Mama over the telephone and she told me it was Michael's time. The nurses at the AIDS hospice said we would know because his breathing would change; it would become nonrhythmic and sputtering, and then, finally, he would take one last breath and be gone.

And that's what was happening.

I had just returned from seeing Michael and the rest of my family for Thanksgiving. Now, on his last night, November 28, 1995, I sat in the dark in my house in Southern California, wondering how much time he and I had lost while the Simpson trial was allowed to drag on. I walked down the dark hallway and rummaged through some books for the videotape I'd shot just a few days earlier. I pulled up the picture on the camera's eyepiece, the sound turned low like a whisper.

On the videotape, my sister Debbie and I bring a plate of Thanksgiving food to Michael, who is resting at a convalescent home, reclined on a white sheet, his long black hair streaked with angry gray. Paralyzed on his left side, Michael bounces his right foot up and down, a sock with his name—"M. Darden"—stenciled on it. His eyes are dreamy, milking over; he's been blind only for the last month.

On the tiny screen in front of me, my sister Debbie sits on the bed with him and tries to feed him yams, Mama's dressing, and sweet potato pie. Michael loves Mama's dressing. But he just stares toward a window that he can't see. "Remember Mama's rolls?" Debbie asks. Michael takes one and holds it in his hand, but after a time, it is too heavy and his arm falls against the pillow.

"Why won't you eat?" Debbie asks.

His voice comes from somewhere in his chest and it is little more than the breath that forces it. "I can't swallow." He won't turn his head away from that window. Maybe he sees something out there, something the rest of us can't see yet. He is wearing pants but they look empty. He weighs 70 pounds now and he tugs at the diaper that sticks out of his pants.

When he was still fighting, Michael and I had talked about this— about my filming him. He asked me to do it to keep a record of what the disease did to him, "so other people can see how this makes you suffer." Still, it was hard to keep the camera on him. He had a brain infection and headaches so severe he would grab his head and scream for hours. Once, the convalescent center didn't know what to do and so they called the police.

The camera moves around the room, to the window, some flowers, and back to Michael. A sheet of paper on his bedstand reads: "Patient cannot feed himself."

As if on cue, Michael tries to eat, still stubborn, still standing up to whatever authority is in front of him, even if that authority is nothing more than a hand-lettered sign. He holds a wavering fork as if it weighs 100 pounds and tries to guide a bit of dressing into his mouth. But he doesn't make it and Debbie has to help him. And then she leaves for a while and I set the camera down, to say good-bye. I tell him that I will see him on the other side. Michael looks eighty, hollow and brittle, mouth twisted up, mustache filled with bits of food, almond-shell eyelids heavy and ready to close.

Then the tape ran out and I was alone again in my house. And Michael was gone.

In my garage are more than twenty boxes that I have taken from my office, boxes filled with letters and gifts from people who watched the trial and were moved somehow by the things that I said or did.

Of course, not all of them were favorably moved.

There is a card with a crude drawing of a black man running through a watermelon patch and a suggestion that I lost the case on purpose. Another letter begins, "It is the Niggers that are Racists: Not the White Man." Another, "This O. J. trial is nothing but a nigger hunt and you're no more than a token black puppet for whitie." And more,

"How can any African American have any respect for you and your family. You're a disgrace!"

I would like to say that the letters don't hurt anymore, but that isn't true. But, thankfully, only a fraction are so angry. Most are like the letter sent by a Vietnam veteran who enclosed an honorary membership to his army unit and expressed his gratitude for "the fine job you did." He included a fading, twenty-year-old photograph of his unit—ninety-four men of all races stacked five deep like a football team. Six of them were killed in Vietnam and twenty-five were wounded, he writes. "Even though I did my best, never cowered, nor let my fellow soldiers down I still felt like I could have done more."

People often ask how I feel. That is how I feel.

There were some dark days after the verdict, when my mistakes and my sacrifices gnawed at me from two different directions. During those times, some of the letters made me feel better, like one that came from an entire family:

> I don't know if you ever read the book or saw the movie *To Kill a Mockingbird*. There was a scene where the lawyer lost a case due to a racist jury. After the courthouse cleared, there was a small crowd in the balcony, including the lawyer's two small children. As the lawyer cleared his desk and left the courthouse, an old man said to the children, "Stand up, children, your father is passing by."
>
> I just want you to know, Mr. Darden, when you left the podium unable to finish your statement, my family & I stood— to honor you for your courage, your dignity and your integrity.

There is a third category of letter, which usually starts out, "I am a white woman from . . ." or "I am an Asian man from . . ." They are from families in Texas, a man in Vermont, and a woman from Bad Axe, Michigan, who wrote, "I'll be the first to admit I'm ignorant about race relations. To be honest, I'm not sure if I'd be considered prejudiced or not." These letters often ask for help in understanding the verdict or comprehending how a country can be so easily fractured by something as common as a murder trial.

These are also some of the people I see when I am traveling across the country, lecturing at colleges. They seek me out as if I might be able to explain the verdict to them or explain where everything went wrong. They want to know why many white people and many black people appear to have different views of justice.

After a lecture in Massachusetts, a woman—a young girl, really—took my arm and told me that she was beaten by her boyfriend and that she is still afraid. This sort of thing happens often as well, in letters and in person. This girl began crying when I asked if she had left him. Yes, she said.

"Good. Stay away from him. And whatever you do, don't let him back in your life."

At home, in Carson, I turn off the television whenever I see anyone talking about the Simpson case. When Asshole began doing interviews in early 1996, I refused to watch and I toss the newspaper aside when he is on the front page. I have heard reports of some of his lies—Nicole bruised her own face in 1989?—but I don't care to listen. He has always valued his public image more than the people in his life, and I suppose he will go on forever haunting his empty estate, monitoring the television channels, looking for someone who is talking about him, so he can call up and try again to deny what he is.

I won't listen. He had his chance to testify and he chose to let a team of lawyers make his statement instead, a statement that he is bigger than the law and that the lives of his ex-wife and her friend are worth roughly $6 million in legal fees.

After the trial, I took a leave of absence from the Los Angeles County District Attorney's Office and accepted an associate professorship at Southwestern University School of Law. There, I am encouraged to see young, idealistic people who look at the law as a calling. For myself, I doubt I will ever practice law again.

Marcia and I talk on the telephone and see each other every once in a while. We talk about our kids, but we rarely discuss the case. For some people who were drawn in by this case, it is more difficult to let go. Ron Shipp comes over to have a soda, watch a basketball game, and talk about whether he should move out of L.A. Faye Resnick calls to tell me that she is afraid and that she hopes her life will get back to normal. And

Kim Goldman comes by sometimes, to ask what she should do with her anger and to tell me that she misses her brother.

I told Kim once that the last thing I wanted to do was write a book about this case. As the trial wound down, I had noticed that one of the defense lawyers appeared to be at work on a book already, typing on a laptop computer in court. I did not want to profit that way from the deaths of these two people.

"It's not like that," Kim said. "You have a chance to do something worthwhile, to help people see what happened here." I promised to try.

On October 2, 1995, we received word that the jury had a question. Most of the attorneys had taken the day off, and so Bill Hodgman and I took the elevator down to Department 103, as the jury listened once more to the testimony of Allan Park, the limousine driver. We watched the jury, looking for hints about the first couple of hours of deliberations. It seemed a good sign that they wanted to hear from one of our most effective witnesses, yet I still had the bad feeling I'd carried with me for more than a year.

When the jurors had heard enough, they retreated to the jury room and we gathered our things to go. It seemed like only ten minutes later that Judge Ito was motioning us to the bench.

"You go," I said to Bill. I watched Hodgman walk up to the bench, where Ito flipped a sheet of paper sideways for Bill to see. He turned and made eye contact with me, and I struggled out of my chair and made my way across the courtroom to the bench, my eyes making straight for the sheet of paper. The note said that they'd reached a verdict.

On the way out of the courtroom, Carl Douglas and I shook hands. "Man," he laughed, "you know it's not guilty. No way they gonna convict my boy in just a few hours."

I spent the night in the presidential suite of the Westwood Marquis Hotel, lying on top of the covers, staring at the ceiling. Marcia and I would escape here separately during the trial sometimes, and I lay there the night before the verdict was announced getting a fitful couple of hours of sleep, my eyes snapping open repeatedly and focusing on the digital clock on the nightstand. The next morning, Gavin de Becker offered us the use of his bulletproof car, but the guys from the D.A.'s investigative bureau would have been put out.

"Don't worry," they said. "We can protect you."

Marcia and I were ferried in separate cars—escorts in front and back—through downtown L.A. We passed buildings that strobed the morning sun and it seemed as if everyone in the city was out on the street. At Spring Street, I could see and hear helicopters swarming above us and by the time we reached Temple, I saw that the street in front of the CCB was blocked off at both ends. Between the barriers, the long block was completely filled with people—like a one-block, self-contained parade. We drove up to the building, through screaming crowds, the faces blurring as they flashed past. Packs of people ran through the streets and seemed to scream for no reason; I had never seen anything like it—except perhaps in old pictures of V-J Day, after World War II.

"Give us Fuhrman!" some of the crowd chanted. "Send out Fuhrman!"

I will always remember the war room the way it appeared to me that day. Lawyers and clerks were dressed up in their best, happy that their work was finally coming to a close, confident that we had won. Everyone except Cheri Lewis and me was optimistic, saying that it had to be a guilty verdict. The jury had asked for Allan Park's testimony, and such a quick verdict could only mean they had understood the overwhelming nature of the evidence. The pundits were saying much the same thing. But when people asked my opinion, I just shrugged. I didn't want to spoil this moment, and so I savored a few minutes of victory with people who had long inspired me with their dedication and hard work.

In the courtroom, the anticipation was a sharp pain in my chest as we stood for the verdict. At 10 A.M., with 90 percent of the televisions of America tuned in, with commerce pausing to look over its shoulder and the entire world holding its breath, Judge Ito asked Simpson to rise and his clerk, Deirdre Robertson, began reading the verdict. "We the jury . . ."

Afterward, I was numb, riding through the throng in the back of a car, trying to imagine how they could come to a reasoned decision in just four hours. It was impossible. They owed it to the people of California to weigh the evidence and reassess the testimony and they hadn't.

If they had just gone over the case and tried to answer their doubts with testimony from the trial, then they still could have come back with a not guilty verdict, and I would have accepted their decision. But that didn't happen. Twelve people could not make an honest assessment of nine months of testimony in just four hours.

Instead, they did just what Johnnie Cochran asked them to do. It was that look in their eyes, the one I'd recognized from the beginning. It was the juror who gave Simpson a black power salute.

They sent a message.

In December, a group of black community leaders held a tribute in my honor at the Afro-American Museum in L.A. I was moved and honored by the event. Sponsored by Los Angeles County supervisor Yvonne Brathwaite Burke and the Langston Bar Association, the tribute drew about one thousand people. Among the speakers was Johnnie Cochran, who used the event to say that he was still on his "journey to justice." He made his peace publicly with me by saying he had "developed a lasting respect for this man and his integrity."

When it was my turn to speak, I thanked the black leaders who had gathered. As I stood on the dais, I recalled Cochran's warning that I was "making it hard for us to get you back in. . . ." On a television news program earlier that week, he'd said he was looking forward to "welcoming me back to the community."

I talked about Ron and Nicole and my duty as a prosecutor. I talked about crime victims and the desperate need that our community had for black prosecutors. And then I said, "You don't have to welcome me back into the community, because I never left."

That day, I came to pay homage to the idea of African-American unity, to make peace, but also to reassert that no one man can say what it is to be black. We can only be unified in our diversity. There is no one black experience, no black political party, no one notion that represents the "correct" African-American opinion. I stood up to remind my brothers and sisters that we have battled too long the limitations put upon us by others because of our color, only to replace them with our own limitations because of our color.

Perhaps I had to be "kicked out" of the black community to understand my place in it. But sometimes the view is much better from outside.

I found myself in a place between black perception and white perception, in a borderland where I can see both sides through eyes that are clearer than any I've ever imagined. At first, this place frightened me because I thought I was alone. But like someone whose eyes adjust to a dark room, I can see many others here now.

I see Colin Powell struggling against the opportunity to go further than any black man before him. In him, or in the next Colin Powell, there exists a day when black people won't be able to blame the Man anymore, because the Man will be black. When that day comes, we will support a Colin Powell, not necessarily with our votes—because we don't have to agree with him to support him—but with our tolerance and understanding.

I see in this borderland thousands of everyday black professionals, people whose achievement is a testament to their work and their refusal to be limited by their white guidance counselors—or by their black cousins.

W. E. B. Du Bois said that we were all of two worlds—part African and part American. It is only in the middle where we can be free to be both, to move in the world of American laws and culture without forsaking our African heritage. And we must be free. That has always been the prize.

As a young man, racism seemed to me a single-edged knife, one that whites used to hold blacks down. Now I see that our own racism can be as dangerous and insidious as that which we have battled for centuries. I see racism in people who purport to represent all African Americans. I see racism in a community that refuses to hold one of its own responsible. I see racism in myself. It is wrong. It has always been wrong. We cannot defeat their racism with our own; we cannot defeat bigotry by cheating justice.

When you are the subject of prejudice, you are enslaved by it. And you are just as enslaved when you practice prejudice. I can see now that freedom from the shackles of slavery and freedom from having to conform because of the color of your skin are one and the same.

There is much work to do. Somehow, we have allowed the murder trial of a simple football player to define race relations in America. We must all find more worthy causes and more significant points to debate—a moral and ethical center for the civil rights movement. If there is no other common ground, we must at least agree that there is more important business to attend to.

That is where I will have to make my final peace with Johnnie Cochran, on some path where we agree that justice is the true destination.

As for the jury, I bear them no ill will. It is the system that I hold in contempt, the criminal justice machine that allowed this thing to become something it wasn't.

I will lose no more sleep over O. J. Simpson because he will be judged again one day.

And my legacy?

I understand that some black prosecutors have a name for the pressure they feel from those in the community who criticize them for standing up and convicting black criminals.

They call it the "Darden Dilemma."

It's probably not the future I dreamed of on those summer nights on my parents' porch, but there is a truth behind it that makes me proud.

I hope that, because of the things I have done, my children and their children will find it easier to challenge the status quo and to stand up for what is right. I hope that someone will nod someday after hearing their last name and say, "Your father, he was a good man."

All any of us can do is try to improve the world that we pass on.

In Michael's last hours, my sisters Debbie and Anita were with him, along with his wife, Carolyn, and our brother-in-law Doyle.

I am most grateful that Mama was there. Michael would have wanted to be with our mother, who has always been the quiet rock in our family and has seamlessly taken Nanny's place as the source of both strength and forgiveness.

When Michael's chest began to rattle and his breathing slowed to a whisper, Mama took his hand. "It's OK," she said. "God loves you."

Crying, Mama recited the Twenty-third Psalm to him from memory: "The Lord is my shepherd; I shall not want. He maketh me to lie down in green pastures; he leadeth me beside the still waters. He restoreth my soul: he leadeth me in the paths of righteousness for his name's sake. Yea, though I walk through the Valley of the shadow of death, I will fear no evil; for thou are with me; thy rod and thy staff they comfort me.

"Thou preparest a table before me in the presence of mine enemies: thou anointest my head with oil; my cup runneth over. Surely goodness and mercy will follow me all the days of my life: and I shall dwell in the house of the Lord forever."

She stroked his hair and said good-bye. "It's OK to let go now. It's OK to go home."

And so he did. Finally at 10:28 A.M., Wednesday morning, November 29, 1995, Michael Darden died. His wife tried to close his eyes, but they snapped back open; apparently, Michael left his stubbornness behind.

Two days later, we lowered him into the ground in a sixteen-gauge steel coffin. He wore one of my suits, a blue one. With my family gathered around, an associate pastor at Michael's church said a few good words about him and some things that made us all feel better.

I have always been proud of my brother and I was proud of the way he died. Despite all that he had been through—the pain he caused his parents and the pain he endured himself—my brother showed courage in the face of death and he walked toward it the way he lived his life, unafraid and without a single complaint.

Later, I stood on my parents' porch and tried to conjure up a kid's daydream of what the future would hold, hoping that in it, I would realize what to do now. Instead, I remembered sitting on the porch during so many sunsets, watching Michael walk away from me, strutting up the street in his starched jeans, looking for his cool friends, leaving me behind with my head in my hands. I wished I could go with him; I always wanted to go with Spider.

But Michael told me that I had to stay behind, that I had things to do that he could never even imagine. Now, after his funeral, I watched the sun go down and thought about the words the preacher had said: Everything bad passes and we are all headed for a better place.

I know that he is right.

AFTERWORD

Time and distance. It would be nice if those two things could heal the wounds left over from the murder trial of O. J. Simpson. But this case is unique and sometimes I wonder if it isn't just plain evil. As time goes on, the shadows from this murder only touch more people, the anguish it causes only intensifies, the mistrust it breeds only spreads. For just about anyone involved in this case, it seems, time and distance aren't enough.

And yet we all move on. I live in a different home now, a bright, open, two-bedroom house in Ladera Heights, and I teach at Southwestern School of Law in Los Angeles. To the students there, I am simply "Professor Darden." It is tonic every time I hear those words.

The students crowd into the simple, urban classrooms where I teach, listen attentively, and offer refreshingly idealistic answers to every question, every scenario. I am energized each day to see the law through their young eyes, to see it as a path to justice and not as a meaningless stage, a place where truth is blocked by manipulation, and where the sweet fruits of civil rights and black unity are used cynically to free criminals.

It has been more than a year now since O. J. Simpson was acquitted in the murder trial of his ex-wife Nicole Brown, and her friend Ronald Goldman. The shock waves of this case continue to amaze me. When it was over, I prayed for a little time and a little distance—for myself, for the people involved in this case, and for the untold number of people profoundly affected by it. I hoped that a year would soften the sharp feelings that so many people felt. But as the case continues to reverberate in American culture, I am reminded of the many families of murder victims with whom I worked during my career as a prosecutor. Perhaps, for the first time, we're feeling what victims' families feel—what the Gold-mans and Browns feel—a loss that seemingly can never be dulled.

The case hasn't gone away.

In the last year a straight-forward double murder has profoundly changed the way many people look at race in this country, the way they see the criminal justice system, the trust they place in police, lawyers, and the media.

I have watched as this case continues to take an incredible toll on my friends and colleagues in law enforcement, as it continues to carve an angry swath right through Los Angeles, through a city that for too long has seemed one incident away from more riots.

There are times I miss the prosecutor's office—the camaraderie and the knowledge that we were always out there, working together, doing the right thing. But I haven't missed the pettiness, the lack of support, and the jealousy of a few of my former colleagues in the wake of the Simpson case. Sometimes I think this case has spoiled everything it touches, my old office included. I suppose after working myself sick for a year, I was too tired to listen to after-the-fact second-guessing of the prosecution team from a few people within our office; to the anger over small bonuses that Marcia Clark and I received; to the criticism of the book deals she and I signed, like crabs angry at a couple of other crabs who managed to scurry out of the pot.

I talk to Marcia on the phone every couple of weeks.

Her custody battles are finally behind her and she is barreling ahead with her life the way only Marcia can. I will always feel a deep friend-ship with her and I have told her that if she ever needs anything, I will be there before she can finish dialing my number. But I suppose she and I have drifted apart a little bit and anyone who has gone through an exhausting, bitter ordeal like that will understand why. When people are drawn together by intense circumstances, the relationship can some-times fade with the intensity. I guess the closest analogy is the experience of people who serve together in the military and then lose touch when it is over. Sometimes the only thing you can do is move on.

Even though Marcia and I were on the front lines most days, dozens of other people in the Los Angeles County District Attorney's office bear the scars from that case. My old boss, Gil Garcetti, was hit like no one else. What should have been a simple reelection campaign for him in

1996 became a fierce battle with a person whose credentials aren't even close to Gil's. Even though he won, Gil continues to be caught between white anger over Simpson's acquittal and black anger over the prosecution of the case and the actions of Mark Fuhrman. I empathize with him very much. I know what it's like to be in the middle.

Most of the rest of the Simpson prosecution team is still there, handling less-publicized cases, but cases in which the victims' grief is no less severe and the bad guys are no less bad. I still admire their commitment and their honor and I miss them.

I am immeasurably proud of the minions, the clerks I hired for the Simpson case. They are all lawyers now. They all passed the bar and most of them have decided to stay with the prosecutor's office, scattered by the winds to the different offices throughout Los Angeles County. I talk to them occasionally about the cases they're working on and they exude a real sense of purpose and morality. They are still the good guys.

As are the officers in the Los Angeles Police Department. In the last year, I went to bittersweet retirement parties for two of the best detectives I've ever worked with—Phil Vannatter and Tom Lange. It pains me every time I turn on the television and hear one of Simpson's old lawyers accuse those two fine cops of lying and conspiring to frame O. J. Simpson. At their retirement parties, we laughed and talked about their long, distinguished careers, about their successes and the years they devoted to this city. And we talked about Simpson. Driving home after their retirement parties, I would have given anything for their careers to have ended differently.

The Los Angeles police, like cops everywhere, have had to deal with the fallout from this case and from the racist lies of Mark Fuhrman. I am outraged by the disrespect with which law enforcement officers are being treated in courtrooms across the country because of one blustery, ignorant cop.

Still, there is no evidence that Fuhrman planted any evidence. In the end, he may have done more than anyone on the Dream Team to free O. J. Simpson. And his perverse help for Simpson seems to be unending. As they chose a jury for the civil suit brought against Simpson by the victims' families, there was Fuhrman in court—and on television for all the jury candidates to see—pleading nolo contendere—no contest—to perjury.

I am often asked how I believe the civil case will be resolved. I am encouraged to see the judge in the civil case exerting the kind of control over his courtroom that Lance Ito should have used in the criminal trial. And I think the burden of proof in a civil case (a preponderance of the evidence vs. proof without a reasonable doubt in a criminal case) will serve the plaintiffs well. In the end, the attorneys for the Brown and Goldman families should be able to prove that O. J. Simpson was responsible for the deaths of Nicole and Ron.

But this is Simpson. The only guarantee is that the case will be strained and strange. That it will go on longer than it should. That it will continue to divide people.

In the last year, this case has been rehashed in several books that retrace the prosecution of Simpson, at least a couple of them blaming prosecutors for Simpson's release. I have acknowledged that we made errors in strategy and in the courtroom. It seems to me such books—one written by a former prosecutor who spent no time in the courtroom—contain little new information.

Blame. That's all they contain.

Perfect prosecutions just don't happen. And I don't believe a perfect prosecution in this case would have necessarily made a difference in the face of a jury eager to acquit, a judge drunk with attention and power, witnesses holding back information, and defense attorneys willing to drive a stake through America's fragile race relations just to free a double murderer.

Other books and media reports have offered more information that incriminates Simpson, some by his own inner circle. They dribble out new bits of information that they mysteriously forgot to tell prosecutors when it really counted. People who were silent when it could have made a difference or who helped Simpson now seem to demand credit for standing up and telling the truth.

And so we've seen the likes of Kato Kaelin on television, saying that he now believes Simpson is guilty and that Nicole was terrified of the man she had married. Robert Shapiro distances himself from Simpson and decries the use of "the race card." Robert Kardashian appears on television to say that he "had doubts" about Simpson's innocence, that the blood evidence worries him, and that he has trouble sleeping at night.

Yet this is the same Kato Kaelin who coyly dodged questions and who stuttered and strained to not incriminate his friend Simpson. This is the same Robert Shapiro who gathered the Dream Team and set in motion the racial aspects of their defense. This is the same Robert Kardashian who refused to testify in the case, claiming lawyer-client privilege. He seems to have no trouble stepping away from his client now. I just shake my head. These are people who want it both ways. They want to make their money and get their friend acquitted and then they want to say that they didn't mean it, that they should still be invited to the same parties, that they shouldn't lose any clients or friends who are disgusted by their shifty ethics.

Well, there was a chance for these people to contribute to real justice and they—like others—chose instead allegiance to a killer. I don't doubt that Robert Kardashian has trouble sleeping. I just wonder how some of his other friends and lawyers do it.

Still, some of the new information that has come out in books and other media reports is intriguing:

Simpson's lawyers acknowledge that he failed a lie detector test with almost the worst possible score. It's certainly not surprising. We'd heard that he failed such a test, but since it was administered by the defense team, by Shapiro, there was no way to have it introduced into evidence.

Defense sources acknowledge that they redecorated Simpson's house for the visit by the jury. They took down all the photographs of white people—including a naked photo of Paula Barbierri—and replaced them with pictures of blacks. They even hung a famous school integration painting by Norman Rockwell. At the time, we strongly objected that the house had been rearranged and we were overruled by Judge Ito.

The National Enquirer ran an old photograph of Simpson wearing Bruno Magli shoes identical to those which left bloody footprints outside Nicole Brown's condominium. From the time the tabloids got to Jill Shively—the woman who saw Simpson driving away from Nicole's house the night of the murder—they have continued to ruin some of the best evidence of Simpson's guilt. It was always impossible to compete; we couldn't pay for information.

Simpson's defense attorneys also have written books. Yet they still don't offer a defense for their client. They still don't give an alibi or explain the overwhelming blood evidence. They slip the issue with faulty logic: Mark Fuhrman is a racist, therefore O. J. Simpson didn't kill his wife and her friend.

And what about Simpson himself? His testimony in the civil trial was practiced, but its logic was laughable. He has never offered a believable story to cover his whereabouts the night of the murder. His contention that he never beat Nicole, never hit her, never hurt her, was offensive. Who can think of those photographs of Nicole—her face puffy and darkened, the fear in her eyes—and believe that he never hit her. Who can remember her frantic diary entries—"He continued to beat me as I kept crawling toward the door"—and believe that he never hit her. Who can recall her chilled voice on the 911 tape the night he broke into her apartment or the words she told police—"He's going to kill me!"—and believe that O. J. Simpson never touched his wife.

And yet he skates through life, playing golf, with no shortage of people to treat him with the deference and respect he's always wanted. He seems to have some supernatural power that watches over him. And it ain't Jesus.

I am amazed to see how some in the black community embrace Simpson. I will say it again: This is not a case about civil rights. It never was. The only rights in this case that were violated were those of Ronald Goldman and Nicole Brown.

Martin Luther King often said that the civil rights movement was successful because it had the moral high ground. We are in danger of losing that, of separating the movement from the quest for justice. It should pain any African American to see O. J. Simpson offered the protection of the same banner that ended slavery, that broke segregation; the same movement that continues to work to make America a fair place. We shouldn't offer him shelter in such a hallowed place. He is a killer.

The worst part of the last couple of years has been watching the nightmare continue for the Brown and Goldman families. If we had won, this would all be behind them. Instead, they are still in courtrooms, fighting for Simpson to be held responsible, fighting for Nicole Brown's children. Both families continue to carry themselves with poise and with honor. When I think about the injustice, I don't think about O. J. Simpson; I think about those two families.

I guess that just leaves me. It's been an awful and wonderful two years for me, a time when I achieved some clarity and perspective in the midst of a horrific murder case and a time when I learned to adjust to my own loss of privacy. I now have a job that affords me more time to do the things I've wanted to do: to write, teach, and travel; to spend time with my daughter, Jenee. She is getting ready to go off to college and I burst with pride as I watch her grow up. I have some warmth and space now, some time and distance from the events that carved a deep hole in me. Yet I have a bitter taste in my mouth that I think will be with me forever. It is that bitter taste which has caused me to speak out more about the Simpson case and to comment on the civil trial.

I have traveled across the country to talk about this book and this case and I have been lifted by the support I have received, by the people who feel close to me because of *In Contempt.* I have found other people in the same constricting place where I spent the last two years—between white perception and black expectation. I've received cards and letters and, while I haven't been able to answer them all, I intend to try and I thank everyone who has taken time to write me.

Sometimes someone will call me a hero and it always causes me to blush and to become uncomfortable. I wish it were true. I wish I had done something heroic. I wish there was something heroic to be done, but there wasn't. I just did my job and I survived. It is tragic and fitting that there were no heroes in this case, except maybe Ron Goldman.

I've also been thinking a lot about my brother Michael lately. I miss him. I think back to the days before he died, when he was blind, when his fear was hardening into resolve, when he looked me squarely in the eyes, as if he could still see, and told me not to worry about him, and not to worry about myself, that God would watch over us both, that He would provide us all with a measure of peace.

I hope Michael was right about that. There are so many people now who could use such reassurance, people divided by the Simpson murder case, people haunted by its injustice, and people raw from loss. It's what I pray for now—not just time and distance—but peace.

—Christopher Darden
Los Angeles
December 1996

ACKNOWLEDGMENTS

I would like to sincerely thank:

Lou and Juditha Brown and the entire Brown family, and Fred, Patti, Kim, and the rest of the Goldman family. Your strength and resolve these past two years inspired us all. Thanks for believing in us, and may God bless you all.

My colleagues in the Los Angeles County District Attorney's Office, the finest group of prosecutors, clerks, and minions ever assembled: William Hodgman, Cheri Lewis, Scott Gordon, Hank Goldberg, Lisa Kahn, Brian Kelberg, Lydia Bodin, Darrel Mavis, David Wooden, Alan "Big Papa" Yochelson, Allen Field, Falomi Pierson, Stanley Williams, Dana Escobar, Diana Martinez, Jonathan Fairtlough, Kenneth Lynch, District Attorney Gil Garcetti, Cathy Ozawa, and Margie Budden; Patti Jo Fairbanks; and the minions: Tracy Miller, Natalie Agajanian, Melissa Decker, Kathy Behfarin, Susan Dozier, Lisa Fox, Michael Price, Leticia Minjares, Matthew Gibbs, and Tom "Ratman" Ratanavaraha; to my colleagues in the San Diego County District Attorney's Office, Woody Clarke and Michael Runyon, and in the Alameda County District Attorney's Office, Rockne Harmon. I miss you guys. I could never have made it without each of you.

The L.A. County District Attorney investigators who assisted in the investigation and protected me from harm: Michael Stevens, Dana Thompson, Pat McPherson, Steve Oppler, Jack Gotterman, George Mueller, Bill Guidas, Brian Hale, Wil Abrams, Ken Godinez, Mike Armstrong, and Lieutenant Gary Shramm.

My friends at the LAPD: Phil Vannatter, Tom Lange, Jerry Stephens, Bud Arce, Ron Phillips, Nancy Claiborne, Captain William Gartland, and all the "Roys" at Robbery/Homicide Division. You did the best you could.

My lifelong friends Dr. Gloria Alibaruho and attorney Patricia Ector. Gloria, thanks for helping to shape me into the man I've become. Pat, for more than twenty years you've always been there for me, a phone call away. I love you.

To Gavin de Becker. Thanks for being there for me at crunch time.

Marcia, Marcia, Marcia! Keep running and don't ever look back. You deserve the best life has to offer.

Mama and Daddy, Eddie and Jean Darden; my sisters Angie, Edna, Debbie, Roz, and Anita; my brother Larry; the in-laws, Bob and Doyle; my nieces and nephews, Jeannie and Vernon, Malcolm and Ruby, Doyle, Alex, and Andrew, and Lil' Robert; the Robertsons, Fred, Linda, and Lil' Christopher. I know that this case wreaked havoc in your life too, but you stood firm—like a family should. I apologize, and I'm proud of each of you.

Thanks for hanging in there for me.

Duane and Evelyn Orange, Sarah, John, Mellie-Mel, Dayna, Raymond, and the rest of the Saturday morning workout crew.

To my friend Norman Brokaw, chairman and CEO of the William Morris Agency, and to my literary agent, Mel Berger; to Linda, Mary, and Dana, and everyone else at William Morris, thank you for your guidance. We did it our way—with dignity and class.

My lawyers, the Fleischers—Susan and Mark. You guys owe me one hundred bucks. To old friends Clarence Bolton, Maurice Sullivan, Fred Jackson, Luis Silvestre, Calvin Cazenave, the Jackson family, Daryl

Austin, and the John F. Kennedy High School class of '74—you people are the best.

To radio 92.3 FM KKBT "The Beat." To the "House Party," John London, Shirley Strawberry, Dennis Cruz, and the rest of the crew. Thanks for the airtime. I've been waiting to exhale for months. You let me breathe again.

My editor and publisher, Judith Regan; we were meant to be together. Thanks for giving me a chance to say what needed to be said. To the dedicated Regan Books team: Kristin Kiser, Jennifer Gates Hayes, and John Rossetti, and to all the HarperCollins staff who were so helpful.

Pathenia, in Jenee you've given me a wonderful gift. And to my daughter, Jenee, thanks for being the best daughter a father could have. I love you.

A SPECIAL THANKS

"The last thing I want to do is write a book," I said as I looked over the rim of my glasses at another struggling writer. It was a goofy-looking white kid from Spokane, Washington, named Jess Walter. I had a vision. I wanted to write a book about race and justice. A book that would remain on bookshelves and in libraries for the next hundred years. I couldn't imagine how this guy Walter could help me achieve my goal.

"What do you know about black people?" I asked as I perused a copy of his last book, *Every Knee Shall Bow.* "Well, I brought written recommendations from my only two black friends," he said wryly.

I just looked at the guy. Somehow I knew that he was the one.

No one will ever know or appreciate the long hours, the hard work, and the primitive conditions in which we worked together, taking what was in my heart and putting it in words so that others could understand.

Jess, you're a gifted writer. A writer's writer. One of the best I've ever read. And at age thirty you've yet to reach your full potential. I could not have completed this project without you. When I told Judith Regan that you were the next Hemingway, she agreed, then asked if there was anything else I wanted to say about you. There is. You're also my friend. Thanks for everything and a special thanks to your wife, Anne Windishar, and your lovely daughter, Brooklyn. May God bless and keep you.

ABOUT THE AUTHORS

CHRISTOPHER DARDEN is a writer, lecturer, law professor and practicing attorney. He is a sixteen-year veteran of the Los Angeles County District Attorney's Office, where he was a prosecutor in the O. J. Simpson murder trial. He has tried thirty-six murder cases before juries and is a former Associate Professor of Law at Southwestern University School of Law and a former faculty member at California State University, Los Angeles.

Darden practices law and specializes in the areas of criminal defense, employment discrimination, and civil rights. He has provided legal commentary for CNN, CBS, ABC, NBC, FOX NEWS, and various legal, political, and entertainment shows. Darden has published four novels and one nonfiction book. He currently lives in Los Angeles with his wife, Marcia. You can learn more about him at www.christopherdarden.com.

JESS WALTER is the recipient of the Edgar Allan Poe Award and was a finalist for the National Book Award in 2006. He is the author of six novels, a collection of short stories, and a non-fiction book. He lives with his wife and daughter in Spokane, Washington.